Increasing Language Skills of Students from Low-Income Backgrounds

Practical Strategies for Professionals

Second Edition

Celeste Roseberry-McKibbin, PhD

PLURAL
PUBLISHING
— INC. —

SAN DIEGO
OXFORD
MELBOURNE

PLURAL PUBLISHING
INC.

5521 Ruffin Road
San Diego, CA 92123

e-mail: info@pluralpublishing.com
Web site: http://www.pluralpublishing.com

49 Bath Street
Abingdon, Oxfordshire OX14 1EA
United Kingdom

FSC
www.fsc.org
MIX
Paper from
responsible sources
FSC® C011935

Typeset in 11/13 Garamond by Flanagan's Publishing Services, Inc.
Printed in the United States of America by McNaughton & Gunn

Library of Congress Cataloging-in-Publication Data

Roseberry-McKibbin, Celeste.
  Increasing language skills of students from low-income backgrounds : practical
strategies for professionals / Celeste Roseberry-McKibbin.—2nd ed.
      p. ; cm.
  Includes bibliographical references and index.
  ISBN 978-1-59756-497-7 (alk. paper)—ISBN 1-59756-497-4 (alk. paper)
  I. Title.
  [DNLM: 1. Language Development Disorders—economics—United States.
2. Language Development Disorders—rehabilitation—United States. 3. Child—
United States. 4. Child Development—United States. 5. Cultural Deprivation—
United States. 6. Poverty—psychology—United States. 7. Schools—standards
—United States. WL 340.2]

  618.92'855—dc23
                                    2012032175

Contents

Preface   *xi*

Acknowledgments   *xxi*

**1 Introduction to Poverty: Variables Affecting   1
    Students' Performance**

Introduction   3
Definitions and Demographics of Poverty   5
Physical and Psychological Effects of Poverty   12
    Prenatal and Birth Issues   12
    Hunger and Malnutrition   17
    Overall Brain Development   18
    Basic Safety Issues   19
    Access to Health Care   21
    Environmental Issues   23
    Instability and Chaos   25
    Hearing and Vision   29
    Emotional Atmosphere of the Home   31
    Understanding Children and Families from Backgrounds   33
        of Situational and Generational Poverty
Conclusions   39
Chapter Highlights   40

**2 Language Skills and Behavioral Characteristics in   43
    Children of Families of Low Socioeconomic Status**

Introduction   44
Factors Affecting and Characteristics of Oral Language   45
        Skills of Low SES Children
    Overview   45
    The Research of Hart and Risley   49
    Follow-up Research on Hart and Risley: Greenwood   56
        and Colleagues
Other Factors Affecting Oral Language Development   57
    Job and Environment-Related Communication Styles   57
    Parental Attitudes Toward Oral Language Stimulation   60

Factors Affecting and Characteristics of Literacy Skills of Low SES Children   61

     Material and Psychological Resources   61

     Phonological and Print Awareness Skills   65

Behavioral Characteristics of Some Children from Low SES Homes   68

Conclusions   72

Chapter Highlights   72

3   Considerations in Assessment of the Language Skills of Students from Low SES Backgrounds   75

Introduction   76

Laws Affecting the Assessment of Children from Low SES Families for Special Education   78

Response to Intervention   79

Preliminary Components of the Assessment Process   80

     Screening   80

     The Case History   82

The Use of Standardized Tests   86

     General Considerations in Using Standardized Tests with Students from Low SES Backgrounds   86

     Formal Test Assumptions   89

     Sources of Bias in the Use of Standardized Tests with Culturally and Linguistically Diverse Students from Low SES Backgrounds   91

     Modifying Standardized Tests for Use with Students from Low SES Backgrounds   92

Language Samples   94

     General Considerations   94

     Informal Evaluation of Language Use   95

Other Alternatives to Standardized Assessment   97

     Legal Considerations   97

     Dynamic Assessment   97

     Portfolio Assessment   101

     Assessment of Information Processing Skills   101

Conclusion   103

Chapter Highlights   104

**4 Practical Strategies for Increasing the Oral   107
   Language Skills of Children from Low SES Families**

Introduction   108
Stimulating Infant Language Development   109
   General Principles   109
   Using Books with Babies   114
Stimulating Language Development in Toddlers and   116
   Preschoolers
   The Importance of High-Quality Preschool Experiences   116
   The Importance of Appropriate Training for Early   122
      Child Care Providers
Practical Strategies for Increasing the Language Skills of   126
   Toddlers and Preschoolers in Natural Settings
   General Principles of Successful Language Stimulation   127
      with Young Children
   Specific Incidental Learning/Milieu Teaching   129
      Techniques to Encourage Language Development
   Increasing Vocabulary Skills   131
   Practical Strategies for Teaching Formal Language   135
      Register in Naturalistic Settings
Increasing Grammatical and Pragmatic Language Skills in   138
   Formal Register
   Increasing Grammatical Language Skills in Formal   138
      Register
   Increasing Pragmatic Language Skills in Formal Register   142
Conclusions   149
Chapter Highlights   150

**5 Practical Strategies for Increasing the Literacy Skills   153
   of Students From Low SES Backgrounds**

Introduction   156
Optimizing Book Reading Experiences for Young Children   158
Increasing Early Preliteracy and Literacy Skills: 164
   Evidence-Based Strategies
   Basic Principles   164
   Increasing Children's Phonological Awareness Skills   165
   Increasing Print Awareness   167
   Additional Strategies for Enhancing Early Literacy Skills   175

Enhancing Literacy Skills in the Elementary Years
and Beyond   179

Increasing Vocabulary Skills for Reading Success   185

Providing Assistance for Students from Low SES   190
Backgrounds with Other Written Language Challenges

Conclusions   195

Chapter Highlights   199

**6   Structuring the School Environment for Optimal   201
Performance of Students from Low SES Backgrounds**

Introduction   203

Current School Conditions and Attempts at Reform   204

Attempts at School Reform   204

Current Conditions in Low SES Schools   208

Teacher Preparation and Developing Professionalism   211

Integrating Schools by Students' Socioeconomic Status   216

School Enhancement: Providing Supportive Programs   220
and Relationships for Students from Low SES
Backgrounds

Parallel Education Systems   220

All-Day Kindergartens   221

Implementing the Arts   222

Providing Supplemental Programs   224

Opportunities for Schools to Connect with Community   228
Resources

Serving Gifted Students From Low SES Backgrounds   232

Conclusions   237

Chapter Highlights   237

**7   Practical Strategies for Enhancing Learning,   241
Motivation, and Self-Esteem in Low SES Students**

Introduction   243

Enhancing Learning: Optimizing the Environment   244

Practical Strategies for Enhancing Whole-Brain Learning   247

Reducing Stress   247

Increasing Memory Skills   249

Contextualizing Language for Children from Low SES   252
Backgrounds

Children from Low SES Families and Language   252
   Learning in School
Increasing Contextual Cues to Enhance Learning   256
Dealing Constructively with Students from the Culture   264
   of Resistance
Enhancing Self-Esteem and Motivation: Providing   273
   Appropriate Learning Incentives
Increasing Student Independence and Self-Direction   279
   Basic Principles   279
   Implementing the Equity Game   281
   Emphasizing Effort Over Ability   282
   Utilizing Multiple Intelligences   285
Conclusions   288
Chapter Highlights   288

8   Poverty and Highly Mobile Populations: Mitigating the Impact of High Mobility and Chaos   291

Introduction   293
Chaos: Definition, Characteristics, and Impact on Students   293
   Characteristics and Impact of Disorder   294
   Characteristics and Impact of Turbulence   296
   Chaos: General Impact on American Children   298
High Mobility and Chaos: Specific Impacts on Schools   300
   and Classrooms
Special Considerations in Serving Migrant Students   301
Serving Students Who Are Homeless   306
   Introduction and Demographic Data   306
   Specific Characteristics and Needs of Homeless   309
   Students and Their Families
   Practical Strategies for Supporting Homeless Students   313
   and Families
Increasing Executive Functioning Skills in Highly Mobile   319
   Students Impacted by Chaos
   Definition and Basic Facts   319
   Practical Strategies for Increasing Executive   322
   Functioning Skills of Highly Mobile Students
Conclusions   336
Chapter Highlights   336

9 **Considerations in Working with Families of Students from Low SES Backgrounds**   **339**

Introduction   343
Low SES Families: Cultural and Social Capital   343
Low SES, CLD Families: Special Considerations in   347
     Service Delivery
     Some General Considerations   347
     Providing Services for Students and Families from   351
       Immigrant/Refugee Backgrounds
     Language and Literacy Practices in CLD Families: 354
       Facilitating an Optimal Language Learning
       Environment for Children
     Facilitating Overall Involvement of Low SES, CLD   363
       Families in Children's Education
Possible Value Conflicts Between Low SES Families and   370
     Middle SES Professionals
Facilitating Foundational Support Services for Low SES   373
     Families: Practical Suggestions
     Supporting Low SES Families in Meeting Basic Needs   373
     Supporting Children from Homes Characterized by   378
       Abuse or Neglect
     Helping Caregivers Provide a Supportive Home   383
       Atmosphere
Conclusions   388
Chapter Highlights   388

10 **Some Words of Encouragement**   **391**

References   *397*
Index   *435*

Preface

*The person who removes a mountain
begins by carrying away small stones.*

Chinese proverb

It was a hot July day, especially driving on the freeway. I was 6 months pregnant and on my way to conduct a language assessment with Susanna, a junior high school student who was struggling academically. Unfortunately, my primary preoccupation was with the possibility of acquiring head lice from this student, as I'd been advised by the referring teacher.

I wanted to be careful not to get too close to Susanna because, in my pregnant state, I couldn't use strong medications to de-louse myself after the evaluation. I thought with dismay how sad it was that avoiding lice was my primary preoccupation as I drove to the school.

The junior high school was situated in a low-income area serving children from homes that typically were crowded, with unsanitary living conditions. Ongoing lice infestations were known to be a real problem among these students. Families often could not afford to buy personal care products such as shampoo, and most could not afford remedies for head lice.

I ruefully pondered the irony that my worry about this possible infestation completely overshadowed my professional concern for Susanna's potential language impairment. I really was not looking forward to this session and wondered if I could do my best for this child. Suddenly, I had an epiphany. For years, an important focus of my practice had been the impact of ethnic, cultural, and linguistic differences on students' cognitive, linguistic, and academic

> development. But what about socioeconomic status (SES)? As Susanna's case made clear to me, a common health problem related to a poverty-level standard of living could well affect the quality of school services provided and thus the scholastic experience of the child. Was it possible that SES, was a bigger factor in school performance than the color of children's skin or the language that they spoke at home?

In fact, a few years before that summer day, I had heard a speaker address this issue at a state convention. At the time, it was intriguing but failed to impress me as worthy of serious consideration. Surely, SES differences between families couldn't make that much difference in children's language and cognitive skills and consequent academic performance. Everyone knew that skin color and language spoken in the home had far more impact on these parameters: or did they?

Because I grew up in the Philippines, a developing country where most of the people were poor, I had been surrounded by poverty during a large part of my childhood (between the ages of 6 and 17 years). In addition, before that, my family also was poor. My pastor father received a salary of $300 to support his wife and four little girls. I recall my mother saving for months to buy a 10-cent potholder. Sometimes, all we had in the refrigerator was mustard and ketchup; I am relieved that, my parents' trust that "God would provide" proved to be well founded.

On our family's journey to the Philippines, we sailed through several ports, one of which was in Hong Kong. I had just turned 6 years of age and still have a vivid memory of anchoring in Hong Kong: People came to our ship in boats holding nets on long poles, which they held up, begging for money from the ship's passengers. My mother explained that these people had no money for food. I recall being filled with dismay, wonder, and sorrow at their plight. This was my introduction to the rank poverty to which I was to be exposed for the next 10 years.

The Philippines, a beautiful country with warm, wonderful people, is the most disaster-prone country on the face of the earth. Typhoons, floods, earthquakes, landslides, and volcanic eruptions are part of regular life. One year a typhoon slammed Tablas, the island on which we lived when I was in third grade. My family's house was a concrete building in a coconut grove about a city block from the beach. Our neighbors' houses were nipa huts, constructed in typical fashion of palm fronds. Tablas had one paved road in those days. When the typhoon hit with winds of up to 100 miles per hour, all the nipa huts literally were blown away. The neighbors took refuge in our house, where they huddled in our living room. The ocean made its way through the coconut grove into our home, and the water in our living room reached almost to my knees before the storm subsided and the water retreated. We wondered if we would make it through. Eventually, the raging typhoon subsided. Not only were our neighbors' nipa huts gone, but the school I attended was too. The whole island was devastated. So, we began to rebuild, nipa palm by nipa palm.

The Filipinos, with their characteristic courage, resilience, and good attitude toward life and all its disasters, shrugged and started their lives over again. They were not angry or bitter; this was just the way life was. All their possessions were gone, and some of their friends and relatives were dead, washed away by massive ocean waves or struck by chunks of wind-borne debris. But their attitudes reflected the ideal of *bahala na*: it's in God's hands; whatever will be will be. I almost never saw a Filipino in despair, a Filipino who had given up in bitterness and resignation. The cheerful, accepting attitudes of the Filipinos in the face of disaster made an impression on me that has remained a model for resilience.

After I returned to the United States and grew up to become a practicing speech-language pathologist (SLP), I pondered upon Susanna, the Philippines, and my own family's situation early in my life. Questions arose. Some of the Filipinos I knew, although they barely subsisted by U.S. standards, were able to rise out of poverty to become lawyers, doctors, and ministers. Although my own parents had experienced poverty, I had earned a PhD; one sister had a bachelor's degree, and two sisters had master's degrees. What made the difference for the Filipinos and my sisters and me? Why did I see that, in the United States, students with language difficulties who were from low-SES backgrounds typically struggled mightily in school and then in adulthood often ended up on welfare? With some exceptions, why did so many of America's poor people succumb to an attitude of resignation and despair, when the Filipinos seemed to bounce back from even the greatest of disasters? Why were the Filipinos so resilient and hopeful, despite all the tragedies they endured, whereas many of the low-SES families I worked with in the United States appeared to be depressed and feeling hopeless by contrast? Why did the Filipinos have such strong family values and love for their many children, whereas the families I saw in the United States were crumbling?

I began receiving answers to these questions when I spent my clinical fellowship year (CFY) in a very-low-income school district in northern California, where, as a 23-year-old graduate of a fine master's degree program in speech pathology, I worked in an elementary school in a very "bad part of town." This was a part of town where you rolled up your windows and locked your car doors as you drove, even in broad daylight. You never stayed at work past dark unless at least one other person was present in the building. The children on my speech-language caseload had stories that I was unprepared for.

There were Raymond and Lee B., whose father had gotten drunk at a local bar and had a fight outside. He was shot, and his killer ran over him several times to make sure he was good and dead. Mrs. B., who had a high school education, struggled to support herself and four young sons on welfare. There was Mary Anne S., a darling first grader who shared with excitement that her father was finally out of jail! There was Tyrone M., whose father made him watch while he beat the family dog to death. There was Natasha B., who concerned school staff: we all regularly checked her for bruises from beatings at home. There was Leonard P., whose mother had abandoned him and his siblings on a road and driven off. No one could locate her. There was Mimi E., whose father came after her second grade teacher with a gun, necessitating a school lockdown. There was Elinor T., an angry second grader who had been bounced from foster home to foster home because her parents could not afford to provide for her. There was William C., who ate ravenously in the school cafeteria because his family was so poor. He had been back and forth in foster care owing to maternal abuse, cigarette burns were not uncommon. When I administered tests of language skills to these children, they routinely got low scores. An experienced friend in the district told me: "Knock one year off the test score expectations to compensate for the fact that these kids live in this particular district."

Although I had grown up in a developing nation, nothing could have prepared me for the situations I encountered during my CFY. In the Philippines, in the rural areas where my family and I lived during those years, we saw so many families rich in love and connections. Although they were materially poor, they were loyal to one another and everyone was cared for: young, old, infirm. There were no convalescent homes. Many families had strong religious connections. Children generally did well in school. Even when families experienced natural disasters such as that described above, they shrugged and rebuilt their lives. Why were the Filipino children so much better off than the children I worked with during my CFY? Why were they so much more resilient? They were all poor—what was the difference?

Several years later, I was fortunate to obtain a copy of Ruby Payne's *A Framework for Understanding Poverty* (2003). This wise educator, who had been a school principal for 30 or so years, had encountered children from every walk of life. Like me, she had worked with everyone from the children of millionaires to those whose families lived in their cars. Her book was a revelation. My professional and personal experiences were finally understandable: I had a framework through which to comprehend my questions over the years. Payne explained the existence of generational poverty (described more in Chapter 1) with its attendant conditions of despair, hopelessness, and reliance on welfare. When I read about this phenomenon, I understood so many of the situations I had experienced as a professional speech-language pathologist.

It is well recognized that to determine what constitutes best professional practice, educators and persons in the helping professions need to examine cultural, ethnic, and linguistic factors as they contribute to children's cognitive, linguistic, and academic performance. But increasingly, especially in the 21st century, it is imperative to examine the contribution of SES to children's performance in these areas. Study after study shows that SES is a far greater variable influencing students' performance than has previously been acknowledged. With the United States' Great Recession that began in 2007, followed by the worse financial crisis since the Great Depression in the 1930s, professionals have encountered increasing numbers of students in the schools who are affected by poverty. The impact of increased numbers of homeless students is especially acute.

The strategies presented in this book are both research based and practical. Using these strategies, professionals who serve the increasing numbers of children from low-SES families in U.S. schools can exert a positive influence on three levels:

1. State and federal policy
2. District and school site
3. Individual

Specific recommendations in these three areas are made throughout this book. As professionals, we can implement these recommendations according to the various roles we play: As advocates for children of low-SES families, we can press for changes in policy at the state and federal levels. As legitimate representatives of the educational system, we can act at the district and school site levels. Finally, as individual professionals who interact with the children served by these schools, we can direct our clinical practice to support their learning and overall development.

The first two chapters of this book describe in detail the *nature* of the challenges experienced in various areas by children from low-SES families. In this second edition, Chapters 1 and 2 have been enhanced by an increased number of scientific studies involving large numbers of subjects to support statements made about the nature of challenges experienced by low-SES children.

Chapters 3 through 9 present specific strategies to support these children: actions professionals can take to make a difference in the lives of the students they serve. Chapter 10 reviews the approaches presented in this book and provides a few final ideas on how professionals can be involved at all three levels of action.

There are some new and extended features in the second edition of this book. I have put chapter highlights at the end of each chapter to provide a synopsis for the reader of the chapters' contents. These highlights can serve as a review/refresher of information that the chapter covered. I have included more stories in this second edition, working to give a human face to the scientific studies that address the needs of low-SES students and their families. There are many new research studies to support claims made in every chapter. There is much more information about children and families who are homeless; unfortunately, the Great Recession has increased this population substantially. There is new information about using Response to Intervention (RtI) with low-SES students, and I have updated technology recommendations by including information about using iPads and YouTube videos with low-SES students and families. There is new information about using books with babies. I have also gone into some detail about the nature of chaos in low-SES children's lives, describing how chaos in highly mobile children (e.g., those who are homeless) can impact language and cognitive skills. I give suggestions for strategies professionals can use at school to mitigate the impact of chaos as much as possible.

Most readers of this book probably already have a broad appreciation of the nature of the problems experienced by children from low-SES backgrounds. Practicing professionals may be impatient with the detailed review in the first two chapters because what they are looking for is solutions, if any exist, and specific practical strategies to use to make a positive difference in the lives of the children they serve. Nevertheless, an increased understanding of the nature and scope of the challenges experienced by these children and their families, as presented in the first two chapters, is important for three reasons: First, broadening our understanding of these issues will inform solutions and strategies for supporting these children and their families to succeed in school and in the wider society. Second, we may become less judgmental about perceived lack of effort and repeated failure in these children and their families as we realize the substantial challenges they routinely face. Third, increasing our understanding of the wide scope of problems faced by children from low-SES families will help us to understand why many of the things we are currently doing produce such limited results. Instead of blaming ourselves as professionals for being unsuccessful, we can know that we are doing our utmost in the face of some very major challenges.

A related consideration is the frustratingly poor results of expensive programs and interventions that have been used in attempts to raise achievement test scores in disadvantaged children. In this vein, I am inspired by a conversation with one of my former school principals, Mike Gulden, at the elementary school where I served part time as a speech- language pathologist. (I work full time as a university professor and part time as a public school clinician). We as an Academic Intervention Team were talking about yet another program we might think about implementing to raise achievement test scores for the children in our school, most of whom were low-SES and culturally and linguistically diverse (CLD); for many of our children, English was a second language. Mike said in frustration, "We've been implementing all these expensive programs, and almost nothing seems to help. We keep throwing thousands of dollars at the kids' problems, and we see so few results." I thought long and hard about his statements, and realized that they reflected the feelings of many professionals across the United States. Why indeed, are results of such programs for children from low-SES families so unimpressive?

Ironically, professionals may feel less frustrated if they have a better understanding of the exact nature and scope of the problems experienced by children from low-SES families. When these children arrive at kindergarten, many of them are so far behind in linguistic development that comprehensive, intensive programs are needed just to bring them to a level very generally commensurate with the levels typical for more advantaged children starting kindergarten. The 5-year-old child from a low-SES family who arrives in kindergarten malnourished, with a history of multiple middle ear infections, prenatal exposure to drugs or alcohol, transiency, and no preschool experience, will need far more intensive intervention just to get to "middle ground" than a 5-year-old from a middle-SES family who has been read to, taken on trips, enrolled in preschool, and talked to a great deal by caregivers. An appreciation of just how disadvantaged many children from low-SES families are by the time they reach kindergarten can allow educators and other professionals to stop blaming themselves for the children's limited gains despite their best efforts. In their work with these children, it is important for professionals not to have low expectations and to avoid a "failure mentality," but they also need to recognize that, no matter how much effort they bring to the problem or how many special programs they implement, some children will make limited progress, if any.

The vast scope of problems that many children from low-SES families bring to school with them can be overwhelming. If these children start school in kindergarten so far behind their more privileged "peers" in so many areas, what good are special programs and intensive, expensive interventions in a vain attempt to level the playing field? Although not all the problems experienced by children from low-SES families can be resolved, and even though their deficits in language development may never be adequately remediated, it is essential to keep trying. Research does indicate that various programs and methods and strategies are effective in increasing cognitive-linguistic development in these less advantaged children and boosting their school achievement, thereby increasing their chances for happy and productive adulthoods.

Implementing the suggestions and strategies put forth in this book will not help every child from a low-SES family. However, some children will be helped. Most chapters represent informal meta-analyses of current research from a wide variety of fields: social work, regular education, special education, social science, psychology, anthropology, speech-language pathology, counseling, medicine, cognitive neuroscience, macroeconomics, multiculturalism, and others.

As mentioned, I have written from a premise of evidence-based practice, basing suggestions on valid research as much as possible. In general, I have avoided advocating strategies based only on anecdotal evidence or armchair advice from some well-known authority. Some suggested strategies are based on such less formal evidence, but on the whole, the strategies in this book are grounded in current research that has proved, with quantitative data, that they actually are effective in increasing achievement for children from low-SES families. It has been an utmost priority for me to develop the content of this book from an evidence-based research vantage point.

Throughout this text, I have re-emphasized key points; repetition is the mother of mastery, and by repeating certain key information, I hope to help readers truly retain this information. This book has been written from three primary perspectives: scientific evidence, my clinical experience, and my experience as a parent of a child who is currently a student in a California public school. I am from a middle-SES background, and for the sake of simplicity I have assumed that many readers of this book will be also. Another assumption is that, if you have picked up this book, you are in an educational or related field. (If you are in an educational or related field, and you are rich, not just of middle SES, please E-mail me at celeste@csus.edu and tell me how you managed to accomplish this.)

In sharing my experience as a parent, I have been open regarding the cost of lessons, services, and material goods for my son. This information is provided to highlight how expensive it really is just to afford one child a middle-class lifestyle in the United States today, or at least in suburban northern California. I wish to note that my husband and I take pains not to overindulge our child with designer clothes, electronic games, and the like. For readers who do not have children or whose children are grown, it may be shocking to see just how much parents spend these days to give their children middle-class advantages in the world, advantages that most middle-class people take for granted.

Before I became a mother, I was rather judgmental toward low-SES parents. They weren't involved in their children's education; I thought they were lazy; they were uncaring. Being a mother, however, has transformed my perspective. Throughout this book, I have attempted to demonstrate, from my own experience, just how much time and effort are required to be an involved parent. It then becomes clear why so many children from low-SES families come from "deprived" homes with "uninvolved" parents. It's easy for frustrated school professionals to pass negative judgment on low-SES caregivers, but this can be remedied by a realization of how much in the way of resources it takes just to provide a child with what many of us consider the "basics." Such resources, typically involving time and money, often are unavailable to low-SES parents.

In 2006, then-senator Barack Obama published *The Audacity of Hope: Thoughts on Reclaiming the American Dream* (2006). In his compelling book, Obama talked about the many holes and cracks in our system at level 1, the macroeconomic level, the state and federal policy level. He discussed how the poor often fall through these cracks, and he rendered an objective yet compassionate explanation of why so many Americans are falling into poverty. Obama suggested ways in which level 1 changes could be made to support these Americans.

I like to think that my own book could be subtitled, "The Audacity of Hope" because that is what it really is about: hope for increasing the language skills and, ultimately, the academic performance and life paths of children from low-SES families in the United States. It is worth re-emphasizing that, as professionals, we will not be able to make a difference in the lives of every child and family with whom we work. Many times, our best efforts will not be enough. Nevertheless, it is important to focus on those "success stories": children whose lives actually have been transformed, those families whose lives truly have been changed for the better because of our efforts. We also need to focus on well-done research that identifies successful, practical strategies, programs, and materials for making a positive difference in the lives of children from low-SES backgrounds.

It is my hope that this book will help the reader "carry away some small stones," to reiterate the Chinese proverb that opens this Preface. And, let us dare to experience the "audacity of hope"—hope for leveling the playing field so that the lives of children from low-SES families can be changed for the better.

Acknowledgments

I am thankful for my terrific support team at Plural Publishing, whose enthusiasm and professionalism have been instrumental in creating the second edition of this book: Angie Singh, Scott Barbour, Martin Hill, Caitlin Mahon, Kaye Tengco, Kaela Martin, and Mandy Licata are gratefully acknowledged.

Many thanks to Mary Martineau and Sylvia Soule, students at California State University Sacramento in the Department of Speech Pathology and Audiology, who were a great help with collecting recent research and data. Thanks too to my colleagues from San Juan Unified School District. Shawna Bailey was a helpful sounding board for my ideas for this second edition. Debra Johnson-Garcia, it is so wonderful to work hand-in-hand with you in the schools, serving these precious kids and learning from each other. I am thankful to my superintendent, Glynn Thompson, for his encouragement, interest, and support.

My university students at California State University, Sacramento are a constant inspiration to me, encouraging me to expand my work in reaching underserved children and families. I have been so touched by the stories of some of my university students from low-SES backgrounds, who have faced enormous odds to obtain a college education that the average middle-SES student takes for granted.

The children and families I have worked with in Elk Grove Unified and San Juan Unified School District have put human faces on research studies and great quantities of data I have plowed my way through in order to write a book that is scientific and evidence based in nature. The children are my reason for writing this book; may they be enriched and may they benefit from my and others' efforts to help "level the societal playing field" so that they may have equal opportunities for a high quality of life that every human being hopes to enjoy.

Last, but not least, I thank my husband Mike—for always being there.

To my son Mark
My greatest joy and inspiration
I thank God
For your heart of love and compassion
And your strong drive to bring justice to those in need
With all my love

1

Introduction to Poverty: Variables Affecting Students' Performance

If there are amazing graces on this earth, I believe that they are these good children sent to us by God and not yet soiled by the knowledge that the nation does not love them.

Jonathan Kozol
Amazing Grace

Mr. and Mrs. H have relocated from Mexico to work as agricultural laborers in California. They work hard in the fields. They have no health care insurance but do not want to use welfare; this does not fit with their value system of hard work and emphasis on family cohesiveness. One day, Mrs. H realizes that she is pregnant. She and her husband are overjoyed—their first child! They hope for several more.

As the pregnancy continues, Mrs. H. is tired beyond what she thinks she should be but cannot afford prepregnancy checkups. It is very hard to work outside all day in 100-degree temperatures as a pregnant woman, and one day she collapses. They have no health insurance; she is rushed to the nearest emergency room. After a 2-hour wait, she finally is able to see a doctor, whom she has never met before. After a series of tests, she is told that she has gestational diabetes. She needs to attend classes on how to control this, and she needs to conduct a blood test four times a day. She needs to take specific medication.

Mrs. H. cannot take a break to conduct a blood test four times a day; her employer would not stand for it. She would lose her job if she attended the diabetes classes, which are held two mornings a week at the local hospital. Even if the couple could survive financially on Mr. H.'s paycheck alone, they have only one car, and she can't take it to the hospital because her husband needs it to get to work. She and her husband cannot afford the medication that she needs. Her gestational diabetes goes untreated.

Marcos is born 2 months premature, and he has to be in the neonatal intensive care unit (NICU) for the first 6 weeks of his life. Mr. and Mrs. H. are heartbroken that they do not get to hold him. Mrs. H. would like to nurse Marcos, but she can't. She realizes that she eventually will need to bottle-feed him. This is very difficult for her, because in Mexico, almost all mothers nurse their babies. At work, Mr. and Mrs. H. cannot stop thinking about their baby who lies alone in the NICU. When they go home at night, Mrs. H. cries herself to sleep.

Another first-time mother, Dr. M., is a White university professor. She and her husband also were overjoyed to find out that she is pregnant. Dr. M. is in her 30s, so she is careful to keep up with her prepregnancy care. After a checkup in the first trimester of her pregnancy, Dr. M. is informed that she has gestational diabetes. She is shocked; so is Mr. M., her husband.

Dr. M., who was raised in Southeast Asia, believes in Western medicine; however, she also is open to herbal and nutritional remedies. Through consultation with her doctor and some alternative health care professionals, she is able to find the right combination of safe herbs, vitamins, and healthy foods to treat the gestational diabetes. A blood test at her local HMO clinic reveals that the gestational diabetes has resolved and is no longer present.

Mark is born full term at a healthy weight. His parents take him home. His mother has quit her job to stay home and care for him full time. The couple can afford to do this, although the family budget is much tighter now. Dr. M. is able to nurse Mark, and he is a beautiful baby who brings his parents much joy. Visitors come to the house, bringing flowers for the new mother and presents for Mark. He is off to a great start in life.

INTRODUCTION

As the population of the United States grows and changes, professionals who work with children, particularly in public schools, are realizing that part of helping these children succeed is recognizing and respecting their ethnic, linguistic, and cultural backgrounds (Lopez, 2012). Professionals are increasingly recognizing, however, that socioeconomic status (SES) may be an even more important factor in understanding children's and families' behavior and in helping the children succeed in school and, eventually, in life (Paul & Norbury, 2012. Turnbull and Justice (2012) stated that:

> Often the term diversity brings to mind the cultural differences that arise from religion, race, ethnicity, country of origin, and ability or disability. However, in many countries, substantial cultural differences exist between people who are economically advantaged and those who are disadvantaged. (p. 106)

SES issues often have a greater impact on children's and families' behavior and values than ethnic, linguistic, or cultural factors (Haynes & Pindzola, 2012). Although these factors are important, understanding SES issues may be even more helpful to professionals who work with students and their families (Paradis, Genesee, & Crago, 2011).

This chapter introduces some basic facts about poverty and its effects on learning as considerations in the choice and application of practical strategies to help at-risk children from low-SES homes. (Such strategies, aimed at increasing the language skills of these children and thereby maximizing their academic achievement, are the subject of later chapters.) The well-recognized goal of educators and other professionals who work with children is to help students eventually become successful, productive members of society. Some background information about students and families from low-SES households is presented next.

First, it is important to realize that poverty in the United States has grown in both extent and magnitude. The Reagan Administration guaranteed that the "truly needy" would be provided for by the "social safety net." Despite these assurances, social welfare programs were deeply slashed in the 1980s and the 1990s. The Great Recession, beginning in 2007, has left the United States in a situation of economic hardship unparalleled since the Great Depression of the 1930s. More than a year after the recession officially "ended" in 2009, the U.S. unemployment rate remains at over 9%; the nationwide overall poverty rate climbed to 15.3% in 2010 from 14.3% in 2009. The number of people living in poverty has reached an all-time high in the United States, despite its position as one of the world's wealthiest nations (U.S. Bureau of the Census, 2010).

In the 21st century, the United States has the highest rate of poverty for children of all developed nations, as much as five to eight times higher than in other industrialized countries (Woolfolk, 2008). Approximately 50% of these children live in deep poverty: their families have incomes 50% below the poverty threshold. In 2010, the Bureau of the Census indicated that overall, 32% of children in the United States lived in poverty. Poverty continues to plague our society, despite decades of national effort and trillions of federal dollars spent trying to combat it (National Center for Policy Analysis, 2009).

Entire books have been devoted to why so much poverty exists in the United States. Here, a brief examination of two major contributing factors is sufficient. First, the globalization of the world economy has caused many entry-level, unskilled, blue collar jobs in the United States to be exported overseas. This trend leads to diminished benefits and lower pay in many jobs found in the United States (Howard-Hobson, 2002).

Second, the United States is experiencing, and has already experienced, an ongoing macroeconomic shift from a manufacturing to an information-based economy (U.S. Bureau of the Census, 2010). In today's knowledge-based economy, eight of the nine fastest growing occupations in this decade require technological or scientific skills. To fill the jobs of the future, most workers need higher education. In an information-based economy, workers must have relatively high levels of oral and literate language skills. Without such skills, these potential workers, for whom few unskilled blue collar jobs are available, will be condemned to poverty and probably the welfare rolls.

The number of Americans with only a high school degree who were working went from 74% in the year 2000 to 65% in 2010. For Americans who had less than a high school degree, 52% of them were working in the year 2000; this number declined to 41% in 2010. Thus, in just 10 years, the percentage of workers with a high school education or less declined in our country (Camarota, 2011).

According to the Bureau of U.S. Labor Statistics (2012), in terms of newly created jobs in the United States, 37.6% will require a Bachelor's degree or higher. "Some college" or an Associate's degree will be required for 27.7% of those jobs, while 26.2% will require a high school diploma with no college. Only 8% of jobs will require less than a high school degree. In terms of current unemployment rates, 14.5% of the unemployed have less than a high school diploma, whereas only 4.1% of those with a Bachelor's degree or higher are unemployed. The ranks of the unemployed with less than a high school diploma, then, are 3 to 4 times higher than those of persons with a Bachelor's degree or more (Bureau of U.S. Labor Statistics, 2012).

In sum, the United States is facing a bifurcated employment future: at one end, there are willing but unskilled laborers who are seeing their employment prospects undermined by workers in developing countries. At the other end is a technically competent, highly educated workforce who is prepared for the demands of an increasingly globally oriented workplace.

DEFINITIONS AND DEMOGRAPHICS OF POVERTY

In the year 2011, federal poverty level was $22,350 for a family of four, $18,530 for a family of three, and $14,710 for a family of two (Addy & Wight, 2012; National Center for Children in Poverty, 2010). Children represent 24% of the U.S. population, yet they comprise 34% of those who live in poverty. Between the years 2005 to 2010, the number of children living in low-SES families went up (Figure 1–1). In 2005, 40% of children lived in low-SES families; in 2010, 44% lived in low-SES families. Forty-eight percent of children under the age of 5 years live in low-SES homes.

Status	2005	2010	Percent change/ increase
Low Income	28,598,752	31,862,267	11%
Poor	13,270,233	15,516,423	17%

Figure 1–1. Percentage change in numbers of children living in poverty, 2005 to 2010 (National Center for Children in Poverty, 2012).

Parents of these low-SES children vary in their educational levels. Eighty-five percent of children living in poverty have parents with less than a high school degree, whereas 65% of low-SES children live with parents who have only a high school degree. However, children of parents with college degrees can suffer from poverty also; 30% of low-SES children live in homes where at least one parent has some college education (Figure 1–2). Thus, although there is a positive correlation between having educated parents and being less likely to live in poverty, having one or two parents with some college education does not guarantee that children will avoid being poor.

Unfortunately, poverty disproportionately affects children of color (Reynolds & Fish, 2010). According to the United States Bureau of the Census (2010), income levels for Hispanics and Blacks nationwide decreased faster than incomes for Asians and Whites. Black households typically earned approximately 60 cents for every dollar earned in White households in 2010. The National Center for Children in Poverty (2010) indicated that 31% of White and Asian children live in poverty, whereas 64% of Black children and 63% of Hispanic and American Indian children live in poverty (Figure 1–3).

Some states are more impacted than others. For example, in California, in 2011, an estimated 2.2 million children lived in poverty.

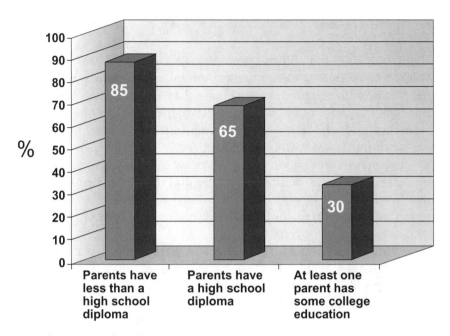

Figure 1–2. Children living in poverty: parents' educational levels (National Center for Children in Poverty, 2012).

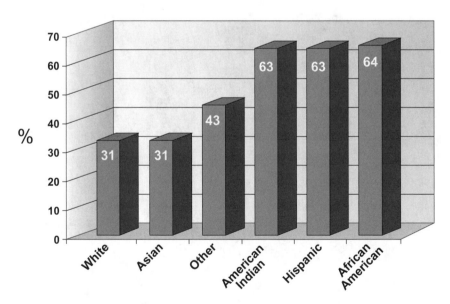

Figure 1–3. Percentage of children in low-income families by ethnicity (National Center for Children in Poverty, 2012).

Children of color in California were four times more likely than White children to be born into economically fragile households. In California, 32% of White children were classified as "income poor" compared to 69% of Hispanic and 71% of African American children. Eighty-two percent of poor children came from homes where at least one parent was working (Posnick-Goodwin, 2011).

The numbers of children in poverty vary according to geographic region (Figure 1–4). Children in the South (48%) and West (45%) are most likely to live in poverty; in the Northeast, 36% of children are poor. Children in urban and rural areas are especially likely to experience the effects of poverty.

Being raised in poverty is related in part to the structure of the family; changes in this structure have occurred in past decades. In 1950, 22% of all householders were not married. Between 1990 and 2000, the number of families headed by single mothers increased by 25% to more than 7.5 million households (U.S. Bureau of the Census, 2000). Over 38% of births are to unmarried women (Hamilton, Martin, & Ventura, 2007). Of these, approximately one-half are to mothers

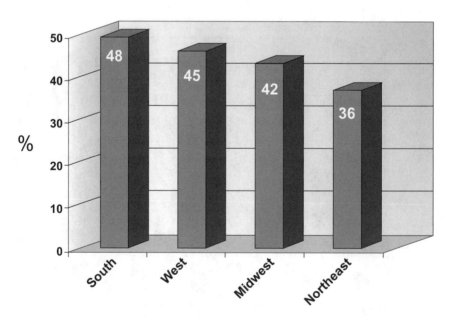

Figure 1–4. Percentage of children in low-income families by geographic region (National Center for Children in Poverty, 2012).

who are cohabiting with their partners; only about half of those relationships culminate in marriage (Lichter, Quian, & Mellott, 2006).

Single-parent families have fewer resources than any other types of families, and poverty is more common in these families (Barrett & Turner, 2005). As Corcoran (2001) has stated:

> Growing up in a single-parent family is associated with less schooling, more male idleness, higher rates of teen births, and more psychological and behavioral problems . . . single-parent families have fewer economic and community resources than do two-parent families . . . even after controlling for race, ethnicity, family size, parental schooling, and family income, growing up in a single-parent home matters for children's futures. (p. 128)

Female-headed households are vulnerable to poverty; many of the women do not have more than a high school diploma or a GED (American Psychological Association, 2012). Children in married-couple families are much less likely to experience poverty than children who live in homes headed by single mothers (Ispa, Thornburg, & Fine, 2006). In 1997, 49% of children in female-householder families lived in poverty, compared with 10% of children in married-couple families. In 2009, married households reported median incomes of $71,830, while female-headed households had earnings of $32,597 (National Women's Law Center, 2011). This is partly because all levels of educational attainment, median female wages in the United States are 30% to 50% lower than male wages at equal levels of educational attainment (U.S. Bureau of the Census, 2000). The proportion of females aged 18 to 64 years with incomes below the U.S. Census poverty thresholds is higher than that of males.

Working-age females in the 70 largest U.S. cities surpass males in their rate of high school completion and match males in rate of attaining a bachelor's degree; unfortunately, this has not translated to sufficient labor market gains to offset higher poverty rates. Being raised in a female-headed family doubles the risk that a child will drop out of high school, triples the risk that that a girl will have a birth out of wedlock, and increases by 40% the risk that young men will be idle (Corcoran, 2001).

For women of color, the situation is even more challenging. In the year 2010, 7.7% of African American and 8.5% of Hispanic women worked in jobs that paid at or below minimum wage, as compared to

4.3% of White men. African American and Hispanic women are more likely to be heads of households than White women (Pungello, Iruka, Dotterer, Mills-Koonce, & Reznick, 2009). Because these women statistically are more likely to be single mothers and earn less than White men, they and their children experience disproportionate hardship in America's economy (National Women's Law Center, 2011).

It is important to realize, however, that in some cultures, family members provide more intergenerational support for one another than family members do in mainstream culture. For instance, African Americans have been found to provide more intergenerational support than Whites (Goode, Jones, & Jackson, 2011). Thus, in discussing risks for children in female-headed households, it is essential to take into account the amount of intergenerational support that is available to these single mothers. In families in which such support is available, even without a father living in the home, children may be shielded from some of the risks that accompany living in a female headed household where such support is not available.

Being raised in poverty puts children at risk in a number of areas. Children from low-SES homes are more than three times as likely to drop out of high school. Girls from low-SES families are more than twice as likely as girls from middle-SES families to have a teen birth and are 2.6 times more likely to have had an out-of-wedlock birth. Boys and youth from low-SES homes work fewer hours per year, have lower hourly wages and annual earnings, and spend more weeks idle in their mid-twenties compared with boys and youth from middle-SES homes (Corcoran, 2001).

Minorities are overrepresented at all levels of the juvenile justice system; racism and poverty play major roles in this situation. A new report by Amnesty International and Human Rights Watch found that at least 2,225 prisoners in the United States currently are serving sentences of life without parole for crimes they committed as minors. This type of sentence is rare internationally; a total of 12 child offenders are serving life terms in Tanzania, South Africa, and Israel. African American youth are serving life without parole sentences at a rate that is 10 times higher than for White youth. If teenage offenders live to age 70 years and die behind bars, taxpayers will pay more than $6 million to keep them locked away (Hubner, 2006).

It is urgent that conditions in the United States change to prevent these kinds of sad, shocking situations. In the Preface, three basic levels of support that are available to low-SES children and their families were delineated (Figure 1–5):

1. Macroeconomic levels of support; federal and state policies that support the poor;
2. District and school site–based support;
3. Individual/personal effort on the part of professionals who work directly with low-SES students

As noted in the Preface, many educators and other professionals who work with children become discouraged because they are trying to provide support at levels 2 and 3 when level 1 support is so inadequate. Without massive changes in level 1 support, changes at levels 2 and 3 will always be very challenging to accomplish. But it is essential to start somewhere. Throughout this book, these three levels of support needed by children and families from low-SES homes constitute a common theme. Such support is necessary to effect

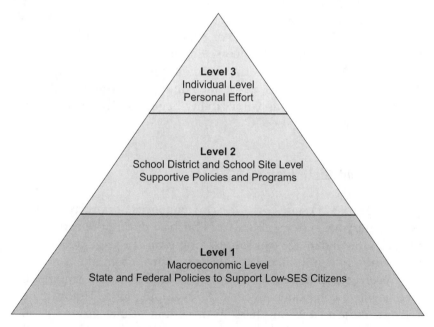

Figure 1–5. Three levels of support for low-income/low socioeconomic status (SES) children and their families.

permanent changes in the lives of these children and their families. Changes need to begin with addressing the physical and psychological effects of poverty.

PHYSICAL AND PSYCHOLOGICAL EFFECTS OF POVERTY

Professionals must recognize that it is important to never equate poverty with dysfunction. As Fazio, Naremore, and Connell (1996) have stated:

> Lack of money alone is not sufficient to put a child at risk for either academic failure or language problems. It is only when lack of money is associated with inadequate nutrition, inadequate medical care, or unstable living conditions that poverty becomes a risk factor. (p. 623)

For many children living in low-SES homes today, lack of money is associated with the foregoing conditions (Owens, Metz, & Farinella, 2011). As a group, low-SES children experience more acute problems than middle-SES children. For example, they are more likely to witness violence and experience seeing a parent arrested (Buckner, 2008). When children live in these conditions, they are more vulnerable to language problems, academic failure, and eventually the welfare rolls (Table 1–1). This vulnerability begins before many of them are even born.

Prenatal and Birth Issues

Long (2005, p. 321) states that "the consequences of poverty can harm a child's nervous system, either from birth or during the early formative years. Such damage can lead to long-term language deficits from which the child is unlikely to recover." Low-SES mothers may not have received prenatal care. Moreover, malnutrition in the mother can have negative consequences for the developing fetus. Unfortunately, statistics indicate that mothers from certain ethnic groups receive less prenatal care than others; this also affects children from low-SES households beginning in utero (Table 1–2).

Table 1–1. Potential Negative Effects of Poverty

Lack of Food	Neighborhood Problems
Low birthweight	Increased violence
Related birth defects	Exposure to crime
Anemia	Inferior schools
Learning problems	Post-traumatic stress syndrome
Lower test scores	Lower achievement
Stunted physical growth	Fewer job opportunities
	Fewer places for children to play, explore, and learn about their world
	Increased aggressive behavior

Housing Problems	Family Stress
Homelessness	Parental depression
Increased lead poisoning, asthma	Conflict between parents and between parents and children
Increased illness	
Utility shutoffs	Abuse and neglect of children
Increased middle ear infections	Less effective parenting
Frequent moving	Marital strain and breakup
Crowded conditions leading to less rest, more stress	Child aggressiveness, behavior problems, delinquency
More play-related injuries	

Fewer Learning Resources	Lack of Cognitive and Linguistic Stimulation
Less quality child care	Lower educational level of caregivers
Fewer books	
Fewer neighborhood libraries	Fewer print and literacy resources in homes and in neighborhoods
Fewer extracurricular activities, hobbies, family trips	Higher stress on caregivers; less emphasis on educational activities
Home, work responsibilities take priority over school work	Lower levels of oral language interaction between caregivers and children
Financial barriers to college	

Source: American Psychological Association, 2012; Fogle, 2013; Kayser, 2012; Neuman, 2009; Paul and Norbury, 2012; Roseberry-McKibbin and Hegde, 2011.

Table 1–2. Demographic and Health Characteristics of Births According to Race of Mother, 2004

Characteristic	White non-Hispanic	Hispanic Origin	Asian/Pacific Islander	American Indian	Black non-Hispanic
Prenatal care beginning 1st trimester	88.9%	77.4%	85.6%	69.9%	76.5%
Prenatal care beginning 3rd trimester/ no care	2.2%	5.4%	3.0%	7.9%	5.7%
Smoker	13.8%	2.7%	2.2%	18.2%	8.4%
Preterm infant	11.5%	12.0%	10.6%	13.7%	17.9%
Low or very low birthweight infant*	8.40%	7.99%	9.04%	8.78%	16.84%

*Low birthweight is birthweight of less than 2,500 grams (5 lbs., 8 oz.). Very low birthweight is birthweight of less than 1,500 grams (3 lbs., 4 oz.).

Source: National Center for Health Statistics, 2004.

Low-SES mothers are more likely to have premature babies. Prematurity is associated with a host of learning and cognitive problems (Roseberry-McKibbin & Hegde, 2011). Children who are born prematurely are at risk for abuse and neglect because their neurological immaturity leads to difficult, erratic, and unpredictable behavior (Paul & Norbury, 2012). Low birthweight infants, who usually are premature, are at risk of impaired development across a wide range of areas, including delayed cognitive-linguistic development and delayed motor and social development. They are more likely to fail or repeat grades.

Neuman (2009) discusses the fact that in order to work for the best possible outcomes for low-SES children, we must get women into care before the baby is even born. She describes one study in Elmira, New York, where a nurse visitation program was developed. Nurses visited 90 mothers and their families in their homes during pregnancy and during the next two years of the children's lives. The same nurse came to each home every time, and young mothers were able to develop real relationships with the nurses. Nurses gave advice and support in all areas. In a 15-year follow-up of the children involved in the Elmira study, there was less drinking, drug use, and crime among the children in this sample as compared to similar peers whose families were not involved in the program. The group who was involved in the program had 59% fewer arrests than similar peers. Subsequent studies in Denver and Memphis found that nurse-visited children were better prepared to enter school; they had better language and cognitive skills than nonvisited children.

It was found that the home visits were extremely helpful; mothers often expressed that they felt discriminated against at doctors' offices. When nurses visited homes, they understood the mothers' circumstances much better. For example, nurses found that some mothers could not let their babies play on the floor because of rats and cockroaches. By actually visiting homes, nurses were able to tailor their recommendations to mothers' individual situations.

Mothers who abuse cocaine and other drugs tend to be from low-SES backgrounds (Paul & Norbury, 2012). Children in poverty are more likely to be exposed, in utero, to nicotine, alcohol, and illegal drugs (Farah, Noble, & Hurt, 2005). These substances can cause a wide variety of linguistic, academic, and physical problems, including fetal alcohol syndrome.

The following case example is based on a real-life family situation:

Debbie is a White woman from a low-SES background who had six children; she is now a great-grandmother at the age of 60 years. One of her granddaughters had a son, Scotty, who is now 23 months of age and not saying any words. Debbie is actively involved in this child's care and is concerned that Scotty's language development might be a little "slow." In a consultation with a speech-language pathologist (SLP), Debbie shared that the boy's mother, a recovering drug addict, was on methadone during her entire pregnancy. Scotty was now in the care of his biological father, who regularly smokes marijuana—even when he is driving with Scotty in the car. Debbie wondered if it is bad for Scotty to be around a marijuana-smoking father. She also wondered if her daughter's taking methadone during the whole pregnancy had caused Scotty to incur permanent brain damage.

The SLP agreed that Scotty needed a speech and language evaluation as soon as possible. She also recommended that Child Protective Services (CPS) intervene to remove Scotty from his pot-smoking father's custody. Debbie was reluctant to take these steps: she would not be supported by her granddaughter, who refused to accept intervention from such agencies; moreover, for unclear reasons, the attorney in this case had stated that if CPS became involved, he would quit. Debbie asked the SLP what she should do. The SLP confirmed that chronic exposure to marijuana smoke could have adverse effects on the brain. She reemphasized her belief that despite what the attorney had said, CPS should be involved with this case; she also suggested that Scotty should be removed from his father's care. Debbie agreed that would be best.

Later, the SLP began to worry that Scotty's father, who had a history of violent behavior, might react in anger to efforts to remove his son from his custody. She was concerned that his anger could extend to attempts at revenge on herself and her family for her support of Debbie's actions. She telephoned Debbie and asked her to keep her involvement anonymous; Debbie readily promised not to give Scotty's father any relevant information. Clearly, however, the safety of the SLP and her family depended on Debbie's keeping her promise.

In hindsight, the SLP realized that she should have limited her involvement to her original recommendation for a speech and language evaluation for Scotty. She recognized that her protective instincts as a clinician and a parent had prevailed, however, and that she probably had overstepped professional boundaries in recommending that CPS intervene.

Meanwhile, Scotty remained in his father's custody. The court had previously ordered Scotty's father (who does not hold down a job) to take Scotty to speech-language therapy; the father refused. When the father was not home, Scotty was watched over by his alcoholic grandmother, who punished him when he did not change his own diapers. Scotty repeatedly got splinters in his feet from wearing no shoes and was not given a coat to wear even in 45-degree weather.

After a prolonged court case, Scotty's mother eventually was awarded custody of her son, much to Debbie's relief. She remained concerned because Scotty still was not speaking but was happy that he was at least safe from abuse. Unfortunately, Debbie just learned that Scotty's mother deserted him and left town with friends. No one can find her, and Scotty is back with his father.

This example drives home the point that in low-SES homes where drugs are involved, children can experience negative effects in many areas. In addition, clinicians who work with families from these homes need to remember to proceed cautiously, being ethical without overstepping their professional boundaries.

Hunger and Malnutrition

Hunger and malnutrition, which usually accompany poverty, lead to decreased cognitive development. In 1996, Brown and Pollitt stated that it was estimated that 12 million children in the United States had diets that were significantly below the recommended allowances of nutrients established by the National Academy of Sciences. According to Brown and Pollitt, childhood malnutrition produces permanent, structural damage to the brain. The American Psychological Association (2012) reported that homeless children especially are twice as likely to be hungry as their housed peers.

Between birth and the age of 2 years, the brain grows to approximately 80% of its adult size. Malnutrition during this period of growth is especially devastating. This devastation occurs partly because small children who are malnourished frequently crawl and walk slightly later than average; this limits their exploration of their physical and social environments. Bloom and Lahey (1978) defined language as a system of symbols used to represent concepts *formed through exposure and experience* [italics mine]. When children's exposure and experiences are limited, their language is negatively affected. Other negative effects of malnutrition include inadequate brain growth, illness, and lethargy, withdrawal and delayed intellectual development (Brown & Pollitt, 1996). Children who are hungry have difficulty concentrating in school.

American children living in urban poverty are at risk for iron deficiency and protein-energy malnutrition, which involves shortages of both calories and protein. Both of these conditions can impair children's brain functioning. Low stores of iron render children more susceptible to environmental lead and its effects.

Overall Brain Development

In terms of brain development, cognitive neuroscience has helped to explain the persistence of generational poverty (Blair et al., 2011; Farah et al., 2005). Children's experience of the world is very different in low versus middle SES communities. Most children from middle-SES homes have many opportunities to explore the world and to be exposed to novel places, people, and ideas. Conversely, children from low-SES homes have fewer of these opportunities; what they do experience often is stressful (Cutuli, Wiik, Herbers, Gunnar, & Masten, 2009).

Powerful effects on the human brain have been recognized for both psychological stress and environmental impoverishment. According to Farah and associates (2005),

> . . . lower SES children show a kind of sad precocity compared with middle class children in their first-hand experience with violence, death, and the criminal justice system. Preschoolers growing up in the inner city know to fear the neighbors from the local crack house. By elementary school, they recognize the sound of gunshots and by middle school they know about prison because a relative has been there. (p. 2)

Psychological stress causes the secretion of cortisol and other stress hormones, which affect the brain in numerous ways, specifically by altering the anatomy and physiology of the brain (Blair et al.,

2011; Cutuli et al., 2009). The developing, immature brain is especially sensitive to these effects. The area of the brain most affected is the medial temporal area, needed for memory. Basically, an impoverished and stressful childhood can have a negative impact through neuroendocrine mechanisms that affect memory. When children's brains are negatively affected by environmental impoverishment and stress, they are ultimately denied many social and economic opportunities, and thus, another generation of children of low SES is born.

Basic Safety Issues

Many children from low-SES homes live in unsafe neighborhoods. The poor cannot afford to relocate to communities that are close to available jobs, and they can afford housing only in disadvantaged neighborhoods that provide fewer good role models, less social control, lower-quality schools, fewer job networks, and higher crime rates and more gangs. As stated, children may be exposed to violence. Because some low-SES neighborhoods are not safe, many parents keep their children indoors. When children are indoors, they tend to watch a great deal of TV, some more than 6 hours a day (Barton, 2004). By some estimates, in some inner-city homes, the television is on 11 hours a day (Obama, 2006).

In terms of national averages, TV viewing among children is at an 8-year high. On average, children ages 2 to 5 years spend 32 hours a week in front of a TV. Children between 6-11 years of age spend about 28 hours a week in front of the TV, and 71% of 8 to 18 year olds have a TV in their room. By the time the average American child is 18 years old, he or she will have seen 200,000 violent acts and 16,000 murders on TV (University of Michigan Health System, 2012).

When children are watching TV, they are not getting cognitively and linguistically enriching experiences that can support them in school. In my own clinical practice as a speech-language pathologist, I encountered a Chinese second grader from a low-SES family who was struggling in school. His records indicated that as a preschooler who was cared for by his grandparents while his parents worked, he watched approximately 10 hours of TV each day.

In the following case example based on a real-life middle-SES family, everyday life provides exposure to numerous experiences not available to children who live in poverty.

> My husband, son, and I live in a middle-class home across the street from a lovely park. Though Mark is not allowed to go there alone, often the three of us will walk there on weekends. Mark sees the changing of the seasons, meets new friends on the playground, and plays by a creek. He sees various animals (we live in a somewhat rural area) such as dogs, sheep, rabbits, and horses. When we are at the park and I am filled with gratitude that it and its attendant experiences are available, I simultaneously think of children in neighborhoods in the unsafe part of town, where they must remain indoors and not experience the things my own child is experiencing.

Professionals must recognize that children from low-SES homes may not have what ordinarily are considered "basic" experiences, such as going to parks, because some neighborhoods are not safe; again, parents must keep their children indoors, watching TV.

Even middle-SES neighborhoods also may be becoming less safe, resulting in more TV and computer time for children. Two brief case examples from real life follow.

> One friend of mine (her twin sons are Mark's age) and her husband live in a nice, middle-SES neighborhood. One day when her boys were 3 years old, they were playing in the front yard. Catherine looked up from the living room to see a strange car stop and the driver try to get one of the boys into the car. She ran outside and chased the stranger away. After that, it was Nintendo and videos—inside where the boys could stay safe.
>
> Another friend lives in a lovely home across from a middle school in a nice neighborhood. When her son (also Mark's age) was 5 years old, he would play in the yard. Middle school students would come and throw dog poop laced with straight pins at this boy, hitting him in the face while he played. A large fence was put around the house, and the little boy was allowed computer games indoors.

Shocking as these stories may seem, they are true; they illustrate that, at both middle-and low-SES levels, children are increasingly unsafe in their own yards. In response, their parents keep them inside, staring at computer and TV screens. At least during this "screen time," reason the parents, the children's physical selves are out of harm's way. The impact of "screen time" on other aspects of children's development is considered later in the chapter.

Access to Health Care

Because of barriers such as lack of transportation and money, many low-SES families are unable to visit doctors or medical facilities for care. Transportation problems are very real for many low-SES adults, who often must rely on others for rides to appointments. In addition, many low-SES families tend to be unaware of health care services that are available, especially if these families do not speak English or have recently immigrated to the United States. Some families are intimidated by the process of using medical care and are unaware of the importance of ongoing care, especially preventive care. Even when enrolled in medical care programs, low-SES families often are less apt to use it. In addition, the SES of a geographical area can influence the available supply of health care professionals (Borrell, Beck, & Heiss, 2006). Thousands of low-SES families are does not have health insurance; this varies from city to city (Table 1–3).

Consequently, low-SES children often receive inconsistent well-baby care. They are less likely to have contact with physicians at an early age and are less likely to have recommended vaccinations (Chen, Martin, & Matthews, 2006).

Dental care is reduced for many children from low-SES homes. Untreated caries (cavities) are prevalent. Students with toothaches tend to be more inattentive and distractible in class and during tests than are students with healthy teeth. Johnson and Johnson (2002) described their findings in children in a third grade classroom at a low-SES school in Louisiana. Many children complained of tooth pain; some were in tears because they hurt so much and had never seen a dentist. Every day, students reported stomachaches due to hunger. Some children had earaches and were in so much pain they couldn't concentrate in school.

Table 1–3. Income, Poverty, and Insurance in the United States

INCOME		POVERTY		INSURANCE	
$46,326 (U.S. median income in 2005, up 1.1% from 2004)		**37 million** (number of people in poverty in 2005, unchanged at 12.6% from 2004)		**46.6 million** (number of people without health insurance in 2005)	
Cities with the highest median income, 2005 (population 250,000 or more)		**Cities with lowest poverty rates, 2005** (population 250,000 or more)		**States with highest #s of uninsured people, 2004–2005**	
1. Plano, Texas	$71,560	1. Plano, Texas	6.3%	1. Texas	24.5%
2. San Jose	70,921	2. Virginia Beach	7.4%	2. New Mexico	20.6%
3. Anchorage	61,217	3. Anchorage	9.5%	3. Florida	20.3%
4. Virginia Beach	58,545	4. San Jose	10%	4. California	19%
5. San Francisco	57,496	5. Anaheim	11.7%	5. Oklahoma	19%

Source: U.S. Bureau of the Census, 2005; American Community Survey, 2006.

In the case study that opens this chapter, I shared that, when I was pregnant with my son Mark, I was diagnosed with gestational diabetes. Thanks to a combination of excellent medical care and alternative medicine therapies, this quickly resolved, and my pregnancy proceeded uneventfully to a normal birth. Mark was born a healthy, full-term baby with a high Apgar score. Today he is a happy, successful eighth grader with a bright future ahead of him.

For mothers from low-SES backgrounds, however, outcomes can be much less fortunate. The following case example is based on a real-life family that I worked with in my job as a public school speech-language pathologist.

Mrs. N. was in her 30s when she became pregnant with Kevin. The N. household consists of an extended family,

> including a grandmother and Mr. N.'s brother and his wife; the N.'s are from Vietnam and have no health insurance. Several family members are employed, but only in low-paying jobs, and the household has difficulty making ends meet. Mrs. N., who speaks little English, was diagnosed with gestational diabetes. It went uncontrolled, and Kevin was born with many medical problems. Moreover, Mrs. N. went blind as a result of her diabetes. Today, Kevin demonstrates a low IQ and significant cognitive-linguistic deficits. His future, as well as that of his family, is uncertain.

The differences between middle-and low-SES families, as exemplified by Mark and Kevin and their mothers, are clear. For an English speaking mother from a middle-SES background who has health insurance and access to good medical care, it is reasonable to expect a good pregnancy outcome with birth of a healthy baby. The experience of a mother from a low-SES background, especially if such "basics" are lacking, may fall far short of an optimal outcome. Mrs. N. had none of those things, and her son will pay for it for the rest of his life.

Environmental Issues

Poverty is associated with increased exposure to certain harmful environmental pollutants such as lead. Lead poisoning is more common in children who live in older houses with lead-soldered pipes and lead paint, which are common in many inner-city areas. Hispanic low-SES children especially are very vulnerable to lead exposure, as 80% of Hispanics live in areas that don't meet the ambient air quality standards of the U.S. Environmental Protection Agency (Kayser, 2012). Antoniadis, Gilbert, and Wagner (2006) recently discussed the hazards of lead, pollution, and other neurotoxicants in children's environments. These investigators point out that, in small infants, the blood-brain barrier is immature, not fully developing till after 6 months of age. Exposure to neurotoxicants is especially devastating during this time.

There is growing evidence for a link between neurotoxicants such as lead and cigarette smoke and disabilities (Hepp, 2011). Children who have greater concentrations of lead in their blood often demonstrate long-term neurological impairments, behavior problems, reading disability, hyperactivity and distractibility, and lower school achievement, as well as diminished cognitive abilities (Kayser, 2012). They may show stunted growth (less than normal height for age), as well as behavioral problems in early adolescence. Children from low-SES families also are at greater risk for exposure to particulate air pollution and ambient noise.

When children are older, lead exposure in schools can occur through cracking and peeling paint that produces lead dust, as well as use of older drinking water systems with leaded pipes. Lead dust may be inhaled or inadvertently ingested by children, teachers, and administrators. High levels of lead in the blood can result in encephalopathy. As stated, low levels of lead in the blood can result in behavioral difficulties and cognitive impairment, as well as low intelligence test scores and lowered academic performance. Other potential effects of lead in the blood, even at low levels, are problems with balance and hearing. Contaminated house dust is a significant source of lead exposure for children who live in urban communities. Thus, low-SES children are at risk for increased lead exposure, both at home and at school.

The following case example is based on my own clinical experience.

> Alyssa G., a 7-year-old third-grade girl from a low-SES family, was referred for evaluation after transfer from a neighboring school district, where she had been in a self-contained special education classroom. I and the other members of the team were asked to conduct updated psychoeducational assessments of her current levels of performance.
>
> According to Alyssa's file, she was the youngest of five children. Concerns about her behavior included the following: She was off task 95% of the time; she ran off when not supervised; she had low cognitive-linguistic skills; she exhibited gross and fine motor delays; and she had an oral fixation that included licking tables and desks. She also had a history of middle ear infections, as well as skin and scalp problems. Alyssa ate dirt as a toddler and was diagnosed with lead poisoning.

I found Alyssa to be eager to please during the testing session. She had a sunny disposition, and the team members all enjoyed working with her. She exhibited a profile of profound language impairment in all areas, with some being lower than others. Alyssa also had significant bronchial congestion; her records did not state whether or not she had received treatment for this congestion.

With regard to congestion, children from low-SES homes tend to suffer from chronic impairments, for example, as indicated by higher rates of hospitalizations for asthma (Chen et al., 2006). Asthma is provoked partly by breathing fumes from the low-grade heating oil often used in low-income housing, as well as from buses and diesel trucks, which are more numerous in low-income neighborhood. Asthma also may be associated with allergic reactions to excessive dust, mold, cockroaches, and second-hand smoke, all of which are more prevalent in low-income housing.

Many asthmatic children refrain from exercising and consequently are less physically fit and more sedentary. They frequently have trouble sleeping at night, resulting in fatigue, irritability, and possible problem behaviors the next day. Children from middle-SES families usually get treatment for asthma; many children from low-SES families do not. Naturally, this affects their ability to learn. Many asthmatic children have single mothers who are employed outside the home. If these mothers try to take time off from work to care for the medical needs of their asthmatic children, they may lose their jobs (Ispa et al., 2006).

Instability and Chaos

Many low-SES children are at risk for difficulties linked to the instability and chaos/disorder in their lives. Vernon-Feagans, Garrett-Peters, Willoughby, and Mills-Koonce (2011) studied the role and results of chaos, poverty, and parenting as these factors related to children's language development. Vernon-Feagans et al. defined two basic constructs under the rubric of chaos: turbulence/instability and disorganization/disorder. Turbulence/instability is related to changes in settings and relationships in the home and unpredictability of routines. Disorganization/disorder relates to clutter, excessive crowding, and high noise levels. In this study, the constructs of instability and disorganization (chaos) were examined in relation to their impact on parenting practices and language skills of children in a rural low-SES area.

Vernon-Feagans et al. (2011) stated that in many rural areas, jobs are found less often in farming and more in the service sector where there tend to be nonstandard hours and low wages. Often, families must commute long distances to work and child care facilities. The presence of poverty, irregular work hours, and distance between work and services can create increased chaos in the lives of children. Families may move more frequently, and more persons may be added to the household in order to sustain the economic viability of the family. Because parents spend long hours working and commuting, more persons may especially be added to the household to care for young children. In addition, in some homes, there may be a frequent change of domestic partners, creating added chaos and instability to children's lives.

Chronic noise, residential crowding, a high volume of people coming in and out of the house, messiness of the house, and other factors related to chaos can impact children's language and cognitive development in several ways. First, these children may be compromised in their ability to develop joint attention skills, which are foundational for language development. Joint attention is especially important for word learning. Second, children exposed to chronic chaos and lack of predictability in family routines may show diminished use of appropriate conversational skills and knowledge of rules of discourse because no one in their household has time or energy to conduct sustained interactions. Third, children may withdraw if they are bombarded by too much stimulation. Withdrawal negatively impacts emotional, cognitive, and linguistic growth.

Studies of chaos and its impact on parenting skills have linked chaos to poorer parenting skills and poorer interaction with children. Greater chaos is associated with less giving of objects to children, more parental verbal interference, and more ignoring a child's attempts to communicate. Excessive amounts of noise and crowding are related to less responsive and stimulating parenting. Studies have found that the more crowded a home, the poorer mothers' language is with their children. The language used by these mothers is more negative, less complex, and less sensitive than language used by mothers who are not living in chaotic conditions (Vernon-Feagans et al., 2011).

In the study by Vernon-Feagans and colleagues (2011), the Family Life Project (FLP) was designed to study young children and their families who lived in three counties in Eastern North Carolina (Black South) and Central Pennsylvania (Appalachia). The FLP adopted a developmental epidemiological design in which sampling procedures were used to recruit a representative sample of 1,292 children. A number of home visits were conducted: the first occurred when children were 2 months old, and the next visit occurred when the children were 6 months old. Subsequent visits occurred when the children were 15, 24, and 36 months of age. During the home visits, interviews were conducted and observations were made. Interviewers videotaped interactions between children and adult caregivers. At 36 months of age, children were given an expressive and receptive language test.

The results of this study indicated that disorganization was a significant predictor of receptive and expressive language. In this study, both household density and ambient noise were major factors in young children's having receptive and expressive language delays. As a variable, disorganization contributed substantially more variance in predicting expressive and receptive language skills than poverty or maternal education. Vernon-Feagans et al (2011) noted that chaos may have its greatest effect at early ages in the area of language development.

Chaos in the form of constant TV noise in the background of many homes has been shown to impact children's developing language. In the study by Vernon-Feagans et al. (2011), the TV was turned on for 4 or more hours a day. Christakis and colleagues (2009) conducted a study where they had children wear a digital recorder on random days for up to 24 months. A software program incorporating speech-identification technology processed recorded files to analyze the sounds children made and the sounds they were exposed to. The authors used conditional linear regression to determine the association between audible television noise and variables of interest. They found that each hour of audible TV noise was associated with fewer conversational turns between children and adults in the home, fewer child vocalizations, and vocalizations of shorter duration. They concluded that audible TV is associated with decreased exposure to discernible human adult speech and decreased child vocalizations. In sum, the more TV the child is exposed to in the home, the fewer opportunities there are for meaningful language comprehension and production.

Chaos can impact children's social and emotional skills also. Recent evidence has suggested that instability (moving, changing schools, having a parent with changing partners, having people in and out of the home) is related to depression and externalizing problems in adolescence (Evans & Wachs, 2010). The U.S. Bureau of the Census (2010) reported that in 2010, due to the economic recession, about 5.9 million young adults between ages 25 to 34 lived with their parents (up from 1.2 million before the recession). Thus, the number of young adults living at home has almost quintupled in the last several years. The presence of these young adults adds to crowdedness in homes, and consequent possible displacement of other family members.

In sum, it appears that chaos early in life impacts children's developing language skills the most. As children grow older, the effects of chaos spread to create emotional and social problems as well. Professionals must be aware of chaos, its impacts, and consequences at all levels of children's development.

My son Mark was friends with Jason W., a middle-SES boy from preschool. Jason's parents were educated and both held full time jobs. Mrs. W. had three adult children from her first marriage; Jason's father was her second husband. One adult child, Natalie, had a baby out of wedlock and moved in with Jason and his family. Jason, who was 4 years old at the time, had to give his bedroom to Natalie and the baby. He slept in a sleeping bag on his parents' bedroom floor for approximately one year while Natalie went to night school to learn a trade so she could move out and support herself and her child. Mrs. W. became very preoccupied with her full time job, adult daughter, and infant grandchild living in the home. At times, Jason would be at preschool from 7:00 in the morning till 6:00 in the evening. His life was substantially disrupted by his adult half-sister and her baby moving into his home and taking over his room.

Hearing and Vision

In comparison with children from middle-SES homes, children from low-SES homes have twice the average rate of severe vision impairment (Rothstein, 2004). One possible reason for this is inadequate prenatal development resulting from maternal malnutrition and inadequate prenatal care. Visual deficits may also occur because children from low-SES families are more likely to watch a great deal of television, as previously mentioned; watching TV does not develop the visual depth perception, tracking skills, and eye-hand coordination skills that are critical to success in reading and writing.

Christakis, Zimmerman, DiGuiseppe, and McCarty (2004) established that, between the ages of 1 and 3 years, each hour of daily television that a child watches increases by 10% the risk that he or she will have attention problems, as well as possible vision problems. According to the National Center for Education Statistics (2005), 42% of African American fourth graders watch 6 or more hours of television a day, compared with 13% of White fourth graders. As an overall national average, it is estimated that in 51% of households, the TV is on "most" of the time (University of Michigan Health System, 2012).

As noted earlier, for students from low-SES families of all ethnic backgrounds, it makes sense that if they live in low-SES neighborhoods with safety issues, that watching TV is one of the few safe ways for children to spend their time. Unfortunately, also as stated, these children can develop difficulties with attention, depth perception, and eye-hand coordination. Visual tracking problems, which are highly related to success in reading, are not uncommon. These types of vision deficits are not caught with routine vision testing that occurs in public schools.

Most schools (including the one my own son attends) screen vision using the Snellen chart, developed in 1862 by Hermann Snellen to test the vision of soldiers in the Civil War. Students are asked to read this chart, which screens them for nearsightedness. Most students are never tested for farsightedness or for visual tracking difficulties; these problems are most likely to affect academic performance (Rothstein, 2004). Many students pass "vision screening" perfectly, with results indicating 20/20 vision, but they cannot track horizontally. If they cannot track horizontally and sweep from left to right and then back to the next line on the left again, their ability to read is greatly reduced. Reading comprehension and fluency are negatively affected, and students often fall further and further behind.

In the following case example, additional vision testing proved crucial to allowing development of essential school skills.

> My own son Mark was reading at grade level in kindergarten, but I always got the sense that he was memorizing the books rather than decoding them. In first grade, his teacher was concerned that his reading comprehension was lower than his intelligence and high verbal skills would indicate. At the time, Mark was receiving occupational therapy for some gross and fine-motor delays. The occupational therapist referred us to a developmental optometrist. Results of her testing showed that Mark could not track horizontally at all. We went to weekly vision therapy for one and one half years and did nightly eye exercises; Mark now reads at grade level, and recently said the words that every parent lives to hear: "Mommy, I love to read!" His comprehension has greatly improved. At the beginning of his third grade year, Mark's reading score was a 3.4 (third grade, 4 months). At the end of his first trimester, his reading score was a 5.1 (fifth grade, 1 month). By fourth grade, he was approaching a 7th grade level of reading.
>
> Neither my husband's nor my insurance covered vision therapy. The total cost for vision therapy, not counting car mileage and gas money to get to the optometrist each week, was over $6,000.00. As a middle-SES married mother; I was able to afford this through careful budgeting.

Most low-SES families could never hope to even begin to afford this type of treatment for their children; even if the families have insurance, most insurance companies do not cover the cost of vision therapy such as Mark received.

Even if all children, especially those from low-SES homes, who needed such therapy could be identified, the evidence shows that despite vision testing leading to optometric referrals, parents are less likely to follow through on therapy for the child. If and when these children get prescriptions for lenses, they obtain the eyeglasses and wear them to school less frequently. Another disadvantage faced by many children from low-SES homes who have untreated vision problems is that they may end up misplaced in special education classes.

The disproportionate referral and placement of some low-SES students to special education may reflect, in part, a failure to detect vision problems that are not uncovered on routine screening. Vision problems, even if the child's vision is technically 20/20, make it difficult to read, see the chalkboard (or whiteboard), and copy from the board onto a piece of paper.

Children from low-SES homes are more prone to middle ear infections than children from middle-SES homes for several reasons. First, many low-SES homes have poor heating and sanitation, thereby increasing the chances of sickness and accompanying ear infections. Second, as noted earlier, many low-SES families do not have health insurance; they cannot afford to take their children for treatment of such infections. Children with untreated middle ear infections often have a host of problems: reduced hearing, difficulty paying attention, and eventual difficulties in academic subjects in school.

It is very important for professionals to be aware of both hearing and vision abilities of students from low-SES homes. If these abilities are compromised, succeeding linguistically and academically will be difficult indeed. It is important for professionals to help low-SES families become aware of free or reduced-cost health care services that are available to correct these problems.

Emotional Atmosphere of the Home

It is well documented that in low-SES homes, caregivers' stress levels tend to be higher; maternal depression is common (Barrett & Turner, 2005; Grzywacz, Almeida, Neupert, & Ettner, 2004; Owens et al., 2011; Pungello et al., 2009; Turnbull & Justice, 2012). Parents' experience of more physical and emotional problems leads to more common conflicts between parents and children; such conflicts can include abuse and neglect (Ispa et al., 2006; Roseberry-McKibbin, 2007). Economic pressure increases spouses' psychological distress; low income and daily economic difficulties can provoke anger, sadness, and pessimism about the future.

As spouses become more emotionally distressed, they often interact in a less supportive and more irritable way, increasing the level of marital conflict in the home. With increasing economic pressures, spouses may isolate themselves from family and friends. Spouses who receive social support from friends and family, however, are better able to support each other and manage their situation (Robila &

Krishnakumar, 2005). Thus, professionals can consider helping low-SES parents find sources of social support so that they can better manage their homes and interact more positively with their children. This kind of support is discussed in greater detail in subsequent chapters.

When low-SES parents feel stress and other negative emotions, they may interact with their children verbally and emotionally in an unsupportive manner. Compared with higher-income mothers, lower income mothers often show lower levels of warmth, responsiveness, and sensitivity when interacting with their children (Fish & Pinkerman, 2003; Pungello, Iruka, Dotterer, Mills-Koonce, & Reznick, 2009; Vernon-Feagans, Pancsofar, Willoughby, Odom, Quade, & Cox, 2008) For example, Hart and Risley (1995) found that children from welfare homes received two scoldings for every one encouragement, whereas children in professional homes received one scolding for every six encouragements. As discussed in later chapters, a high proportion of essentially negative feedback has a profound effect on the language skills and self-esteem of children from these homes.

Lynch and Hanson (2011) emphasize that, as the old adage says, money can't buy happiness, but it can buy creature comforts and supports that make life easier. Being financially secure does not make one a good parent, but it provides access to many things that support good parenting. These things can include books and other literacy materials, high-quality preschool, trips to interesting places, and other advantages that children enjoy when their parents have money. Parents who are financially comfortable often find it easier to be supportive of their children. By contrast, parents who experience a great deal of stress on an ongoing basis, related to lack of financial resources and psychosocial support, may have less emotional energy for interacting with their children in positive ways.

The following case example from my own experience shows how such stress can affect parent-child interactions.

> One sunny day I was enjoying an ice-cream cone with my 5-year-old son, sitting outside the ice cream parlor. We heard a ruckus, and a low-SES mother with three small girls arrived at their beaten-up older car parked directly in front of the ice cream store. The mother, young and clearly much stressed, was shouting at her girls that they were disobedient. She jerked them into the car and was so angry that she

was shaking the youngest one hard as she shoved her into her car seat. This child (who probably was only 2 years old) began crying loudly in fear and pain.

I jumped up from my chair, ran over, and gently put my hand on the mother's shoulder. "Can I help?" I asked quietly. "Looks like it's been one of those days." "No," she said, "they just need discipline. Thanks anyway." She calmed down considerably and was much kinder to her daughters, knowing that I was watching her. After they drove off, my son, who also had been watching, looked very sad. "Why was that mommy being so mean to her children?" he asked. How to explain to him the tremendous stress that low-SES parents experience? I wondered what would happen to the children when they reached home.

Understanding Children and Families from Backgrounds of Situational and Generational Poverty

A common assumption among middle-class professionals is that all children and families from low-SES households are "poor." According to Payne (2003), however, two major types of poverty can be recognized: situational and generational. *Generational poverty* is defined as poverty affecting a family for two generations or longer. Usually welfare is involved. *Situational poverty* occurs for a shorter time and usually is the result of a circumstance or particular set of circumstances (e.g., death, illness, divorce). (My own parents experienced situational poverty when my father earned $300 a month as a young minister with a wife and four small children; fortunately, our family's circumstances improved as his earning power increased in later years.)

In situational poverty, people tend to demonstrate an attitude of "pride," reflecting a belief in their ability to manage their own survival and to effect change in their lives, and may refuse to accept offers of help, regarded as "charity." In generational poverty, a common attitude, reflecting the very real lack of resources and absence of a belief that things can change, is, "I'm stuck here, so the world owes me." Table 1–4 summarizes some of the differences in the practices and value systems of persons from a middle-SES background and those from a background of generational poverty.

Table 1–4. Contrasts Between Low- and Middle-SES Values and Practices

Value/Practice	Middle Class	Poverty (Generational)
World view	Seen in terms of national setting.	Seen in terms of local setting; home, neighborhood are your world.
Time	To be valued; punctuality is critical. Future is important.	"You get there when you get there;" The present is most important; survival is key.
Destiny	We all have choices; strong sense of personal efficacy; internal locus of control	External locus of control; weak sense of personal efficacy; "whatever will be will be;" "You can't fight City Hall."
Education	Crucial for making money, getting ahead in life, being comfortable and respected	Valued and respected in the abstract; not emphasized as a reality or as an obtainable or practical goal
Life priorities	Achievement, possessions, status	Entertainment, relationships, survival
Money	To be managed, saved, invested	To be spent, especially on things that bring pleasure in the moment
Religion	One of the accoutrements of life; special times and places such as church, Bible study that fit particular time slots in a busy, activity-filled schedule	May be center of much of life; priest/pastor is the key authority figure; church is a central place for worship, socializing, connections, spending a great deal of time
Language	Formal register is used; language is used to meet needs, get ahead in life	Casual register is used; language is used for survival and to entertain
Interaction style	Quiet is valued; conversational partners do not interrupt, but politely wait their turn	Constant presence of background noise; interruptions during conversation are common and expected

Table 1–4. *continued*

Value/Practice	Middle Class	Poverty (Generational)
Entertainment	Viewed as reward for hard work; money is used for education and life comforts; leftover money is for entertainment after other priorities are met	Plays crucial role; highly valued; may take precedence over education, other abstractions because the present is all we have; why not enjoy life right now? Live in the moment.
Discipline	Punishment/negative consequences are delivered so that the person will change their behavior; "Don't be sorry, be different."	Punishment is not about change; it is about penance and forgiveness; person's behavior continues as before.
Organization/ planning	Life is carefully scheduled into time slots. Structure is crucial; calendars, iPads, and other organizational devices proliferate. Organization is central.	Organizational/planning devices virtually nonexistent; clutter is common; structure is not valued. Planning ahead is not common; "living by the seat of your pants" is typical.

Source: Adapted from Haberman, 1999, 2005; Hart and Risley, 1995; Lynch, 2011; Neuman, 2009; Payne, 2003; Roseberry-McKibbin, 2007; Sue and Sue, 2013.

With regard to the impact of living in generational poverty, Beals, Tyree, and Barker (1994) have stated:

> One of the most profound consequences for a child living in [generational] poverty is the development of a short-term value system, of living without regard for the future. Growing up in an extremely low income household instills a dim outlook for the future. Impoverished children deal with immediate concerns on a daily survival level. They and their caretakers are rarely motivated to consider long-range educational plans. . . . Across the nation, educators are trying to devise and implement creative ideas and methods to respond to this concern. (p. 112)

Many families who live in generational poverty believe that the present is most important; there is a need to survive today. The future is uncertain, and consequently planning is not important. Thus, if a child with a language delay is surviving today as a 3-year-old in the home and neighborhood, the family may not see the importance of early intervention: of planning for 2 years into the future when the child is in kindergarten. Professionals need to be aware that such families may not be interested in services that are offered, especially early intervention services for young, at-risk children.

With regard to surviving in and living for the moment, a story related by Payne (2003) is both entertaining and instructive: At one school, teachers found out that a certain low-SES family had no refrigerator. They banded together and contributed money to buy a refrigerator for the family. Shortly thereafter, the children in this family disappeared from school for a week. When they came back the next Monday, teachers asked them where they had been. The children replied that they had been camping. Where had the money for camping come from? From the sale of the refrigerator! The family felt like they were under such stress that they needed a vacation; the proceeds from the sale of the refrigerator paid for this much needed, well-deserved, week-long vacation.

Not only do many families in generational poverty believe that the present is all that is important; many of them also have an external locus of control. Persons with an *internal locus of control* believe that they can shape their own fate; reinforcements are contingent on their own actions. Persons with an *external locus of control* believe that the future is determined primarily by luck and chance; reinforcing events occur independently of their own actions. Thus, if professionals make recommendations for intervention, home programs, and the like, families may not carry out these recommendations because they do not believe that they can change either their present or their future. (If it's all up to fate, what's the use?)

As a related consideration, low-SES families may have a limited sense of *personal efficacy*. Personal efficacy is a psychological construct that describes an individual's sense of personal power (Lynch & Hanson, 2011). Most people of middle-SES backgrounds believe that barriers to personal happiness or success can be overcome by perseverance and hard work. People with a strong sense of personal efficacy feel empowered: they perceive that they have influence over their own lives. These individuals are more likely to seek out prevention and intervention services.

Individuals with a limited sense of personal efficacy may not seek out prevention or intervention services because they automatically assume that their actions will not make a difference. Low-SES, non-White clients, for example, may believe that hard work and perseverance are insufficient to overcome the barriers created by poverty and race (Sue & Sue, 2013). (After all, you can't fight city hall.) Lynch (2011) states that initial lack of opportunity caused by sociopolitical barriers and discrimination can become a vicious cycle, with despair and anger being prevalent. She points out the reality that inequities and discrimination still exist; these barriers make it harder for some families than others. For example, in the year 2011, there were 1,018 active hate groups in the United States and over 11,500 online sites in the United States that promoted hate and terrorism (Lohr, 2010; Southern Poverty Law Center, 2012).

Payne (2003) has described other characteristics of many families from backgrounds of generational poverty. One of the greatest differences between these families and middle-SES families is in their life priorities: their value systems, which affect all of their actions. Many families in generational poverty place the highest value on entertainment, relationships, and survival. As noted earlier, for persons who live in poverty, the future is uncertain, so why plan for it? Enjoying the moment as much as possible is paramount.

At a professional workshop I conducted in St. Louis, Missouri, the educators who attended reported that even the poorest of families they worked with had iPods, VCRs, cell phones, and other relatively sophisticated electronic equipment. These families may not have had food or school supplies in the home, but most of them had the latest in electronic equipment, equipment that is crucial for entertainment. A speaker at a convention I attended recently described how many low-SES families she worked with did not have the "basics" of life, but they all had iPhones (Blevins, 2012).

Payne (2003) also describes the language used by many persons from backgrounds of generational poverty; this topic is addressed in greater depth in subsequent chapters. A relevant consideration here is that in most middle-SES homes, a formal language register is the norm. Language is used to meet needs and to "get ahead" in life (e.g., obtaining an education and a high-paying job). In many homes of generational poverty, family members use a casual language register.

In casual language register, language is used for survival and especially for entertainment. As addressed later, one reason many children from low-SES families have so much difficulty in school is that they bring this casual register with them from home. Teachers and textbooks use language in the formal register, however. This mismatch between children's language and school language can be the root of various behavioral and learning problems.

In families living in generational poverty, discipline and punishment are not about change; they are about penance and forgiveness, and the person's behavior continues unabated. By contrast, in middle SES families, discipline and punishment are about change. Punishment or negative consequences for certain behavior reinforce the need for the person to change the behavior; otherwise, the punishment will re-occur. As Payne (2003) points out, this difference can make it difficult for school personnel who deal with some students from low-SES homes; when these students are punished, they may not realize that behavioral changes are called for. Professionals may have to deal with this directly.

In middle-SES homes, life often is highly structured. A typical mid-week morning might start off with the mother laying out the day for the child. I can think of so many conversations I had with Mark, when he was younger, that went something like this: "Today Daddy will take you to school because I need to be at work early. But I'll pick you up right after Art Club, and then we'll go to karate. After karate, we'll come home; if you get all your homework done with a good attitude, we can take the dog to the park. We'll have dinner around 6 o'clock." Mark also received a weekly allowance for picking up his toys, keeping his room clean, feeding the dog, and clearing the dinner dishes. His allowance was not forthcoming until I had checked to make sure that all tasks have been done. In many middle-SES homes, organization, planning, and structure are critical to smooth functioning.

By contrast, many low-SES homes lack consistent structure and routine (Ispa et al., 2006). Clutter is common, and cleanliness and hygiene may not be valued, as illustrated in the following case example from real life.

A well-meaning couple used to rent nicely maintained apartments to low-SES families of different ethnic groups. No matter what the ethnic background of the families, the couple was horrified to find that many of them "trashed" the living units, and as the owners they repeatedly had to pay for repairs. In addition, these families often accumulated piles of pizza boxes and other take-out containers (with numerous cockroaches) and other detritus of daily life that were never removed from the premises.

In one apartment recently vacated by a low-SES family in which the father was very obese, the couple found that his sheer weight had broken two toilets. He had failed to notify them of the damage, but evidently the toilets continued to be used!

In short, the lifestyle of these families, who had come to these apartments from situations of deep poverty, seemed to reflect a lack of any sense of "ownership" of the living units they inhabited. This attitude may have been a kind of survival mechanism: they were able to ignore problems they felt powerless and perhaps too embarrassed to deal with (broken toilets) and focused on meeting more immediate needs (pizza).

In point of fact, many low-SES families live in very clean homes that they maintain with pride. In many homes of families from backgrounds of generational poverty, however, day-to-day survival is foremost; cleanliness, structure, routine, and organization are not an integral part of family life.

CONCLUSIONS

Poverty in the United States is on the rise. Children from low-SES homes are vulnerable to its effects in many realms. To address these challenges, many experts have called for level 1 changes—at the macroeconomic level, entailing changes in state and federal policies (Chiu & Khoo, 2005; Ehrenreich, 2006; Farah et al., 2005). As Paul and Norbury (2012) have stated, we need to attack poverty at its base.

Professional educators can work actively toward community, state, and federal government action to support reduction of teen pregnancy, job training, Head Start programs, and other educational efforts that can prevent problems from happening. At level 1, state and federal laws and policies are needed that ensure physical health and safety for all infants, lead abatement in homes, and other such changes (Farah et al., 2005). Another important focus is the elimination of homelessness.

According to Neuman (2009), what schools cannot do is to offset the inequities in society that disproportionately place some children at much greater risk of negative outcomes. Educators and other professionals who work with children need to advocate for reducing poverty, enhancing employment opportunities, and creating communities that promote a high quality of life for all.

At levels 2 and 3, Payne (2003) and Sue and Sue (2013) point out that it can be frustrating for middle-SES professionals to work with children and families from low-SES households because of value conflicts. Middle-SES professionals typically value an internal locus of control and a sense of personal efficacy. So, it is very easy to judge these students and their families as being lazy, uncaring, and uninvolved because of their aforementioned attributes of an external locus of control and weak sense of personal efficacy. With a better understanding of the circumstances that many low-SES families find themselves in, however, professionals can be more compassionate, less judgmental, and more effective in their ability to help meet the needs of these children. This book is devoted to exploring ways in which this can be accomplished.

CHAPTER HIGHLIGHTS

- Poverty is increasing in the United States, especially in wake of the Great Recession that began in 2007.
- This increase is due to a variety of factors. Two major ones are related: first, the shift of entry-level, unskilled, blue-collar jobs being exported overseas has left fewer of these jobs for American workers. Second, in the United States, increasingly numbers of newly created jobs require at least some college education.
- Poverty disproportionately affects persons of color. Families headed by single mothers are highly vulnerable to poverty. Children in these families are vulnerable to a variety of problems, both during childhood and later in life.

■ Physical and psychological effects of poverty include:
1. Prenatal and birth issues
2. Hunger and malnutrition
3. Overall brain development problems
4. Basic safety issues
5. Limited access to health care
6. Environmental issues
7. Instability and chaos
8. Hearing and vision problems
9. Difficulties in the emotional atmosphere of the home

■ Students generally come from a background of situational or generational poverty. In situational poverty, poverty is temporary due to circumstances; there is a proactive attitude of improving these circumstances. In generational poverty, welfare usually is involved; poverty is a lifestyle accompanied by a belief that one "cannot fight City Hall."

■ There are three levels of support available for children and families in poverty: (1) macroeconomic level (state and federal laws and policies), (2) district and school site–based support, and (3) individual/personal effort of professionals who serve low-SES students and their families.

■ Through increasing support at all three levels, the lot of children and families in poverty can be improved.

2

Language Skills and Behavioral Characteristics in Children of Families of Low Socioeconomic Status

The only source of knowledge is experience.

Albert Einstein

Mark is now 2 years old. Mark's mother brings him with her to many places, including the food market. She has taught Mark to say, "Thanks, and have a nice day!" He was able to say this at approximately 22 months of age, much to the astonishment and amusement of the checkout clerks. Mark has an expressive vocabulary of 200 to 300 words. His mother has taken a job outside the home, teaching at a local university.

While his mother and father work, Mark attends a small preschool, housed in the teacher's home, that provides a caring, supportive environment. The back yard is large, equipped with a sandbox and a great deal of interesting play equipment. Mark frequently brings home art projects that he has done at "school." He has good friends at the preschool, with whom he also interacts in regular play dates scheduled by his mother.

Marcos also is 2 years old. Both of Marcos' parents are employed outside the home as seasonal agricultural workers.

Marcos now has a baby brother, and the children are cared for by Marcos' grandmother, an elderly woman who speaks only Spanish to them. This is an asset to the children, as the ability to speak Spanish is becoming increasingly valued in the United States. The neighborhood is not entirely safe, so Marcos mainly stays inside the house, which has a very small back yard.

Marcos watches TV for about 5 to 6 hours a day while his grandmother cares for the baby, cleans, and cooks. No neighborhood children are nearby for Marcos to play with. Marcos' grandmother, mother, and father are nonliterate, and there are no books in the house. Marcos' grandmother is thankful that he is a "good boy" and watches TV while she takes care of the baby and the home. When his parents finally get home in the evening, they are very tired; although they love their children, they have very little energy to play with them or talk with them.

INTRODUCTION

A number of factors have been found to affect language development in children from families of low socioeconomic status (SES). Key factors include the family's SES and the educational level of primary caregivers (Hammer & Rodriguez, 2012; Vernon-Feagans et al., 2011). The research of Hart and Risley (1995), as well as that of other experts, has shown that low SES children are talked to less in their early years than are middle SES children (Greenwood, Thiemann-Bourque, Walker, Buzhardt, & Gilkerson, 2011; Reynolds & Fish, 2010). By 3 years of age, a major difference in the number of words that low and middle SES children have been exposed to has been recognized.

Authorities have speculated that in terms of reading achievement of children who live in poverty, the primary negative influences of poverty fall into two categories: material resources and psychological resources. Low SES homes frequently are lacking in both. Language difficulties of low SES children may lead to difficulties with behavior.

In this chapter, language and behavioral characteristics of low SES children are described based on studies linking low SES status to poorer linguistic and behavioral outcomes for children from backgrounds of poverty. The description of these characteristics lays a foundation for later chapters, where evidence-based practical strategies for intervention are described.

FACTORS AFFECTING AND CHARACTERISTICS OF ORAL LANGUAGE SKILLS OF LOW SES CHILDREN

Overview

No causal relationship between poverty and language impairment in children has been demonstrated. Some low SES children come from homes where they receive good language stimulation. Others, however, show problems in language learning and development (Pruitt, Oetting, & Hegarty, 2011). As discussed in Chapter 1, families who live in poverty often face conditions such as hunger, overcrowded and unclean housing, unsafe neighborhoods and schools, and limited access to health care. Research shows that, although not directly causing language impairments, these variables, in addition to low educational levels of caregivers, often are associated with lower language skills in children from low SES homes (Hammer, 2012; Nelson, 2010; Paul & Norbury, 2012).

Research over the decades has shown that the SES and educational levels of caregivers are highly related to children's oral and literate language development (Hammer & Rodriguez, 2012; Owens, 2012; van Kleeck, Lange, & Schwartz, 2011). Wulbert, Inglis, Kriegsman, and Mills (1978) compared the interactional styles of middle and low SES mothers and their children. They found that lower SES mothers, regardless of ethnic background, tended to use shorter, terser sentences with their children and to use language more to discipline their children than to explain things to them. This finding was confirmed by Ispa et al. (2006). Adams and Ramey (1980) found that mothers with less education used fewer questions and more imperatives in speaking to their children. Nittrouer (1996) noted that regarding low SES children, much evidence indicates that the amount of parental language directed at these children is diminished when compared with that of middle SES children. "The effect of SES on child-directed language is consistent across ethnic groups and is independent of the dialect being learned . . . these reported differences were observed both in the United States and in Great Britain" (Nittrouer, p. 1062). According to Nelson (2010), children in low SES families are more engaged in talk about practical, day-to-day concerns than in talk that revolves around stories, games, and other nonessential, enriching activities.

One of the most extensive studies ever completed regarding children's oral language production was conducted by Loban (1976). Loban conducted a 13-year longitudinal study with 211 typically developing students between kindergarten and grade 12. The students were grouped as follows: (1) Group A consisted of subjects rated high in language ability, (2) Group B consisted of subjects rated low in language ability, and (3) Group C contained a random group of subjects who were was representative of the group as a whole.

Subjects in the high-proficiency language group spoke effectively, fluently, and freely. These subjects were considered to be good, focused listeners. They used a varied vocabulary and adjusted their speaking pace to listeners' needs. Subjects in the low-proficiency language group had sparse vocabularies. They frequently were unaware of listeners' needs. When they spoke, they appeared faltering and hesitant; their language rambled and did not appear to have a specific goal.

On an annual basis, Loban (1976) conducted an oral interview with all subjects and measured their language in communication units. He defined a communication unit as an independent clause with its modifiers. From grade 3 onward, he collected one or more written compositions from the children. Loban had two primary research questions: (1) Does growth in language follow a predictable year-by-year sequence? (2) Are there differences (over the years) between subjects in the high-proficiency language group and subjects in the low-proficiency language group?

Loban's findings were as follows (1976). First, the subjects with a high average number of words per communication unit also were rated highly by their teachers on a checklist of language skills. Second, subjects spoke and wrote in units that were similar in terms of average length. Third, students who had superior oral language skills in kindergarten and first grade, before they learned to read and write, were the same students who had excellent reading skills by sixth grade.

A fourth finding was a strong correlation between membership in the high-proficiency language group and SES; the higher the SES of the students, the more likely they were to be in the high-proficiency language group. Similarly, there was a correlation between low SES and membership in the low-proficiency language group. Loban (1976) found that SES, not ethnic background of the subjects, affected membership in a language skills group (high or low proficiency): "Minority students who came from securely affluent homes did not show up in the low proficiency group. *The problem is poverty, not ethnic affiliation*" (p. 23) [italics mine].

Research has found that SES is more critical to a child's language development than ethnic background, and the factor most highly related to socioeconomic status is the mother's educational level (Dollaghan et al., 1999; Greenwood et al., 2011; Owens, 2012). As Hammer and Rodriguez (2012, p. 33) stated, "Maternal education affects children's language and literacy development . . . Children of more educated mothers have larger vocabularies and more advanced language abilities than children of less educated mothers."

Maternal education has consistently been shown to positively relate to children's vocabulary development especially (Pan, Rowe, Spier, & Tamis-Lemonda, 2004). In comparison with their middle SES peers, children from low SES families often have been found to have smaller vocabularies and less advanced language development (Biemiller, 1999; Lubliner & Smetana, 2005). By the time middle SES children with well-educated parents reach third grade, they know approximately 12,000 words. Children with less educated parents who don't talk with them very much have vocabularies of approximately 4,000 words: one-third the size of middle SES children's vocabularies. Thus, educators need to start very early in building the vocabulary skills of low SES children so that they will not fall so far behind their middle SES peers (Snow & Juel, 2005).

Dollaghan and associates (1999) compared children's scores on different measures of language with respect to maternal education in three categories: less than a high school graduate, a high school graduate, or a college graduate. These investigators found that maternal education correlated positively with children's mean length of utterance, the number of different words the children used, and the children's scores on a test of receptive vocabulary. Their scores on this test increased significantly with the mother's increased educational level.

Maternal educational level impacts the nature of conversations between mothers and children. Low SES parents are less likely to respond to their children's utterances; when verbal interaction does occur, it is more likely to take the form of directives (which end the interaction) than inquiries, which keep the interaction going (Nittrouer, 1996; Owens, 2012). For example, a low SES child may state: "I'm hungry." The parent may reply: "Here—eat this." A middle SES parent may say: "You're hungry? What would you like to eat? You can have a hot dog, or some applesauce, or yogurt. Which would you like?"

Along these lines, Woolfolk (2008) gives the following example, which contrasts the ways in which a low SES mother and a middle SES mother may work with a child on a jigsaw puzzle:

Low SES MOTHER: "No, put that piece over there!"

MIDDLE SES MOTHER: "What shape is that piece? Can you find a spot that is straight like the piece? Yes, that's straight, but look at the color. Does the color match? No. Look again for a straight, blue piece. Yes—try that one. Good for you! You finished the edge."

Clearly, the middle SES child is benefiting from verbal elaboration, problem-solving opportunities, conceptual development, and encouragement to take initiative. The low SES child is getting none of these opportunities. Over time, the difference between the two mothers' styles will dramatically affect how their children perform in school, where verbal elaboration, problem solving, and conceptual development all are highly valued.

In terms of oral language stimulation in low SES homes, research supports the fact that low SES parents provide less of this stimulation than middle and upper income parents (Smith, Landry, & Swank, 2000; Turnbull & Justice, 2012). Smith and colleagues found that the amount of verbal stimulation provided to children, along with SES, was significantly related to a child's verbal skills at 5 years of age. Children from low SES homes who had received less verbal stimulation had lower verbal skills at 5 years of age than those noted in children from middle SES homes who had received more verbal stimulation.

My husband and son, Mark, and I recently visited the charming colonial town of Williamsburg, Virginia. We entered the governor's mansion tour with our group; the guide was explaining how in the old days, people could not enter the mansion without an escort. The three-year-old middle SES girl in her mother's arms behind us piped up. "What's an escort, Mommy?" I listened as the mother patiently gave a full, rich explanation complete with several examples. At the end, the mother quizzed the little girl: "Now, what did Mommy say an escort was? You tell me what the word 'escort' means."

The Research of Hart and Risley

In terms of children's oral language development, probably the most extensive research project ever undertaken was that of Hart and Risley (1995). These researchers from the University of Kansas were troubled by the mediocre results of a curriculum they had helped design at the Turner House preschool in a predominantly low SES neighborhood in Kansas City. The 4-year-old children at Turner House did not make the language (especially vocabulary) gains that were expected to result from a language stimulation program.

To find out why, Hart and Risley (1995) decided to explore what the circumstances in children's homes between birth and 3 years of age: the years *before* children came to preschool. Their goal was to discover what was happening in children's early experiences that could help explain the "intractable differences in rates of vocabulary growth we saw among 4-year-olds" (p. 191).

In what proved to be a ground-breaking study, they began by identifying 42 "normal" families; there was no spousal abuse or problems with drugs or alcohol. All but eight of the families had two parents in the home on a regular basis. In all but one of the families, the father or another adult male was regularly involved in the family's daily life. Each SES category included both white and African American families.

The families ranged from highly educated upper class families living in affluent suburbs to welfare families living in deteriorating neighborhoods; most families were in the middle of this range. Hart and Risley (1995) designated three categories of SES: (1) welfare, (2) working class (blue collar), and (3) professional. The study focused on the home environments of 1- and 2-year-old children, specifically looking at interactions and language stimulation within these homes.

Hart and Risley (1995) conducted sequential monthly hour-long observations in the home of each family over a period of almost 2½ years. They concluded that SES made an overwhelming difference in how much talking went on in a family. The family factor most strongly associated with the amount of talking in the home was not ethnicity, but SES.

Hart and Risley (1995) found that higher-SES parents simply talked more to their children. According to their findings, all of the high-quality features of interaction and language were present in the daily parenting that all children experienced; however, the amounts differed. Increased amounts of talking provided some children with a great deal more experience with nearly every high-quality feature of interaction and language.

Some interesting differences were found in the amount of talking that went on in homes when the children were very young. Hart and Risley (1995) counted the number of utterances per hour addressed to the baby when the subjects were 11 to 18 months old. In the 13 homes where the parents had professional and managerial occupations, 482 utterances per hour were addressed to the baby.

In the 10 middle SES homes where parents worked in offices and hospitals, 321 utterances per hour were addressed to the baby. In the 13 lower-SES families in which the parents were working in factories, construction, and services, 283 utterances per hour were addressed to the baby. In the 6 families on welfare, 197 utterances per hour were addressed to the baby (Figure 2–1). Thus, there was a 285-utterance per hour difference between professional and welfare homes.

Hart and Risley (1995) extrapolated that in a 365-day-year, children from professional families would have heard 4 million utterances and children from welfare families would have heard 250,000 utterances. Children from working class or blue collar families fell in between. The researchers stated that even by 3 years of age, the difference in the vocabulary knowledge between children from welfare and professional homes was so great that in order for the welfare children to gain a vocabulary equivalent to that of children from working class homes, these welfare children would need to attend a preschool program for 40 hours per week where they heard language at a level used in the homes of professional families (see Figure 2–1).

Hart and Risley (1995) showed that on average, professional parents spoke more than 2,000 words per hour to their children. Working class parents spoke about 1,300 words per hour to their children, and welfare parents spoke about 600 words per hour. At 4 years of age, children of professionals had vocabularies that were almost 50% larger than those of working class children and twice as large of those of welfare children. By age 4 years, the children from professional homes had heard a total of 45 million words; the children from working-class homes had heard 26 million words, and the poverty children had heard 13 million words (Figure 2–2).

Hart and Risley (1995) also recorded how often parents verbally reprimanded or encouraged their children. They broke down sentences used by the parents into three distinct types: (1) *question* (e.g., "Can you tell me where the dog is?"), (2) *affirmation* ("What a good, smart girl!"), and (3) *prohibition* ("Bad girl! Quit that!"). As mentioned in Chapter 1, toddlers in professional homes received an average of six encouragements per reprimand. Working class children got two encouragements per reprimand, and welfare children received one

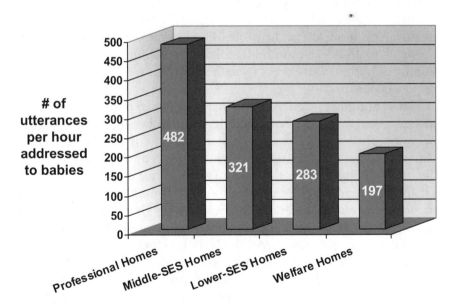

Figure 2–1. Frequency of talking to babies by socioeconomic status (SES). (Based on Hart & Risley, 1995, pp. 62–63.)

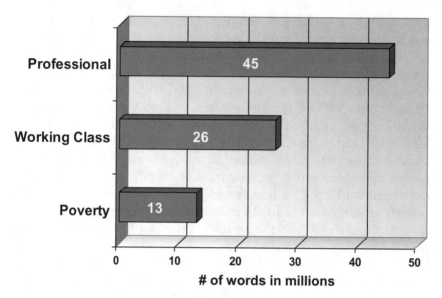

Figure 2–2. Total number of words heard by children up to the age of 4 years at three different family income levels. (Based on Hart & Risley, 1995.)

encouragement for every two reprimands. In the homes of welfare children, negative imperatives such as "don't," "stop," and "quit" were heard much more often. In professional homes, more than 80% of feedback to 13- to 18-month-old children was affirmative; in welfare homes, almost 80% of parents' feedback to 13- to 18-month-old children was negative.

Hart and Risley (1995) found that middle SES parents were "both nice and strict" (p. 83). For example, one mother named the "right" behaviors she wanted from her child, counted to three while the child chose to engage in the right behaviors or not, and sent the child to his room when he did not choose to engage in the behavior she had set forth. Overall, the researchers found that middle and upper SES parents involved the children in decisions by giving them a chance to voice a counterargument, an alternative, or even an excuse. They stated that when parents provide such choices for very young children, the children gain experience with a variety of discourse functions.

Parents can definitely go too far, however, in allowing their children voices and choices. In my personal experience as a mother, I can recall sometimes being exhausted by interactions with my 3-year-old son. One day, weary from the arguing, I resorted to a simple and classic statement of fact: "You have to do this because I'm the mommy and you're the boy." He frowned and said angrily, "No—I'm *not* a boy—I'm a superhero!" In hindsight, I recognize that I frequently gave him too much leeway in voicing counterarguments and in making choices. It has been my experience that many middle SES parents behave as I do, however.

It is interesting to view Hart and Risley's findings in light of findings, discussed in later chapters, that in many schools serving predominantly low SES families, the children are told strictly what to do and are not given a voice or room to verbally engage with teachers about alternatives. Evidently, this pattern begins very early in the lives of children from low SES families. In many homes, a mentality of "You'll do it because I said so" seems to predominate among parents and caregivers. In homes in which the caregivers have more money and education, children hear more well-elaborated explanations. As Hart and Risley point out, it takes a great deal more language (and, I might add, energy) to give a child an explanation than it takes to give a command. Consider the following scenario:

CHILD: Mommy, I want ice cream.

LOW SES MOTHER: No!

CHILD: Why, Mommy?

MOTHER: I said *no!*

CHILD: Mommy, I want ice cream.

MIDDLE SES MOTHER: Not right now.

CHILD: Why, Mommy?

MOTHER: We are having dinner soon. If you eat ice cream now, it will fill up your tummy and you will not have room for growing food like chicken and vegetables. Remember, growing food helps you become tall and strong. We will have growing food first, and ice cream after that.

In a related vein, Hart and Risley (1995) saw differences between families which reflected the cultural priorities that parents casually transmitted through talking. In the professional homes, the culture seemed to prioritize relationships, names, and recall. Parents seemed to be concerned with preparing their children to participate in a culture that emphasized analytic problem solving and symbolic skill. To prepare their children for advanced educations, the parents spent effort and time developing their potential. They asked questions, challenged their children, encouraged their children to engage with adults, and used affirmatives to encourage their children to listen.

By contrast, in the welfare families,

> the lesser amount of talk with its more frequent parent-initiated topics, imperatives, and prohibitions suggested a culture concerned with established customs. To teach socially acceptable behavior . . . obedience, politeness, and conformity were more likely to be the keys to survival. Rather than attempting to prepare their children with the knowledge and skills required in a technical world with which the parents had had little experience, parents seemed to be preparing their children realistically for the jobs likely to be open to them, jobs in which success and advancement would be determined by attitude, how well the children presented themselves, and whether they could prove themselves through their performance. (Hart & Risley, 1995, pp. 143–144)

Another thing Hart and Risley (1995) discovered in their research was how busy upper SES families were, and how isolated welfare families were. In upper SES families, even parents who worked outside the home volunteered time to school, church, and community activities. At-home upper SES parents talked on the phone a great deal, visited friends, went shopping, and took siblings to special activities. The children in these upper SES homes watched TV shows such as "Sesame Street," designed to stimulate development in many areas of learning, and had rooms full of books and toys.

By contrast, the welfare families were quite isolated. In single-parent welfare families without a car or telephone, a parent could be virtually cut off from all opportunities for interaction with other adults. Hart and Risley (1995) stated that for some parents, "their closest and most interesting friends seemed to be the characters on soap operas" (p. 69). The researchers also noted the welfare parents' resilience, their perseverance in the face of repeated humiliations and defeats, the joy they took in their children, and their desire for their children to succeed in school. However, these parents did not turn on the TV to "Sesame Street," take the bus to special places such as the zoo, or talk with their children frequently.

In a follow-up study, Hart and Risley (2003) found that the measures of accomplishment from data gathered when children were 3 years old predicted third grade school achievement. Vocabulary use at age 3 was predictive of measures of language skills and reading comprehension scores at 9 and 10 years of age.

Hart and Risley (1995, 2003) concluded that the first three years of life are tremendously important in terms of the child's future in a variety of areas. At age 3, the children from all homes had become like their parents. It was obvious, noted the researchers, why a few hours of intensive intervention at 4 years of age had so little impact on the magnitude of the differences in cumulative experience that resulted from those first three years. By age 2, the growth and mylenization of nerve cells is almost complete. By 4 years of age, cortical development is largely accomplished. The years before age 2 are the time when environmental stimulation and input may have the greatest influence on cortical development.

According to Hart and Risley (1995, 2003), the problem of skill differences among children by the time they enter school is much larger, more important, and more intractable than has generally been realized. As discussed in Chapter 1 the macroeconomic changes in today's society have made nonskilled jobs less available, and the United States has become an increasingly technological and information-based economy. Hart and Risley (1995) stated that the early language experiences of children may be most important for the symbolic and language-based analytic competencies that are necessary for an advanced education and participation in the current economy. These competencies probably will become more important as society increasingly polarizes into technological and service sectors.

The advantages gained by the children of college-educated professionals may, unfortunately, suggest the evolving of a distinct subculture in this country, one in which adults pass on to their children the symbolic thinking and problem-solving skills that are foundational for well-paying adult careers and that are so hard for outsiders to acquire in mid-life. A trend toward separation into subcultures jeopardizes children's chances for upward mobility and may have the unhappy effect of polarizing American citizens, as well as increasing the numbers of low SES individuals (Hart & Risley, 1995). As discussed in more detail in Chapter 4, early intervention programs probably are the best way to prevent these untoward effects.

Follow-Up Research on Hart and Risley: Greenwood and Colleagues

Greenwood et al. (2011) described how it was important for research to follow up on the results of Hart and Risley (1995). In a follow-up study by Greenwood and colleagues, the LENA system for auto-mated record, analysis, and reporting (Infoture Foundation, 2008; Xu, Yapanel, Gray, & Baer, 2009) was used to replicate Hart and Risley's original study. The purpose of the study was to replicate and extend some of Hart and Risley's findings using LENA digital recording and automated processing technology instead of language samples tran-scribed by humans.

The participants in this study were English-speaking families with typically-developing children between 12 to 20 months of age. Families were recruited from communities in Missouri and Kansas. Thirty of the original 37 families completed the study. Socioeconomic status was determined by educational attainment of mothers, who reported a mean educational attainment of 16 years. The parent read-ing achievement assessment scores were more than one standard deviation above the mean. Seventy-seven percent of the families were European American, 10% were African American, and the remainder were Pacific Islander, Asian, and multiethnic.

Repeated measures were collected during the study, which lasted 10 months (Greenwood et al., 2011). The subjects' first measurement occasion occurred at different ages within the 12 to 20-month inclu-sionary age range. Audio recordings were collected in the children's homes for 12-hour durations at least once a week; this was in contrast to Hart and Risley's audio recordings, which were collected once a month for 1-hour durations. Parents in this study were requested to make recordings at least once a week but no more than three times a week.

Participating families were given a T-shirt with a pocket specially designed to hold the LENA Digital Processor (LDP), an unobtrusive digital audio recorder. When in the pocket, the LDP was turned on by the parent in the morning to make a 12-hour recording. The recordings collected enabled the following parameters to be assessed: adult word count, child vocalizations, and conversational turns. At the beginning of the study, each child was given several language measures.

To address research questions, the content of 8,640 recording hours was analyzed. Several important results emerged. First, a result not found by Hart and Risley showed that the amount of talk directed to children was highest at two times of day: in the early morning, beginning at 7:00 AM, and in the late afternoon-early evening. Talk dropped to near zero at 7:00 PM. There was a definite bivariate trend or rhythm of talk, which appeared to be associated with the daily routines in families' sleep-wake and feeding-care cycles.

Unlike Hart and Risley, Greenwood et al. (2011) did not find that there was a significant difference in talk as related to family SES. However, a result similar to one found by Hart and Risley was that mothers with more than a high school education said 514.8 more words to their children per day than mothers who had attained less education. The children of the more educated mothers were more responsive, producing 193.7 more vocalizations and 47.6 more conversational turns than did children in families with a high school education. Greenwood and colleagues found that adult females rather than males provided the majority of daily words that the child heard.

In sum, the results of a study by Greenwood et al. (2011) supported previous research which linked the educational level of mothers to children's amount of talk as well as amount of turntaking. A new finding from this study was that the amount of talk was strongly associated with times of day where routines were occurring: feeding, bathing, and other child care activities.

OTHER FACTORS AFFECTING
ORAL LANGUAGE DEVELOPMENT

Job and Environment-Related Communication Styles

Rothstein (2004, 2006) notes that many low SES parents have jobs in which they follow routines and are told what to do. Middle and upper-middle SES parents often have jobs that require divergent thinking, collaboration with others, and creative problem-solving skills. Rothstein speculates that the types of jobs parents have contribute to the way in which they interact with their children.

As supported by considerable research, low SES caregivers tend to give more commands and orders, whereas middle SES caregivers tend to engage in more discussion and problem solving with their children. This difference could be a function partly of caregiver educational level; it also could reflect the types of careers and jobs that low and middle SES caregivers tend to have.

Kohn (1969) found that parents who were closely supervised at work (e.g., parents in low-paying jobs) were more likely to base punishment on their children's actions, regardless of the children's intentions when the actions were performed. Parents whose occupations required creativity and decision making were less likely to punish their children if the children's intentions were desirable, even if things did not work out as intended.

For example, a child may try to bring a glass of juice to his tired mother sitting on the couch. If the juice spills on the floor, a mother in an occupation requiring decision making and creativity may praise the child for his thoughtfulness and help him clean up the spilled juice. A mother who is closely supervised at work, however, may berate her son and slap him for spilling the juice, even though his motive was to help his tired mom.

As discussed in Chapter 1, low SES parents are more likely to hit or spank their children (Ispa et al., 2006). They give more prohibitions. For example, a low SES mother may say: "Put those scissors down right now!" A more middle SES utterance in the same circumstance may be: "Why don't you hand me those scissors so you won't get hurt?" (Hymowitz, 2005). Intrusive and controlling behaviors may be especially detrimental to children's language development. These behaviors include verbally controlling children with unnecessary, repeated directions, unnecessarily restraining children, and disrupting the child's efforts at communication with the adult's own bids for attention. Pungello et al. (2009) found, in their study, that caregivers' intrusive and controlling behaviors undermined children's confidence and automony, and impacted their language use. Tamis-LeMonda, Shannon, Cabrera, and Lamb (2004) found that negative intrusive parenting was related to language outcomes at three and four years of age.

I will never forget visiting a mother and her twin toddlers one afternoon in a low SES area of northern California. I politely declined a glass of wine because I was driving, but she poured herself some in a nice, delicate wine glass. During our conversation, the twins made repeated bids for attention and continuously attempted to grab their mother's attractive, shiny wine glass. She did not move the glass out of their way; instead, she constantly slapped their hands and berated them for getting too close to the fragile, expensive glass. They were admonished many times to "Stop that!" and "Stay away!" It was one of those situations where I was afraid to offend the mother by gently suggesting that she merely move the glass out of the children's reach and get them some age-appropriate toys and books to play with; after all, I was a guest in her home and this was a social visit, not a professional meeting.

Neuman (2009) discusses in detail how low SES children are more strictly controlled due, in part, to environmental issues. She describes how many low SES families have limited access to places such as stores; grocery shopping can take about four hours by the time the family takes public transportation to the store, shops, and returns home via public transportation. As Neuman states (p. 17), "Routines are not routines in poor neighborhoods." Thus, in addition to working long hours in low-paying jobs, parents are forced to take a great deal of time completing daily living chores that most middle SES people do quickly. Because of these added hours of being away from their children, parents leave children alone or with relatives or friends. In their attempts to establish some clear boundaries to protect their children, parents end up restricting children's autonomy. They often use strict obedience and punitive measures when trying to keep children from straying too far. "The verbal give-and-take so common in middle-class homes is replaced by absolute authority" (Neuman, p. 17). Thus, children have fewer chances to develop higher-order language skills involving negotiation, discussion, and compromising, all skills favored in higher paying white collar jobs.

The style of parent-child interaction impacts the way that low SES children interact with their peers and eventually authority figures in the school and workplace. As discussed in later chapters, professionals need to give these children ranges of discourse styles and vocabulary choices that are acceptable in more formal situations outside the home.

Parental Attitudes Toward Oral Language Stimulation

Children's language skills also are affected by overall parental attitudes. Hymowitz (2005) has examined middle SES and low SES parents' attitudes toward language and education.

> In middle-class families, the child's development—emotional, social, and these days, above all) cognitive—takes center stage. It is the family's raison d'etre, its state religion. It's the reason for that Mozart or Rafi tape in the morning and that bedtime story at night, for finding out all you can about a teacher in the fall and for Little League in the spring, for all the books, crib mobiles, trips to the museum, and limits on TV. It's the reason, even, for careful family planning; fewer children, properly spaced, allow parents to focus ample attention on teach one. Just about everything that defines middle-class parenting . . . consciously aims at education or child development . . . the child-rearing philosophy among the poor and much of the working class is "natural growth." Natural growth believers are fatalists; they do not see their role as shaping the environment so that the Little Princes or Princesses will develop their minds and talents, because they assume that these will unfold as they will. As long as a parent provides love, food, and safety, she is doing her job. . . . Talking or reading to a young child or taking him to the zoo are simply not cultural requirements . . . [when we encourage low SES young mothers] to talk to their babies, they often reply, "Why should I talk to him? He can't answer me." Mothers describe playing with or cuddling a baby or toddler, obligatory in suburban homes, as "spoiling." (Hymowitz, 2005, pp. 5–7)

In a study of White and African American parents, Lareau (2002) found that low SES parents from both groups believed that children were subordinate to adults. Parents did not negotiate with children; they issued directives. Children's wishes did not guide or inform adult actions, and physical discipline was emphasized. Low SES White and African American parents believed that in order to thrive, all their children needed was safety, food, and love. In contrast, middle SES White and African American parents had highly structured daily routines for their children. They enrolled their children in many activities. These middle SES parents preferred verbal rather than physical approaches to discipline, and engaged in lengthy dialogues where language was used for reasoning and problem-solving.

It must be remembered, as we are saying throughout this book, that low SES parents courageously deal with multiple stressors that impact their interactions with their children (Hammer, 2012). These stressors not only impact oral language interactions. Factors that impact the oral language development of low SES children often also have an impact on the development of their literacy skills.

FACTORS AFFECTING AND CHARACTERISTICS OF LITERACY SKILLS OF LOW SES CHILDREN

Material and Psychological Resources

Research evidence indicates that in addition to having depressed oral language skills, low SES children may be at risk for difficulties in literacy and academic skills as well (Barone, 2006; Fazio, Naremore, & Connell, 1996; Turnbull & Justice, 2012; Ukrainetz, 2013). As noted earlier, from a macroeconomic standpoint, it is important to consider the ramifications of low literacy in the United States today.

Generations ago, when the U.S. economy was primarily industrial and agricultural, many jobs were available that did not require literacy skills. However, in today's information-based economy, low literacy has much greater socioeconomic consequences. In the information economy, low literacy leads to poverty much more than it did in the agricultural or industrial economy. Low literacy can lead to unemployment, crime, welfare dependency, homelessness, and other negative sequelae.

Research has shown that in many low SES households, children are not read to as much as they are in households with a higher SES. Authorities (e.g., Duncan & Brooks-Gunn, 1997; Foster, 2002; Neuman & Celano, 2006) have speculated that in terms of reading achievement of children in poverty, the primary negative influences of poverty fall into two categories: material resources and psychological resources. *Material resources* refer to parents' access to literacy materials such as books, paper, writing implements, and other materials which help foster preliteracy and literacy skills. *Psychological resources* refer to the quality of the home environment and mother-child interactions involving stimulating learning opportunities and activities.

In terms of material resources, parents often lack the disposable income to afford print resources. In addition, resources may be unavailable in their neighborhoods. For example, Neuman and

Celano (2001) analyzed four Philadelphia neighborhoods and found great disparities in access to print resources for low and middle SES children. In poor communities, only one book title was available for every 300 children. In middle SES communities, 13 book titles were available per child. School libraries in low SES neighborhoods average one-half as many books as school libraries in middle SES neighborhoods. Public libraries in low SES areas often have more limited hours of operation than libraries in middle SES communities (Neuman, 2009).

In a study of the number of books in the homes of various families, Bradley, Corwyn, Pipes-McAdoo, and Garcia-Coll (2001) found that across all ethnic groups, nonpoor children were much more likely to have 10 or more developmentally appropriate books in their homes than their low SES counterparts. Fish and Pinkerman (2003) showed that the number of children's books in the home at 4 years of age was significantly related to children's language performance during kindergarten. Davis and Banks (2012) point out that for low SES children from culturally and linguistically diverse backgrounds, the challenge is twofold: a) affording books at all, and b) finding books in the children's languages if they speak a language other than English.

Sharif, Reiber, and Ozuah (2002) showed that the more young children were read to, the better their receptive vocabulary skills were as they developed. Luster, Bates, Vandenbelt, and Peck Key (2000) showed in their study that the more a child was read to at a young age, the higher the child's scores were on a standardized receptive vocabulary test. Adams (1990) found that the average number of hours of one-on-one picture book reading (involving a caregiver and the child) that children experienced before kindergarten was estimated at 25 hours for low SES children and between 1,000 and 1,700 hours for middle SES children.

Children who are not read to have less experience with different, new, and more sophisticated vocabulary that exists outside of their day-to-day encounters. This may lead to, among other things, difficulty with decontextualized language and vocabulary for low SES children.

White, Graves, and Slater (1990) found that the reading vocabulary of a third grader from a low SES family averages 5,000 fewer words than that of middle SES peers. McGregor (2004) noted that low vocabulary skills can affect reading achievement: "Children from impoverished environments exhibit severe disadvantages when it comes to incidental learning. Compared to their high-vocabulary peers, they have more words to learn (fast map) and more words to elaborate (slow map) from any given passage" (p. 305).

Schools' difficulty in overcoming the disadvantages of children from less literate homes is a universal reality, not a failure peculiar to the United States. The number of books in children's homes consistently predicts their test scores in almost every country surveyed. For example, low SES Turkish immigrants in Germany have few books in the home and suffer a school achievement gap, as do Okinawans in Japan, Algerians in France, and Caribbean, Pakistani, African, and Bangladeshi students in Great Britain (Rothstein, 2006).

As mentioned earlier, low SES mothers often have not had the benefit of education, and this limitation can affect available psychological resources, which in turn affects the way they read to their children (Britto, Brooks-Gunn, & Griffin, 2006; Heath, 1983, 1986; Rothstein, 2006). Some studies have shown that regardless of ethnic background, educated mothers read to their children more than non-educated mothers (Rashid, Morris, & Sevcik, 2005). In addition, there seem to be differences in the atmosphere created in the homes of low and middle SES parents; this can have an impact on children's willingness to read (Rashid et al., 2005; Turnbull & Justice, 2012).

Baker, Mackler, Sonnenschein, and Serpell (2001) found that a positive affective atmosphere during shared reading activities between mothers and children had a beneficial effect on the child's reading activity in third grade. Better educated mothers were found to generate more positive affective interactions during shared reading than those during shared reading with less educated mothers. A positive affective atmosphere during shared reading can promote increased engagement in and enjoyment of reading for the child (Baker et al.). Britto et al. (2006), in studying reading practices of low SES African American mothers with their preschoolers, showed that preschoolers whose mothers provided them with guided participation and high levels of support demonstrated greater expressive language use and greater school readiness when compared with children who received low levels of maternal engagement in reading activities.

Rothstein (2006) states that when working class parents read aloud, they are more likely to tell children to pay attention without interruption or to name letters or sound out words. When they ask their children questions about a story, the questions tend to be factual, for example, asking for memory of events or names of objects. Parents who have higher degrees of literacy tend to ask questions that are creative, predictive, or interpretive (e.g., "What do you think will happen next? Why do you think the girl liked her new school better than her old one?").

Van Kleeck, Gillam, Hamilton, and McGrath (1997) examined the type of language used by middle-class mothers and fathers when they were reading to their children. These investigators found that over 60% of the language the parents used was at the level that their preschoolers had already mastered, and 40% was at a level that would challenge the children. Using lower level language a greater percentage of the time gave the preschoolers a knowledge base from which to operate; language above their current abilities tested and challenged their language weaknesses.

When the parents read books to their children that the children had never heard before, there was an increased level of abstract language and also new vocabulary that stimulated conversation. Thus, middle-class parents appeared to consistently use language, during reading, that had many ideal characteristics for promoting their children's literate language skills.

Payne, Whitehurst, and Angell (1994) found a strong correlational relationship between children's language and the literacy environment of their homes, especially with regard to the following parameters: frequency of parents reading to their children, number of picture books in the home, frequency of the child's requests to be read to, frequency of visits to the library, and the child's age when shared reading began. Children with higher-level language skills were read to frequently, had begun reading with their parents very early, visited the library often, and had many picture books in their homes. Thus, like other studies, Payne and colleagues' study showed that home literacy practices had a strong impact on children's language skills.

Raikes, Pan, Luze, Tamis-LeMonda, Brooks-Gunn, Constantine, Tarullo, Raikes, and Rodriguez (2006) conducted a study of 2,581 low SES mothers and their reading patterns with their children. About half the mothers reported reading daily to their children. At 14 months of age, the odds of reading daily increased by the child being female or firstborn. At ages 24 and 36 months, the odds of reading daily increased by maternal education or verbal ability and by the child being firstborn or enrolled in Early Head Start. White mothers read more than African American or Hispanic mothers. For children who spoke English, concurrent reading was associated with comprehension and vocabulary at 14 months of age, and with cognitive development and vocabulary at 24 months. A pattern of daily reading for the English-speaking children predicted children's cognitive and language skills at 36 months. Raikes et al. concluded that path analyses suggested reciprocal and snowballing relations between children's vocabulary and maternal bookreading. The more the children were read to, the greater their vocabularies and overall cognitive and linguistic development.

Phonological and Print Awareness Skills

Other predictors of a child's reading ability that relate to SES also have been recognized. According to Neuman (2009), research has shown that low SES children may enter kindergarten knowing only one or two letters; middle SES children may know all 26 letters when they start kindergarten. Within the first few weeks of kindergarten, low SES children find themselves easy targets for kindergarten retention.

Dodd and Carr (2003) carried out a study in the United Kingdom in which they examined young children's letter sound development at three levels: letter sound recognition, letter sound recall, and letter reproduction. They found that children from upper SES backgrounds had significantly higher scores on all three tasks than children from lower-SES backgrounds. They also found that children from lower-SES backgrounds had more difficulty with letter reproduction than letter sound recall, whereas those from upper SES families had similar scores on the same two tasks. Other research has documented that low SES children often have difficulty in the areas of phonological awareness and print access (McDowell, Lonigan, & Goldstein, 2007; Paul & Norbury, 2012; Vernon-Feagans et al., 2011).

A positive correlation has been found between children's access to print in the home environment and children's emergent literacy knowledge (Ukrainetz, 2013). This is particularly true of written language awareness. As noted earlier, a family's material resources greatly influence children's access to print. Poorer families cannot afford books and many other written materials. Justice and Ezell (2001) observed that children living in low SES homes showed low proficiency in many aspects of written language awareness. These included letter discrimination, knowledge of directionality of print, and print function. A possible reason for these low skill levels is that the low SES children in the study had fewer early literacy experiences.

Some parents may not prioritize literacy practices in the home. Marvin and Mirenda (1993) asked parents to rate their home literacy experiences. They found that low SES parents and parents of children with special needs rated literacy experiences as less important than other activities. These activities included self-help and daily living activities (e.g., brushing teeth, getting dressed) as well as spoken communication. Relative to other children, low SES and special needs children had less access to literacy-related materials. In addition, the parents of these two groups of children did not hold high academic expectations for their children.

In-home literacy practices may differ in terms of families' ethnic backgrounds as well. In 2005, 60% of children aged 3 to 5 were read to daily by a family member. Asian and White, non-Hispanic children were more likely to be read to than were their Hispanic and Black, non-Hispanic peers (Forum on Child and Family Statistics, 2006). This can impact children's emergent literacy skills (Table 2–1).

Low SES parents from some culturally and linguistically diverse backgrounds may not view reading as "their job." In many cultures, parents' responsibilities and schools' responsibilities are sharply delineated. The parents are responsible for love, discipline, and providing basic needs. They are not to interfere with the school or try to carry out educational tasks at home (Kayser, 2012; Roseberry-McKibbin, 2007, 2008). These parents have so much respect for schools and educators that, in order not to interfere, they believe that they should leave reading and other "school-type" tasks to educated professionals with expertise in academic training for children. For example, Madding (2000), in a study of Mexican mothers in southern California, found that they viewed their job as being responsible for loving their young children and providing for their physical needs. They viewed reading and other educational type tasks as the school's responsibility and they respectfully stayed within what they perceived were their boundaries. More is said about this in Chapter 9.

Family structure also has an impact on reading practices. Children living with two parents are more likely to be read aloud to every day than are children who live with only one parent or with no parent (Federal Interagency Forum on Child and Family Statistics, 2003). As noted, low SES households often are maintained by single women; they may be too tired or overwhelmed with the demands placed on them to read to their children.

Table 2–1. Characteristics of Children and Families from Mainstream and Culturally Diverse Backgrounds

	White, Non-Hispanic	Hispanic	Black, Non-Hispanic
Population			
% of U.S. children	64	16	15
Family SES and Background information			
Rate of adolescent births per 1,000	14	53	45
% of low-birthweight infants	6.8	6.5	13.1
% of children living in poverty	9	27	30
% of children living in 2-parent home	77	65	38
% of mothers with a bachelor's level education	20	8	8
% of fathers with a bachelor's level education	23	9	5
% of children with a parent working all year on a full-time basis	84	73	65
Children's Skills and School Readiness			
% of 3- and 4-year-olds recognizing all letters	21	9	16
% of 3- and 4-year-olds identifying all colors	84	55	63
% of 3- to 5-year-olds read to every day	64	42	48
% of 3- and 4-year-olds writing their first names	48	37	42
% of 3- and 4-year-olds holding pencils properly	90	91	94
% of 3- and 4-year-olds writing and drawing	65	55	67
% of children 5+ years owning fewer than 10 books	3	31	27
% of children 5+ years owning 50+ books	47	19	13

Source: Based on Federal Interagency Forum on Child and Family Statistics (2003).

If low SES children experience delayed language as a result of intrinsic language learning disabilities or lack of appropriate environmental input or stimulation, their behavior can be affected in ways that may present additional difficulties for these children. It is important for professionals to be aware of the behavioral characteristics of some low SES children.

BEHAVIORAL CHARACTERISTICS OF SOME CHILDREN FROM LOW SES HOMES

As borne out by my own extensive clinical experience, many low SES students are respectful, well-behaved, and courteous. As professionals, speech-language pathologists and other educators should never stereotype low SES children in terms of one particular pattern of behaviors. However, research does point to certain trends of which educators should be aware, including the fact that language and behavioral skills usually are inextricably intertwined.

If children have difficulties with language skills, problems with behavior are often not far behind (Johnson, Beitchman, & Brownlie, 2010). According to Neuman (2009), children who experience chronic poverty and persistent family economic hardship are likely to have difficulties with peer relationships, including psychopathology, school dropout, and delinquency. Parent and teacher reports indicate that children may externalize their anger through fighting, lashing out, and manifesting difficulties controlling their emotions and getting along with others. Problematic patterns of social behavior characterized by poor communication skills may become ingrained, increasing children's risk for substance abuse and eventual negative encounters with juvenile justice and prison systems (Armstrong, 2011; McCormack, Harrison, McLeod, & McAllister, 2011; Redmond, 2011).

Payne (2003) has pointed out that in many low SES neighborhoods, children need to be able to fight to survive. There is a lesser emphasis on verbal negotiation and problem-solving, and more of an emphasis on use of physical aggression to solve problems, make bullies back off, and generally remain safe. Unfortunately, these same behaviors get children into trouble in school. As recommended by Payne, professionals can tell children that there are two sets of behaviors: home/neighborhood behavior and school behavior. At school, people solve problems through talking, not using their bodies to fight. Subsequent chapters discuss this issue in more depth. Nevertheless, "tough" low SES students may need to be that way to survive in their homes and neighborhoods.

In addition, low SES children often live in neighborhoods with an increased likelihood of violence, so they are more likely to witness violence themselves. As a result, they have an increased chance of adopting aggressive behaviors themselves (Murphy, 2011). Low SES children also are more likely to have transient peer groups; these children do not have the opportunity to develop stable friendships that can help them avoid problems such as aggressive behavior.

An increasing amount of research shows that preschool children who grow up in low SES homes are at increased risk for developing behavioral as well as language and academic difficulties later in life (Ispa et al., 2006; Kaiser, Qi, Hancock, & Foster, 2002; Woolfolk, 2008). Low SES children enrolled in Head Start programs have been shown to have higher than expected levels of externalizing behaviors and internalizing behavioral problems. Examples of externalizing behaviors are oppositional behaviors (e.g., running away, lying), physical aggression (e.g., biting and kicking), weak attention skills, hyperactivity, and impulsive behavior. Internalizing behaviors include problems of an introverted nature such as worrying, social withdrawal, and depression.

Qi and Kaiser (2004) studied the language and social skills of 60 low SES children enrolled in Head Start programs in Tennessee. The children represented different ethnic backgrounds, and all spoke English as their dominant language. In one group, the children had typical language development. In the other group, the children had language delays.

Qi and Kaiser (2004) found that children with language delays had poorer social skills and exhibited more problem behaviors on most but not all measures in comparison with the children whose language was developing normally. These investigators suggested that children who both are from low-income families and are language impaired are at risk for social and behavioral problems, and recommended that in intervention, professionals may wish to incorporate social skills training that includes conversational strategies for improved interactions with others.

Miles and Stipek (2006) found that poor literacy achievements in low SES children in first and third grades predicted relatively aggressive behavior in third and fifth grades, respectively. These authors suggested that because academic and social development are inextricably linked, efforts to improve skills in one domain will be more effective if attention is given to the other domain also.

When mothers experience poverty, depression and decreased maternal sensitivity are likely to result (La Paro, Justice, Skibbe, & Pianta, 2004). If mothers are depressed and less sensitive to their children's needs, then the children's language development may be negatively affected. Behavior also may be affected. It is important for professionals to work closely with low SES mothers to optimize their relationships with their children so that the children can grow in linguistic and socioemotional skills. This issue is addressed more fully in Chapter 9.

Recently I was working at a low SES school where I assisted the full-time speech-language pathologist, Barbara, with evaluations. I had tested a child and was writing a report at the computer in a corner of the room. In a different section of the room, while I typed, Barbara was attempting to hold a meeting with the caregivers of Donte M. Donte, a charming 4-year-old with a wide grin, was delayed in every area: speech, language, motor, and cognitive skills. Barbara was meeting with the school principal, social worker, and Donte's caregivers, his maternal aunt and her husband. Donte and his sister "Beyonce" (so she demanded to be called) were the products of pregnancies where their birth mother abused drugs and alcohol. Unfit to care for the children, she was forced to give them up for adoption to her sister and her sister's husband. The sister and husband told the team that they did not know what to do. They would put Donte and Beyonce in a room full of toys; 10 minutes later, the room and its contents were completely destroyed.

Having no child care, Donte's aunt and her husband had brought him and Beyonce to the meeting at the school. Barbara gave the children some play materials that they could entertain themselves with during the meeting. The children enjoyed the play materials for 2 to 3 minutes, but were soon bored and beginning to cause a ruckus that interrupted the very important meeting that was being held. Sitting at my computer writing the diagnostic report I needed to complete, I knew what was called for. I stopped writing my report, hit the "save" button, got up, and began engaging with the children, hoping to give the personnel in the meeting some extra time to talk and accomplish their goals.

After about 2 minutes of looking at the new (and, I hoped, engaging) materials I presented, Donte and Beyonce began yanking open cupboard doors and grabbing cupboard contents, throwing things on the floor. Horrified, I got the kids out of the room so that their commotion would not interrupt the meeting further. They lasted for 2 to 3 minutes in the little hallway outside the room with some materials I provided, but were soon bored and began to create such a commotion that I took them to the kindergarten playground. They ran around excitedly as I tried to direct them toward the play equipment and tricycles. They ran swiftly towards the gate, which led onto a busy street, and had the gate unlatched in seconds. They ran into the parking lot. Panicked, I ran as fast as I could after them. Fortunately, I was able to catch up with them and corral them back into the fenced-in playground, locking the gate very tightly to make sure this wouldn't happen again. The children raced off in all directions; when I looked back at them after my back was turned for a few seconds, I saw a heart-stopping sight. Beyonce had Donte standing on top of a tricycle to reach the drinking fountain; the tricycle wobbled precariously under his weight. Sprinting toward them at top speed, I tried to ignore the visions of lawsuits flashing through my head as I imagined Donte falling off the tricycle, hitting his head and knocking out several teeth. Thankfully, I was able to grab him before he fell. I lifted him to safety.

That was the longest 45 minutes of my life. I kept waiting and hoping in vain for Barbara to come out and signal that the meeting was over and that I was off the hook, free to go back inside my air conditioned speech room and sit down to the relief of my computer and the comfort of writing my diagnostic report. But Barbara never came. The meeting went on and on. Eventually I did bring the children back to the speech room, where the meeting was coming to a final, long-awaited conclusion. I was so grateful that both children were in one piece, and I tried to imagine what it was like to care for them on a daily basis. The children were so sweet, but wow, *what* energy! My heart went out to their aunt and her husband, both good, caring individuals who were doing the best they could under very challenging circumstances.

CONCLUSIONS

Living in poverty often has an impact on both the oral and literate language skills of children. Although parents do the best they can in their circumstances, by the age of 4 to 5 years, middle and upper SES children have linguistic advantages and skills that far outweigh those of low SES children. For professionals who try to help low SES children succeed linguistically and academically, the road can be long indeed, especially if they are not able to start helping these children until they arrive in kindergarten.

However, as grim as this picture may seem, research has shown that the proverbial die may not be as rigidly cast as statistics would indicate. Subsequent chapters explore potential solutions and practical strategies to support low SES children as they attempt to catch up with middle SES children in oral and written language skills. Also discussed are strategies for helping low SES children behave in ways that will help them achieve the best possible success in school and, eventually, the world of work.

CHAPTER HIGHLIGHTS

■ There is no causal relationship between poverty and language skills. However, two factors that are consistently linked to child language outcomes are maternal education and family SES.

- Children of low SES backgrounds, especially those whose mothers have not had the benefit of ongoing formal education, tend to have reduced oral and literate language skills. The number of words spoken in the home is consistently linked to SES and maternal education level in families.
- The research of Hart and Risley showed that by age 4 years, children in poverty in their study had heard 13 million words; children in middle SES homes had heard 45 million words. Low SES parents gave many more prohibitions than affirmations. In middle SES homes, more affirmations were given; in addition, middle SES parents gave their children many more choices than low SES parents.
- Hart and Risley concluded that the first three years of a child's life are critically important language-wise; vocabulary use at age 3 was predictive of language skills and reading comprehension scores at 9 and 10 years of age.
- Greenwood and colleagues replicated and extended Hart and Risley's findings using digital recording. The most talk directed to children occurred in the early morning (around 7:00 AM) and in the late afternoon-early evening. Mothers with more than a high school education spoke to their children more and took more conversational turns with them than mothers with a high school education or less.
- Research has indicated that many low SES parents have jobs where they follow the same routines and are strictly controlled. Middle and upper SES parents tend to have jobs requiring divergent thinking and creativity. Parents' jobs influence the way they interact with their children.
- Due to variables such as having jobs where they are strictly controlled as well as living in dangerous neighborhoods, low SES parents may control their children more tightly and engage in more punitive measures than middle SES parents who live in safe neighborhoods.
- Many middle SES parents prize language stimulation in the home; they prefer verbal approaches to discipline and are more likely than low SES parents to engage in enrichment activities for their children. Low SES parents may assume that their children's talents will unfold without extra encouragement and active development.

- For low SES children, low literacy skills are commonplace. These low skills can be linked to a lack of material resources (e.g., books) and psychological resources (e.g., a positive affective reading environment in the home).
- Home literacy practices differ along several parameters, including resources (indicated above) and cultural beliefs and practices of individual families.
- The behavioral characteristics of low SES children range along a wide continuum. Chronic poverty and persistent family hardship put children at risk for behavior problems and negative sequelae in adult life.
- Professionals who work with low SES children may need to prioritize social skills training, literate language development, and overall oral language development.

3

Considerations in Assessment of the Language Skills of Students from Low SES Backgrounds

The journey of one thousand miles begins with the first step.

Japanese proverb

Marcos is in second grade, and Mark has just entered first grade. Both boys are struggling with reading. Despite Mark's excellent oral vocabulary and high phonological awareness skills, his first grade teacher is concerned about his reading comprehension. Because English is Mark's primary language, testing with a variety of measures of reading comprehension can be expected to give valid results. These tests indicate that his reading skills are lower than expected for his grade level. In the course of evaluation for this and other factors, Mark also has additional vision testing, which shows he will benefit from specialized vision therapy. This therapy leads to a substantial improvement in his reading skills. In third grade, he now reads for enjoyment, above grade level.

Marcos is having great difficulty with reading. Although his primary (and dominant) language is Spanish, he is assessed by school personnel with measures that are all given in English. As might be predicted, he does not perform well.

The evaluation team notes environmental issues of poverty and truancy, and the fact that only Spanish is spoken at home, and recommends that Marcos not receive any special services. The team decides to give him "more time" to develop his reading skills. He continues to struggle in class, falling farther and farther behind.

INTRODUCTION

A strong relationship between SES and performance in school has been recognized (Paul & Norbury, 2012; Woolfolk, 2008). Students from high-SES families of all ethnic backgrounds have higher levels of achievement on tests and stay in school longer than students from low SES families. Poverty during a child's preschool years appears to have the greatest impact, and the longer the child lives in poverty, the greater the impact on his academic achievement. Even when the educational levels of parents are accounted for, the chance that children will be retained in grades or placed in special education increases by 2 to 3% for every year they live in poverty (Sherman, 1994).

Because children from low SES families tend to struggle academically at a higher rate than children from homes with more abundant financial resources, classroom teachers may refer less advantaged children to special education programs at a correspondingly high rate (Woolfolk, 2008). The result is that children who do not belong in such settings often end up in "Special Ed"; moreover, these programs include excessive numbers of children from low SES families. An important contributing factor is that many standardized tests of language and cognitive skills are biased against students from low SES backgrounds. Even if children from low SES homes are developing in a typical fashion, they may still be incorrectly identified as having cognitive or language impairments and may be inappropriately placed into special education programs (Murphy, 2011).

In an important study (mentioned earlier) by Fazio et al. (1996), some children from low SES families were found to score lower on language and cognitive tests than the normative sample, but this was not due to an underlying language impairment. Of 12 children who scored lowest on tests of language in kindergarten, 7 were later found to be typically developing students who did not have true language impairments. Because of the effects of poverty, these children were incorrectly labeled as "language impaired." As they became acculturated to the school environment, their scores on tests of language skills improved.

One of the most intransigent problems in special education has been the disproportionate number of culturally and linguistically diverse (CLD) students enrolled in special education services (Battle, 2012). Unfortunately, achievement gaps between CLD students from low SES backgrounds and white students from middle-SES backgrounds can be observed as early as kindergarten (Hosp & Reschly, 2004). Race and poverty overlap considerably in the United States, and it has been suggested that disproportionate CLD referral to special education may be more linked to SES than to race (Sibka, Poloni-Staudinger, Simmons, Reggins-Azziz, & Chung, 2005).

In order to prevent situations such as overplacement of students from low SES backgrounds (especially CLD students) in special education, it is important to assess these children's skills in a comprehensive and nonbiased manner. Ideally, professionals can use a combination of procedures known to be less biased: (1) Implementing Response to Intervention, (2) conducting a screening, (3) gathering a thorough case history, (4) evaluation of related areas such as vision and hearing, (5) modified use of appropriate standardized measures, and (6) use of nonstandardized, informal measures such as information processing tasks.

As discussed throughout this chapter, a key point for professionals to remember is that most formal, standardized tests assess a student's *knowledge base*; many students from low SES backgrounds have a compromised knowledge base as a result of their environmental circumstances. This chapter presents strategies for avoiding labeling students from low SES homes as needing special education (e.g., speech-language therapy) when their knowledge base is compromised but their underlying language-learning ability is intact. Two key federal laws pertain specifically to the assessment of children from low SES homes for potential special education services; these are discussed next.

LAWS AFFECTING THE ASSESSMENT OF CHILDREN FROM LOW SES FAMILIES FOR SPECIAL EDUCATION

On December 3, 2004, President Bush signed into law the *Individuals with Disabilities Education Improvement Act of 2004* (IDEA 2004), also known as Public Law (P.L.) 108-446. This new version of the original IDEA places greater emphasis on the use of prereferral services to prevent unnecessary referrals to special education and to minimize overidentification of children from certain backgrounds. School districts are now permitted to use up to 15% of their federal funds annually, combined with other funds, to develop and implement coordinated early intervention services.

IDEA 2004 has a specific focus on children in kindergarten through third grades who have not been technically identified as needing special education but who may need additional support to succeed in the general education classroom environment. A particular focus is on early intervention for students who are having difficulty developing their basic reading skills.

The newly reauthorized law also emphasizes that CLD students often are overrepresented in special education, so individual states will be asked to account for this situation if it is true for them. The law indicates that states will be required not only to keep track of how many "minority" students are being identified for special education but also to provide coordinated, comprehensive, early intervention programs for students in groups that are overrepresented (e.g., minority students).

Another federal law affecting services to students from low SES backgrounds is the *No Child Left Behind Act* (NCLB) (U.S. Department of Education, 2002), which attempts to correct inequities as summarized by Silliman, Wilkinson, and Brea-Spahn (2004):

> This sharp increase in enrollment [in American public schools] coexists with a crisis of illiteracy in America, which is particularly regrettable given the changed sociodemographic characteristics of American classrooms. A growing achievement gap exists among (1) minority and nonminority students, (2), those from poorer vs. richer families, (3) those whose native language is English, in contrast to those whose first language is not English, and (4) those identified for special education services versus those in regular education. (p. 99)

The No Child Left behind Act addresses these inequities in several ways. First, it requires students with disabilities to participate in state accountability systems for reading and math in grades 3 through 8. In other words, students with disabilities must take standardized state achievement tests along with their typically developing peers. Accommodations are allowed for students with disabilities, as are alternate assessments that include information similar to that on the standard forms.

The No Child Left Behind Act also requires that schools must show adequate annual progress toward achievement of proficiency in math and reading by *all* students (including those from low SES backgrounds); otherwise, the schools will face penalties. Finally, the No Child Left behind Act mandates that teachers use scientifically based instruction in their classrooms.

Ideally, under the mandates of No Child Left Behind, only students with true potential special needs would undergo formal assessment for special education. In order to ascertain whether or not a special education assessment is even necessary, many schools are implementing a Response to Intervention (RtI) model.

RESPONSE TO INTERVENTION

Because of the numbers of students who are struggling in their classrooms, many schools are implementing a model of *response to intervention* (RtI). RtI integrates assessment and intervention within a multilevel system designed to prevent failure, reduce behavioral problems, and maximize student achievement. Schools use multiple sources of data to identify students who are at risk for poor learning outcomes. For these at-risk students, schools provide evidence-based interventions, monitor student progress, and adjust the nature and intensity of the interventions depending on students' responsiveness or lack thereof (National Center on Response to Intervention, 2012). Students who initially do not respond to RtI are provided with instruction that becomes progressively more individualized and intense (Long, 2012; Rudebusch & Wiechmann, 2011). If they do not respond to this more intense and individualized RtI, then they are usually referred for special education assessment and placement. A major advantage of RtI is that it tries to prevent failure through offering support *before* a child receives special education (Davis & Banks, 2012).

The school where I work uses an RtI model that is typically applied as follows. If children in the early grades are struggling, professionals (such as the resource specialist) work with them in the classroom setting, giving them extra academic support in areas where they especially need it. If the children receive this extra support for a certain period of time (for example, six months to a year) and perform consequently perform academically in a manner commensurate with that of their peers and grade level expectations, then it is assumed that they do not need screening (and eventually in-depth assessment) for possible special education services. If the children do not show an optimal response to intervention—if they continue to struggle, show learning difficulties, and fall behind their classmates—then screening and eventual in-depth special education assessment are considered.

When a low SES student is having difficulty in the classroom, it is ideal to use an RtI model to assess the student's ability to learn when provided with instruction. Many low SES students are at risk for being mistakenly diagnosed with language impairments or learning disabilities because they do not come from environments that provide experiences that match schools' expectations. If struggling low SES students benefit from RtI and have enhanced academic performance, schools can safely assume that these students' original struggles were rooted in an environmental mismatch between home experiences and school expectations, not an underlying language impairment or learning disability. However, if RtI is not sufficient to boost students' performances to acceptable levels, then the special education assessment referral process begins. This process often begins with a screening.

PRELIMINARY COMPONENTS OF THE ASSESSMENT PROCESS

Screening

Screening is the process of quickly and efficiently obtaining a general view of a child's skills. In screening, the professional decides if: (1) more, in-depth assessment is needed, or (2) the child's skills appear to be developing in a typical fashion and no further assessment is needed at this time. For example, children's language skills may be screened.

In some school districts, screening for language skills in all kindergartners is automatic. It is relatively common for many kindergartners from low SES families to begin school before they have turned 5; they may not speak English at home, and many have never been to preschool. Screening these children at the beginning of kindergarten undoubtedly would lead to many overreferrals for in-depth, comprehensive assessment for possible language impairments. In many cases, however, most of these children are performing in a satisfactory way in the classroom by the end of kindergarten. Nevertheless, children whose performance is less than satisfactory often are not referred for screening until the end of the year or even in subsequent grades. Screening also should include hearing screening. The following case example illustrates the importance of including this component of screening.

One second grade teacher referred an African American student, Maleah, to me for in-depth language testing. The teacher was concerned about the Maleah's classroom performance and overall academic skills. Maleah showed excellent performance on the language tests I gave her, and most of her scores were above average. Maleah's school records indicated that she had passed a school group hearing screening which was administered by the school nurse.

I decided to read the records more carefully, and I found an audiogram from an audiologist at a local hospital. The school nurse had made an error. Hospital audiological testing records indicated that Maleah was almost completely deaf in her left ear. I made several suggestions to the classroom teacher, who said, "Oh—sit her front and center in the classroom? Great idea—thanks! I hadn't thought of that!" The new seating position helped Maleah immensely, and her work improved. This brief true story illustrates that another important consideration in such screening is obtaining accurate results.

Early literacy screening also is crucial for children from low SES homes. Justice, Invernizzi, and Meier (2002) have described an effective approach:

> One of the most effective strategies for preventing reading difficulties is ensuring early and accurate identification of those children who are experiencing difficulties in attaining critical early literacy skills . . . the prevention of literacy problems can be realized only if early literacy skills are assessed before children become immersed in the mechanics of conventional literacy instruction . . . [at-risk children include those who] exhibit limited English proficiency, reside in a low-income household, have a parent with low educational attainment . . . Children impacted early by such circumstances often show less proficiency on early and conventional literacy tasks as compared to children from middle and upper income households . . . both socioeconomic status . . . and familial history of reading difficulty have emerged as particularly powerful predictors of literacy achievement. (pp. 85, 87)

In summary, screening is a quick and efficient way to determine whether a child needs more in-depth, comprehensive evaluation for a possible language impairment, or whether the child is developing typically and does not need any further evaluation. Professionals can automatically screen children, especially at the kindergarten level, or screen only children who are specifically referred by teachers or parents. If the results of a screening indicate that a child needs to undergo an in-depth evaluation, then it is best to start with the case history.

The Case History

When a student from a low SES background is struggling in school, it is essential to gather a detailed case history before any type of in-depth special education evaluation takes place. The case history, ideally, should yield detailed information that helps professionals understand the child, his or her background, and any variables that may be contributing to reduced academic performance. Professionals can examine the students' records, talk to caregivers, and confer with teachers.

Research has shown that in terms of gathering a case history as part of an assessment, professionals can effectively use parent report with young children from low SES families as long as it is used in conjunction with other measures (Pan et al., 2004). Pan and colleagues suggest triangulating data, for example, when evaluating the language skills of a young SES child from a low SES family, a professional can use parent report, spontaneous language samples, and appropriate standardized assessment tools.

The importance of the case history in the assessment process is highlighted in the following case example based on a real-life clinical situation.

I'll never forget LaVera T., a first grader whom I "inherited" on my caseload at a new school. She was from a low SES family; her kindergarten teacher had reported that LaVera was not performing adequately in the classroom. As I worked with LaVera, I sensed that something was not right about her special education label of "speech-language impaired." During the intake evaluation, I noticed that LaVera, who had a charming grin and a quick mind, learned new information quickly. I wondered how this child had qualified for speech-language services in the first place as a kindergartner.

Some digging in LaVera's files — and conversations with her — revealed that she had started kindergarten a little early, at 4 years and 10 months of age. She had never been to preschool. Her home (where the adults received welfare), consisted of a small house occupied by a father and three biological mothers; LaVera was one of 12 children also living there, who all belonged to the three mothers and the one father. After gaining an understanding of LaVera's background, I talked with her first grade teacher, who reported that generally, LaVera was performing at grade level academically. She was in the lowest third of the class but seemed to be "catching on." The teacher saw no real reason to be concerned about LaVera's school ability.

I dismissed LaVera from speech-language therapy. Here was a clear case of a child who had normal underlying language-learning ability; her environment was a strong factor in her "low" academic performance in kindergarten.

> It could be argued that no harm was done in this case. Therapy to boost LaVera's language skills certainly did not hurt her; in fact, it probably helped. But is it legal and ethical to label a child like LaVera as "Special Ed"?

An important consideration is that in qualifying children for any type of special education, professionals are putting a label on them, a label that often follows them for years. A wide range of nonspecial education support services are available, as discussed in subsequent chapters. The point here is that when students from low SES families are not performing up to academic expectations, the first step is to obtain a detailed case history, to avoid inappropriate referral of these children for special education services.

In gathering data for a detailed case history, it is important to look for the following parameters:

- *Family living patterns.* Has the family been homeless for any period of time? Is there a history of migrancy or frequent moves from one geographical region to another? This is, of course, related to educational history. Children whose school attendance has been sporadic often have concomitant academic problems.
- *Description of the language/academic problems.* Such descriptions may include both the parent's and the teacher's points of view.
- *Information about the child's language behavior.* Is the language behavior considered to be within or outside the norms for that particular cultural and linguistic community?
- *Prior assessment and treatment* for the language/academic problem. It is especially important to consider whether or not nonspecial education services have been used before a special education referral.
- *Family constellation and communication patterns.* Does anyone else in the family have a communication disorder? Do the adults in the home have enough time to talk and read with the child? Who lives in the home?
- *Prenatal, birth, and developmental history.* Was there maternal use of drugs, alcohol, or tobacco, or any other prob-

lems, during pregnancy? Were there difficulties with the birth process?

- *Medical history.* Hearing and visual acuity are of special concern; also, has there ever been a diagnosis of attention deficit hyperactivity disorder (ADHD)?
- *Patterns of language use in the home.* Does the family speak a language other than English? What languages are spoken by whom? Has the child had English exposure before school enrollment? Has the child been exposed to formal language register in preschool? Do the adults in the home use formal or casual register to communicate?
- *Educational history.* It frequently is very useful to look in the child's "cum" (cumulative) file for information. This often-overlooked rich source of information can be very helpful in deciding whether or not a student needs a special education evaluation.

In the public schools, each child has a "cum" file. This file contains information about the child such as health history, report cards, teacher comments, results of vision and hearing screenings, and other important information. A very helpful part of gathering a case history is examining the contents of the child's "cum" file for any notations of problems or patterns on report cards.

Jonathan L. was referred by his teacher for evaluation for possible language problems. Before screening, I took a look look at his "cum" file. The file contained a note from Jonathan's mother in which she referred to a restraining order in place against his father. In addition, Mrs. L. wrote: "I am disabled. My children all have special education needs. Is it possible that all my children could be put on the same track [for a year-round school]?" The family history of a restraining order was potentially important information, because Jonathan's language and academic problems may well have been related more to his environment than to underlying language impairment or other issue that would be an indication for special education. Moreover, tracking the children as requested by Mrs. L. could relieve stresses at home, potentially benefiting Jonathan (as well as the rest of the children).

As mentioned, it is a good idea to review students' report cards to discover any patterns to areas of difficulty over the years, or any pattern in teachers' comments. For example, if a student has a genuine special education need (that has not been addressed), there will be teacher notes on report cards often contain relevant teacher notes each year: "Trang tries hard, but has difficulty following directions"; "Trang struggles to express himself verbally and often cannot find the word he is looking for." A careful reading of the contents of a student's "cum" file often will answer many questions for the professional evaluating the case: an investment of just 10 or 15 minutes. Review of the file should be done before the student's caregivers are interviewed.

After appropriate screening and obtaining a thorough case history, the professional may decide that the student does not need further evaluation. If special education testing is necessary, however, standardized tests often are used.

THE USE OF STANDARDIZED TESTS

General Considerations in Using Standardized Tests with Students from Low SES Backgrounds

For various reasons, many professionals use standardized, norm-referenced tests of academic, language, and cognitive skills when evaluating children from low SES families for possible special education services. Standardized tests provide a quantitative means of comparing a child's performance with the performance of large groups of children in a similar age category (Haynes & Pindzola, 2012). Many professionals believe that the use of standardized, norm-referenced tests is required by federal and state law. As discussed later, however, the relevant legislation, IDEA 2004, actually does allow the use of nonstandardized, informal measures when appropriate. Nevertheless, most professionals are comfortable with obtaining numbers, with comparing the performance of the students they test against the performance of the students upon which the tests were normed.

Adler and Birdsong (1983) recommend that when choosing standardized tests to use with children from low SES families, professionals ask the following questions about each test:

1. What was the size of the standardization sample?
2. Was the sample selected from different geographical regions or from only one part of the country?

3. Are members of the sample all from large cities, or are some from rural areas?
4. How was SES of the members of the sample determined?

Once these considerations have been addressed, it is then important to keep in mind potential pitfalls in using these types of tests with students from low SES backgrounds (Haynes & Pindzola, 2012).

First, Payne (2003) makes the case that standardized tests (e.g., IQ tests) assess a student's *acquired knowledge*: the knowledge accumulated from many different types of life experiences. Specifically, many IQ tests assess *crystallized intelligence*, which reflects the knowledge bank that a student has when he or she walks through the door. Most IQ tests do not assess *fluid intelligence*, or the underlying ability to learn and think. A similar problem is inherent in tests of language skills: They assess a student's acquired language knowledge but often do not assess a student's language-learning ability: ability to learn when provided with instruction (Roseberry-McKibbin, 2007).

It is especially difficult to measure IQ in CLD students because most IQ tests are standardized on monolingual, English-speaking students. Many experts have criticized the practice of using IQ tests with CLD students (Commission on Excellence in Special Education, 2001; Sue & Sue, 2013).

Many standardized tests have content bias against students from low SES backgrounds. *Content bias* occurs when the examiner uses activities and items that do not correspond with the child's experiential base or background. For example, a child from a low SES family living in Texas probably has never been exposed to an ice-skating rink. A test item that refers to an ice-skating rink would be biased against that child. In another example, certain language tests in common use assume that children have exposure to zoos. Although visiting a zoo may seem like one of the basics of childhood, many children from low SES families have never had this experience. Other examples of content bias are found in various tests; the students being tested have simply never been exposed to those concepts.

Items on standardized tests also may have *value bias*. This occurs when test items assume a value system that is different from the child's. Wyatt (2002) gives the following example: On a standardized test, the only acceptable, correct answer to the question, "Why should you brush your teeth?" Is, "Because you can get cavities if you don't." An African American child, however, might answer: "Because my momma told me to." This answer would be consistent with the child's value system; however, it differs from what is expected by test protocol.

The vast majority of standardized tests also contain language *register bias*. As noted elsewhere, many students from low SES backgrounds come to school using casual language register; they may have difficulty with tasks that involve formal language register. A related consideration is that these children often have difficulty with decontextualized language; their casual language register often is heavily reliant on context.

Most standardized tests are written and administered in formal language register. The test tasks are highly decontextualized:

"Tell me everything you can about a *dog*."

"Listen. I am going to say 4 words. I want you to tell me which two go together, and why they go together. Let's try one: *apple, broom, grape, cat.* Which two go together? That's right—apple and grape go together because they are both fruits."

Such tasks may be especially difficult because they are completely decontextualized from things or concepts the child has personally experienced.

Formal language register also requires the ability to effectively use Mainstream American English (MAE) grammar. This can put students from low SES backgrounds at a disadvantage. For example, one popular test of language skills gives children scenarios and asks them what they would do to solve a given problem. For instance, a child may be shown a picture of a boy who has fallen off his scooter and now has a bleeding knee. The child is asked what the boy should do now.

Even if the content of the response is correct, the child can only be given full credit for the response if it also is grammatically correct and complete. For a response of, "He ain't happy—needs to call his momma and git him a Bandaid," for example, the child is given only partial credit for the answer. As discussed in subsequent chapters, language in casual register often is "truncated" and grammatically incorrect by MAE rules. Children from low SES families who use this type of language often are penalized by standardized tests of language skills because again, the tasks are decontextualized and demand that answers be given in formal register that conforms to the rules of MAE.

Formal Test Assumptions

When using standardized tests to assess students from low SES backgrounds, professionals need to remember that the development of these tests has grown out of a middle class, literate, Western framework. Formal testing for children is generally conducted on the basis of the following assumptions (Roseberry-McKibbin, 2008):

- the child will feel comfortable enough with the examiner in the testing situation to perform optimally and to the best of his or her ability.
- the child will be willing to guess even if he or she is not sure of the answer.
- the child understands the test tasks (e.g., fill-in-the-blank, describe a picture).
- the child will follow the cooperative principle by performing to the best of his or her ability and by trying to provide answers that are relevant to the situation.
- the child will attempt to respond even if the test tasks do not make sense.
- the child has been exposed to the information and background experiences inherent in the content of the test.
- the child is proficient in verbal display of knowledge.

These assumptions do not hold true for many students from low SES backgrounds. As noted previously, in many low SES homes, a mentality of, "You'll do it because I said so!" prevails. Children are to be seen and not heard. Children may not be given choices or asked to elaborate verbally. Such home attitudes certainly can affect performance on a standardized test, where the child is expected to feel comfortable with the examiner, perform to the best of his or her ability, and be proficient in verbal display of knowledge (telling orally what the child knows).

In addition, many children from low SES families have not been previously exposed to "schoolish" type tasks such as labeling pictures, doing flashcards, or reading books. Most standardized tests require students to have at least some degree of familiarity and comfort level with such tasks.

If test tasks do not make sense, students are expected to try their best anyway. But if they are from low SES homes where they have not been encouraged to take risks, especially verbal risks, as in using words to solve problems and explain their reason for doing something, many students from low SES backgrounds will "shut down." They may have been punished in their homes for asking "why" or for questioning authority.

As stated previously, research shows that many middle-SES parents prepare their children for a world of symbolic thinking and problem solving. Low SES parents, on the other hand, may be preparing their children for service-level jobs that do not necessarily require this type of symbolic thinking and problem solving (Hart & Risley, 1995). If students from low SES backgrounds are from these types of homes, guessing at test tasks that do not make sense will be unfamiliar. Again, as borne out by my own clinical experience, students may "shut down" and answer "I don't know."

Qi (2006) brings up another issue that pertains to using standardized tests with children from low SES families. According to this investigator, research indicates that in assessment of the language skills of children from low SES families, professionals need to recognize that problem behaviors may be associated with language abilities as measured by performance on standardized tests.

Professionals should be aware of the possibility that lower standard scores may be related to disruptive behaviors that affect children's test performance, thereby putting into question the validity of these tests. When children exhibit noncompliant behavior during testing, the professional must discontinue testing and regain their cooperation before testing continues. Qi (2006) recommends that professionals can: (1) allow children to take breaks, (2) use instructions that are easy to understand, and (3) use behavioral methods such as stickers to motivate children to complete testing.

The following case example presents one such approach to motivate children to give full cooperation in the testing process.

> Recently, I was requested to assess the language skills of Juan, a Mexican second grader from a low SES, non-English-literate family whose academic performance was rated very poor by his teachers. Accustomed to failure, Juan was challenging to motivate in terms of completing test tasks. I knew that I was asking him to do things during

the assessment session that were hard for him. To address these challenges, I began by setting out a silver "prize box" with many attractive toys in it. Next, I did two things.

First, I directed Juan's attention to the prize box before I started testing and told him that if he would hang in there with me, he could choose any toy he wanted at the end. Then I gave him a choice: either get all the testing over with at once, or do some now and, after a long break, come back to the speech room to finish up. Like most children, Juan liked the idea of "getting it over with," receiving a toy, and not having to come back.

Juan worked very well for me, and the assessment session was highly satisfactory. This "carrot and stick" approach often is the most effective for children from low SES backgrounds—especially those whose extraneous behaviors may interfere negatively with testing and compromise the validity of test results.

Sources of Bias in the Use of Standardized Tests with Culturally and Linguistically Diverse Students from Low SES Backgrounds

As noted, professionals nationwide have become increasingly sensitive to the fact that many standardized tests are not appropriate for use with students from low SES homes; researchers over the decades have criticized this practice (Bailey & Harbin, 1980; Crowley, 2004; Evard & Sabers, 1979; Haynes Pindzola, 2012; Long, 2012; Roseberry-McKibbin, Brice, & O'Hanlon, 2005; Wolfram, 1983; Wyatt, 2012). This applies especially to CLD students from low SES backgrounds, including students who speak African American English. Some standardized tests are appropriate for use with these students (Craig & Washington, 2002, 2004a), but others are not. Many experts have described standardized tests' biases against students who speak African American English; this includes academic achievement tests and IQ tests, as well as specific tests of language skills (Terrell & Jackson, 2002; Thomas-Tate, Washington, & Edwards, 2004; van Keulen, Weddington, & DuBose, 1998).

For example, a test of grammatical competency may include the following item: "Listen to this sentence—tell me if it is correct or incorrect: *The girl, she be ridin' her bike.*" The answer is "incorrect"; however, this sentence as worded is consistent with the rules of African American English. An African American English speaker who answered "correct" would be marked wrong on that item. Johnson (2005) showed that standardized tests that contain third person singular -*s* in either production or comprehension items may be biased against children who speak African American English. A new instrument on the market, created specifically for use with African American English speakers and adaptable for use with other children as well, is the Diagnostic Evaluation of Language Variation (Seymour, Roeper, de Villiers, & de Villiers, 2003). This test is gaining in popularity as an excellent measure for use with students who speak African American English.

Many authors have discussed sources of bias in the use of standardized tests with CLD students (Haynes & Pindzola, 2012; Roseberry-McKibbin, 2008; Wyatt, 2012). The sources of bias include those described previously. Special emphasis is needed on the fact that for many of these students, English is a second or third language. Thus, assessment of skills needs to occur in these students' first languages.

Modifying Standardized Tests for Use with Students from Low SES Backgrounds

If standardized tests are so inappropriate for use with students from low SES homes, why use them at all? Why not use solely informal assessment? In fact, in my own clinical practice, informal assessment procedures and materials are used primarily, if not entirely, with these students, with excellent results. Unfortunately, most professionals feel uncomfortable with this approach.

Across the United States, many educators and other professionals who work with children report that in their particular school districts, they are pressured to use standardized tests with all children, even though federal law technically does not mandate this (as discussed later). In addition, most professionals are more comfortable with standardized tests than they are with the uncertainties of informal, nonstandardized means of assessment. In any case, it is established practice to use standardized tests with students from low SES backgrounds.

Accordingly, authors have made recommendations for modifying standardized tests (Roseberry-McKibbin, 2008; Wyatt, 2012). These recommendations are summarized as follows:

1. Allow students extra time to respond.
2. Explain or rephrase confusing instructions, especially if the formal, decontextualized language of the instructions is confusing.
3. Give extra practice items, examples, and demonstrations, especially for students from low SES backgrounds who have limited exposure to testing-type situations.
4. Omit biased items that students are likely to miss (e.g., items depicting concepts or things that these students have not likely experienced before).
5. Continue testing even after the ceiling has been reached. Some students, especially those whose families have moved frequently, may have "pockets of knowledge" that can be tapped only by continuing to test, even after the formal test ceiling has been reached.
6. Devote more than one session to the testing. This is especially important for students from low SES backgrounds, who typically take some time to "warm up" to an unfamiliar adult.
7. Don't be afraid to use token reinforcers and prizes to motivate students to do their best.
8. When students first come for assessment, begin with the tasks that are the most familiar or easiest to do: pointing to pictures or talking about common subjects such as their families or friends, for example. In my own clinical experience, picture-pointing tasks, although certainly not common in most low SES homes, often help students feel comfortable and gently ease them into the formal testing situation. Because the examiner usually is a stranger, this gives them time to "warm up" and not have to talk to him or her right away. It is intimidating for many students from low SES backgrounds to come to an unfamiliar room with a stranger and immediately be put on the spot to talk as much as possible, so beginning with silent pointing tasks and easing gradually into test tasks that demand verbal output can be very helpful.
9. Within professional boundaries, don't be afraid to be warm and caring. As noted elsewhere in this book, many students from low SES backgrounds respond best to an adult who is warm

and caring and takes a personal interest in them. Although this sounds obvious, I think that many of us, with our busy schedules and numbers of children to deal with, tend to forget a "personal touch" tailored to the attributes of these children.

Traditional approach:

PROFESSIONAL: Leilani, let's get started. I am going to ask you to listen carefully and tell me what each one of these words means.

Tailored approach:

PROFESSIONAL: Leilani, thank you for coming. I'm glad you are here with me to talk, point to pictures, and earn a prize from the prize box over there. While I am getting my things together, tell me about your family. Do you have brothers and sisters? [*Student answers.*] What are your favorite things to do at recess time?

I find that being warm, supportive, and nurturing works much better for children from low SES backgrounds than being cool and distant. Many of these children seem to need a nurturing, interested, warm atmosphere to feel comfortable in the assessment setting, especially when the examiner is attempting to gather language samples.

LANGUAGE SAMPLES

General Considerations

Because standardized tests often are biased against students from low SES backgrounds, language samples can be used to evaluate their ability to communicate. As mentioned, many of these students use casual register, so the formal register of standardized tests is unfamiliar. Language sampling provides opportunities for students to express themselves in the mode in which they are the most comfortable: casual language register.

In the gathering of a spontaneous language sample, the professional (usually the SLP) converses in an informal manner with the child and tries to draw him or her out to interact as much as possible. The goal is to evaluate parameters of language based on the language the child uses during these interactions. Ideally, language samples should be *representative*: They should give the professional a picture of what the child's language is like in different daily situations in the "real world" context.

Many ways to evaluate language samples are available. Formal programs can be used to obtain detailed analyses of students' language content, form, and use. Sometimes clinicians evaluate language samples informally. Owens (2012) gives a detailed description of both formal and informal methods for language sample analysis.

Formal methods of language sample analysis usually assess students' morphological and syntactic skills in depth. This approach can work well for students from low SES backgrounds who speak MAE. For those who do not speak MAE, who use casual register or even a dialect of English, in-depth analysis of morphological and syntactic skills can be biased. Accordingly, in obtaining a language sample in a child from a low SES family, the primary focus of the assessment should be the child's ability to communicate meaning in naturalistic situations: the child's skills in language use.

Informal Evaluation of Language Use

With students from low SES backgrounds, it is essential to analyze their interactions in natural communication situations with peers from similar linguistic, cultural, and SES backgrounds. Their interactions with adults also can be evaluated; however, in view of the fact that these students may not trust adults, especially unfamiliar ones, it may be best to observe them interacting with peers with whom they are comfortable.

Again, the goal is to evaluate the students' semantic and pragmatic skills and ascertain if they are effective communicators in their day-to-day environments. Of note, if the student uses casual register effectively with peers, even if he or she does not display a command of "appropriate" formal English register, the student probably does not have a language impairment. In assessing the student's ability to communicate effectively in casual register with peers, the following parameters can be evaluated to indicate the possible presence of language impairment (Roseberry-McKibbin, 2008):

▪ The student replaces speech with gestures and communicates nonverbally when it would be more appropriate to talk.

▓ Peers indicate that they have difficulty understanding the student.

▓ The student expresses basic needs inadequately (e.g., cannot even communicate a need to go to the bathroom).

▓ When peers initiate interactions, the student often does not respond.

▓ The student rarely initiates verbal interaction with peers.

▓ When asked a question or engaged in conversation, the student gives inappropriate responses.

▓ The student has difficulty conveying thoughts in an organized, sequential manner that listeners can understand and make sense of.

▓ The student has difficulty appropriately maintaining a topic.

▓ Nonverbal aspects of language are inappropriate (for example, the student does not use appropriate gestures or facial expressions).

▓ The student has difficulty with turn-taking skills; either the student interrupts inappropriately or is passive and does not take a conversational turn when appropriate according to the norms of casual register

▓ The student needs to have information repeated, even when the information is expressed clearly and is thus easy to comprehend.

Again, if a student's language does not reflect differences from the casual register of peers in these areas, that student probably does not have underlying language impairment. If professionals still have questions about the language skills of a student from a low SES background, however, in addition to language samples, other alternatives to standardized assessment can be used to assess whether or not the student's low language (and usually academic) skills are the result of environmental issues or an underlying language-learning impairment.

I was asked to assess the language skills of Juanita, a pretty, low SES first grader from a Spanish-speaking home. Her parents were involved and concerned; they said they were worried because Juanita talked very little, and had been late in her Spanish language developmental milestones.

I brought Juanita to my testing room, preparing to administer several formal Spanish language tests (I speak very basic Spanish). Juanita would have no part of the formal tests. She started crying, an escape strategy that I was well prepared for through prior conversations with her parents and teacher. When she said she wanted to go back to her classroom, I smiled pleasantly and said that she had to stay with me until certain tasks were accomplished. The sobs grew louder. I told Juanita that I was fine with her crying, and that she could cry as long as she wanted, but the tasks still needed to get done. I informed her that she could not go back to class until after she completed the tasks, and I was willing to wait till she was ready. I glanced at the clock, opened a book, and started to read. After more loud sobs, Juanita glared at me angrily, stopped crying, and grudgingly performed several informal receptive language assessment tasks. I was grateful that I had some informal materials available, because completion of standardized tests was definitely not going to happen. (Incidentally, when I saw Juanita in the hallway several months later, she ran up and gave me a big hug. Maybe children do appreciate boundaries after all!)

OTHER ALTERNATIVES TO STANDARDIZED ASSESSMENT

Legal Considerations

As noted earlier in the "Introduction" to this chapter, children from low SES families are vulnerable to being overreferred to special education. The IDEA 2004 specifically places a greater emphasis on decreasing the numbers of students from low SES backgrounds in special education, especially if they are from CLD families. As of July 2005, states were increasingly required to keep track of how many "minority" students were being identified for special education. To review IDEA specifics, states are now required to provide coordinated, comprehensive early intervention programs for children in groups that are determined to be overrepresented, for example, children from low SES homes (Klotz & Nealis, 2005).

IDEA 2004 does not specify the use of either formal or informal tools for assessment of students who are suspected of having special education needs; what it does specify is that a variety of assessment tools should be used, and that the determination of a disability should not rely on a single measure or assessment tool. The key points of federal law are summarized as follows:

1. All children, regardless of handicap, are entitled to a free and appropriate education.
2. Testing and evaluation procedures and materials must be selected and administered in a nondiscriminatory manner.
3. Testing and evaluation materials must be provided and administered in the language or other mode of communication in which the child is most proficient.
4. Accommodations may include alternative forms of assessment and evaluation.
5. Tests must be administered to a child with a motor, speech, hearing, visual, or other communication disability, or to a bilingual child, so as to reflect accurately the child's ability in the area tested, rather than the child's impaired communication skill or limited English language skill.
6. No single procedure may be used as the sole criterion for determining an appropriate educational program and placement for a child; multiple measures must be used.

Federal law is very clear that biased assessment materials and procedures should not be used with children. The law also is clear that it is acceptable to use alternative procedures in evaluating students, as summarized by Kratcoski (1998):

> Evaluations and assessments in school settings have traditionally involved the use of standardized tests . . . to adhere to state and federal regulations.
>
> . . . According to federal regulations, the present level of performance must be presented in terms of objective measurable evaluations to the extent possible. [But] the provisions of P.L. 94-142 IDEA do not mandate specific assessment tools *or even require that standardized*

measures are used . . . tools must display equity, validity, and nondiscrimination . . . and they stipulate a team assessment approach that incorporates multi-measure decisions, and evaluation based on specific educational needs, and a look at the whole child

. . . Traditionally, many professionals have used standardized tests . . . operating from the belief that a *quantitative standard score is mandated by federal law* . . . *however, the law does not exclude subjective or qualitative measures* . . . *it leaves the choice of measurement tools and criteria to the educator.* (pp. 3–10 [italics mine])

Because it is legal to use subjective, qualitative, informal tools for assessment of low SES students' language skills, and professionals are not required to use formal standardized measures, it is important to be aware of other assessment options. These options are summarized next.

Dynamic Assessment

Often when professionals assess students, they use *static assessment*, which involves measuring the student's skills at one point in time to make a judgment about whether a linguistic or cognitive impairment is present. A student's current level of performance in a given area is determined relative to the performance of his or her peers. Thus, a child who has been referred for testing comes to the professional's office and is given several normed, standardized tests, usually in one sitting. The tests are scored, and a diagnosis is made on this basis. But what if an ongoing crisis at home is preventing the child from getting enough sleep, or is upsetting enough to impair the child's ability to concentrate that day? The problem with static assessment is that this approach does not look at a student's ability to learn; it just looks at what he or she knows on any given day.

Dynamic assessment evaluates a student's ability to learn when provided with instruction (Owens et al., 2011; Wyatt, 2012). It examines a student's learning potential (Long, 2012). With this assessment model, instead of asking what the student already knows, the professional asks *how* the student learns. The dynamic assessment model is characterized by a test-teach-retest format that observes a student's ability to learn. In dynamic assessment, the professional looks at the student's *modifiability*, which involves the student's responsiveness to instruction, his or her ability to transfer learning to new situations, and the amount of examiner effort that was required during the assessment. The assumption underlying dynamic assessment is that children with language differences will exhibit good modifiability; those with underlying language disorders will show less modifiability (Haynes & Pindzola, 2012).

When using dynamic assessment with a student from a low SES background, the professional can obtain optimal results by addressing the following considerations with respect to typically developing similar peers:

- Was this particular student slow to learn new information?
- Did he or she have more difficulty learning it?
- Did this particular student require more structure and individualized attention than were needed by similar peers?
- Did this student require instructional strategies that differed from those used effectively with similar peers?

If the answer to most or all of those questions is "yes," then a reasonable conclusion is that the student has an underlying language impairment requiring focused special education services. This conclusion, obtained by means of dynamic assessment, is based on the evidence that the child has difficulty in *ability to learn* overall. Of relevance here is the RtI concept introduced earlier in the chapter. RtI uses the principles of dynamic assessment in that it evaluates a child's ability to learn when provided with instruction.

As one example of the effectiveness of dynamic assessment with CLD children from low SES families, a study by Ukrainetz, Harpell, Walsh, and Coyle (2000) is discussed next. These researchers studied two groups of Native American children. One group was from an Arapahoe background, and the other group was from a Shoshone background. On the basis of teacher report and examiner observation of these children in the classroom setting, the children were labeled as "stronger" or "weaker" language learners. All children participated in a dynamic assessment procedure. Findings of the study showed that differences between pre-and post-test performance and modifiability scores were consistently greater in the "stronger" language group.

Ukrainetz and associates suggested that dynamic assessment may be considered as one valid and reliable way to differentiate language differences from language impairments in CLD children from low SES families. Other researchers have suggested that this approach also can potentially be useful with children from low SES families who speak African American English (Fagundes, Haynes, Haak, & Moran, 1998).

Portfolio Assessment

A portfolio is a container (e.g., a box, notebook, or folder) that holds information about and materials created by a student. Portfolios are valuable because student work samples collected over time allow evaluation of the student's progress in one or more areas. Language and work samples can be reviewed over a period of months to see if the student is progressing at an acceptable rate. If the student is progressing a great deal more slowly than can be expected, then it is possible that he or she has language impairment or other type of special education need. Again, progress of students from low SES backgrounds can be compared with that of peers from a similar cultural and linguistic background. Like dynamic assessment, portfolio assessment also can be involved in an RTI model.

Assessment of Information Processing Skills

Wyatt (2012) states that a major paradigm shift has been made toward the use of processing-dependent measures. Low SES students frequently have difficulty on knowledge-based language measures because of the mismatch between their environment and the expectations of test creators. Processing-dependent measures help circumvent this problem, permitting clinicians to assess whether students have language differences (based on environmental variables) or language impairments. Students with genuine, underlying language impairments are thought to have difficulty with processing-dependent measures that tap their ability to retain the sequential order of information. They also appear to have specific difficulties with tasks that require verbatim, immediate ordered recall. For example, these students have difficulty repeating back lists of nonwords, real words, and digits (Haynes & Pindzola, 2012). They also have difficulty recalling sentences (Dollaghan & Campbell, 1998).

Research has shown that processing-dependent measures such as nonword repetition are effective in distinguishing underlying language impairments from language differences in children who speak English as a second language (e.g., Campbell, Dollaghan, Needleman, & Janosky, 1997; Hwa-Froelich & Matsuo, 2005; Jacobs & Coufal, 2001; Kohnert & Windsor, 2004; Laing & Kamhi, 2003; Thordardottir et al., 2011; Wyatt, 2012). New research shows that processing dependent measures also may be useful for evaluating the language-learning ability of students from low SES backgrounds with a limited knowledge base due to environmental circumstances.

In an effort to determine if knowledge-based measures discriminate against children from low SES families, Enos, Kline, Guillen-Green, Weger, Roseberry-McKibbin, and O'Hanlon (2005) administered a commonly used knowledge-based measure of vocabulary to typically developing children from low- and middle-SES families in the Sacramento area of California. The study was designed to ascertain whether this measure would yield significant differences in the scores of the children from middle- and those from low-SES families.

Results of the study indicated a significant difference between two groups' vocabulary test scores. The average percentile rank score for the subjects from low SES backgrounds was 38; the average percentile rank for the subjects from middle-SES backgrounds was 51. Thus, a 13-point difference was found in the mean scores of the two groups when they differed only by the variable of SES. The investigators concluded that knowledge-based tests may indeed discriminate against typically developing children from low SES families and recommended that processing-dependent measures be used to assess their language skills instead (Enos et al., 2005).

Horton-Ikard and Weismer (2007) studied African American toddlers from middle-and low SES backgrounds. In terms of performance on two standardized vocabulary tests, it was found that low SES children scored significantly lower than middle-SES children. However, the two groups performed similarly on a fast-mapping task involving learning new word meanings. Horton-Ikard and Weismer concluded that, whereas the standardized tests were biased against the low SES subjects, the informal processing task was not. The results of this study support the use of informal processing tasks to assess low SES students in a manner that is nonbiased and truly reflective of their ability to learn language, not reflective of environmental differences as measured by standardized tests.

Engel and colleagues (2008) compared 20 Brazilian children from low- and higher-SES families on measures of working memory and vocabulary. The low SES children performed significantly lower on receptive and expressive vocabulary measures than the middle-SES children. However, both groups performed similarly on working memory measures (Engel, Santos, & Gathercole, 2008). Like Horton-Ikard and Weismer (2007), Engel and associates demonstrated that while knowledge-based measures discriminate against low SES children, processing measures are more fair and accurate measures of these children's language learning potential.

More research needs to be conducted to explore the use of processing measures in assessment of the language skills of low SES children. In preliminary work with processing-dependent measures with children from low SES families, I have had good results in my own clinical practice. These measures are extremely useful because, as Laing and Kamhi (2003) have noted, they do not rely on a child's prior experience or world knowledge. According to Laing and Kamhi:

> The use of processing-dependent dynamic measures . . . is appealing for a number of reasons. They are not biased toward life experience, socialization practices, or literacy knowledge, and they are quick and easy to administer . . . It is very advantageous to use assessment measures that do not rely on a child's prior experience or world knowledge. . . . Performance on nonword repetition and working memory measures has been found to be highly correlated with language impairment and second-language vocabulary acquisition in adults and children. When children perform poorly on processing-dependent measures, there is a high likelihood that they will have some type of language-learning difficulty. (p. 51)

CONCLUSION

Research shows that children from low SES families struggle in school to a much greater degree than do children from middle-SES families. Accordingly, teachers tend to refer less privileged children for special education assessment at a higher rate than for more privileged children. If professionals follow less biased assessment practices, low SES children will be at much lower risk for being misidentified for special education.

CHAPTER HIGHLIGHTS

▨ Statistics show that low SES students tend to be over referred for special education. Because of a mismatch between their home and neighborhood environments and schools' expectations, these students may be inappropriately labeled as needing special education when, in fact, they have normal underlying ability to learn.

▨ Recent federal laws such as the Individuals with Disabilities Education Act and No Child Left Behind have mandated that school districts provide focused, early intervention for at-risk children. These laws also specify that assessment needs to be nonbiased.

▨ Response to Intervention, or RtI, integrates assessment and intervention within a multilevel system designed to prevent failure, reduce behavior problems, and maximize student achievement. If RtI is successful in boosting students' performance to an acceptable level, special education assessment is not necessary.

▨ When professionals attempt to conduct thorough assessments of the skills of children from low SES families, they often begin with screenings. If screenings indicate some potential special education needs, more thorough, formal assessment takes place.

▨ This ideally begins with a case history, where parents, teachers, and others who are familiar with the student are asked specific questions about his or her performance in a number of areas.

▨ Many professionals then use standardized tests to assess the student's skills; these usually are IQ tests and tests of language skills. Standardized tests contain various types of bias against students from low SES backgrounds (especially CLD students), so informal, nonstandardized measures often are preferable for determining the potential need for special education services.

▨ These informal, nonstandardized measures include dynamic assessment, portfolio assessment, and the assessment of information-processing skills. One of the best features of these measures as a whole is that they do not tap a student's underlying knowledge, which is affected by environment. Rather, they assess a student's underlying ability to learn. Professionals also can use language samples to assess students' ability to use language in everyday situations.

Assessment of students from low SES backgrounds for potential special education services continues to be a challenge for many professionals throughout the United States. Increased national use of an RtI model, as well as implementation of less biased informal measures, should help reduce the numbers of low SES students who are mislabeled and inappropriately placed into special education.

4

Practical Strategies for Increasing the Oral Language Skills of Children From Low SES Families

Language is power.
Paulo Freire

Marcos and Mark both are 3 years old. Marcos stays at home with his grandmother and baby brother while his parents work in the fields. He spends most of his days watching TV and entertaining himself as best he can in the small back yard of his home.

No one reads to him because his parents and grandmother do not read or write. The household contains no books and only a few toys. Marcos occasionally plays with the children who live across the street, but they too mostly spend their days inside watching TV. (Because the neighborhood has a history of some minor criminal activity, playing outside is not considered entirely safe, so interaction among the neighborhood children is minimal.)

As he is turning 3, Mark is placed into a well-regarded developmental preschool program. The setting is safe and highly stimulating, with a huge fenced-in play area outside that provides a large sandbox, tricycles, a large play structure, and a spacious yard for running. The staff maintains some animals, a pig, chickens, and ducks, on the premises that the children feed. The children are exposed to music, art, literature, and many age-appropriate sensory learning experiences on an ongoing basis. The staff schedules frequent field trips to interesting places in the community. Mark makes many new friends and forms strong attachments with several of the teachers. His mother volunteers at the preschool, doing everything from helping serve snacks to sweeping the patio. Eventually, at age 5, Mark is moved to a Montessori school for a year of prekindergarten, participating in a program that has a strong emphasis on math, phonics, and building early literacy skills.

At age 5, Marcos is placed into an all-English-speaking kindergarten. He has had no preschool experience. He speaks only Spanish. He has rarely been read to. He can't count. Learning problems, perhaps stemming from prematurity and his mother's untreated gestational diabetes, are beginning to surface.

When Mark is placed into kindergarten at 5 years and 10 months of age, he has been read to for probably 500 to 1,000 hours at home. He has been in preschools with highly enriched environments. His phonological awareness skills are two years above age level. His verbal language skills are quite strong, and he has an extensive vocabulary for his age.

INTRODUCTION

As discussed in Chapter 1, the macroeconomic changes in today's society have made nonskilled jobs less available, and the economy has become increasingly technology- and information-based (U.S. Bureau of Labor Statistics, 2012). To revisit the research findings of Hart and Risley (1995), the early language experiences of children may be most important for the symbolic and language-based analytic competencies that are necessary for an advanced education and participation in the current economy. These competencies probably will become more important as society increasingly polarizes into the technological and service sectors.

According to Hart and Risley (1995), the problem of skill differences among children by the time they enter school is much larger, more important, and more intractable than generally has been realized. Early intervention is key because infancy is a neurologically critical period during which cortical development is influenced by the amount of central nervous system activity that is stimulated by experience. According to Neuman (2009), 85% of brain development is accomplished by three years of age. Research supports beginning language stimulation in infancy if possible (Carolina Abecedarian Project, 2006; Fowler, Ogston, Roberts- Fiati, & Swenson, 1995; Loeb, Fuller, Kagan, & Chang, 2004; Paul & Norbury, 2012). This stimulation can be provided by caregivers in the home (e.g., by the mother and others) and by caregivers in outside settings such as daycare programs. Low SES children also benefit when adults around them consciously use specific language stimulation strategies designed to boost expressive and receptive language skills.

STIMULATING INFANT LANGUAGE DEVELOPMENT

General Principles

As stated, it is critical to begin language stimulation as early in life as possible. Even before babies are born, they can hear well enough in utero to distinguish the sound of their mother's voice. After babies are born, maternal warmth and responsiveness are strong predictors of future language development and emotional security (Hamer, 2012). Maternal responsiveness is especially related to vocabulary development.

Furey (2010) examined the number of words in the vocabularies of matched 16- to 18-month-old children from low and middle SES families. She discovered, among other findings, that at 16 months of age, low SES children had expressive vocabularies of 83 words; middle SES children produced 115 words. Thus, at 16 months of age, there was a 32-word gap between low and middle SES toddlers. By 18 months of age, this gap had grown significantly. At 18 months old, the low SES toddlers produced 115 words, and the middle SES toddlers were producing 179 words. Thus, by 18 months of age, the gap had widened; between 16 to 18 months of age, or in 2 months' time, the middle SES toddlers were producing 64 more words than the low SES toddlers. In a 2-month time period, the middle SES toddlers' vocabularies had grown twice as much as the vocabularies of low SES toddlers. In order to help low SES toddlers increase their vocabulary skills, it is ideal for them to attend high quality preschool programs.

Research over the years has consistently shown that high-quality preschool programs portend the best short- and long-term results for at-risk children from low SES homes (Geoffrey et al., 2007). It is especially ideal if these programs can begin when children are infants. Geoffrey and colleagues studied a representative sample of 2,297 Canadian children, conducting the first assessment in infancy (birth to 11 months). The children were followed for four years. When they were between 4 to 5 years old, their receptive vocabularies were assessed. It was found that SES mediated the association between non-maternal care (NMC) and receptive language skills. Full time NMC in the first year of life was associated with higher receptive vocabulary scores among children from low SES families, but not among children from middle SES families. Low SES children were more likely to receive maternal care than middle SES children, and children in maternal care had mothers with higher depression scores than children in full time NMC. The authors concluded that provision of full time NMC during infancy may help mitigate linguistic inequalities between low and middle SES children, serving a protective role in the case of low SES children. They emphasized that, for children from impoverished environments, full time NMC is often ideal.

One highly successful NMC U.S. preschool program, the Abecedarian Project, took place in Chapel Hill, North Carolina (Carolina Abecedarian Project, 2006). Begun in the early 1970s, this longitudinal study followed 111 children from low SES families. Fifty-seven of the children were assigned to a high-quality, year-round daycare program; 54 children formed a control group that did not receive treatment.

The experimental children were in the program from infancy through age 5 years. A major focus of the daycare was a language enrichment program. Each child had an individualized prescription of educational activities, which consisted of games incorporated into the child's day. Activities focused on emotional, social, and cognitive areas of development, but language was especially emphasized. The staff-child ratio for babies was 1:3 and 1:7 for preschoolers. Children were evaluated at ages 12, 15, and 21 years.

At age 21, when compared with their control-group peers, the Abecedarian students had higher IQs, higher reading achievement, and higher math scores; they were less likely to be retained in a school grade, and were twice as likely to go on to postsecondary schools as controls. Compared to controls, the Abecedarian students delayed having a child by two full years. Moreover, mothers whose children participated in the program achieved higher employment and educational status than mothers whose children were not in the program. These benefits were especially pronounced for teenaged mothers.

Data from the Abecedarian Project provided scientific evidence that early childhood education, beginning in infancy, significantly improves scholastic success and educational attainments of low SES children, even into adulthood. The evidence also showed that learning begins in infancy; accordingly, child care officials should be aware of the importance of high-quality care from the very earliest months of life.

These findings are consistent with those of Fowler and colleagues (1995), who studied infants from various cultural and linguistic groups; these infants also varied by socioeconomic status. Even into high school, the performance of the students who began language stimulation programs at 4 months of age greatly exceeded that of the students who began language stimulation at 12 months of age. In follow-up studies of early home intervention programs, it was found that balanced turn-taking in language play during infancy proved to be the most powerful predictor of later language competencies. Parents' skills in turn-taking during language play correlated with children's later Scholastic Aptitude Tests (SAT) scores in high school (Fowler, Ogston, Roberts-Fiati, & Swenson, 1995).

Other researchers have examined the importance of beginning language stimulation in infancy. An important component of this language stimulation is the primary caregiver's (usually the mother's) attitude toward interacting with the baby. As mentioned previously, when mothers experience poverty, depression and decreased maternal sensitivity are likely to result (La Paro et al., 2004). When maternal sensitivity, warmth, and responsiveness increase, babies' language development is supported (Turnbull & Justice, 2012). Word learning has been shown to be faster and more efficient when caregivers are responsive, warm, and engaged in joint attention activities with their children (Vernon-Feagans et al., 2011).

Wallace, Roberts, and Lodder (1998) examined the relationships between aspects of mother-infant interaction and cognitive and communication skills of infants at 1 year of age. These researchers observed 92 African American mother-infant dyads; 70% (64) of them fell below the poverty line. Measures of infants' global cognition, receptive and expressive communication, and communication use were correlated with ratings of maternal sensitivity, responsiveness, warmth, elaborativeness, stimulation, and encouragement of initiative in semistructured play interactions. The most consistent correlates of infant communication measures were found to be the overall quality of the home environment and maternal ratings of elaborativeness and stimulation.

Relations were stronger in middle SES dyads than in low SES dyads. Wallace et al. (1998) found that low SES mothers had lower scores than middle SES mothers on six of the eight caregiving measures. The research of these investigators reinforces the critical importance of support from professionals for low SES mothers, beginning when their children are infants, in providing ideal types of language stimulation and thereby facilitating a solid linguistic foundation.

Bohannon and Bonvillian (2009) state that it is ideal if adults in a very young child's environment talk about something that is concrete and the object of the child's transitory attention. In some studies, mothers who spent more time talking about the object of their children's visual gaze patterns had babies who said their first words earlier and developed larger initial vocabularies than mothers who did not relate their utterances to an object that the child was already focused on.

A study conducted by Tamis-LeMonda, Bornstein, and Baumwell (2001) showed similar results: For infants' language milestones to be met, a responsive and supportive environment was essential. Children from high-responsive homes were 6 months ahead, in language development milestones, than children from low-responsive homes. Children from high-responsive homes could imitate words at 10 months of age; children from low-responsive homes did not imitate words until around 13 months of age. Tamis-LeMonda and associates found that the way mothers spoke to their children affected their language scores. These researchers determined that the types of responses that mothers gave to their infants' vocalizations helped predict timing of first imitations, first words, first 50 words, first combinatorial speech (putting two words together), and first use of language to talk about the past.

The key factor in stimulating the children's language development was maternal responsiveness. How often a mother initiated conversation with her baby was not predictive of language outcomes. The most powerful mechanism for moving a baby from babbling to fluent speech was maternal responsiveness to child-initiated vocalizations and words. Thus, when working with caregivers of infants, we can emphasize that *responsiveness* to infant-initiated vocalizations, words, and actions is key to language growth.

Stated differently, Hamer (2012) describes *contingency* as the extent to which the intended recipient is fully sensitive and responsive toward receiving a form of communication from another person. In communication between parents and babies, the extent to which they are engaged in reciprocal activity forms the basis of contingency. In order for babies to form secure attachments, contingency is important both cognitively and psychologically.

Robinson and Acevedo (2001), in their study of interactions of low SES mothers and their babies, found that one strategy mothers could use to encourage language in their babies was to be responsive in their interactions with the child during emotionally challenging situations. Doing so stimulated the babies' emotional vitality, linked to later language and cognitive development for infants from low SES homes. In this study, babies who scored as having high vitality also scored higher on either the Preschool Language Scale-3 (Zimmerman, Steiner, & Pond, 1993) or the Mental Development Index of the Bayley Scales of Infant Development-II (Bayley, 1993). Babies felt more secure with mothers who were emotionally responsive and available; consequently, their test scores were higher than those of babies whose mothers were more emotionally distant and unavailable.

In terms of stimulating infant language development, the longitudinal study by Hart and Risley (1995) discussed in Chapter 2 explored caregiver-child interactions in welfare, working class, and professional homes. Of interest, across all SES groups (even in the professional homes), the parents rarely looked at books with their babies. In addition, the parents almost never imitated the sounds their infants made (e.g., during babbling). Hart and Risley noted: "We were astonished to see all parents simply wait for their children to say words . . . the parents just let their children practice babbling, apparently sure that words . . . would appear in due time" (p. 55).

This finding suggests that across SES levels, professionals should focus especially on helping caregivers feel confident when looking at books with their infants and responding to babbling and attempts at words, not just waiting for actual words to emerge. Rossetti (2001) has suggested simple language expression activities to use with young children; the caregiver can encourage the child to "play" with words and noises, for example. Table 4–1 lists other practical, easy to implement strategies for stimulating children's language development beginning in infancy.

Using Books with Babies

Many parents and childcare professionals are not aware that exposing babies to books can help begin to build a foundation for later literacy (Bardige, 2009; Paul & Norbury, 2012). Literary language is different than ordinary, daily verbal conversation. It has distinct and memorable rhythms, and generally uses more complex syntax with greater numbers of adjectives and adverbs than ordinary talk. Even very young babies attend to simple stories, songs, and rhymes. When my son Mark was a baby, he would gaze raptly at the Thomas the Tank Engine book I read to him from the day he was born.

Books for babies should be washable, sturdy, easy to hold, and safe to chew on. They should have clear, colorful pictures that caregivers can point to and name. Books should show familiar routines, objects, and actions; they do not necessarily need to tell a story. Books for babies can be home made. By the time babies are six months old, they will attend to pictures, especially pictures of other babies. As they approach their first birthday, many babies will point to familiar pictures in books on command and make appropriate noises for animals in pictures. One of Mark's favorite books was his *Lift the Flap Bible*, especially the story of Noah's ark. At a very young age, he could lift the flaps and make appropriate animal noises for all the animals in the ark.

When caregivers are sharing books with babies, the initial goal is to establish joint attention to the pictures. Caregivers can help book reading to be a language-rich time through strategies such as being face to face during book sharing, labeling and talking about the pictures in the book, and asking questions. Caregivers should especially notice what babies are looking at, and comment upon it. Once the

Table 4–1. Stimulating Infant Language Development

1. Start talking to the baby at birth. Face-to-face contact is ideal.

2. Begin reading to the baby at birth. Simple books with colorful pictures are best. Label common objects and actions for the baby ("Look, *bear*. The *bear* is *eating*.").

3. Ask questions, pausing between them to facilitate later turn-taking skills.

4. Introduce music. Sing to the baby.

5. Introduce a foreign language simultaneously with the native language.

6. Let the baby have a mirror in her crib (made of safe glass). Point out and label her body parts.

7. Use short utterances with simple syntax.

8. Heighten facial expressions, gestures, and intonation.

9. Play turn-taking games such as patty-cake and peek-a-boo.

10. Remember that most newborns focus best on black-and-white objects. Expose them to black-and-white pictures, mobiles, and toys (e.g., pandas).

11. Introduce the baby to rattles that make various kinds of noises.

12. Imitate the sounds the baby makes. Make new sounds.

13. Use greetings and expressions (e.g., "Hi Allyson!" "Bye-bye, Brandon!" "Night-night")

14. Label what the baby is paying attention to or handling (e.g., "That's the *dog*! "You have a *ball*.").

15. Label simple, relevant objects and actions in the baby's daily environment; e.g., *cup, bottle, play, bath, eat*, and so forth.

16. Provide many opportunities for the baby to put simple objects in and out of containers.

17. Plant the seeds of literacy through having literacy artifacts in the environment (e.g., books, newspapers, alphabet designs, T-shirts with slogans, and so forth.

18. Use the same words in daily activities and routines. For example, during getting dressed, label body parts and clothing items. (e.g., "Here are your *shoes*. We'll put your *shoes* on your *feet*.")

19. Tie jingling bells to the crib.

20. Start a scrapbook for the baby—make it out of soft cotton cloth. Cut favorite animals and favorite objects out of fuzzy fabric. Go through the scrapbook and name the pictures.

continues

Table 4–1. *continued*

---

21. When cleaning the house or going on errands, let the baby come along. Describe what you are doing. (I will never forget being stared at in the grocery store as I talked to my baby, describing the contents of shelves in detail. I'm glad I couldn't read people's minds!).

22. Introduce two languages to the baby from birth (if possible).

Source: Adapted from Kaderavek, 2011; Paul and Norbury, 2012; Roseberry-McKibbin, 2007.

baby has been exposed to the book several times, the caregiver can stop on a page and wait for the child to do something like point to a picture. When the child points, the caregiver can label what he or she is pointing to (Paul & Norbury, 2012).

If caregivers begin reading with babies early in infancy, they are more likely to keep reading when children are older. Children will associate book reading with cuddling with their parents and sharing a warm, positive interaction (Bardige, 2009).

STIMULATING LANGUAGE DEVELOPMENT IN TODDLERS AND PRESCHOOLERS

The Importance of High-Quality Preschool Experiences

As noted, it is ideal for low SES children to begin participating in high-quality language stimulation programs when they are babies. The next-best scenario would be for them to participate in high-quality language stimulation programs as toddlers and, finally, as preschoolers. High-quality preschool care enhances social, cognitive, and linguistic development (Bradley, 2010; Snow & Juel, 2005; Woolfolk, 2008) and can be very effective in helping children develop a strong foundation of oral language skills. One reason it is important to address oral language skills in young children is that such skills have been found to be predictive of their later literacy development (McCormack, Harrison, McLeod, & McAllister, 2011). Many low SES families, however, have limited access to high-quality preschool programs that promote oral and preliterate language (Evans, Eckenrode, & Marcynyszyn, 2010; Turnbull & Justice, 2012).

The National Institute of Child Health and Human Development (NICHD) initiated a large-scale longitudinal study of the effects of early child-care arrangements on the development of children (NICHD, 2006). A not unexpected finding was that children (who were studied between birth and 54 months of age) were more likely to experience higher-quality child care if they were from more advantaged families.

These families had, among other characteristics, larger vocabularies, less authoritarian child-rearing beliefs, and higher educational and income levels of the parents. In the early findings of the study, higher quality child care was related to advanced language, cognitive, and preacademic outcomes, as well as better peer and socioemotional outcomes at some ages.

According to Neuman (2009), it is especially important to provide early high-quality programs because by 3 years of age, 85% of a child's core brain structure is formed. However, less than 4% of public investments in education and development have been specifically targeted for early childhood development programs. Neuman states that although spending on public education has increased, funds for early learning have essentially been frozen.

As noted, families in poverty often do not have access to high quality preschool care for their children. Across the United States, child care fees average $4,000 to $10,000 or more a year, exceeding the cost of most public universities in many states. According to the Forum on Family and Child Statistics (2011), in 2010, 48% of children ages 0 to 4 with employed mothers were primarily cared for by a relative. Fourteen percent were cared for in a home-based environment by a nonrelative (e.g., a babysitter or nanny). Only 24% spent most of their time in a center-based daycare arrangement such as preschool or Head Start. In 2007, only 15% of 3 to 6-year-old children in families in poverty were in center-based care as their primary arrangement. Some of this may have been due to the families' cultural background. As we discuss in more depth in a later chapter, some culturally diverse families believe that staying at home with relatives is much better, for infants and young children, than attending a center-based daycare.

There were also differences in the maternal education level of children who were in daycare and those who were not. Seventy one percent of children whose mothers had a bachelor's degree or higher were enrolled in center-based arrangements, compared with 29% of children whose mothers had less than a high school diploma, 43% of children whose mothers had a high school diploma or its equivalent, and 54% of children whose mothers had some college (Table 4–2).

Snow and Juel (2005) discuss the fact that in Sweden, early childhood education is organized to give priority to providing free, very high quality early childhood education to children from the families that are most at risk: non-Swedish-speaking families, families living below the poverty line, and immigrant families. In the United States, it is just the opposite: as described above, at-risk preschoolers are often in the care of relatives or are in informal family/home-based daycare setting. In such settings, often books, curricula, or professionally-trained educators are lacking.

As Rothstein (2006) states:

> Too many low-income children are parked before television sets in low-quality day-care settings. To narrow the academic achievement gap, care for infants and toddlers should be provided by adults who can create the kind of intellectual environment that is typically experienced by middle-class infants and toddlers. This requires professional caregivers and low child-adult ratios. (p. 24)

Such recommendations are highly laudable but will be hard to put into practice until the wages of child care professionals are raised. In one high-quality (and quite costly) preschool (my son's), the teachers

Table 4–2. Enrollment in Early Childhood Care and Education Programs for Children Ages 3 to 6 Years (not yet in kindergarten)

Cultural-Linguistic Group	Percentage of Children Enrolled in Early Childhood Care and Education Programs
Black, non-Hispanic	65
Asian	64
White, non-Hispanic	58
Hispanic	39

Source: Forum on Child and Family Statistics, 2011.

were paid only approximately $14,000 a year, and it was the highest quality preschool I could find.

Preschool teachers and early child educators need to be paid at a level that reflects the expertise needed for the job. Highly motivated, well-educated people can scarcely be expected to embrace a profession that typically pays less than what the average blue collar worker earns. The head of Mark's former preschool shared that she had been a housekeeper/maid before she became a preschool teacher. She told me once, "I got paid more to clean people's toilets than I do to care for their children." Society needs to be sure that preschool teachers and early child care providers are paid in accordance with the increasingly high expectations that today's parents place on them. When these child care professionals are paid what they are worth, then they can invest in training in how to best facilitate children's cognitive-linguistic development.

When I looked for child care for my own son during his early years, I was shocked to find that the differences between child care centers were extreme, even though they were only a few miles away from each other. Less expensive centers often had far fewer enrichment programs and activities (e.g., music, field trips) and far less in the way of literacy materials. The outdoor play areas were vastly different. If outdoor play areas were provided in less expensive centers, they typically were merely concrete-paved slabs with limited space and equipment. By contrast, in high-quality child care centers, outdoor play areas were deliberately designed to promote exploration of varied mini-environments and gross motor development, and abundant opportunities to experience interaction. For $200 more a month, I was thankful to eventually afford a wonderful child care center that provided a great deal of enriching gross motor, play, oral language, and preliteracy activities and materials. As I mentioned before, the outdoor play area, which included lots of grass and a terrific playground, was one of the best I have ever seen in terms of promoting exploration and gross motor development. There were even chickens, ducks, and a pig for the children to feed and care for. I remember thinking to myself at the time how thankful I was to afford a place such as this and not be economically limited to a child care center where the playground was cement with little play equipment and where there were few books and no field trips. Indeed, advantaged families are able to afford far more enrichment for their children even before kindergarten begins. At level 1, the macroeconomic level, our nation needs to support funding for high-quality prekindergarten programs for all children, especially those from low SES homes.

Research has shown that high-quality prekindergarten programs in five states effect significant improvement in children's early mathematical development, literacy, and overall language skills. Children who attended state-funded prekindergarten programs in Michigan, New Jersey, Oklahoma, South Carolina, and West Virginia gained significantly regardless of SES or ethnic background (National Institute for Early Education Research, 2005). Other studies in various states have shown that high-quality prekindergarten programs improve linguistic and cognitive abilities of children from low SES homes (National Institute for Early Education Research, 2005). Researchers are unanimous in their conclusions that failure prevention must begin before kindergarten entry (Neuman, 2009; Norris, 2011; Paul & Norbury, 2012).

High quality daycare centers constitute an excellent resource for preparing children from low SES homes for school success. Children attending these daycare centers often show significantly better behavior, language skills, and mental development than those who are in other care settings such as the homes of untrained friends and family members. It is ideal if high-risk low SES children can attend *compensatory programs*, which are longer, more focused on direct instruction, small in size, and accountable for results (Neuman, 2009).

An extensive longitudinal research study conducted by Loeb and colleagues at Stanford University examined the linguistic, behavioral, and cognitive skills and development of preschoolers who participated in family child care homes, as contrasted with the development of those who were in daycare centers (Loeb, Fuller, Kagan, & Chang, 2004). These researchers found that children in daycare centers scored better on a battery of tests than those who were left with friends or relatives or put into family child care homes while their mothers went to work. In addition, children placed in family child care homes had more aggressive behaviors than those who in daycare centers.

Specifically, the research team conducted two rounds of interviews with 451 families living in Tampa, Florida, and in San Jose and San Francisco, California. The first interview took place when the children were 2½ years of age; the second interview took place when they were 4 years old. The researchers assessed overall behavior and abilities in the home and in daycare settings. At the second interview, 83% of mothers worked outside the home.

Loeb and colleagues (2004) reported that tests of school readiness and cognitive and language proficiency were highest among children who attended daycare centers. The advantages of daycare center participation remained even after adjustment for factors such as the mothers' educational and cognitive levels. Whether or not the mothers had graduated from high school had no significant effect on the children's cognitive development. When the quality of the daycare centers was examined, it was found that children showed more social problems when cared for by providers with less than a high school education.

Children in daycare settings with better-educated teachers achieved higher measures of language skills and school readiness. According to Loeb and colleagues (2004), the findings of this study confirm the fact that for many children from low SES families, high-quality preschool or child care can provide valuable social, cognitive, and linguistic stimulation that will prepare them for school. Again, federal and state governments need to give higher priority to investing in these types of programs.

France pays approximately $7 billion a year, or $5,500 per child, to send nearly all 3- to 5-year-olds to voluntary, all-day preschool. There is a rich curriculum of culture and art. Teachers hold the same credentials and receive the same salaries as elementary school teachers (Posnick-Goodwin, 2001). In the United States, some states have implemented universal preschool or universal prekindergarten. Universal prekindergarten in Georgia has been funded by state lottery since 1995. New York launched a pilot prekindergarten program in 1998. California began transitional kindergarten in 2012. Overall, in the United States, the percentage of 3 to 5-year-olds enrolled in full-day preprimary programs increased from 32% in 1980 to 58% in 2010

(Aud et al., 2012). As encouraging as this seems, as stated, more public funding needs to be provided for early child development programs. This funding, among other things, can involve targeted training for daycare providers.

The Importance of Appropriate Training for Early Child Care Providers

It has been assumed all too often that child care providers and preschool teachers play a relatively minor role in young children's development, and that it is the job of the public schools and special education to serve at-risk children once they enter the public school system. The public schools, however, provide special education services only for the very lowest-performing children, thereby overlooking the nearly 35% of children in the United States who enter kindergarten in the at-risk category (Podhajski & Nathan, 2005). Thus, it is crucial for early child care providers to be given the appropriate training to support them in providing rich cognitive-linguistic stimulation for young children (Turnbull & Justice, 2012).

Very few child care providers are adequately trained to provide language-enriching activities to the children with whom they work (Podhajski & Nathan, 2005). Only 10 states require early childhood care providers and educators to obtain some type of credential or education (Barnett, 2003). Thus, 40 states require no more training than a high school diploma for people to become preschool educators or child care providers. Yet strong evidence shows that children in early child care programs benefit from teacher training and preparation (Cabell et al., 2011; Justice et al., 2010; Wasik, Bond, & Hinman, 2006).

Ruston and Schwanenflugel (2010) studied the effectiveness of an intervention program for prekindergarten children. The adults who worked with the children were trained in techniques for holding language-rich, stimulating conversations with the children. During the study, the adults in the experimental group emphasized use of open-ended questions, linguistic recasts, and use of rare words. Twice a week for 10 weeks, children in the experimental group engaged in 25 minutes of intensive conversation with a trained adult. The control group did not receive this intervention. Pre- and post-measures using the Expressive Vocabulary Test-2 (Williams, 2007) and a language sample showed that children in the experimental group showed greater growth on the EVT than the controls, and also showed greater growth than the controls in lexical diversity.

With many mothers with children younger than 5 years of age in the workforce, a majority of young American children now spend a great deal of time at preschool and in child care center. As was stated earlier, in the United States, 85% of children are placed into some type of outside care during their first year of life. It is essential that professionals who work with these children obtain training to optimize the cognitive-linguistic environments in which these children spend so much time.

Wasik and associates (2006), in a study of training strategies for Head Start teachers, found that often in preschools for children from low SES families, the amount of teacher-child verbal and interchange was minimal, and so was the amount of time that teachers spent reading to children. Accordingly, these investigators conducted an experiment in which they specifically trained Head Start teachers in optimal ways of facilitating children's oral and literate language development. They found that children's oral and literate language skills increased; specific teacher behaviors appeared to be especially highly correlated with this increase.

These effective teacher behaviors included asking descriptive questions, providing feedback to children when they spoke, and using active listening strategies. Asking reactive, predictive, and recall questions outside of book reading also appeared to be related to children's language development. The data from Wasik and associates' study also suggested that teachers' questioning before and after book reading had more of an impact on children's language growth than asking questions during book reading. In addition, children's language development was positively facilitated when teachers made connections between what had occurred during book reading and other classroom activities. ("Let's wash our hands before snack. Remember how Timmy, in the book we read, washed his hands before he ate? Let's wash our hands like Timmy did.")

Wasik and associates (2006) discussed the strategies implemented in their study that were quite helpful for training the Head Start teachers. First, the researchers conducted an intensive professional development intervention that emphasized both conceptual and procedural aspects of literacy and overall language development in young children. During training, the teachers weren't just told what to do; instead, they were also given explanations about *why* reading and talking to young children would be beneficial to the children's language and literacy development. In addition, the teachers had the opportunity to observe demonstrations of the behaviors they were expected to use, to practice those behaviors while being observed, and to receive feedback about their performance. Through this coaching model, teachers had continuous opportunities to practice target behaviors and to confer with an expert trainer about what was effective and what was not.

Wasik and associates (2006) specifically emphasized that teachers were not merely trained through a one-day or week-long work shop with no follow-through. Rather, in this study, trainers spent an average of four hours a month with each teacher in the classroom. Thus, trainers formed relationships with teachers, making it easier to provide feedback that was accepted and utilized. Appropriate feedback was vital to helping teachers consistently and effectively implement the strategies with children; having trainers available to observe and provide this feedback fully addressed this need. Podhajski and Nathan (2005) also found, in their study of providing literacy training to preschool teachers, that this training was best provided by a 2-day training session and a 6-month mentorship program.

More speech-language pathologists (SLPs) are providing services to children in their preschool classrooms. As part of these services, SLPs are providing training to preschool teachers concerning strategies for language facilitation. As de Rivera, Girolametto, Greenberg, and Weitzman (2005) point out, training teachers can extend the SLP's services by enhancing the teachers' skills and ultimately freeing up some of the SLP's time.

SLPs and other professionals can train preschool teachers and daycare providers in techniques for facilitating increased successful peer interactions for children who have difficulties using language effectively. Girolametto, Weitzman, and Greenberg (2004) showed that daycare providers can be successfully trained to facilitate children's interactions with their peers. In their study, the daycare providers attended an inservice session addressing methods for developing peer interaction skills in preschool children and how to set up peer interactions through verbal supports. For example, a caregiver might specifically prompt a child to play with a peer or might praise the child for interacting with a peer. Girolametto and associates (2004) showed that children in the experimental group (those whose daycare providers had been trained) increased their frequency of peer-directed utterances during certain types of play.

Increasing Language Skills of Students from Low-Income Backgrounds

Practical Strategies for Professionals

Second Edition

Girolametto, Weitzman, and Greenberg (2012) examined the efficacy of a professional development program for early childhood educators. Led by a speech-language pathologist (SLP), this program trained the educators in strategies that facilitated emergent literacy skills in preschool children. Specifically, the strategies addressed increasing children's skills in sound awareness, print concepts, alphabet knowledge, and comprehension of decontextualized oral language. The early childhood educators utilized the strategies in naturally occurring classroom interactions. Results of the study showed that educators who received training used more utterances that included decontextualized language and print/sound references than the control group. The children who worked with the trained educators used a significantly higher rate of utterances that included print/sound references and decontextualized language as compared to controls. Girolametto et al. (2012) concluded that SLPs can provide training to early childhood educators that produces short-term changes in facilitation of emergent literacy skills in early childhood settings.

These results are encouraging because today, as stated, so many children spend much of their time in daycare settings. Professionals such as SLPs and others can provide simple suggestions or even inservice training programs for daycare providers to teach them practical methods for helping young children with language problems integrate more with their peers (Justice et al., 2010; Paul & Norbury, 2012). It is my experience that many of these providers are open to suggestions, especially if implementation of the suggestions can help the children behave better. Children with communication problems often get frustrated and throw tantrums, cry, and manifest other disruptive behaviors. When I have made suggestions to daycare providers who work with these children, they have been very eager to implement any techniques which will reduce these disruptive behaviors.

Clearly, research shows that persons who provide care for young children from low SES families need to be trained in strategies for stimulating the children's language development. An encouraging research finding is that, when properly trained, early childhood professionals such as preschool teachers can successfully provide this type of language stimulation. Hale (2004) adds another recommendation for early childhood professionals such as preschool teachers. She notes that if and when they obtain training, this training usually is limited to preschool education. Accordingly, she recommends that preschool teachers receive training that will help them prepare children to segue successfully into kindergarten. Preschool teachers need to articulate with elementary curriculum. This is becoming increasingly important, because the mandates of No Child Left Behind (2002) require that all children perform within a certain range on standardized state and national tests. Certain groups of children from low SES backgrounds are more vulnerable to poor performance on these types of tests than children from other groups, and professionals need to be aware of this.

Craig and Washington (2004b) discussed in detail the effects of poverty on the language and academic performance of African American students. They noted that African American children are more than three times as likely as their White peers to live in poverty and added that they are more likely than majority children to live in families in which the levels of parental education are low. Craig and Washington emphasized that poverty is one variable that is implicated in school reading failure for African American students. They went on to state that "although poverty and its covariables can have profound adverse effects on a child's well-being, recent research indicates that formal public preschool experience may mitigate some of these effects for literacy learning" (2004b, p. 234).

At level 1, society needs to give far greater acknowledgement to the great importance of the job that early child care providers and preschool teachers carry out: that of providing a strong and solid cognitive-linguistic foundation for young children *before* they enter kindergarten.

Ideally, provision of this foundation should begin at birth. If that ideal option is not possible, high-quality preschool programs, staffed by well-trained teachers, can help give at-risk children from low SES families the critical foundational skills they need to be successful in school, and ultimately in life. Thus, today's early child care providers must be well trained, and paid what they are worth.

PRACTICAL STRATEGIES FOR INCREASING THE LANGUAGE SKILLS OF TODDLERS AND PRESCHOOLERS IN NATURAL SETTINGS

The importance of training caregivers, preschool teachers and other early child care professionals in techniques to provide language stimulation for young children cannot be overemphasized. Some specific activities and strategies that can be used are described in this section. These activities and strategies generally are easy to implement within a busy day, and most cost virtually nothing. Some general principles of stimulating language skills in young children are described next.

General Principles of Successful Language Stimulation with Young Children

We have just talked about the importance of training preschool teachers and other early child care professionals to engage in activities that provide language stimulation for young children. In this section, we will describe some of the specific activities and strategies that can be used. Let's begin by looking at some general principles of stimulating language skills in young children.

Language stimulation activities with young children often are successful in a context of play. Caregivers can arrange activities so that targeted outcomes occur naturally. For example, to work on greetings and leave-takings (*hi* and *bye*), puppets or dolls can be used in a play house to model and encourage adoption of these structures. Many preschool children enjoy dramatic play, whereby they role-play various situations while learning new vocabulary and routines for interacting in novel situations.

Adults who interact with children in natural settings must be encouraged to learn to use periods of silence during communicative exchanges and not to force verbal output. As someone who did not grow up in the United States, I have observed that most Americans are uncomfortable with silence and will rush to fill it with words. Many American caregivers and professionals believe that periods of silence during interactions with young children should be avoided. Frequently, however, silence is followed by increased communicative attempts on the child's part (Tabors, 2008; Weitzner-Lin, 2004). If a caregiver bombards a young child with verbalizations, the child can be overwhelmed and become reluctant to take conversational turns (Rossetti, 2001). Also, among some ethnocultural groups such as Arabs, conversational silences are accepted and even expected (Sharifzadeh, 2011). Professionals and caregivers who work with children from these ethnic groups must remember that continuously verbally bombarding them during interactions may be incompatible with the expectations of the culture.

Another general principle of language stimulation involves asking the kinds of questions that will promote language. It is ideal if adults, during their interactions with young children, can avoid yes-or- no questions as much as possible. When the child responds with a yes-or-no answer, there is restricted opportunity for turn-taking. As Rossetti (2001, p. 241) says, yes-or-no questions are "the death of communication exchanges." Instead of asking yes-or-no questions, adults can ask "wh-" (why, where, when, who) or "how" questions or they can use lead-in phrases such as "Tell me about . . . "

Preschool children tend to use significantly more multiword responses to *topic-continuing* and *open-ended questions* used by their teachers. Thus, it is ideal if caregivers can use open-ended and topic-continuing questions to enhance children's language skills. For example, the simple "closed" question, "Do you want juice or milk?" can be framed as an open-ended question: "What would you like to drink?" A similar approach can be used in more complex interactions:

CHILD: I went to the park yesterday with my mommy.

TEACHER: *That sounds like fun! Did you see any special animals at the park?*

CHILD: We saw squirrels.

TEACHER: *What were the squirrels doing when you saw them?*

Preschool teachers might be expected to automatically use these kinds of questions, but in fact, many do not). Teachers in child care centers typically are quite busy, with many children to attend to, and even if they are aware of how to formulate such questions, they may perceive this interaction mode to be too time-consuming to apply on a regular basis. Professionals who encourage preschool teachers to use these types of questions can demonstrate how easy and quick it is to incorporate these types of questions into existing daily preschool routines such as washing hands before lunch, circle time, lining up for recess, and others.

It is ideal if professionals can go into children's daycare settings (such as preschools and homes) and videotape interactions between children and family members or children and early childhood caregivers. On later viewing of these videotapes, caregivers can obtain direct feedback about their interaction patterns with the child. In consultation with the professional, caregivers can voice their opinions about the interactions and give suggestions as to how they can improve their communication with their child. Caregivers also can be asked to identify what is currently working successfully. The professional then can give his or her input.

The caregivers can be videotaped at a later date as they are implementing the specific suggestions that were previously discussed. In this way, caregivers are given continuous feedback and support for improving their communication with their children and interacting in ways that will optimally facilitate language growth. Many of the strategies that facilitate language growth involve milieu teaching techniques.

Specific Incidental Learning/Milieu Teaching Techniques to Encourage Language Development

Toddlers and preschoolers spend most of their time interacting with parents and other caregivers such as child care providers and preschool teachers. Accordingly, one of the best things that professionals can do is provide these caregivers with practical techniques for cognitive-linguistic stimulation, especially during routine activities. We recall from Chapter 2 that Greenwood et al. (2011) found that most of the talk between parents and children in their study occurred during daily routines such as feeding, dressing, bathing, and others. Because routines are generally automatic and occur daily, it is logical that language stimulation activities should occur during these routines. Caregivers and child care professionals can be trained to capitalize on daily routines as opportunities to enhance language skills.

The training and education of people in children's natural environments should focus on two objectives: (1) enhancing the environment to facilitate change in the child's language and (2) helping the caregivers respond within that environment in a manner optimal for facilitating language change. These objectives often can be accomplished through training caregivers and other adults who interact with young children to use naturalistic, *incidental learning/milieu teaching* techniques.

Milieu teaching involves organizing the child's environment with desirable activities and objects that they must request or comment upon in order to receive these activities and objects (Paul & Norbury, 2012). How milieu teaching techniques can be successfully used with at-risk, low SES toddlers and preschoolers is discussed next (Roseberry-McKibbin, 2007).

In the technique of *responsive interaction*, the adult works within environments that are arranged to engage the child in relevant activities (for example, washing hands before snack time at preschool). The adult follows the child's lead, establishes joint attention, and engages in interaction. For example, when the child arrives at the sink because it is his turn to wash his hands, he may say, "I want soap." The adult can *comment*: "Let's put soap on your hands because they're dirty." Then the adult can ask (*question*): "Were you playing outside in the sandbox?" If the child answers, "No," the adult can say: "OK—I bet you were playing in the dirt over by the swings" (*comment*). "Are you going to play again in the dirt after snack?" (*question*).

In the technique of *incidental teaching,* the adult to carefully observes the child and identifies "teachable moments." For example, if the child reaches for a book, the adult can say, "You want to look at that book"—thereby engaging the child's attention and providing a label for what the child is doing. As with responsive interaction, incidental teaching requires that the adult establish joint attention with the child and follow the child's lead.

Another example of incidental teaching comes from my own experience as a mother. When my son was 2 years old, we could look out the window into our yard and see squirrels chasing each other.If he was the first to see the squirrels, he would point and call out in great excitement: "Kwerl, Mommy! Kwerl!" I would go to look at the squirrels and say something like "Yes! Wow! Look at those two brown squirrels! They are chasing each other around the oak tree." In this way, I was using incidental teaching: establishing joint attention with my son, following his lead, labeling what he was seeing, and adding language.

Within responsive interaction and incidental teaching situations, caregivers can use several specific language stimulation strategies to further expand children's language skills. In the technique of *self-talk*, the professional describes his or her own activities during play or interaction with the child. Self-talk often is used in conjunction with focused stimulation (described later). Self-talk can be very useful with children who are unwilling to interact with the caregiver. As noted, children from low SES homes have not heard nearly as many words spoken as have children from middle SES homes. Thus, an easy and often overlooked technique for increasing the number of words heard by these less privileged young children is the technique of self-talk.

For example, when it is time to go outside, the caregiver can say:

> It is time to go outside. It is cold, so we will get our coats. Please get your coats and put them on. Jackie, I am helping you button up your red coat so that you will be warm. I will help Howard put on his blue coat so that he will be warm too. Now that everyone has their coats on and buttoned up, we will go outside.

The technique of *parallel talk* is similar, but when using this technique, the professional plays with the child and comments on the objects the child is interested in and about what the child is doing in general. The professional provides a running commentary on the child's actions. For example, if the child is playing dress-up, the professional can say: "You picked the doctor costume! Look—you have a white uniform and a stethoscope. It looks like you are going to take care of some sick people. I bet your doctor does a good job of taking care of you when you are sick. I'm so glad we have doctors to give us medicine and help us feel better."

Joint routines involve repetitive, routinized activities that are often used with young children for language stimulation. For example, many children love peek-a-boo or patty-cake. Caregivers also can create their own routines and encourage children to use the words and phrases along with them when the routines are memorized. This helps children expand their language use.

Again, a number of informal, easy-to-implement strategies are available for providing additional language stimulation to young children from low SES families in everyday settings (Paul & Norbury, 2012; Roseberry-McKibbin, 2007). Some strategies that are specifically focused on certain types of language skills are considered next. An important set of strategies relates to helping young children from low SES homes increase their vocabulary skills before they begin kindergarten.

Increasing Vocabulary Skills

Strategies to increase vocabulary in children from low SES families are detailed in subsequent chapters, so only a brief introduction is presented here. As noted in Chapter 2, even by age 3, children from low SES homes have been exposed to far fewer vocabulary words than those encountered by more advantaged children. No matter what the age of the child, it is extremely important to build his or her vocabulary skills (Pan, Rowe, Spier, & Tamis-Lemonda, 2004; Turnbull & Justice, 2012). Barone (2006) comments that for the low SES children she studied, low vocabulary skills for older elementary children frequently hampered their reading comprehension. Fortunately, there is research evidence to support the efficacy of appropriate vocabulary training strategies (Montgomery, 2007).

Peterson, Jesso, and McCabe (1999) trained low SES mothers to spend more time engaging in narrative conversations with their children. Mothers also were trained to ask more context-eliciting and open-ended questions. Children in the intervention group showed significant improvement in their vocabulary skills immediately after the intervention. A year later, they demonstrated improvement in narrative skills.

Beals (1997) studied mealtime conversations of preschoolers and their families. Conversations that incorporated unfamiliar words contributed to children's learning of those words. Of the 1,631 exchanges around unfamiliar words reported in the study, two-thirds of the words were used contextually in ways that helped the children learn the meaning of the words. Thus, the adults created a context for learning of vocabulary. Children's frequency of use of these unfamiliar words was positively correlated with scores on the Peabody Picture Vocabulary Test–Revised (PPVT-R) at 5 and at 7 years of age.

Experts have recommended early intervention that involves a massive buildup of content knowledge (Bardige, 2009; Hirsch, 2003). Young children can learn social vocabulary as well as basic school concepts such as the alphabet, colors, numbers, and shapes. When students are learning new words, it is ideal to provide them with concrete experiences to accompany the learning of the new words. For example, if a student is learning what *grapes* are, touching and eating grapes are highly reinforcing. If concrete experiences are not available, research shows that the next best way to teach is through the use of play objects if possible (e.g., plastic grapes), followed by pictures and then words themselves (Wolfe, 2001).

Many low SES students have difficulty learning vocabulary words because the words initially are presented in the abstract. For example, typically a child is presented with the printed word g-r-a-p-e-s, told that grapes are fruit, and asked to memorize the word—and spell it correctly on Friday's spelling test. If children can handle objects or even see pictures, however, they are much more likely to learn words and retain them.

Wolfe (2001) emphasizes that students often remember words better if they act them out or draw pictures, or both. Students can play a game such as Pictionary or do pantomime when they are reviewing words. Using technology, such as an iPad with apps for increasing vocabulary, is often effective as well, but not in all cases.

I have been using an iPad for about a year now with students in the school district where I work part time. I do assessment and intervention for students from preschool through high school; many are low SES. They represent various cultural and linguistic backgrounds. Some are on the autism spectrum. As a clinician, I have found that the iPad is highly effective in engaging students' interest; I have successfully used iPad vocabulary apps with students from ages 3–18 years. My teenage students on the autism spectrum have especially been interested in iPad apps; with some, use of the iPad is the only way I can create opportunities for joint attention and persuade them to interact with me. Use of book apps to increase vocabulary skills has been highly successful. For example, there is an app that tells the story of Peter Rabbit. There are tabs on each page that students can move; on one page, blackberries descend from the sky and can be "popped" by the student pressing them with their fingers. Students from ages 3 to 18 years love this app and are engaged by it.

Caution needs to be utilized, however. Several weeks ago I went to a preschool classroom with low SES 3 to 4-year-olds who have extensive special needs. The theme for the week was farm animals, and I had pre-selected apps that embedded farm animals into vocabulary activities. Sitting at a small table with four very active boys, I confidently opened the first app, a book about farm animals, and began to read. William, one of the boys (born to a mother who used drugs during pregnancy) started banging on the iPad and then physically assaulting Jose, the child next to him.

I tried to intervene, but William kept going. I could see that Jose was about to start crying. In the meantime, another boy began to bang on my iPad keyboard, causing a key to fall off. I jumped up, went around the table, picked William up, and seated him on my lap, away from the other boys. With one arm firmly around him, I "turned pages" on the iPad with the other hand and tried to continue my literacy activity. William jumped out of my lap, ran away, and joined another group. I ran after him, leaving my iPad unguarded in front of the other three boys in the group (not a good move). When I was sure William was OK in a different group, I rushed back to my original table where the other three boys were gleefully manhandling my iPad. Needless to say, I shut it and hastily got it out of the way. Later, the classroom teacher diplomatically told me that I was lucky that none of the kids had grabbed my iPad and hurled it across the room.

The next week, my iPad stayed far away in a locked room while I worked with the children in a small group at the sandbox. We focused on vocabulary goals using plastic farm animals in the sand, and the children loved pouring sand on top of each animal as we named it. Afterward we washed our hands in a bucket of water. William was entranced with the water, and could not get enough of feeling it on his hands while we finished our vocabulary activity. Hmmmm . . . which was best, an expensive iPad with all its fancy high-tech apps, or a box of sand and a bucket of water for encouraging vocabulary development?

In sum, I love using technology for encouraging development of vocabulary skills in low SES students. However, I have found that with certain students, good old-fashioned materials, such as sand and water, are best!

In addition to working to increase the vocabulary skills of young low SES children, professionals can also teach them to use formal language register. This will help prepare them for school, where formal language comprehension and expression are expected.

Practical Strategies for Teaching Formal Language Register in Naturalistic Settings

As noted by Payne (2003) and others, many low SES children come to school using casual language register. As discussed later in this chapter, when children are school-aged, more direct techniques can be used to contrast casual and formal language register. When children are young, when they are toddlers and preschoolers, more naturalistic, indirect methods can be used to teach and encourage the use of formal language register. This is helpful because children from low SES homes who are exposed to and learn to use formal language register before they start kindergarten will have the distinct advantage of being conversant with the language of the school setting: the language of the teachers and books to which they eventually will be exposed.

In the technique of *focused stimulation*, if a child needs to work on a particular language structure, the professional repeatedly models that structure in hopes of encouraging the child to use the structure. Usually, this is done during a play activity that the professional has prearranged for the express purpose of modeling the target structure. For example, if the child needs to work on appropriate use of present progressive *-ing*, the professional may use a grocery store setting (ideally with realistic toys) to address this, using running commentary as follows:

> See the people shopp**ing**? That man is look**ing** at the ice cream. I bet he's think**ing** about what flavor he wants. The woman stand**ing** over in the vegetable section is decid**ing** whether she wants tomatoes or radishes. Maybe at home tonight, she will be mak**ing** a salad and us**ing** the vegetables in it. Oh, look, at the cash register, customers are stand**ing** in line wait**ing** for their turn to pay.

In the technique of *expansion*, when a child makes an incomplete utterance, the professional expands it into a more grammatically complete utterance that more closely approximates formal language register. For example:

CHILD: Me wash hands.

PROFESSIONAL: Yes, you will wash your hands.

The professional does not add any extra information to the child's utterance; he or she just models the child's sentence with added grammatical information. In the technique of *extension*, the caregiver comments on the child's utterances and adds new information to them. In an extension, both grammatical and semantic information are added:

CHILD: Me wash hands.

PROFESSIONAL: You will wash your hands before snack time because you were playing in the dirt.

CHILD: He runned real fast yesterday.

CLINICIAN: Oh, he ran real fast yesterday to get away from someone?

Research shows that once children have received a correction such as this, they are three to eight times more likely to repeat the correction than at any other time in conversation (Link & Bohannon, 2003). Studies have examined the effects of these types of corrections on children's subsequent grammatical development. They found that when adults used corrective replies, both immediate and long-term improvement in grammatical skills resulted. The improvement was particularly noticeable when the corrections followed actual errors (Saxton, 2000; Saxton, Gallaway, & Backley, 1999; Saxton, Kulcsar, Marshall, & Rupra, 1998).

Roberts and Kaiser (2011), in a meta-analysis of research studies addressing the effectiveness of parent language interventions to increase their children's language skills, found that extensions were very useful, effective, and easy to teach. In accordance with previous research, Roberts and Kaiser found that extensions were especially helpful in increasing children's morphosyntactic skills. Turnbull and Justice (2012) stated that children who hear complex syntax more often in their environment produce greater amounts of complex syntax at younger ages than children who hear complex syntax less often.

For children who use casual language forms that do not match the norms of formal language register, caregivers also can use the more direct *mand-model* technique. The caregiver uses attractive games, toys, books, or all of these in creating a naturalistic play situation. Then, he or she establishes joint attention with the child to a particular item such as a game. The game provides the opportunity for the caregiver to "mand" a response from the child and correct the response if needed, with appropriate reinforcing praise.

CAREGIVER: Let's play Hi Ho Cherry-O. How many cherries do you want on your tree?

CHILD: I be wantin' 10.

CAREGIVER: OK—now say "I want 10 cherries for my tree."

CHILD: I want 10 cherries for my tree!

CAREGIVER: Good! I like how you said that so well. Here are your 10 cherries.

For encouraging the use of a wider variety of formal language register forms, *recasting* also is an excellent technique. In recasting, the caregiver expands the child's utterance into a different type of utterance. The caregiver changes the modality or voice of the sentence, rather than simply adding grammatical or semantic information, for example:

CHILD: Doggy barking. [declarative]

CAREGIVER: Is the doggy barking? [change to interrogative or question]

CHILD: The mommy makin' dinner.

CAREGIVER: The dinner is being made by the mommy. [change to passive voice]

The technique of *sabotage* (Fey, Long, & Finestack, 2003) involves having the caregiver disrupt the environment or environmental routines somehow to encourage children to use accurate, full, formal language register structures. For example, if a child always says, "I ain't gonna . . . ," the caregiver can teach, "I'm not going to . . . " Then, later, the caregiver can have a puppet say, "I ain't gonna . . . " and the child is rewarded for each time she notices the puppet saying, "I ain't" instead of "I'm not."

INCREASING GRAMMATICAL AND PRAGMATIC LANGUAGE SKILLS IN FORMAL REGISTER

Increasing Grammatical Language Skills in Formal Register

As noted earlier, many students from low SES backgrounds come to school speaking in casual language register; this often involves, among other things, the use of nonstandard English grammatical structures (Adler, 1979; Anastasiow & Hanes, 1976; Anastasiow, Hanes, & Hanes 1982; Campbell, 1993; van Keulen et al., 1998). For example, White children from Appalachia frequently use grammatical structures that are not consistent with those of Mainstream American English (MAE). If children come to school speaking an nonstandard form of English as part of using language in casual register, the difficulty is that textbooks and teacher classroom talk all occur in formal register, which includes, among other things, the use of MAE. It is important for teachers and clinicians to help such children become bidialectal: comfortable in speaking both their "home language" and "school language" (Adler, 1979; Campbell, 1993; Paul & Norbury, 2012; Roseberry-McKibbin, 2008).

Adler (1979) eloquently outlined the logic of this approach:

> Three solutions [to students' nonstandard dialect use] have been proposed. The first of these maintains that nonstandard dialects . . . are inferior modes of communication and, as such, must be eradicated. This solution is based on invalid assumptions about language, and thus it can be dismissed. A second solution, recognizing the fact that no dialect is inherently better than any other, proposes that teachers merely leave the students' languages alone, appreciating the various dialects for what they are . . . those who tell us to leave these dialects alone accuse [others] of racism. . . . This view overlooks three important considerations, however. First, "standard" English is the language of mainstream society; without a command of it *one is isolated from that mainstream* [italics mine]. Second, "standard" English is the language of instruction in the schools . . . without knowledge of it, problems in reading and in school are likely to occur. Most importantly . . . because of standard written grammar, Americans can read books written by Australians and vice versa. Therefore, there seems to be only one possible solution—bidialectalism. This solution assumes that students

should learn . . . "standard" English while maintaining the dialect of their nurture. (p. 174)

It is interesting to me to read these words, written more than three decades ago. I agree with Adler (1979), and advocate a "bidialectal" approach, advocated by most professionals today where students are shown that they can use either of two legitimate ways to communicate, depending on the specific environment (Turnbull & Justice, 2012).

Adler described the notion of "functional bidialectalism," defined as expanding children's language to include facility with both the native and the second dialect. This entails *communicative competence*, or the ability to use either dialect appropriately in various settings according to the demands of the social situation. Campbell (1993) and Adler (1979) recommended that professionals can actively draw children's attention to the "home" and "school" ways of talking. Adler recommended use of the terms *standard* and *nonstandard* with students. The terms *home way* and *school way* (Campbell, 1993) seem preferable, however, because they are less pejorative.

Anecdotally, an international perspective on this subject reveals that children in most countries learn the "home dialect" and "school dialect." In Germany, for example, students may speak Schweitzer Deutsch or Schwabischer Deutsch at home; in school and in business, they must speak Hoch Deutsch (the "high German" taught in high school and college classes). In some China provinces, Taishanese is spoken; children must learn and use Mandarin in school. In many homes in the Middle East, spoken dialects of Arabic are used. In school, classical Arabic is taught. My own experience as a child living in the Philippines puts the whole issue into perspective: In the town of Odiongan in the Philippines, my sisters and I spoke standard English at home, Odionganon with our friends, and another dialect, Hiligaynon, in church, and we learned Tagalog (the national Filipino language) in school, for our family and many others, this was perfectly natural. It puts this whole discussion into an international framework when we as professionals realize that throughout the world, most children have a "home" and "school" language.

In most countries, no stigma is attached to the "home language." The home language is just that, a language used in the home and neighborhood. Children and the adults around them routinely accept that in school, they will learn the school or business language: the language they will eventually use as members of the larger society. In the United States, however, the "home languages" of some children are routinely stigmatized. I never experienced that growing up; however, I recognize that here in the United States, children's use of "home languages" can be a very emotionally and politically charged subject. Professionals who work with children are in good position to help remove any emotion from this discussion, and in their own practice, they need to maintain awareness that in most parts of the world, children routinely learn the concepts and functions of *home* and *school* language, with no accompanying negative emotions or stigma. These children can be described as confidently bidialectal.

In working with children to help them become confidently bidialectal, it is important to initially accept their language as it is, praising efforts at communication. Professionals can model standard forms of English. Then they can use contrastive analysis to point out differences in home and school ways of speaking. For example, the teacher can write sentences on the board:

He work hard.

He works hard.

The teacher then describes how these two sentences differ.

The professional also can conduct discrimination drills, in which pairs of words or sentences are presented to students and then they are asked to tell whether the pairs are same or different. For example:

Teacher Stimulus	*Student Response*
1. He work hard. He works hard.	1. different
2. He work hard. He work hard.	2. same
3. Paula likes leather coats. Paula likes leather coats.	3. same
4. She prefers movies. She prefer movies.	4. different

Adler describes translation drills, another practical idea for helping students learn the "home way" and the "school way":

Teacher Stimulus	*Student Response*
1. He work hard.	1. He works hard
2. Robert play ball.	2. He plays ball.
3. Ms. Jones teach English.	3. Mrs. Jones teaches English.

A variation of this drill is for students to translate using the "home way." For example:

Teacher Stimulus	*Student Response*
1. He works hard.	1. He work hard.
2. She likes shopping.	2. She like shopping.
3. The man drives very fast.	3. The man drive very fast.

Adler (1979) gave specific examples of methods used in the Knoxville (Tennessee) Head Start program to prepare White Appalachian preschoolers from low SES families for the demands of MAE-speaking public school kindergartens. Special situations were used to facilitate communication between "home talk" and "school talk." Hand puppets were used in the early stages of the program (e.g., both a "home" puppet and a "school" puppet were provided). Later on, pictures representing a school or an everyday environment were presented; the children identified particular speech and language patterns as being appropriate to each. Finally, children engaged in role-playing; they could be a mother, father, teacher, businesswoman, or other role. Adler gave an example of the kinds of things that Head Start teachers said to preschoolers:

General Instructions

Sometimes we talk in different ways when we are in different places. At rest time we sometimes talk differently from other times during the day [e.g., we use our quiet, indoor voices at rest time and our outdoor voices at recess]. Today we are going to learn two kinds of talking: "everyday [home] talk" and "school talk." Is everybody ready to play? (p. 148)

At that point, the teacher may place a picture of a tree and a house on a flannel graph board, and a picture of a school on another part of the flannel graph board. Then the teacher can put "school talk" words under the picture of the school, and "everyday talk" words under the picture of the house and the tree. As variations, the teacher sometimes may present familiar sounds such as a siren and a school bell and identify them as everyday and school sounds. Art work also may reflect school and home (everyday) pictures.

The Head Start teachers especially focused on "home" vocabulary that could get children into trouble when they entered elementary school. For example, many of the children used the words "I need to piss" when they wanted to go to the bathroom. Teachers explained that at school, the request is given as "I need to use the restroom" or another acceptable variant.

Adler and colleagues found that this bidialectal-bicultural approach was highly successful in teaching preschoolers MAE in a nonpejorative way. Elementary classroom teachers also can use the bidialectal-bicultural approach to help students from low SES backgrounds become confident in use of both "home" and "school" language to communicate in the appropriate settings (Paul & Norbury, 2012).

Increasing Pragmatic Language Skills in Formal Register

Children from low SES families using casual language register may demonstrate differences from the norms of MAE in their use of social language, or pragmatics, as well as in their grammatical patterns. Hart and Risley (1995) observed that the caregivers in professional homes transmitted to their children an upper SES style of communicating, with its care for courtesy and distinctions in status. Caregivers in lower-SES homes often did not make these distinctions. As a result of these differences in styles of communicating in the home, low SES children may communicate too informally in settings such as school. As described in Chapter 2, low SES children on the whole do not receive as much conversational stimulation at home as middle SES children do. The language they are exposed to may contain some negative elements, including many prohibitions and intrusions. Thus, these children may not be skilled at meeting the formal language register expectations of courteously initiating interactions with others, expressing feelings appropriately, and taking turns in conversations without interrupting. They may also have difficulty with formal language register expectations in areas such as eye contact, speaking in a linear and sequential manner, and using verbal negotiation and problem-solving strategies.

In the early life experiences of children from low SES homes, it is important for professionals to intervene early to help them learn to socialize competently and successfully with their peers (Paul & Norbury, 2012; Qi & Kaiser, 2004). Much has been written about intervention for young children who have difficulties with pragmatics, or social skills. These children are at increased risk of being viewed negatively by their peers; many of these children also do not have reciprocal friendships. Problematic patterns of social behavior characterized by poor communication skills may become entrenched, increasing these children's eventual risk for substance abuse and possible incarceration as adults (Armstrong, 2011).

In order to help low SES children increase their social language skills, professionals can support them in learning how to communicate with appropriate courtesy as well as in how to initiate interactions with others. In one study, the researchers looked specifically at the difficulties that children with language problems had with entering peer groups and initiating play (Nungesser & Watkins, 2005). These researchers found that for their young subjects, these aspects of pragmatics skills were enhanced by the use of picture symbols that visually depicted social rules, characterized as "Steps." For example, Step 1 used a picture of a stick figure with a speech balloon that said "walk" (the step was "Walk over to your friend"). Step 2 had a simple picture depicting the rule, "Watch your friend." The picture for Step 3 depicted, "Get a toy like your friend is using." The Step 4 picture depicted, "Do the same thing as your friend," whereas Step 5 showed, "Tell an idea." The results of the study showed that the children with language problems became more successful in their peer interactions as a result of the use of picture symbols depicting social rules.

Brinton and Fujiki (2011) suggested an effective strategy similar to that proposed by Nungesser and Watkins (2005) for helping children to join groups effectively: WALK (approach—get close enough to see), LOOK (observe what is going on), SAY SOMETHING NICE (comment on the task, make a validating comment), PLAY (stay with the play). Teaching low SES children these steps for joining a group according to the rules of formal language register are helpful, especially if they come from chaotic home environments where the only way to successfully call attention to oneself is to engage in negative behavior.

Some low SES children, exposed to negative verbal interactions in the home, may have difficulty communicating their feelings appropriately. Dodge, Rice, and Grimm (2010) developed a resource, called Kimochis, for supporting social skills, especially the appropriate expressing of feelings. Kimochis are "feeling" plush toys that are part of a program that teaches seven keys to successful communication (e.g., "choose words that help instead of hurt"). Anecdotal evidence has shown that young, low SES children especially benefit from this program because it is simple, attractive, and hands-on. Children love holding the toys, which depict various emotions, and concrete activities using the toys help them absorb the rules of communication better than abstract, verbal instructions.

In addition to learning the appropriate communication of feelings, low SES students need to be taught turn-taking skills In some low SES groups, interrupting during conversations is expected (Payne, 2003; Roseberry-McKibbin, 2008). Students who interrupt in school, however, are penalized for that behavior. In my own clinical practice, use of a "speech ball," a fuzzy red soft ball that a child gets to hold when he or she is speaking, has been very successful in teaching how to wait for a turn to talk. When the speech ball is in use, the only person who can talk is the one holding the ball. Everyone else needs to listen silently and attentively, waiting for a turn to talk.

Professionals can model and encourage use of more formal register in communicating, as in the following real-life case example:

> To demonstrate the use of formal register, one idea I used with great success with elementary school children was to have them be "newscasters," interviewing each other with the use of formal greetings, leave-takings, questions, and answers. Being on a very limited budget, I made a "microphone" out of an empty toilet paper roll covered with newspaper. Because this group happened to contain all boys, I made a black construction paper bow tie that they taped to their shirts when they were the "interviewer." All questions and answers had to be stated in formal language. The children enjoyed the activity immensely, and I found it very instructive to see how they met the challenges posed by the requirement to speak in formal register. I scaffolded the task for them and modeled formal register. Near the end of the therapy session, I asked the boys to review the techniques we had discussed for appropriate use of formal register in interactions. I will never forget Jason's answer: "Don't wander off when someone else is talking."

Effective use of formal register also involves appropriate eye contact. Research in Chicago showed that many inner-city ghetto parents warn their children to avoid eye contact with strangers and to develop a tough outer demeanor when encountering people on the streets. Although these behaviors are helpful for ghetto survival, they hinder successful interaction and relationships in mainstream society (Wilson, 2006). Professionals in schools can help children from these backgrounds learn to be bicultural in their pragmatics skills. Being tough and not making eye contact works in the neighborhood; at school, and in future job settings, other behaviors are needed. In formal language register, eye contact is important.

Payne (2003) makes the point that when people use casual register, they tend to "talk in circles," meandering around a topic and eventually getting to the point. In formal register, the pattern of communication is linear, and the idea is to get to the point as efficiently as possible. Students from low SES backgrounds who use the meandering style of casual register in their speaking and especially their writing are at a true disadvantage. In school, they will irritate teachers and be marked down for "disorganized writing." As adults, they will irritate potential employers during interviews.

When my son reached third grade (in a well-regarded middle SES school), his teacher introduced a program, called Step Up to Writing (Auman, 2003), aimed at helping the students develop their writing skills. My son's first assignment was to write an "accordion paragraph" about Halloween. This was only one of several new literacy-related concepts presented in this fairly recently developed program, and as a parent, I had to spend quite some time to familiarize myself with these specifics.

Table 4–3 diagrams two different kinds of writing covered in the program. (The expectation is that third grade children will learn how to write this way.) A quick look shows how linear and sequential the writing is. Many students from low SES backgrounds could not be expected to perform well in this program, which has a distinctly "middle SES" flavor.

Professionals who work with the social language skills of children from low SES homes can expand their practice beyond teaching a more linear, sequential manner of communication. In terms of casual register communication style, inappropriate comments from these children can be turned into "teachable moments." Rather than reacting in disapproval (or shock if the comment was especially inappropriate), professionals can introduce contrastive analysis into the situation

Table 4–3. Linear and Sequential Writing: Giving Information and Telling Stories

Telling a Story	Conveying Information
Beginning	Introduction
↓ ↓ ↓	↓ ↓ ↓
Middle	Body
↓ ↓ ↓	↓ ↓ ↓
End	Conclusion

Source: Adapted from Auman, M. (2003).

by writing down students' utterances in one column (home language) and formal register alternatives in the other column. Table 4–4 provides an example of how this may be done.

Making teachable moments out of students' casual register utterances, with use of contrastive analysis, avoids moralizing, blame, and negative judgment. A constructive approach brings students' language into a metalinguistic realm and presents them with better, more acceptable alternatives. Even if students do not use the formal register alternatives right away, if at all, they will at least have a bank of alternative choices on which to draw in the future.

Regarding formal and casual register social skills, it is worth noting here that to resolve conflicts, some people in poverty use their fists. Professionals need to recognize that children from low SES backgrounds may not survive well without this strategy; however, the children also can be taught specific strategies of verbal negotiation and problem solving. Then they will have two sets of behaviors to choose from in a specific situation. This is in keeping with a general goal of education: to provide students with a variety of solutions and strategies from which to choose, depending on the situations they find themselves in.

Table 4–4. Formal and Casual Register: Contrastive Analysis ("Home" Talk and "School" Talk)

Casual (home)	Formal (school and business)
Gimme that apple!	May I please have that apple?
Dude, those shoes s-ck.	Those shoes look different from the ones you usually wear.
When is recess anyway?	What time is it? I'm looking forward to recess.
You're late.	Was there a lot of traffic? I'm glad you made it.
My homework's not done.	I'm sorry I did not finish my homework; may I please bring it in tomorrow?
Let's see *you* do it.	Will you please show me how to do this?
Forget it, -itch.	This is pretty hard for me; will you please explain it?
You're wrong, fool.	We can agree to disagree.
Cut it out, man.	I am uncomfortable with that; please stop.
Do it this way.	I would recommend . . .
I hate you.	I don't like this. May we discuss it?
Leave me alone.	May I have some privacy?

A relevant analogy can be found in the practice of karate, of which I have some knowledge because this was one of my son's activities for 5 years. Like "a jewel in your pocket," says his instructor, karate is never to be used outside the dojo unless truly necessary. The children studying in his dojo have been coached endlessly, as follows: If another child is trying to pick on or bully you, use your words—"Stop it!" If he or she persists, walk away. If the other child still persists, find an adult. If no adult is around and the child is actually hurting you physically and will not stop, *then* you can use your karate skills.

It was very instructive for me to warm the bench for the five years of Mark's karate lessons and see him learning conflict resolution skills, and a set of choices for how the children can respond if someone is trying to hurt them. It seems obvious that many low SES children can benefit from exactly this type of instruction. Table 4–5 presents an example of a method that can be used to help children problem-solve and use their words as a first alternative if another person is trying to hurt them.

Experts have discussed the use of social skills groups to provide students with strategies for positive conflict resolution and problem-solving (Armstrong, 2011; Brinton & Fujiki, 2011). Social skills groups can help students identify their emotions; they can be given the vocabulary to describe these emotions. When they are able to articulate their feelings, identify their emotions, and solve problems, anxiety and aggression are reduced.

Table 4–5. Conflict Resolution Skills for Children: "Words First" Self-Protection Protocol

---

How to Protect Yourself

If another child is trying to hurt you . . .

1. Use your words. Tell him, "No! Stop it!" Look him in the eye.

2. If he will not stop, walk away from him.

3. If he follows you and still will not stop, find an adult.

4. If there is no adult around, and your words have not worked, it is OK for you to defend yourself.

If a grownup who you don't know tries to grab you . . .

1. Yell, "Danger! Stranger!" as loudly as you can.

2. Run away.

3. Find a safe grownup. Try to pick someone wearing a uniform.

4. If there is no grownup wearing a uniform, find a mommy with kids. Ask her to help you.

5. If none of these things work, it is OK for you to defend yourself by kicking or hitting the grownup so that you can get away and be safe.

An additional strategy that can help students resolve conflicts through words is to learn to use validating comments (Brinton & Fujiki, 2011). Validating comments are compliments, encouragements, and other verbalizations that make other people feel valued and appreciated. As we have said, many low SES children come from homes where they were and still are repeatedly exposed to intrusive, negative behavior by caregivers. These children have heard many prohibitions and putdowns; when they use these with other children outside the home, conflict is created. I have had to actively teach such children to use validating comments as part of my intervention strategies to increase their effective use of social language.

> I was recently playing Candyland with a small group of low SES boys as part of a language activity in therapy. Patrick, a child with substantial social skill challenges, had a strong tendency to be a bad sport and make negative comments when he wasn't winning a game. I was able to seize upon a teachable moment for helping Patrick make validating comments: when he finally won Candyland Antonio, another boy, spontaneously hugged him and said, "Nice job, Patrick." Antonio was the ideal role model!

CONCLUSIONS

Because low SES children are vulnerable to oral language deficits due to environmental issues, it is important for professionals to do everything possible, in the early years, to build these children's oral language skills. By building oral language skills, professionals can provide children with a solid base for the literate language of school and the workplace. As noted in the beginning of the chapter, "Language is power." One of the best ways to empower children from low SES homes is to work to increase their language skills beginning at birth, and to continue to build language throughout the school years.

CHAPTER HIGHLIGHTS

▨ It is critical to begin as early in life as possible to provide language stimulation opportunities for children from low SES families. These opportunities ideally should begin in infancy. Maternal warmth and responsiveness are especially important for language development.

▨ Caregivers can successfully expose babies to books. This exposure helps babies begin to build very early preliteracy skills, which will serve as a foundation for later, formal literacy instruction.

▨ Research has found that well-trained child care providers in high-quality early education settings can provide children with cognitively and linguistically rich environments that will provide a critical foundation for their later participation in formal schooling.

▨ Research converges upon the fact that young low SES children will probably receive better cognitive and linguistic stimulation in high quality daycare centers than in informal home settings with untrained caregivers. More public funding needs to be directed to the provision of high quality early childhood development programs.

▨ Caregivers can use specific techniques to provide language stimulation for children. Milieu teaching techniques that can be implemented are responsive interaction, incidental teaching, self-talk, parallel talk, joint routines, focused stimulation, mand-model, and sabotage.

▨ No matter what the age of a child from a low SES family, it also is critically important to build vocabulary skills. Vocabulary ideally should be learned through presentation of concrete objects and experiences to help new words to be learned in context.

▨ Many low SES children use casual language register to communicate with others. While casual register is appropriate within these children's homes and neighborhoods, it may not be appropriate for use in more formal settings such as school and, eventually, work settings. Professionals can help children to become confidently bidialectal, using casual and formal language register in appropriate settings.

Professionals can train children to use home language and school language, employing techniques to differentiate the two. Formal register or school language involves use of mainstream grammar, conventions of courtesy, appropriate use of eye contact, and competent turntaking. School language also involves communicating in a linear, sequential fashion.

Training students in formal language register or school language also involves helping these students learn appropriate, acceptable conflict resolution skills.

5

Practical Strategies for Increasing the Literacy Skills of Students From Low SES Backgrounds

*The limits of your language are
the limits of your world.*
Ludwig Wittgenstein

Mark is in kindergarten, and Marcos is in first grade. Both are struggling with reading and writing. Marcos can barely read. Writing is hard for him too. Spelling is especially difficult, and his teacher sends home a deficiency notice in all areas of written language. His parents don't understand exactly what the note says, but they know it isn't good. A student study team (SST) meeting is arranged with a Spanish-speaking interpreter present. Marcos' parents manage to get two hours off from their jobs in the fields. They are informed by their boss that if this happens again, they will be fired.

The members of the SST include the school principal, a speech-language pathologist (SLP), the classroom teacher, and a resource specialist. Among other things, the SST strongly recommends that Marcos' parents read to him every night. Their hearts sink. They are nonliterate but are too embarrassed to admit this to the SST. The school principal takes this occasion to give Marcos' parents a mild scolding for his truancies, and the classroom teacher emphasizes that they need to help him more with his homework. They nod silently, knowing full well that they are not able to provide this kind of help.

They are sorry about the truancies, says his mother, but sometimes Marcos' little brother is sick and they need Marcos to stay home and take care of him while they work. Marcos' grandmother has passed away, and they have nowhere else to turn. They see the disapproving looks on the faces of the SST members. The resource specialist tells them that Marcos appears to be "unmotivated"; perhaps they could talk to him? No special education services are offered. Marcos' parents leave the SST meeting in despair, wondering what they can do to help their child. They can't think of anything.

Despite Mark's excellent oral language skills, including a very sophisticated vocabulary, reading is difficult for him. His mother knows that she and her husband have provided all possible home support for development of their son's reading skills; for one thing, they have spent many hundreds of hours reading to him, starting when he was an infant.

Nevertheless, Mark struggles mightily with writing as well as with reading. At report card time, the kindergarten teacher tells Mark's parents that he rates the lowest in the whole class in several written language areas. In a rather accusatory tone of voice, she suggests that "something is going on at home" that is affecting his school performance. Mark's parents are heartsick. They have worked very hard to give their only child every advantage, making many sacrifices in their careers as well as in their personal lives. How is this situation possible after all the enrichment Mark has experienced? His mother volunteers in his classroom each Friday. She struggles to hold back tears as she grades the homework for the class; Mark's writing stands out as being much sloppier and more problematic than that of the other children.

In desperation, Mark's mother takes him to an occupational therapist for evaluation. On tests of fine motor and visual motor skills, Mark scores only in the first percentile rank for his age. No wonder he constantly cries and tells his mother: "I'm stupid; I'm a loser; I'm the worst kid in school." Mark's parents had no idea that he had these kinds of special issues. His mother enrolls him in weekly occupational therapy sessions (at $60.00 an hour), and takes him to therapy each week. She begins using a writing program at home with him called Handwriting Without Tears (Olsen, 2003). Occupational therapy and Handwriting Without Tears help Mark substantially, and he is promoted to first grade.

Three months into first grade, the occupational therapist recommends that Mark be assessed for visual tracking skills, even though a school vision screening program reported that Mark's visual acuity was 20/20. His mother takes him to a developmental optometrist, who confirms that Mark has profound visual tracking problems that are affecting his reading and writing. More bad news! Fortunately, Mark's mother is able to change her work schedule to allow her to take him to weekly vision therapy (at $85.00 an hour) in addition to his weekly occupational therapy. She helps Mark do the prescribed eye exercises every night. Mark's mother also enrolls him in weekly horseback riding lessons ($40.00 per 1/2 hour) because she has read that sometimes this can be helpful for children with his types of learning needs. Although Mark's reading and writing both improve immensely, his first grade teacher recommends tutoring, and his mother finds an excellent tutor for the summer before he enters second grade (Price tag; $50.00 an hour). Mark starts second grade, confident and ready to do well in school. Total price tag of all services from kindergarten through second grade (including lost income from professional opportunities Mark's mother turned down so she could drive him to his weekly therapies): $10,000 to $15,000. She is very grateful that she has a flexible job and the money to afford all the services Mark needs. She realizes that she is in a small minority of parents who have the types of resources that are available to her and her son.

INTRODUCTION

Research over the decades indicates that low SES children, for many reasons, are at risk for written as well as oral language deficits (DiLorenzo, Rody, Bucholz, & Brady, 2009; Fogle, 2013; Iglesias & Rojas, 2012). In a review of research on literacy development in English language learners in the United States since the 1980s, Genesee and Riches (2006) found that SES was correlated with performance on a number of literacy measures. Specifically, these investigators found that students from low SES backgrounds scored significantly lower than students from higher-SES backgrounds. Although SES itself is not a causal factor in written language deficits, research confirms that it is associated with a variety of other factors, as discussed earlier (e.g., lower educational levels of caregivers, lack of books in the home) (Lopez, 2012; Paul & Norbury, 2012; Turnbull & Justice, 2012). Professionals who work with children recognize the importance of solid literacy skills for future employment prospects in today's information-based, technological economy. Children who have difficulty learning to read are at great risk for academic failure and eventual vocational difficulties.

It is well documented that children who read poorly in primary grades often remain poor readers for the remainder of their educational experience (McDowell, Lonigan, & Goldstein, 2007; Neuman, 2009). The prognosis for poor readers does not improve with age, as documented in a longitudinal study showing that 74% of children identified as poor readers in third grade remained poor readers in ninth grade (Francis, Shaywitz, Stuebing, Shaywitz, & Fletcher, 1996). Children who live in poverty and read below grade level by third grade are three times as likely to not graduate from high school as students who have never experienced poverty (Hernandez, 2011). Such children are at risk for school failure, low self-esteem, delinquency, drug abuse, and social and relational problems.

The negative trajectory of failure continues into adulthood: Poor reading ability has been correlated with limited occupational opportunities and decreased economic success. Even mild or moderate reading disorders can lead to significant deficits in academic learning over time. Lack of literacy proficiency can have severe short- and long-term consequences for adolescents and young adults. Low literacy achievement is correlated with a generally underprepared workforce, underemployment, welfare dependency, and crime (Moran, 2010).

Poor early literacy proficiency is the single strongest predictor of both high school dropout rates and future prison occupancy (Cain, 2004). Moran (2010) describes how states like California and Indiana factor in the number of third graders who are not reading at grade level when planning future jail construction. A penitentiary in Richmond, Virginia, accurately predicts the number of prison cells to prepare by the number of students in local public schools who are reading below grade level in second grade (Williams, 2002). For example, with a count of 450 second graders who read below grade level, the penitentiary makes plans to have 450 prison cells ready within a decade to house the poorly adapted young adults these failing children will become. The cost is very great to both individuals and society. Thus, it is critical to prevent reading difficulties and their far reaching negative sequelae when children are young. It is ironic that taxpayers spend more money to keep adults behind bars than they spend on early prevention programs to help the same people become productive, tax-paying citizens. Apparently, Americans are more comfortable paying for prisons than for early intervention programs for at-risk children.

The U.S. Department of Education (2001) found that 46% of children entering kindergarten came from family backgrounds with one or more risk factors for limited skills and knowledge. These risk factors included living in a single-parent household, having a mother with low educational achievement, coming from a non-English-speaking background, and living in poverty. The performance of children with one risk factor lagged behind the performance of their nondisadvantaged peers on assessments in mathematics and reading. In the group of children with multiple risk factors, nearly half performed in the lowest quartile. These children usually did not know names of letters and were unaware of sound-letter associations. Similar results have been reported across a range of literacy and language skills in both the United States and the United Kingdom (Duncan & Seymour, 2000; Locke, Ginsborg, & Peers, 2002).

As stated previously, students from low SES backgrounds, especially those who are culturally and linguistically diverse (CLD) are overreferred to special education programs. Early intervention to prevent such overreferral is essential. By shifting attention and resources to earlier stages in the educational process, professionals can help improve children's outcomes. This would be much better than the current wait-to-fail system, in which children are not given help until their academic performance is so dramatically low that they end up qualifying for special education services. It is important to begin promoting development of oral and written language skills early in life. In Chapter 4, we discussed strategies for promoting oral language development. This chapter is devoted to strategies for promoting literate language in low SES students, with special attention to techniques that are supported by scientific evidence.

OPTIMIZING BOOK READING EXPERIENCES FOR YOUNG CHILDREN

Snow and Juel (2005) define literacy as the capacity to construct and express meaning through writing, reading, and talking about texts. Literacy is a prerequisite to formulating new ideas and to acquiring information. Snow and Juel believe that reading with children is important because the kind of language used in reading and the kind of language used in informal, daily conversation are different. Conversational language often is contextualized. Reading is contextualized in early books, but eventually decontextualized language is used. In addition to promoting decontextualized language skills, reading expands children's vocabularies (Montgomery, 2007). A goal of educators is for children to know 80,000 words by the time they graduate from high school, and reading is extremely important in acquisition of this vocabulary.

All professionals are aware of the importance of encouraging caregivers and early childhood professionals to read with young children (Maxwell, 2012). For low SES children, there are special challenges in the implementation of this recommendation. First, caregivers may have low levels of education themselves; reading might be a challenge for them personally. Second, low SES parents may be so stressed with providing the "basics" of daily life that reading is not a priority. Third, there may not be access to appropriate children's books. Hamer (2012) states that the number of picture books in the home has been positively linked to children's expressive and receptive language. Familiarity with storybooks has been associated with growth in young children's vocabulary and reading skills.

Rodriguez et al. (2009) conducted a longitudinal investigation that focused on the language and literacy environments of 1046 children from low SES families across the children's first three years of life. Children's cognitive and language abilities were examined at 14, 24, and 36 months of age in relation to the frequency of their participation in literacy activities, the quality of mothers' engagements with their children, and the availability of age-appropriate learning materials. Literacy experiences at each of the three ages studied explained unique variance in children's 36-month cognitive and language skills. Rodriguez et al. concluded that with low SES young children, it is important to target multiple aspects of their literacy environments, starting in the first year of life, to support their cognitive and linguistic development.

It is ideal for professionals work to systematically increase children's participation in daily book-reading routines. Paul and Norbury (2012) give a variety of suggestions for caregivers and preschool teachers to promote emergent literacy skills in young children. Paul and Norbury's ideas are especially relevant for families who may be too busy to set aside specific times for emergent literacy activities during the day. These activities can be worked into the daily routines of busy parents.

First, Paul and Norbury (2012) emphasize that books should contain simple pictures that can be described or labeled with just a few words. Caregivers can "read" these simple books with their children whenever they find themselves with a few extra moments, for example, while waiting at the bus stop or in the doctor's office. Caregivers also can draw attention to and talk about print. For example, they can show the child the day's shopping list or read various signs (e.g., at the grocery store, at the dentist's office). At the breakfast table, caregivers can even read words on cereal boxes.

Adults who use shared or *joint book reading* use systematic storybook reading to stimulate language in children. Reading books with children provides opportunities for practice and repetition of certain words and phrases. For example, in the well-known joint book reading routine of "Brown bear, brown bear, what do you see? I see a _____ looking at me!" the adult uses a predictable pattern to help fill in words. Adults also can use books that are not predictable but are read so often that children eventually can fill in the words from memory. Although a simple task, shared storybook reading helps children achieve a sense of story grammar, enhance their vocabularies, and develop phonological awareness skills that are foundational to reading success.

Nelson (2010) emphasizes that while it is important for teachers to read with children, it is especially important for parents of low SES children to read with them as well. In my experience, some low SES parents feel inadequate about their literacy skills. Although it is tempting to give them long lists of evidence-based reading strategies to use during reading times with their children, experience has taught me that it is best to keep it as simple, and do-able, as possible. To that end, Nelson recommends that we can teach parents, during reading with their children, to CAR: *comment* on your child's interests, *ask questions* about those interests, and *respond* to your child's utterances by adding more information. For example, if a parent and child are reading the book *The Lion King*:

PARENT: I see that you are looking at how Simba likes to play with Nala near the water. (*comment*)

PARENT: Do you think they are going to get into trouble if they go into the elephant graveyard? (*question*)

CHILD: I think Zazu might get mad.

PARENT: Yes, Zazu will get mad if they go into the elephant graveyard because it is dangerous there. (*respond*—add information)

Researchers have cautioned both professionals and parents not to force children to participate in shared storybook reading activities if the children are not interested. Studies suggest that a significant factor in learning to read is the individual child's motivation to read. Accordingly, forcing children who are not interested in reading materials to participate in such activities when they would rather do something else may have far-reaching negative effects (Fey, Windsor, & Warren, 1995; Kaderavek & Boucher, 2006; Kaderavek & Justice, 2002).

Fey and colleagues (1995) suggested that if children seem uninterested in shared book reading experiences, adults may need to modify their styles of reading and storytelling. These researchers recommended the following modifications: (1) getting the child actively involved through choral reading, completion of cloze sentences (e.g. "The sun shines during the "), open-ended questions, and story re-telling; (2) providing feedback in the form of sentence recasting, requests for clarification, and integration of story content; and (3) focusing joint attention on a mutually pleasurable story experience.

Kaderavek and Boucher (2006) provided additional suggestions for specific modification:

Shared book reading may not be a positive interaction for the highly active child. Book reading with emergent readers is not dialogic; it is an inherently passive task since the child is the "listener" and not the "reader." Shorter books, books with highly dramatic or exciting story themes, and manipulative books (books with flaps, movable parts, etc.) Might be appealing to children who are very active . . . very active children may also benefit from acting out stories and participating in dramatic play activities of story themes. (pp. 17–18)

In my first SLP position, I learned this the hard way. As a 23-year-old new Master's degree graduate working in my first job in a low-income school district, I read to children as I had been taught to do in my coursework. But many of the children, especially the kindergartners and first graders, became bored and restless during the reading. Eventually it dawned on me that most of the children had never been read to before kindergarten. Sitting politely and quietly, listening to an adult reading from a book with few pictures, was not in their experience. These children responded quickly and positively with a high level of interest, however, when I provided shorter books with many colorful pictures and features like buttons that they could press to produce corresponding sound effects. My clinical experience bears out the observations of Kaderavek and Boucher (2006): With low SES children who are unaccustomed to being read to, traditional methods of quiet, passive, sitting and listening to stories may be ineffective. It is ideal for professionals as well as home caregivers to "jazz up" literacy experiences in the ways described.

Roberts, Jurgens, and Burchinal (2005) examined how four specific measures of home literacy practices and a global measure of the quality and responsiveness of the home environment during the preschool years predicted children's language and emergent literacy skills between 3 and 5 years of age. The four measures were shared book reading frequency, maternal book reading strategies, children's enjoyment of reading, and maternal sensitivity. The subjects in this study were African American children and their mothers from low SES homes. The researchers found that the strongest predictor of children's language and early literacy skills was the global measure of overall responsiveness and the support of the home environment.

As discussed previously, low SES mothers with less education may not always promote a positive affective reading environment during shared reading activities with their children. In addition, they may not interact in optimal ways to promote literacy development (e.g., they don't ask higher-level questions). Wells (1986) conducted a longitudinal study of 32 children from high, middle, and low SES homes. He found that many of the challenges experienced by children from low-SES homes were the result of the low value parents placed on literacy, as evidenced by the absence of books in the home and parents' limited use of literacy skills.

As previously stated, I have found that many low SES parents are intimidated by the thought of reading with their children because they themselves struggle with reading. For some parents, reading brings back memories of failure and shame. Thus, professionals need to sensitively and appropriately make reading appear to be fun, appealing, and desirable as a shared activity for parents and children. To this end, professionals can make short DVDs that demonstrate how to make shared reading activities positive; the DVDs also can demonstrate strategies that increase children's reading comprehension, reading fluency, phonological awareness skills, and overall awareness of print. Because many low SES families have DVD players, short DVDs of this nature may be extremely helpful for promoting literacy practices in these homes.

An idea that I am working on now is the use of short YouTube videos that parents can watch on their phones. Anecdotally, my colleagues and I have found that even in low SES families, many parents own iPhones. YouTube videos, free of charge for parents with Internet access, can be watched over and over again. The goal of the 3- to 4-minute YouTube videos is to demonstrate practical ideas, for reading with children, that parents can implement immediately. As I have spoken with members of low SES, culturally and linguistically diverse communities about the appropriateness and desirability of short YouTube videos promoting shared reading strategies, the response has been uniformly enthusiastic. Formal research will determine the efficacy of using short YouTube videos to promote parent-child shared reading with low SES, diverse families.

In one research study on encouraging low SES parents to read with their children, Sharif, Reiber, and Ozuah (2002) studied the effects of a literacy intervention program called Reach Out and Read (ROR) that was administered to inner-city preschoolers and their parents over a 3-year period. At the end of this program, an 8-point difference in receptive vocabulary scores was found between children who had participated in this program and children who had not. These researchers speculated that a possible reason was that the parents in the control group came to a clinic where staff handed out books for reading but did not provide instructions on how to increase literacy in their children. The parents in the experimental group were videotaped reading to their children during home visits and therefore may have become more aware overall of positive reading behaviors that made a difference in their children's literacy. Nevertheless, the point is that evidently it's not enough to just hand parents books; they need specific instruction in best literacy practices.

Whitehurst, Arnold, Epstein, Angell, Smith, and Fischel (1994) examined the impact of dialogic reading strategies on literacy and language development in children from low SES families under three conditions: in day care, at home, and in both settings. *Dialogic reading* is a method of reading picture books in which adults become active listeners who ask questions, add information, and promote the use of children's descriptive language; children are provided with multiple opportunities to talk and engage in conversation.

During the 6-week intervention, day care teachers read for approximately 10 minutes each day, and parents were given books to read at home (Whitehurst et al., 1994). Both teachers and parents were trained in dialogic reading techniques. The results of the study indicated that, on formal vocabulary tests, the children who scored the highest were those who had engaged in dialogic reading in both the home and the preschool settings.

Dyadic interactive strategies during book reading may differ depending on the cultural and linguistic characteristics of families and their SES (Anderson-Yockel & Haynes, 1994; Kaderavek & Justice, 2002; Roseberry-McKibbin, 2007, 2008). For example, Anderson-Yockel and Haynes (1994) studied book reading experiences in mothers and preschool children from European and those from African American backgrounds. Results of this study showed that African American mothers asked many fewer questions than did European American mothers, and African American children thus exhibited a higher proportion of spontaneous verbalizations during shared book reading experiences. European American mothers asked more questions of their preschool children, resulting in more question-answering in the children. When professionals work with parents of young children, it is important to take into account the parents' cultural practices. More is said about this in Chapter 9.

INCREASING EARLY PRELITERACY AND LITERACY SKILLS: EVIDENCE-BASED STRATEGIES

Basic Principles

Wasik et al. (2006) noted that preliteracy skills consist of complex interrelationships among code-related and oral language skills. As discussed in Chapter 4, oral language skills play a critical role in laying the foundation for a child's literacy skills. Oral language is an essential precursor to reading (Hamer, 2012).

Reading also involves *code-related skills*, which include knowledge of conventions of print (e.g., the knowledge that print goes from left to right), letters and letter sounds, beginning forms of writing, and phonological awareness). Code-related skills also have been termed *emergent literacy skills* by some researchers. *Emergent literacy* is the set of concepts, behaviors, and skills of young children that precede and develop into conventional literacy. Emergent literacy is the foundation for later reading and writing (Kaderavek, 2011). For most children, the foundation of emergent literacy is acquired from approximately birth to 6 years of age, or the time preceding formal reading instruction.

Emergent literacy is composed of two different but highly interrelated areas of development: phonological awareness and print awareness (DiLorenzo et al., 2011; Justice, Chow, Capellini, Flanigan, & Colton, 2003). Phonological awareness refers to the child's ability to realize that words are made up of sounds, and that sound segments can be manipulated in words and represented by symbols or letters (Paul & Norbury, 2012). Rhyming, syllabication, and sound blending are all examples of phonological awareness skills (Goldsworthy & Pieretti, 2012). Print awareness "describes the implicit and explicit knowledge children acquire concerning the fundamental properties of print, such as the relationship between print and speech and the functions and forms of particular language units (e.g., letters, words, punctuation marks" (Justice et al., 2003, p. 320). Both print awareness and phonological awareness are critical to later literacy, and children from low SES backgrounds are at risk for deficits in both of these areas (Turnbull & Justice, 2012). Thus, professionals need to actively target these skills in intervention.

Increasing Children's Phonological Awareness Skills

Professionals may need to focus especially on increasing the phonological awareness of children from low SES families. Because research consistently shows that low SES children have disadvantages in this area, it is clear that they would be helped by interventions to increase their skills. Phonological awareness skills constitute a very important precursor to reading (Goldsworthy & Pieretti, 2012). Phonological awareness ideally is targeted in the preschool years to prevent delays in the acquisition of reading skills during the elementary school years.

Kaderavek (2011) states that there are two basic ways to target phonological awareness and other emergent literacy skills: (a) *embedded intervention,* and (b) *explicit intervention.* Embedded intervention is less direct than explicit intervention. Using embedded intervention, professionals work to enhance children's phonological awareness and other emergent literacy skills within meaningful classroom interactions and activities. For example, preschool teachers can provide "literacy artifacts" in their classrooms such as magnetic drawing boards, stapled paper books for writing and drawing, crayons, and other items. They can be display print around the classroom at the children's eye level, for example, teachers can post calendars, letters of the alphabet, and small posters with writing on them, all of which help enhance children's awareness of print (Paul & Norbury, 2012).

Explicit intervention is much more direct and emphasizes sequenced, structured adult instruction. The adult works to directly enhance literacy through selecting specific targets and guiding the child through activities designed to help him learn those targets. Kaderavek comments that, although explicit intervention is not as naturalistic as embedded intervention, both types of intervention are needed to actively engage children to foster literacy development. Koutsoftas,

Harmon, and Gray (2009), in a study with low SES preschool children, concluded that explicit instruction in emergent literacy skills is necessary in order to see measurable gains.

Specific techniques to develop phonological awareness skills in children have been detailed in other sources (DiLorenzo et al., 2011; Goldsworthy & Pieretti, 2012; Nelson, 2010; Turnbull & Justice, 2012). Several such techniques are summarized here:

- Count the number of words in a sentence.
- Identify the number of syllables in a word.
- Identify the number of sounds in a word.
- Identify words that rhyme.
- Demonstrate sound blending skills (e.g., the adult says "c-a-t—what word is that?").
- Identify the first sound in a word (e.g., "Jose, what is the first sound in the word dog?").
- Identify the last sound in the word (e.g., "Maria, what is the last sound in the word car?").

Professionals can use enjoyable activities to help children develop their phonological awareness skills. Rhythm sticks and clapping can be used to emphasize the number of sounds or syllables in words. Professionals also can use rhymes; Dr. Seuss books are excellent for this purpose. Children can recite or sing the rhymes and act them out. As rhymes are recited, sung, or read, children can clap or shake a shaker for each word or syllable they hear. These are just a few of the many ideas available for increasing children's phonological awareness skills (Roseberry-McKibbin, 2007). As a clinician, I have discovered that the younger the child, the more he or she will enjoy things like music and rhythm sticks. The goal is to actively involve the child and to make phonological awareness activities fun!

Ukrainetz, Ross, and Harm (2009) studied schedules of phonemic awareness treatment for kindergarteners. In one schedule, the students were seen for intervention three times a week from September through December. In another schedule, the children were seen once a week from September to March. There were large, maintained gains for children seen via both schedules. It was found that gains made from the short, intense treatment condition were similar to those made in the longer, less intense treatment condition. Ukrainetz et al. concluded that both schedules of intervention were effective in boosting children's phonemic awareness.

Saint-Laurent and Giasson (2001) conducted a study to assess whether teaching phonological awareness and other emergent literacy skills in a classroom environment to kindergartners from low- and middle SES homes would improve scores on various aspects of pre-reading skills. Four experimental groups and two comparison groups were used in the study. Pre- and post-testing scores for the experimental groups were higher than those for the comparison groups on measures of invented spelling, phonological awareness, and reading orientation at the end of kindergarten. Children in the experimental group who had included phonological awareness training along with an early literacy program scored the highest on phonological awareness measures at the end of the year. The authors noted that these gains did not last into first grade, however, and suggested that phonological and literacy training needed to continue into first grade for maintenance of the gains made in kindergarten.

Increasing Print Awareness

In terms of written language or print awareness, Justice and Ezell (2001) examined the written language awareness skills of preschool children from low SES homes. A battery of six measures was administered to assess skills in print awareness, word awareness, graphic awareness, and metalinguistic awareness. Analysis of the children's performance on the battery revealed that they had substantial knowledge gaps across all four dimensions of written language awareness. In a separate study (2002), these researchers found that intervention with preschool children from low SES families that focused on increasing print awareness was successful in enhancing the children's overall performance in this area.

In a study by Justice, Pullen, and Pence (2008), it was found that during reading, preschoolers only looked at print about 5 to 6% of the time when adults did not explicitly reference print. However, when adults referenced print explicitly, children looked at print in the storybook about 12.5 times when the adult read the book verbatim, 17.7 times when the adult made nonverbal references to print, and 21.2 times when the adult made verbal references to print.

On the basis of their findings, Justice and colleagues (2008) recommended that SLPs and other professionals should implement early screening programs to identify children with difficulties in written language awareness skills before they begin kindergarten. These professionals also should work to stimulate early literacy skills. Such skills may include increasing the children's knowledge of the names of letters and improving their book reading conventions. Table 5–1

Table 5–1. Written Language Awareness Attainments During the Preschool Period

By the time they are 6 years old, children should be able to:

- display interest in reading and sharing books
- hold a book right side up
- identify the front and back of a book
- identify the top and bottom of a page
- look at and turn pages from left to right
- know that text runs from left to right
- identify where the title is on the cover of a book
- identify titles of favorite books
- distinguish between pictures and print on a page
- know where the story begins in a book
- identify letters that occur in their names
- print the first letter of their names
- recite the first 10 letters of the alphabet
- point to the first letter in a word
- differentiate uppercase from lowercase letters
- use terms such as *letter, word, alphabet*
- point to words individually as they are read
- identify the space between two words
- respond to signs in the classroom
- recognize common environmental signs such as a stop sign
- recognize and read some signs in the environment (e.g., Boys, Girls [with regard to restrooms])
- ask for help to "read" signs in the environment

Source: Adapted from Justice and Ezell, 2001; Paul and Norbury, 2012.

lists attainments in written language awareness that children should have mastered by the age of 6 years. Professionals can use this list to guide them in assessment and intervention with children from low SES families who may be at risk for reading problems.

Justice and colleagues (2003) examined the relative efficacy of two approaches to emergent literacy intervention for 4-year-old children experiencing multiple risk factors (including poverty). Both approaches involved 12-week intervention programs. Children's emergent literacy knowledge was evaluated three times during the course of the research project: at pretest, midway through the program, and at posttest. Children were randomly divided into two groups. After group assignment, children then participated in a 12-week emergent literacy intervention program conducted in two 6-week segments. The order of the segments was counterbalanced across the two groups. Thus, every child received 12 weeks of intervention. However, one group received Approach a followed by Approach B; the other group received Approach B followed by Approach A.

In Approach A, the comparison approach, the children completed a 6-week segment consisting of biweekly 30-minute sessions conducted with small groups. These sessions incorporated adult-child shared storybook reading. At the beginning of each session, an adult read a storybook to the children. The adult used different strategies to promote children's verbal involvement and active participation in the storybook reading. After the storybook was read, the adult led the children in a story re-telling activity.

In Approach B, the experimental explicit intervention program, each child completed a 6-week segment consisting of biweekly 30-minute small group sessions. These sessions were designed to engage children in activities that would direct their attention to the phonologic features of oral language and the orthographic features of written language. Each session consisted of phonological awareness games, alphabet recitation, and name writing.

Both types of interventions were found to be of benefit (Justice et al., 2003). Preschool children exhibiting multiple risk factors, including poverty, showed substantial emergent literacy growth during the 12-week period that included both Approach A and Approach B. In the areas of alphabet knowledge, phonological segmentation, and rhyme production, children's task performance more than doubled. The most profound positive changes in the children's literacy skills, however, occurred during Approach B, the experimental explicit intervention program. The researchers stated that during Approach B, "substantial, widespread change was observed, encompassing all areas examined. In contrast, performance changes during the comparison program [shared storybook reading] were notably modest, with only phonological segmentation showing significant change" (2003, pp. 328–329).

According to Justice et al. (2003), for young children at risk of developing literacy problems, including those from low SES backgrounds, it is most efficacious to provide explicit intervention focused on specific areas of skill development such as name writing, rhyming, and letter naming. Explicit intervention in areas such as these provided more widespread positive change than literature-based (storybook reading) activities in which literacy goals were more generally and less explicitly targeted.

As further support for the effectiveness of explicit intervention for increasing early literacy skills, the Commonwealth of Virginia has all kindergarten children undergo a comprehensive screening of literacy skills at the beginning and at the end of the school year (Justice, Invernizzi, & Meier, 2002). Children who are identified as at risk at the beginning of the year are given additional, intensive instruction during kindergarten; this instruction is geared toward promoting early literacy skills as a foundation for later grades. Preliminary research evidence showed that this intervention was effective (Invernizzi & Robey, 2001, cited in Justice et al., 2002). As stated earlier, Kaderavek (2011) supports the assertion that explicit intervention is necessary for promoting literacy-related skills in young children.

In other research examining emergent literacy skills in low SES children, Dodd and Carr (2003) conducted a study that assessed 83 children who all had completed first grade in mainstream primary schools. These schools were located in Newcastle upon Tyne in the United Kingdom. The children, who were from northeast England, all spoke British English and were Caucasian. Their average age was 5 years and 6 months. The study included 41 subjects from upper SES backgrounds and 42 subjects from lower-SES backgrounds. Testing and background checks verified that none of the subjects had hearing, sensory, or intellectual problems. All children were assessed in three areas encompassed by the term *knowledge of letter-sound associations*: letter-sound recall, letter-sound recognition, and letter reproduction skills.

For the letter-sound recall task, each child had to label the phonemes of 24 graphemes and 8 digraphs. The examiner, for example, would point to the letter t and say: "Do you know what sound this letter makes?" The letter-sound recognition task in this study required children to indicate the appropriate corresponding letter from an array of 16 letters. For example, the examiner said: "Can you show me the *t*?" For the letter reproduction task in this study, the child heard a letter spoken and then printed that letter (e.g., "James, write *t*.")

Dodd and Carr (2003) found that SES affected the children's performance on all three tasks. Children from upper SES backgrounds performed significantly better than children from low SES backgrounds. Children from high-SES backgrounds performed equally well on the letter-sound recall and the letter production task. Children from low SES backgrounds had more difficulty with the letter production task than with the letter-sound recall task. The researchers summarized their findings as follows:

> The results indicate that despite compulsory implementation in the United Kingdom of the National Literacy Strategy (1998), formal instruction has not obviated the influence of SES. This result may reflect the difficulties that children from lower SES backgrounds face when they enter school. Statistics . . . indicate that at school entry, children from disadvantaged backgrounds are more likely to have poorer health, to be less socially adept, to have low motivation to learn, and to know few letter names and letter-to-sound associations. *From their first literacy lesson, they are disadvantaged* [italics mine]. (p. 135)

Why are SES differences so profound in the development of letter-sound knowledge, especially letter reproduction? These researchers speculated that among other things, low SES children's ability to print letters is affected by their lack of opportunity for preschool learning and their lack of access to resources such as paper, pencils, and a table top, as well as a caregiver to encourage effort and provide models (Dodd & Carr, 2003). Lack of opportunity for preschool learning was viewed as especially salient to low SES children's lack of skill in letter reproduction.

An important clinical implication of the study by Dodd and Carr (2003) was that children from low SES backgrounds are more likely to need greater emphasis on the foundational skills of emerging literacy: skills such as printing and letter-sound associations. Like Justice and her colleagues, these researchers recommended that children be screened for early literacy abilities such as phonological awareness and letter-sound knowledge. Children in need of intervention could be identified and served appropriately to prevent future literacy failure.

Duncan and Seymour (2000) and Hecht, Burgess, Torgesen, Wagner, and Rashotte (2000) showed that knowledge of the three letter-sound association tasks described in Dodd and Carr's (2003) study was the best predictor, in the early school years, of later literacy. In situations in which large groups of children are at risk for failure to acquire adequate literacy skills, Dodd and Carr suggested that professionals such as SLPs and others might work with teachers to provide phonological awareness training that includes helping children specifically develop the three skills described in this research.

One successful strategy for enhancing children's phonological awareness and overall emergent literacy skills is *print referencing* (Justice & Ezell, 2004; Justice et al., 2008; Justice, Skibbe, & Ezell, 2006). This evidence-based strategy can be used by professionals to enhance the emergent literacy skills of young children. Print referencing refers to an adult's use of verbal or nonverbal cues to direct a child's attention to the functions, features, and forms of written language during shared storybook reading.

The following examples of such cues are based on a fictitious book *Quack Quack Duck*:

- The adult can track print while reading, for example, when beginning the reading session with "The title of this book is *Quack Quack Duck*," the adult can track a finger under the title.
- The adult can ask a question about the print, for example, "Which word do you think says *water?*"—and have the child point to the word he or she thinks says *water*.
- The adult also can *comment about print*, for example, "The author of this book is *Jane Johnson*"—while pointing to those two words.

Empirical evidence has shown that print referencing is an excellent way to facilitate children's written language awareness skills, and that this strategy can be applied in children from CLD as well as low SES homes (e.g., Justice & Ezell, 2000, 2001, 2002; Justice et al., 2008; Lopez, 2012). Parents and others in these children's environments can be trained to use print-referencing behaviors during reading.

Justice and Ezell (2000) conducted a study on use of print referencing with typically developing 4-year-old children and their parents. Parents in the experimental group were trained to read to their children using five print-referencing behaviors aimed at promoting children's interactions with print. Parents were shown a 7-minute training video to help them comprehend and implement these print-referencing behaviors. The five print-referencing behaviors were three verbal references to print (comments, questions, and requests about print) and two nonverbal references to print (pointing to print and tracking print while reading). Examples of verbal references to print follow: "Show me the longest word on this page." "Show me just two words on this page." "Where is a word that begins with *r*?"

Results of the study showed that parents who were trained specifically in print-referencing behaviors showed a significant increase in their use of these behaviors when reading with their children. This phenomenon was not observed in a control group of parents who had not been trained. Parents in the experimental group reported that they experienced significantly higher levels of satisfaction with the impact of their shared book reading sessions on their children's knowledge of print concepts as well as knowledge of the alphabet. Table 5–2 gives examples of use of print referencing during child-mother storybook reading.

Justice, Kaderavek, Fan, Sofka, and Hunt (2009) studied the efficacy of accelerating low SES preschoolers' literacy development through classroom-based teacher-child storybook reading and explicit print referencing strategies. Examples of explicit print-referencing strategies used in this study were as follows:

> "This M in the red block is an uppercase letter. See how this uppercase letter is different than these lowercase letters?" "This word is the. This word is in this book all the time—can you help me find it?"
>
> "This is the letter K. It is in the words *kangaroo* and *kick*."
>
> "This is the title of the book. It tells us the name of the book."

The results of the study indicated that children whose teachers used explicit print-referencing strategies showed larger gains on three standardized measures of print knowledge than children whose teachers did not use these strategies.

Justice, McGinty, Piasta, Kaderavek, and Fan (2010) conducted a study to determine the effectiveness of explicit intervention for print referencing with 4- and 5-year-old children. Children were assigned to

Table 5–2. Examples of Use of Print-Referencing Cues During Shared Storybook Reading

Book Reading Transcript	Print-Referencing Cue
MOTHER: The name of this story is *The Five Clowns*. (mother tracks her finger under title)	Tracking print
CHILD: (pointing to title) That says *The Five Clowns*.	
MOTHER: Right! Good! Which word do you think says *clowns*?	Question about print
CHILD: (points to *five*) This one.	
MOTHER: Good try. But that says *five* (points to *five*). This word says *clowns* (points to *clowns*).	Points to print; comments about print
CHILD: What does this say? (points to author's name)	
MOTHER: (points to author's name) That says *Bill Smith*. He is the author, the one who wrote this book.	Points to print; comments about print
MOTHER: Point with me to the two words— *Bill Smith*.	Request about print
CHILD: (Points to the words *Bill Smith*)	
MOTHER: Show me where the B is in the author's name.	Request about print.
CHILD: Here it is (points to the B in *Bill*)	
MOTHER: Let's read the story together.	

Source: Adapted from Justice and Ezell, 2004.

two conditions. The control group of children were read to by teachers, but there were few-no explicit references to print. The children in the experimental group were read the same set of books as the controls, but the teachers integrated explicit references to specified print targets in each session (120 read-aloud sessions conducted in their classrooms over a 30-week period). Results of the study showed that children in the experimental group had significantly higher print knowledge scores at the end of the study than the controls. Justice et al. concluded that explicit, print-focused read-alouds positively impacted children's literacy development.

Additional Strategies for Enhancing Early Literacy Skills

In addition to targeting phonological and print awareness skills, it is also is important to work on children's reading comprehension, even when they are in preschool. In one study involving Head Start preschoolers, van Kleeck, Vander Woude, and Hammett (2006) had adults read books to the children and ask both literal and inferential questions using scripts that were embedded throughout the text. The study's results showed significant differences between experimental and control groups on pretest and post-test measures of literal and inferential language skills. The researchers suggested that, although it is important to increase at-risk preschoolers' phonological awareness skills as a foundation for later decoding skills, it is at least as important to facilitate their foundational reading comprehension skills.

After writing the first edition of this book and continuing to practice as a part-time public school clinician with low SES students, I had sharply increased awareness of how many of them did not have books at home. In 2008, I began collecting gently used children's books to give to some of the low SES children I worked with. They were allowed to keep the books, not just borrow them and bring them back. When my mother Bev Roseberry (a teacher) passed away in 2009, I kept the collection going in her memory. This project continued to grow; as of this writing, I have been privileged to collect and donate over 20,000 gently-used children's books to low SES children all over my geographic area. Books have been given to Head Start families, families utilizing the local crisis nursery and receiving homes (for neglected and abused children), a local school that serves homeless children, elementary schools in high-poverty areas, organizations that serve families in crisis, and others. It has been very gratifying to see children's excitement and hear stories about how grateful they and their parents are to actually be able to own books that are permanently in their homes.

Where have all these books come from? As a university professor, I have offered my students extra credit on exams for bringing new or gently used children's books. Mindful of students' budgets, I have emphasized that they can shop at garage sales or thrift stores. My students have been incredibly generous, and most of the books have come from them.

My church has been another excellent source of children's books. I attend a large local church, with wonderful pastors and people who love to give to those in under resourced communities. My church has donated over 3,000 children's books as of this writing.

Another source is friends, acquaintances, and family members. I have been amazed at how, when I began putting the word out, so many people came forward with books. Dozens of times, I have heard the words, "Oh wow! I have sooo many children's books sitting at home (or a relative's home) that are just gathering dust. I'd love for you to have them!" My patient husband has finally, in resignation, realized that his garage will never be the same, what with boxes of books in it all the time.

For readers who would like to collect children's books to use with low SES students you work with, I suggest the above ideas. If you or a relative belongs to a service organization like the Rotary, Lion's Club, and so forth, this is another good potential source. The books are out there—all you have to do is ask—and clear out some space in your garage!

Because many low SES families do not have books in the home (as previously discussed), encouraging students and families from low SES backgrounds to utilize local libraries is another strategy that professionals can use to encourage the development of literacy skills. It is well known that access to high-quality libraries can have a positive impact on the literacy skills of all children. Allen (2010) describes the success of local libraries in Australia in reaching low SES parents and successfully encouraging them to read to their children through workshops, provision of supplies, mentoring, and modeling of successful reading strategies.

Neuman and Celano (2006), in their study of improving quality and quantity of library access for students from low SES backgrounds in Philadelphia, made an interesting discovery supporting Payne's (2003) statement that such students need role models outside the home to encourage and mentor them.

One librarian participating in the study took on a role largely outside that of a traditional librarian. She greeted children by name as they arrived, gave them hugs, and asked about their day. She spent extra time showing them resources, giving additional guidance for successful reading, as well as how to appropriately use the computers. She also held three story hours a day. She started chess clubs and writing clubs and created a neighborhood directory.

> In this setting, children received additional supports in the form of more potent, caring, content-driven interactions that significantly affected the amount, type, and quality of reading experiences. . . . These observations, along with others that followed later, have important implications for the training of librarians to work in different community contexts and ongoing professional development. Libraries may wish to consider interventions and trainings that strategically focus on affect and attachment, informal instruction, guidance, and careful monitoring very early on, beginning in preschool . . . (Neuman & Celano, 2006, p. 199)

Thus, it is not enough to just have more libraries. Children from low SES backgrounds need librarians who can develop personal relationships with them, serve as role models, and provide mentoring over time.

Our local Orangevale Library, though small, has a thriving outreach program for children. For some years, a trained therapy dog named Delilah would come each month with her owner, and parents could sign up their children for a 15-minute time slot to read with her (at no cost). In Mark's early elementary years when reading was such a struggle, sessions with Delilah the dog proved positive and nurturing; these sessions helped Mark feel good about reading. Through the years, librarians at Orangevale Library have helped Mark with school projects, assisting him in finding resources in areas of interest. Because I frequently go the Orangevale Library to buy used children's books for children at the elementary school I serve at part time, I have noticed signs advertising Russian reading sessions that local families can access for free. I continue to be impressed by our local library's strong emphasis on reading out to children in the community.

Neuman (2009) discusses Reach Out and Read (ROR; mentioned earlier). This program, now located in over 2,000 hospitals and health centers in all 50 states, shows low SES parents and children the pleasures of reading together (Reach Out and Read, 2012). The results of ROR show that literacy-promoting interventions by pediatricians can dramatically improve the language scores of young children. Studies from 19 clinical sites in 10 states report a tenfold increase in parents' reading aloud with children when they participate in ROR; in addition, these studies show statistically significant increases in references to reading as one of the three most favorite things that parents do with their children.

Use of appropriate technology for increasing phonological awareness and emergent literacy overall can be very valuable to young children, including those with mild disabilities. One option is *computer-assisted instruction* (CAI), in which a computer is used to present instructional tasks. Many software programs are available for intervention. As one example, some clinicians use Earobics (Cognitive Concepts, 1997–2003), a CD program that presents colorful, interactive games emphasizing skills such as auditory attention and sequential memory, sound-symbol correspondence, overall phonological awareness skills, and others. Specific Web sites especially enjoyed by children include http://www.primarygames.com and http://www.starfall.com. The latter focuses especially on promoting early literacy skills.

The increasingly popular iPad has thousands of apps, or applications, that promote phonological awareness and other literacy-related skills. If schools can afford to purchase iPads, these can be used successfully with students to increase their interest in reading-related activities.

ENHANCING LITERACY SKILLS IN THE ELEMENTARY YEARS AND BEYOND

Professionals who work with children need to put a great deal of effort into early prevention and intervention reading programs for children from low SES families. Hopefully, such programs can prevent reading failure in later years. In a longitudinal study of the reading skills of children from low SES families, Chall, Jacobs, and Baldwin (1990) assessed children in grades 2, 4, and 6 and then conducted follow-up evaluations in each group for 2 years. The most significant finding of the study was that children from low SES families showed deceleration of their reading skills beginning in fourth grade. Skills related to knowing word meanings or vocabulary were the first and strongest to decelerate. Reading comprehension itself was not negatively affected, however, until sixth grade, when comprehension began to decline.

Chall and her colleagues (1990) speculated that perhaps in fourth grade, the students were able to use context to compensate for their weakness in vocabulary skills. But when the reading material incorporated too many difficult words and became more abstract, the students' comprehension decreased. Thus, these researchers recommended that professionals who work with children from low SES families focus on increasing literacy skills, especially vocabulary and reading comprehension skills, in these students. This emphasis is especially important as children stop learning to read and begin reading to learn (Chall & Jacobs, 2003).

Research has found that two of the factors associated with higher reading achievement in children were: (1) the frequency with which teachers read aloud to students and (2) the frequency of sustained silent reading (SSR) in school. In one study, children who experienced daily SSR scored much higher than those who had it only once a week (Trelease, 2006). When students read, they must use both silent and oral reading experiences to stimulate the frontal lobes of the brain (which are heavily involved in higher level thinking).

Wolfe (2001) examined PET scans obtained while a student was engaged in reading. When the student was reading aloud, the PET scan showed activity in the motor area of the brain, with little activity elsewhere. When the student read silently, however, significant frontal lobe activity occurred: much more so than when the student read aloud to others. Thus, again, it is important for all students to be given time for SSR, as well as for reading out loud.

Many professionals wonder how to help older students from low SES backgrounds with reading difficulties. One way is to ensure that these students have appropriate foundational phonological awareness skills. To this end, Swanson, Hodson, and Schommer-Aikins (2005) carried out a study whose goal was to examine posttreatment outcomes after systematic, direct phonological awareness instruction for seventh grade poor readers from low SES, Spanish-speaking backgrounds. The treatment group of 35 students participated in 12 weeks of small group sessions that emphasized phonological awareness at the phoneme level and incorporated explicit linkages to literacy. The students received approximately 45 hours of instruction; they were seen daily for the 12-week period and participated in 60 sessions.

At the end of the 12 weeks, the treatment group was compared with an equivalent nontreatment group of students who were waiting to receive the 12 weeks of instruction. Posttreatment results showed that the experimental group showed significantly higher scores in such skills as phonological awareness, word identification, word attack, and word and passage comprehension. The researchers concluded that seventh grade poor readers from bilingual, low SES backgrounds can profit from systematic, direct instruction that emphasizes phonological awareness and is linked to literacy (Swanson et al., 2005).

With older students from low SES backgrounds who have reading problems, instruction often begins at a level that is too high for them. It bears repeating that phonological awareness skills are a critical component of students' literacy foundation; this is true for older as well as younger students. Research has focused on younger students; such studies need to be replicated and extended with other adolescents from low SES backgrounds who are poor readers in order to verify that time focusing on increasing underlying phonological awareness skills is time well spent.

In a particularly ironic case, I will never forget an anecdote told to me by a speech-language pathologist in a workshop I conducted in Los Angeles: a 14-year-old student from a low SES background could not read but had amassed $14,000 by stealing expensive cars. He had experienced repeated failure in school, and had finally given up trying. With excellent street smarts and mechanical skills, he was able to figure out how to easily break into cars and steal them.

A difficulty for most professionals who work with adolescents from low SES backgrounds who are poor readers is that by the time these children reach adolescence, they may be turned off to reading because it is so difficult for them. Professionals need to be especially proactive with these adolescents. Nippold, Duthie, and Larsen (2005) studied the leisure activities and free-time preferences of older children and adolescents. They found that the most popular free-time activities were watching TV or videos, listening to music or going to concerts, playing computer or video games, and playing sports. Reading was "moderately popular" (p. 93). These investigators found that during the 11- to 15-year age range, interest in pleasure reading declined. Boys were more likely than girls to report that they spent no time in reading for pleasure.

According to Nippold and colleagues (2005), the amount of time spent reading predicts word knowledge. Because word knowledge is so important to academic success, it is important for school-aged children and adolescents to spend time reading a variety of materials. Reading a variety of materials is especially important in vocabulary development for older students. Nippold et al. recommended that professionals work collaboratively with parents, teachers, and other professionals to encourage strong literacy habits in all students. Examples of relevant interventions include the following:

1. Organize book clubs at school; these clubs can have different themes such as Harry Potter and others.
2. Provide specific incentives such as prizes for reading. For older students especially, increasing their motivation to read is crucial

3. Encourage students to visit the school library and take books home.
4. Provide blocks of class time each day (e.g., 25 minutes) for SSR when all students are required to read material of their choice.
5. Encourage parents to read with their children at home and discuss what they have read.
6. Encourage parents to support the school library.
7. Explore with students their reasons for rejecting certain types of material and help them acquire reading materials that engage their interest.

In another research project designed to motivate older students to read more, Paterson and Eliot (2006) implemented an experimental cross-age tutoring program that paired struggling ninth grade readers (some of whom were bilingual) with struggling second and third grade readers. The ninth grade tutors were instructed in reading strategies for use with the elementary school students. It was found that early in the program, the tutors tended to rely directly on strategies learned from lesson plans given to them by instructors. As the tutors gained confidence, however, they began making their own decisions about teaching strategies based on the needs that they perceived in their elementary school "pupils."

The elementary school children made measurable gains in their reading skills. The ninth graders showed improved attitudes and motivation toward reading, with a favorable impact on subsequent performance in all of their classes. Administrators, staff, and teachers at the high school and elementary schools played important, supportive roles. Paterson and Eliot (2006) concluded that cross-age tutoring programs such as theirs can improve students' attitudes toward reading, increase motivation, and provide opportunities to perform in supportive, structured academic environments.

Many other creative ways can be devised to provide incentives for students to read more. At Mark's previous elementary school, the principal and the librarian challenged the students to collectively read greater than 1 million minutes over the school year. As an incentive, the principal, truly a dedicated professional, promised to allow himself to be "dipped in goop and covered with feathers" if the 1-million-minute goal was met. All parents had to keep track of the number of minutes that they read with their children at home and turn in report sheets each month. Because the students succeeded and met the goal of 1 million minutes, at a special assembly held at the end of the year, the school principal was indeed dipped in goop and then covered with feathers, much to the delight of the students! For the next year's incentive, he danced in a tutu in front of the whole school when the students met their reading goal, a performance also very well received by the entire audience, children and adults alike.

Before reading, professionals should try to engage students in pre-reading activities such as skimming the text, reading the title of the book, and eliciting predictions of what the book will be about; also of benefit are developing questions about things to look for in the story and (if possible) telling the story in the students' primary language first if English is their second language. If students have the "big picture" before they try to decode the words in a story, they frequently will comprehend the story much better. Looking at the pictures in the story first, before reading, also can help children to get the "big picture" before they begin to decode the words. It is important that professionals link students' background experiences and knowledge with the reading; as much as possible, the reading should be related to students' lives. When students engage in pre-reading activities such as skimming the book, talking about the pictures (if there are any), and relating content to their own experiences, their reading comprehension will be enhanced.

For students with reading problems, direct teaching of strategies and skills is especially important Students with reading comprehension problems should be directly taught specific strategies that don't compete with decoding (a very hard skill for most of these students to master). For example, students can pause at least at every paragraph to re-read what they have read or paraphrase it. Many poor readers do not like to read because they feel inadequate; they believe that good readers can read something once and comprehend everything. Students with reading problems need to be reassured that strategies like pausing, re-reading, and paraphrasing will be helpful to them and will not make them look "dumb." These students also may need support with skills in decoding polysyllabic words.

At the school where I used to work, we used a reading program called REWARDS (Archer, Gleason, Vachon, & Isaacson, 2007), which is available for use in academic and other settings. REWARDS, an acronym for Reading Excellence: Word Attack and Rate Development

Strategies, is an intensive, short-term-intervention reading program that is specifically designed for students who have mastered basic skills associated with first and second grade reading levels but read slowly or have difficulty reading longer words. REWARDS supports students through the use of flexible strategies for decoding multisyllabic words to build reading fluency and accuracy. The REWARDS program is especially suited for use with students who are struggling in the classroom and have not yet been evaluated for special education. Basically, the REWARDS program is a form of response-to-intervention that has been most successful with students from low SES backgrounds. REWARDS is a non-special education, noncategorical intervention to help at-risk students avoid the need for special education services.

One other strategy I have used is to drill with students so that they can quickly and automatically read the 20 most common words in English print (Table 5–3). If students must stop and sound out these words each time they come upon them, reading will be slow and tedious indeed. I have written these words on index cards; at the end of a therapy session, I take 2 to 3 minutes to drill my students in reading the words quickly. Anecdotally, I have had excellent success in helping low SES kindergarteners (even English Language Learners) to read the words fluently and easily by the end of the kindergarten year.

Montgomery (2007, 2011) recommends that professionals use Fry's (2004) 1,000 instant words as a guide for teaching students the most common English words used verbally and in print. The first 100 of Fry's words account for 50% of the words students encounter in reading, so time is well spent in helping students learn these words thoroughly (Graves, 2006).

Table 5–3. 20 Most Commonly Occurring Words in Print

• the	of	and	a
• to	in	you	is
• that	it	at	he
• for	on	are	as
• with	his	they	be

Increasing Vocabulary Skills for Reading Success

For students in schools, vocabulary acquisition demands are very great. Children begin first grade with a spoken vocabulary of about 6,000 words; they learn 36,000 more spoken words by 12th grade. They still need 55,000 words for printed school English. State curriculum standards expect students to demonstrate ability to understand and fluidly use learned words. Because vocabulary learning affects all academic learning, difficulties with vocabulary can negatively impact learning across the curriculum (German, Schwanke, & Ravid, 2012).

Experts document the fact that students with less-developed vocabularies have more difficulty with reading, and that low SES students are vulnerable to vocabulary deficits (Hammer & Rodriguez, 2012; Montgomery, 2007; Paul & Norbury, 2012; Snow & Juel, 2005). These deficits have been linked to variables we have discussed previously, including lower maternal education levels in many low SES homes and lack of extended discourse in these homes (Hammer, Farkas, & Maczuga, 2010). Horton-Ikard and Weismer (2007) reported that low SES African American children are especially challenged in this area due to their disproportionate representation in areas of high poverty. Thus, an important component of reading development for students from low SES backgrounds is to increase their vocabularies, as discussed previously. Lovelace and Stewart (2009) stated that:

> Children from low SES backgrounds are often limited in experiences needed to build background knowledge for vocabulary growth because individual choices and experiences provided to these children overall are more limited than for groups with greater economic resources. Because experiences are limited, the potential for gaining word knowledge from a variety of opportunities is predictably reduced for these children. These early differences in children's vocabulary knowledge have shown that even a small disadvantage grows into a larger one and becomes difficult to ameliorate without intervention. (p. 168)

I agree with the above statement. Restated, many low SES children have small vocabularies, and it is challenging to teach them new words because they have a paucity of prior life experiences and concepts to link the new words with. I believe that schools struggle so much with teaching new vocabulary to low SES students, who have difficulty learning and retaining the new words, because often new words are introduced once or twice briefly. The students are expected to use fast mapping skills to learn the new words immediately without repeated exposures to the words and active engagement in the learning process. Hoover and Storkel (2005) state that word learning depends, in part, on other sounds and words the child already knows. How a new word relates to those existing words (neighborhood density) positively influences the speed of learning.

As an example, let's say that a kindergarten teacher is introducing zoo animals to the class. She is talking about *zebras, elephants, tigers*, and so forth. Middle SES children will probably learn the animal names immediately (if they don't already know them) because they have been to the zoo, been read books about the zoo, and learned about the zoo in enriched preschool programs. For these middle SES kindergarteners, one or two exposures to the zoo animal vocabulary words are sufficient.

For low SES children, learning the zoo animal vocabulary is a much different process. Most of them have never been to a zoo. Many have not been in high-quality preschool or center-based care situations where zoo animals were introduced. They may not have been read to at home as the middle SES children have been. Thus, when words such as *zebras, elephants, tigers* are introduced, these words are completely unfamiliar. Low SES children have no prior experiences to link these new words to.

Again, low SES children need have repeated exposures to words and active engagement in the learning process. Instead of briefly introducing words one time and moving on, professionals can help low SES students by using extended mapping strategies and providing links between new and previously learned words (Turnbull & Justice, 2012). These strategies can be used during both oral and literate language activities. Children need multiple exposures to new words in order to effectively understand and retain these words, and they learn new words through extended discourse which can involve discussions about books (Montgomery, 2007). Montgomery provides extensive and varied activities to promote vocabulary development in children; some of these involve use of storybooks.

Use of storybooks to increase vocabulary skills in young children can be very effective. For example, Justice, Meier, and Walpole (2005) carried out a study in which they used storybooks to foster vocabulary growth with at-risk kindergartners with low vocabulary knowledge. In the study, the adults who read books to children used a vocabulary word elaboration strategy, utilizing multiple exposures to words, that was shown to be effective. This strategy had three steps: (1) read the words in context, (2) define the word, and (3) use the word in a supportive context. For example (Justice et al., p. 23):

ADULT READS TEXT: "They came down to a *marsh* where they saw a muskrat cleaning his house."

ADULT PROVIDES DEFINITION: "A *marsh* is a very wet place where there are wet lands covered with grasses."

ADULT USES WORD IN SUPPORTIVE CONTEXT: "Like last summer when we took a boat through the *marsh* and we saw lots of birds and alligators."

Again, for at-risk young children with low vocabulary skills, this strategy proved to be effective in helping the children enrich their vocabularies.

The research of Lovelace and Ryan (2009) with low SES culturally and linguistically diverse kindergarteners showed that vocabulary instruction was most effective when children used the words meaningfully in multiple contexts. In this study, new vocabulary words were "learned deeply" (not just on the basis of 1 to 2 exposures) through various games and activities where the words were repeated often. New words were also connected with children's prior life experiences when possible.

Like Lovelace and Ryan (2009), Turnbull and Justice (2012) commented that merely exposing children to new words through reading is not enough. Students learn words more quickly and retain them better when professionals provide elaborated discussions about the meanings of words in context. Professionals can prime words in discussions before a passage or story is read, and students can actively practice using new words in sentences rather than just passively reading sentences containing new words. Taken together, research findings converge upon the fact that for effective vocabulary learning to take place, low SES children need multiple exposures to the words; they benefit from varied activities that actively engage them in word learning. Again, multiple exposures and active engagement are key (Roseberry-McKibbin, 2001).

As stated, active engagement comes when students can relate new vocabulary words to their prior experiences. Biemiller (2003) states that in order to connect new vocabulary words to children's prior experience, we link these words to those children already know. For example, if a child says, "I will look for my backpack," we can say, "You will **search** for your backpack. **Search** is a fancy way of saying **look for**." In another example, a student might say, "I have to do my homework." We can say, "You are **required** to do your homework" and extend the discussion from there. We can use butcher paper or whiteboards to keep a list of the known and new words so they can be reviewed with students.

An iPad app I use for this (that the students really enjoy) is called Fancy Nancy. Each Fancy Nancy app involves a story about a girl and her adventures; new, fancy, sophisticated synonyms for ordinary words are learned in a fun, entertaining way. For example, when Fancy Nancy visits her neighbor, the neighbor is reading about *movie stars*: Fancy Nancy calls them *celebrities*. When Nancy visits her neighbor, she likes to wear gloves, a hat, and a lot of jewelry; she calls these *accessories*. In each Fancy Nancy book/app, the new, fancy, sophisticated words are introduced in an memorable, interesting manner. The students I am currently using this app with don't seem to realize that they are actually learning and being drilled on new vocabulary words!

A free online resource that can be used to teach more sophisticated synonyms to students starting in around third grade is Freerice (http://www.freerice.com). This Web site teaches vocabulary through multiple choice items using synonyms, and there are 65 levels (Level 1 is the simplest; Level 60 is the most complex). For example, an item will say:

Lucky means the same thing as:

    A. Bored
    B. Fortunate
    C. Fatigued
    D. Happy

For every correct answer the student clicks on, 20 grains of rice are literally donated to the United Nations World Food program and given to a hungry person somewhere in a developing country. I have found that children love this Web site, and so do adults! If the player gets an answer wrong, the correct answer is highlighted and then the item is presented again in a few minutes. For older students, this works so much better than being told by a teacher or other authority figure that they are wrong. The Web site keeps presenting the question until it is answered correctly, no matter how many tries it takes. As the player learns more words, the Web site gradually makes the questions more challenging. Anecdotally, I have heard many positive and enthusiastic comments about Freerice from a wide variety of individuals of different ages.

> Anecdotally, I have had some low SES speech and language students on my caseload bring their classroom language arts books to therapy. Using these classroom books for my therapy, I have helped the students learn new and unfamiliar vocabulary in the stories currently being read in the classroom. We have engaged in active learning through discussions, writing sentences, and linking new words with the children's prior experiences. What has been highly effective is having students draw pictures of new words they are learning. I will never forget a group of 5th grade boys who brought their language arts books to therapy; the class was studying the story of Paul Revere. On the first page alone, there were a dozen or so words the boys did not know: *belfry tower, steed, aghast,* and others. I remember so clearly wondering to myself how in the world these boys were going to comprehend the story and pass a test on its contents when they did not understand so many of the words on the very first page!

Lubliner and Smetana (2005) examined the effects of a multifaceted, metacognitive vocabulary intervention on the vocabulary achievement and reading comprehension of fifth grade children in one of California's lowest-performing Title I schools. This intervention, Comprehensive Vocabulary Development (CVD), provided fifth graders from low SES families with 12 weeks of instruction in a metacognitive approach to vocabulary instruction.

Instruction focused on two kinds of metacognitive knowledge: management of thinking (self-regulation) and self-appraisal of cognition (self-monitoring). The overall goal of instruction was to help students monitor their comprehension of words and implement word-learning strategies to increase comprehension of texts. Teachers were trained in CVD, and they used it for 12 weeks with students. Strong gains were made in metacognitive skills, vocabulary achievement, and reading comprehension. Comparisons of Title 1 students' scores and the scores of students in an above-average-performing school revealed large, significant differences between groups before CVD and small, nonsignificant differences after the intervention.

As noted by Lubliner and Smetana (2005), teaching vocabulary to students from low SES backgrounds often is restricted to giving definitions of words while the students sit passively. One extremely helpful part of the CVD approach was the use of clarifying cues to help students actively apply metacognitive strategies to learn new vocabulary. Table 5–4 is an example of a worksheet that students can use to enhance their vocabulary and metacognitive and reading comprehension skills.

In sum, low SES students are vulnerable to vocabulary deficits that can impact their learning across the school curriculum for all their school years. Through repeated exposures to new words and active engagement in the learning process, these students can build up their vocabularies as a foundation for supporting learning across all areas of the curriculum.

PROVIDING ASSISTANCE FOR STUDENTS FROM LOW SES BACKGROUNDS WITH OTHER WRITTEN LANGUAGE CHALLENGES

To re-emphasize, students from low SES backgrounds need support in a number of areas, such as emergent literacy skills, to support the development of written language skills. These students also may need extra support in other areas related to reading and writing. For example, some students may have visual tracking problems, so that they lose their place easily; words "move around on the page."

Many teachers of students with visual tracking problems use the Neurological Impress Method (NIM; Heckelman, 1978). The NIM is a multisensory approach in which the teacher reads aloud while sitting beside and slightly behind the student so that the teacher's voice is clearly audible to the student. The student is instructed to follow the

Table 5–4. Super Power Reading Strategies

Before you read:

Look at the book and chapter titles, headings, words in boldface, and pictures

Highlight key vocabulary words

Read the concluding summary or last paragraph

While you read:

Picture things in your head

Ask yourself questions about what you just read

Predict what will happen next

Use the context to understand what words mean

Mine your memory; ask yourself, "Have I ever seen this word before? Can I remember what it means?"

Ask an expert; does someone in your class know what a word means? Can you figure it out together?

Place a Post-it; if you can't figure out what a word means, put a Post-it in the book and look up the word later in a dictionary or check with a teacher

---

After you read:

Look at the title, headings, pictures, and highlighted vocabulary words again

Ask and answer questions about what you just read

Summarize what you just read in your own words

Source: Adapted from Lubliner and Smetana, 2005; Roseberry-McKibbin, 2008.

reading passage in the book with a finger under each word as it is read out loud. As an adaptation, the teacher can put a finger above each word while the student puts his or her finger under each word, and they read the words aloud together. This approach utilizes the learner's kinesthetic, visual, and auditory senses together during reading. In my own clinical work with students who experienced great difficulty keeping their place during reading, the NIM has been quite successful in helping them not skip words or lose their place on the page.

Professionals also can encourage students with visual tracking problems to place a finger under words as they read (without an adult's help), moving from left to right. This helps students not to lose their place. One very practical idea (from a third grade teacher) is to have students use an index card above the sentence they are reading, not below. In this way, students can keep their place but also scan downward more quickly to the next line.

Professionals also can implement specific strategies to help students improve their writing. *Dictated stories* can be used for improving the written expression skills of young low SES children. Professionals listen to children's stories and write them down. These stories can be about past experiences, a picture the child painted, and the like. The professional writes down the child's story verbatim and later reads it back to the child. Then the child is asked if the story says enough, or if anything else should be added to complete the child's thoughts. Frequently, children wish to expand on their stories. In an atmosphere of encouragement and support, children's stories become much more complex and rich. Anecdotally, I did this with Mark when he was little. For him, there was something very magical about seeing his words on paper and made into a "book" (i.e., with pages stapled together). I still have many of these 'books" that Mark "wrote," and he enjoys looking at them.

As discussed elsewhere, many students from low SES backgrounds bring casual language register to school with them. Writing difficulties are common for these children because in school, writing takes place in formal language register. To help these students move from writing in casual register to writing in formal register, communication of students' ideas initially should be the main focus; then the focus should progress to correct form or mechanics such as grammar and spelling (Ruiz, Rueda, Figueroa, & Boothroyd, 1995).

Often, CLD students from low SES backgrounds experience special challenges in reading because books used in the classroom are written in their second language of English. Professionals can help these students by providing creative ways of accessing print; these strategies are summarized in Table 5–5.

One way professionals can help these students with challenges in written language skills is by recommending relevant computer programs. Some low-income families do own computers; if they don't, the students may be given extra time in the school's computer lab to take advantage of technology resources for learning. Use of the

Table 5–5. Encouraging Literacy Skills in CLD Students from Low-SES Backgrounds

---

- Have CLD students listen to books on tape
- Encourage CLD students to share their languages, cultural heritage, and even songs in their primary languages with the whole class
- Create a multicultural environment in the classroom
- Provide opportunities for students to use English and their primary language in situations both inside and outside the classroom
- Help students find appropriate reading and learning materials for use in the home with family members
- Remember that some students come from homes where the parents are nonliterate; send home wordless books that can be looked at and discussed in the language of the home
- Use tutors or aides who speak students' primary languages to help classroom curriculum become more comprehensible. Student peer tutors can be very helpful.

Source: Adapted from Roseberry-McKibbin, 2007, 2008

Internet is becoming more common in today's schools. The Internet can be especially helpful for CLD students and their parents:

- The Internet provides these parents with a way to link with the schools. This is especially helpful if the parents don't have transportation to the school.
- The Internet has thousands of free resources that can be accessed quickly. It provides a tool that allows students to delve into various subjects in ways that are not possible through any other source.
- Students can link with peers for collaboration and tutoring on school work.
- They can access relevant Web sites in English and the primary language at home; if their parents are unable to help them with their English homework (as is relatively common in CLD families), the students can obtain help from the Internet.

Computers also may be used for word processing. Word processing programs can be very helpful for students from low SES backgrounds that have challenges with writing, especially those who are English language learners. Word processing programs allow students to compose and edit material for school that is free from common errors in grammar and spelling, which reinforces their own writing skills. Today, a great deal of computer software is available to greatly enhance reading and writing for many students. One software program that encourages keyboard skills is Type to Learn (Sunburst Technology Corporation, 2002). There are also iPad apps that encourage writing and boost written language skills.

Text-reading software lets the computer scan text and highlight it either letter by letter or word by word. It also can provide spell checks and definitions of terms. Various types of writing templates are available for specific types of documents such as resumes, reports, and formatted outlines. Visual concept organization software provides graphic organizers for a student's words As expressed by Bender (2004):

> With this increasing emphasis on assistive technology in the schools, teachers must [en] sure that all students—including those from ethnically diverse backgrounds or poorer students—have reading access to assistive technologies that will enhance their learning. . . . For students with learning disabilities . . . assistive technology can be the difference between a successful school experience and an unsuccessful one . . . our students . . . deserve the very best instruction we can provide, and in many cases today, it will often involve assistive technology of one type or another. (p. 348)

An important point in this context is that the writing process involves three types of function: (1) language production, or formulating the ideas to write down, (2) fine motor function, or physically producing handwriting, and (3) visual motor memory, or the ability to see, hold onto the language, and actually write it down. Many students from low SES backgrounds are creative thinkers, but the mechanics of reading and handwriting are so difficult they become discouraged and don't want to write. Professionals can help these students in two ways: through provision of and instruction in use of technology, as previously mentioned, and through the development of fine motor and visual motor skills.

With regard to actual handwriting, many students from low SES backgrounds come to school without the motor skills necessary for typical kindergarten activities. A speaker at a recent convention I attended works in southern California with a very low SES population. In her presentation, she described the children's fine motor skills as "atrocious" (Blevins, 2012). An above-average amount of TV viewing probably contributes to this deficit. In addition, many children from low SES families have not had experience with painting, "coloring," drawing, modeling with clay, drawing with chalk, and other activities involving fine motor coordination regarded as commonplace for children from middle SES families.

In previous times, kindergarten teachers would spend time helping children to develop these types of skills. Today's kindergartens have no time for such corollary development; children must start writing immediately. Some children are not ready and therefore flounder; they may have creative ideas, but putting these ideas on paper is very difficult for them. Table 5–6 shares some practical ideas for developing fine motor and visual motor skills to help students write more effectively.

A program called Handwriting Without Tears (Olsen, 2003) uses a "ball and stick" model for developing handwriting. This program is multisensory, developmentally sound, and highly effective with many types of children, including those from low SES homes who have not had exposure to writing or writing implements. In my own clinical practice, this program has been extremely helpful for elementary school children from low SES families who initially demonstrated fine motor challenges related to lack of experience.

CONCLUSIONS

The ability to read and write fluently is increasingly important in today's highly technical, literate world. Students from low SES backgrounds who have low literacy skills often are doomed to lives of frustration, limited vocational opportunities, and perhaps even crime and incarceration.

As stated at the beginning of this chapter, it makes far more sense to prevent literacy problems early in children's lives than it does to ignore their needs when they are young and then incarcerate them when they are older. The cost to society is immeasurable. Professionals can take an active role in preventing literacy problems and their grim, sad sequelae before they happen. Surely, efforts directed at enriching the literacy skills of students from low SES families will help break the cycle of poverty.

Table 5–6. Practical Suggestions for Enhancing Students' Writing Skills

Primary goals for the child:
- Achieve good shoulder stability
- Achieve appropriate body positioning
- Achieve appropriate pencil grip
- Increase muscle tone in small muscles of hand
- Write with appropriate letter formation
- Succeed in copying from the board
- Succeed in scissor skills/cutting abilities

SHOULDER STABILITY
1. *Write on vertical surfaces*. Write on a chalkboard or dry erase board. Tape paper on wall at shoulder level.
2. *Wheelbarrow walk*. Hold the child's feet and have her walk on her hands. If not stable enough, hold her at the knees.
3. *Wall pushups*. Do pushups against the wall.
4. *Prone or quadruped position*. When playing, watching TV, or reading, encourage lying on the floor propped on elbows.

BODY POSITIONING
1. *90-90-90*. When sitting, the child should sit straight, with hips and knees at a 90-degree position; feet should be flat on the floor.
2. *If the child's feet* don't touch the floor, put books under the feet.
3. *Prone activities*. Do activities on stomach to strengthen trunk muscles.
4. *Seat cushion*—if the child has poor postural control, sitting on a pillow or seat cushion can help posture

PENCIL GRIP
If the child does not use the index and middle fingers and thumb to hold the pencil, try the following:
1. *Pencil grip*. Add a rubber pencil grip to help position the fingers.
2. *Small pencils*. Use a golf/bowling-sized pencil to help promote a three-finger grasp.
3. *Tongs, tweezers, eye droppers*. Use first two to pick up small objects or even cotton balls. Eye droppers can be used to squeeze colored liquid into containers. This strengthens the fingers and promotes a functional pencil grip.

INCREASING MUSCLE TONE IN SMALL MUSCLES OF HAND
Use materials such as:
- Spin toys (e.g., tops, jackstones)
- Playdough, "Silly Putty"

Table 5–6. *continued*

- Squirt bottle for spraying things (e.g., plants)
- Rubber stamps and ink pads for use in creating pictures and designs
- Hole punch
- Stringing, lacing activities
- Art projects—e.g., painting
- Pegboard activities
- "Squishy" balls of various textures—great to squeeze during listening activities

INCREASING SKILLS IN LETTER FORMATION

1. The Handwriting Without Tears (HWT) program www.hwtears.com is a developmental program that uses multisensory lessons and is virtually 100% successful. It's easy, fun, and inexpensive. Some children are confused by the slant and loops of other traditional handwriting programs. HWT letter forms are vertical and convert readily to cursive. HWT is being adopted in various states as well as Canadian provinces.
2. Write letters in various textures such as sand, shaving cream, salt.
3. Cut out letters in sandpaper and have the child trace over them with an index finger.
4. Roll out Playdough to form letters.
5. On paper, place a happy face in the upper left hand corner to orient the child.
6. When you make letters, make them large and have the child trace them with an index finger.

INCREASING SKILL IN COPYING FROM THE BOARD

1. **Vision checkup**. Have the child tested by an optometrist to rule out vision problems.
2. **Close seat**. Have the child sit in front of the class.
3. **Handout on desk**. If there are large amounts to copy, provide the child with a personal handout to copy from.
4. **View finder**. Cut a slit in a manila folder and place the folder over the child's work so that only one line can be seen at a time.

OTHER IDEAS TO INCREASE OVERALL HAND STRENGTH AND DEXTERITY

- Help with washing dishes.
- Help with gardening, planting.
- Help with washing the car.
- Practice identifying small objects in a bag without looking.

continues

Table 5–6. *continued*

- Roll a small ball of clay or Playdough. Using the thumb, roll the ball across the finger tips, from the index to the little finger and then back.
- Using a flashlight, make "finger shadows" against the wall.
- Drop coins one at a time into a slotted top or piggy bank.
- Place coins, on their sides, into Playdough.
- Hang from monkey bars and overhead rings.
- Mix cookie dough by hand.
- Cut anything—paper, Playdough, coupons for Mom and Dad!
- Use clothespins to pick up small pieces of crumbled paper. Pass the paper to each other and drop the pieces into a bucket.
- Squeeze balls of various consistencies and sizes.
- Push pins into foam with a paper design over the top.
- Use playdough to make a dragon and pinch marks on top of the dragon.
- Tear pieces of construction paper into small pieces and glue the different colors of paper on an uncolored picture.
- Make a small mosaic picture by gluing colored rice onto a piece of paper—the child can follow a design or do this freehand!
- Play the pick-up-sticks game.
- Crumble Cheerios or Rice Krispies to make "sand" for pictures.
- Get bubble wrap and have the child pop the bubbles.
- Make candy sculptures—use colored toothpicks and candies to make wonderful creations!
- Using a chalkboard, write or have the child write letters or draw pictures with chalk. Have the child erase each line with small bits of paper towel. The child also can erase with a small piece of damp sponge.
- Have the child tear pieces of clear tape from a dispenser and tape pictures or other objects onto paper.
- Have the child draw on a chalkboard using *small* pieces of chalk—this helps with finger dexterity for writing.
- Roll and shake dice within the palm of one hand.
- Use Leggo blocks to build things.
- Roll and pull taffy.
- Drop marbles, small shells, or other small objects into spaces in an egg carton.
- Stretch a rubber band as far out as possible.
- Poke holes in Playdough with fingers.
- Have the child paint anything—pictures, objects such as ceramic figures.
- Squeeze glitter paint from tubes.

CHAPTER HIGHLIGHTS

▓ Low SES students are vulnerable to written language deficits, especially difficulties in reading. Early reading difficulties often lead to problems later in school. Unfortunately, sometimes a lifestyle of crime and incarceration can result if these difficulties are not ameliorated.

▓ It is important to expose children to books very early in life, beginning when they are babies. Adults who engage in joint book reading activities with children need to be sure that the reading experience is pleasurable and instructive. Adults can use specific strategies for engaging children's interest in books.

▓ Reading engages both oral language and code-related skills. Also called emergent literacy skills, code-related skills encompass the early, foundational behaviors that form the foundation of literacy.

▓ Emergent literacy is composed of two different but highly interrelated areas of development: phonological awareness and print awareness. Phonological awareness refers to the child's ability to realize that words are made up of sounds, and that sound segments can be manipulated in words and represented by symbols or letters.

▓ Print awareness is the knowledge that children gain regarding fundamental properties of print. It involves knowledge of letters, print symbols, and reading conventions.

▓ Low SES children need explicit instruction in both print awareness and phonological awareness. Research consistently supports the fact that this explicit instruction boosts reading achievement.

▓ Other strategies for enhancing literacy skills in low SES children include improving reading comprehension, increasing the numbers of books available to them, encouraging library use, and using computer-assisted technology.

▓ Older students with reading difficulties often need work in phonological awareness skills. They need to be encouraged to view reading as a valuable and desirable activity. Creative incentives can encourage reading.

▓ Professionals must help students build their vocabularies for reading success. In order to help low SES students truly learn and remember new words, professionals must provide repeated exposures to the words as well as active engagement in learning them.

- Professionals can provide special supports for students with visual tracking and fine and visual motor challenges. Technology supports are available to this end. A program called Handwriting Without Tears can provide additional help for students with writing difficulties.

6

Structuring the School Environment for Optimal Performance of Students from Low SES Backgrounds

It takes a village to raise a child.
African proverb

After school, Marcos takes the bus home. Both of his parents are still at work. He struggles to complete his homework; his parents are unable to help him with it because they do not speak English. After attempting unsuccessfully to complete his homework, Marcos spends most of the rest of the day and evening watching TV. Dinner is meager; his parents fight because they are so worried about money. Marcos and his younger brother know better than to speak at the table; their father is tired, and they do not want to incur his wrath.

Marcos and his brother sleep in a crowded bed in the same room. It's cold in the house, but there is no money for heat. Marcos shivers under the thin coverlet and tries to get to sleep. The sound of his parents' arguing comes through the walls, making his younger brother cry. Marcos tries his best to comfort him and wishes he could just get to sleep so he can face another hard day at school tomorrow.

Mark is picked up right after school on Mondays and Wednesdays by his mother, whose department chairperson at the university has given her a flexible work schedule that allows her to take him to his karate lessons (at a cost of $145 per month). Mark's mother feels very grateful for this as she arrives early at the school to find a good parking spot. She chats with other parents who have come to pick up their children. Mark's mother is forging friendships and connections that will last throughout his elementary school experience and beyond.

On the way to karate, Mark and his mother drop by a specialty coffee/fruit drink shop to get him a smoothie (at $2). Karate lasts from 3:30 to 4:15 PM. Since he began karate last year, Mark's grades have improved; so have his overall attitude and level of self-discipline. He is much stronger and physically more coordinated than he was a year ago, with a tremendous increase in self-confidence. His reading is much better, too.

On Tuesdays, Thursdays, and Fridays, Mark spends 1 or 2 hours at the school's Discovery Club, a well-regarded after-school program. He has a network of good friends and nurturing caregivers there, and he often completes his homework there with their help. On Thursdays, he also participates in a club that promotes artistic skills through a variety of media (at a cost of $410 for the year); for Mark, this is the highlight of the week.

Mark and his mother do homework together in the late afternoon and early evening if it has not gotten done at the after-school care center Discovery Club. Mark's mother is able to help him with everything, providing support, encouragement, and a well-lighted, clean place to work. When Mark has finished his homework, he and his mother may go biking in the park or just hang out at home and relax. Later in the evening, after a satisfying hot dinner and a discussion of everyone's day, Mark and both his parents play soccer outside in the spacious back yard. Mark reads for at least 20 minutes before he falls asleep in a soft bunk bed in his own room, surrounded by stuffed animals from special places all over the United States that he and his parents have visited. He sleeps well, waking up the next morning ready for another day of school.

INTRODUCTION

Today's educators experience multiple challenges, both philosophical and practical, as they serve school-aged students. Schools are traditionally middle SES institutions staffed by middle SES professionals, but the number of children who come to school with middle SES values and backgrounds is decreasing. Instead, schoolrooms are increasingly filled with children from low SES families. Since the Great Recession began in 2007, more and more students are living in poverty; their values, cultural practices, and social norms often are at variance with the middle class, traditional ways of education. Accordingly, current school structures and conditions must change to accommodate the needs of the children to be served.

The academic achievement gap between children from low- and middle SES families in the United States has been documented for years (Adler, 1979; Burke, 2012; Kozol, 1995; Rothstein, 2006). Students from high-SES backgrounds of all ethnic groups show higher average levels of achievement on tests. They stay in school longer than students from low SES backgrounds.

According to Terry, Connor, Thomas-Tate, and Love (2010), research shows that there is widely varying achievement among children in American schools, with children from some environments experiencing more difficulty than others. When these children enter kindergarten, achievement gaps are observable even before they start learning to read. According to Terry et al., the most salient child characteristics that predict academic success are race and SES. Non-White, low SES children tend to lag behind White, middle SES children. Thus, unfortunately, it is clear that being non-White and low SES puts children at risk for academic underachievement.

Reardon (2011) examined whether and how the relationship between family SES and academic achievement has changed in the United States in the last 50 years. He found that the achievement gap between children from high- and low SES families was approximately 30 to 40% greater among children born in 2001 than among those born 25 years earlier. He stated that the income achievement gap has been growing in the United States for the last 50 years, and emphasized that this gap is large when children enter kindergarten; it does not appear to narrow as children progress through school.

Unfortunately, low SES students who struggle in school tend to drop out at higher rates than do middle SES students. When students drop out, the cost to themselves and society is very great. The National Center for Education Statistics (NCES, 2011) reported that the median income of persons ages 18 to 67 years who had not completed high school was roughly $25,000 in 2009. In 2009, students from low SES families dropped out of high school five times more often than students from high-income families. The estimated dropout rate was 2.4% for Whites, 4.8% for African Americans, and 5.8% for Latinos. Termed "dropout factories," high schools that graduate disproportionately few students tend to be located in poverty-stricken areas with high rates of crime, ill health, and unemployment. More than 60% of African American students attend schools where greater than 50% of the school population lives in poverty, compared to 18% of White students (Alliance for Excellent Education, 2011).

It is estimated that approximately 12 million students will drop out over the next decade or so, costing the United States approximately $3 trillion. It is also estimated that if dropouts from the class of 2009 had graduated from high school, the U.S. economy would have benefitted from nearly $335 billion in additional income over the course of these students' lifetimes The risk for male dropouts is significant. In 2007, male high school dropouts were 63 times more likely to be incarcerated than those with a Bachelor's degree or higher (Alliance for Excellent Education, 2011).

It is clear that school reforms are necessary, and these reforms must be deep and widespread; society as a whole must participate. As Neuman (2009) stated:

> Placing too many responsibilities, and making too many extraordinary demands on schools as the sole institution of hope, only derails it from its mission of teaching. Rather, schools must be part of the solution—but not the only solution. Other institutions, integrally tied with strengthening early care and education, families, neighborhoods and communities, are important agents of change and must be a part of any equation for improving the lives of disadvantaged children. (p. 181)

CURRENT SCHOOL CONDITIONS AND ATTEMPTS AT REFORM

Attempts at School Reform

Despite ranking fourth in per pupil expenditures among other developed nations, the United States ranks much lower in terms of academic achievement in reading and math. American 15-year-olds are in the middle of the rankings in reading, but are near the bottom of industrialized countries in math, falling behind Slovenia, Estonia, and the Slovak Republic (Burke, 2012). In light of the current situation in our schools, educational reforms have been proposed and enacted. Of all the attempts at school reform in the 21st century, probably none is more controversial than No Child Left Behind (2002), introduced in Chapter 3. The No Child Left Behind Act set out the goal of making all public school students proficient in math and reading by the year 2014. This has proved to be very challenging for low SES schools, especially those in which many students speak English as a second language.

Ironically, as the preparedness of kindergartners has declined, the demands of kindergarten have greatly increased, in large part to respond to the demands of No Child Left Behind. Kindergartners in previous times used to play in the sandbox, sing, take naps, color, and do other activities. Now they are expected to handle a challenging academic curriculum. For example, in my son's kindergarten, children were expected to be reading and writing in the first trimester (by October or November). The children were assigned homework every night that took at least half an hour to complete: spending up to 45 minutes was not uncommon. The class was very rushed, with frequent teacher admonitions to "hurry up!" I personally saw some of these 5-year-olds be penalized for taking too much time in the bathroom.

Hale (2004) states that although the No Child Left Behind initiative can be commended as an attempt to address the problems related to school achievement, this reform does not provide visionary national leadership that shows schools *how* to improve student achievement. Schools have not been given the funds to implement the sweeping curricular changes mandated by No Child Left Behind.

Its methods, in Hale's words "generally consist of politicians pressuring, threatening, or punishing school districts. In this climate of hysteria, school districts are responding with hysterical solutions" (p. 34). Hale notes that many school districts, in an effort to respond to the No Child Left Behind mandates, have pushed curriculum "down"—they are trying to teach students more academic content at lower grade levels. For example, in some places, educators are considering teaching multiplication to second graders and not waiting until third grade. (My own son was doing multiplication at the end of second grade in a California public school.)

Hale's (2004) statement of a "climate of hysteria" is not overexaggerated. As an example:

> In Mark's previous school, concern for children to have high performance on standardized tests reached a point at which children had less access to food and water so that they would have more time to focus on their schoolwork. In first grade, parents were told that their children could no longer eat morning snacks. They were "big boys and girls," able to go for 5 hours or more without food. There was no time for snacks.
>
> Drinking fluids leads naturally to the need to visit a bathroom. But if the children at Mark's previous school drank water when they were thirsty, they were penalized, using the school's token economy system, for subsequent restroom visits. Each visit to the restroom cost 10–20 "Beaver Bucks" because it interrupted the child's work. When parents picked children up at the end of the day, some children would be dehydrated and have headaches because they literally had had no water all day—they didn't want to lose any Beaver Bucks by needing to use the restroom. One child had several urinary tract infections in the course of a year because he would constantly "hold it," not wanting to be penalized for going to the bathroom.

It is important to recognize just how draconian some public schools have become in their quest to meet standards of No Child Left Behind, and generally to just improve high standardized test scores overall. In California, some new schools are being built without playgrounds because the chock-full curriculum leaves no time for play. Children need to "drill and kill" in math, reading, and writing so the school can meet No Child Left Behind's requirements. Many low SES school personnel feel very stressed because of the threat of state takeover if the school's test scores do not come up; teachers feel pressured to administer numerous worksheets to prepare children for standardized testing. These types of measures and attempts to hold schools accountable are counter-productive in that they destroy the pleasure that children, those from low SES families or others, find in learning.

As an engine of educational reform, accountability can help to create a climate for change. Often, however, low SES schools are targeted and teacher autonomy is reduced through top-down reform procedures. In addition, an educational model may be favored over a developmental model. Yet, young children from low SES families may need to be taught through developmental models, at least initially, because they often do not bring to school the cognitive, oral, and literate language experiences assumed by current public school curricula.

Unfortunately, these children are pressured into memorizing information for tests and often are not given hands-on, contextualized learning opportunities that they need as a foundation for decontextualized, "schoolish" activities. As discussed in greater detail in Chapter 7, students from low SES backgrounds, especially those with no preschool experience, need contextualized learning activities as a foundation for decontextualized academic activities; they often do not receive this much needed foundation (Weiner, 2001).

Hale (2004) agrees, stating that strategies that work for students from upper middle SES backgrounds who have high-quality preschool experiences may not work with students who don't have that background. For example, many middle SES, predominantly White families delay their children's entry into kindergarten until they are almost 6 years old. These children go to preschool. Low SES families, however, cannot afford to send their children to preschool, but the parents know their children should be "getting something," so they send them to kindergarten at young ages, believing that their children will reap advantages. This is especially true in many low SES African American families (Hale, 2004). Thus, kindergarten teachers may be confronted with classes that have 6-year-old White children with preschool background and 4-year-old Black children with no preschool background: a challenging situation at best.

As one way to address the difficulties experienced by students from low SES backgrounds in schools, Congress has provided for a specific program to support children from low SES families in public schools. Title 1 of the Elementary and Secondary Education Act provides funding for supplementary services in schools which have large numbers of low SES children. Professionals can explore the possibility of having children from low SES families participate in one or more Title 1 programs for extra language stimulation and academic support. Hale (2004) also recommends that class sizes for primary grade students be reduced. Students from low SES backgrounds can be supported by ensuring that they have good, safe, appropriate class-rooms in which to learn.

Current Conditions in Low SES Schools

Schools that serve children from low SES families can be attractive, modern facilities with clean, well-maintained grounds. I was fortunate enough to work in such a school. The grounds were attractive and well maintained. The equipment was modern and up to date. Unfortunately, more commonly, schools for students from low SES backgrounds may be dilapidated and even segregated (Kozol, 2006; Talbert-Johnson, 2004). Many such schools also put children at risk for lead exposure (Chapter 1 reviewed the behavioral, cognitive, and academic deficits that can result from lead toxicity).

Of relevance here is the research of Johnson and Johnson (2002), who worked with third graders from low SES families in rural Louisiana. These investigators described in detail the physical deficiencies of these children's school.

I recently changed jobs in order to work closer to home. I love my new school district, where I serve part time as an itinerant speech-language pathologist. The school where I am housed, Hazel Elementary, is a lovely old school in a low SES part of the district. Giant oak trees grace the campus, and I feel happy every time I drive into the parking lot. The principal, staff, and teachers are warm and welcoming. I have my own room, which I share with the school counselor and personnel from Child Protective Services. My room is always clean because the custodian, a hardworking and cheerful man, keeps it spotless. However, because the school is old and California is having such great budget problems, upgrades to the facilities are not possible. Heating and air conditioning are issues. When I arrive early at work in the winter, the temperature in my room is often between 37 to 45 degrees. Last Christmas, I told my husband—no jewelry. I wanted a space heater! At the school, we all have them. When I was at work last Friday, it was a hot June day—and I was unable to unlock the door to my room. Bewildered, I told the school secretary about my dilemma. She smiled and shook her head. "Oh, that room," she said. "The heat always makes that door swell. You have to wriggle the key in the lock just right, and then throw your shoulder hard against the door to unwedge it." I started to laugh because I thought she was kidding. She wasn't. Kindly, she walked to the room with me, inserted the key in the lock, threw her shoulder against the door . . . and presto. Politely thanking her for taking time to do this, I mused about how this was really a first in my entire career. Truly, schools in low SES areas don't have the upgraded, modern facilities of schools in more middle and upper SES parts of town!

The walls had not been painted since the construction of the school in 1948. Ceilings were water-stained, and rooms teemed with spiders. Rats and ants were not uncommon. The rooms and hallways smelled of decades of mildew and accumulated dirt. Hot water was not available in the building. Many air conditioner/heating units broke year-round, leaving children either freezing in the winter or sweating in the summer as temperatures outdoors hit close to 110 degrees, with humidity.

One second grade teacher kept blankets in her room to warm the children, many of whom came to school with fevers and high chills. When the teacher tried to call home for sick children to be picked up, no one was available to come. The school provided neither a nurse's office nor cots for children taken ill. The 72 teachers in the building shared one toilet and a small sink: cold water only. During recess one day, a kindergartner relieved herself on the playground because no access to a restroom was provided for the children. There was no playground equipment at all. When these researchers asked a teacher what the children did at recess, she said: "They wrestle" (Johnson & Johnson, 2002, p. 19).

Although dramatic, this situation serves to illustrate the fact that teachers in low SES schools often have limited resources and less professional support than teachers from districts where families have more money. Perkins-Gough (2004) lists common problems experienced in low SES schools: inadequate facilities; dirty, locked, or inoperative student bathrooms; evidence of vermin such as rats and cockroaches in buildings; limited access to computers and the Internet; inadequate science equipment; and insufficient classroom materials and supplies. Disadvantaged students have limited access to up-to-date materials. One teacher described his experience in an inner-city school:

> There was no good place for me to get work done . . . I crossed my fingers every day hoping that the one copier was working. I kept paper in my car for the days when the school ran out . . . (Reinstein, 1998, p. 29)

My first position as an SLP was in a low-income elementary school. I had come from a relatively middle-class school (where I did my internship) with a large, nicely furnished, well-equipped speech therapy room. At my new school, the supplies provided on my first day consisted of one box of crayons, several puzzles with pieces missing, and one dated vocabulary test inappropriate for use with the students in my school. As a 23-year-old new clinician, I panicked. The district had virtually no budget. I ended up spending a significant amount of my meager salary buying supplies for the children, and I found some useful therapy materials I had collected in my graduate coursework. But I was appalled by the vast differences between the two schools.

With regard to school conditions, Chiu and Khoo (2005) conducted a study that examined how resources, distribution inequality, and biases toward privileged students affected academic performance.

In their study, 193,076 15-year-olds from 41 countries completed a questionnaire as well as tests in reading, mathematics, and science. The results of this study showed that students typically had lower scores in countries such as the United States, where clustering of privileged students in nicer schools, greater inequality, and unequal distribution of certified teachers were found. The three countries whose students scored the highest, Finland, Hong Kong, and South Korea, differed in three ways from lower-scoring countries such as the United States.

First, these three countries pursue education policies that give each student equal funding. Second, they mix students of various levels of family SES. Third, they require all new teachers to be certified.

Schools in the United States could improve in each one of these areas; again, in this large-scale international study, it was found that clustering of privileged students and qualified teachers into certain areas or schools had a negative impact on overall test scores in reading, mathematics, and science for students in underresourced areas. Chiu and Khoo recommended that federal governments can mitigate underinvestment in children from low SES families and can increase educational quality by providing universal access to educational resources as well as targeting additional resources for poorer students.

Unfortunately, in the United States, students from low SES backgrounds tend to cluster in the schools with the worst facilities and the most underprepared teachers. As part of structuring the school environment for the success of these students, this vast problem must be addressed at levels 1, 2, and 3: state/federal level, district/school site level, and, when possible, the individual level. Level 1 changes are especially necessary.

Concerning the achievement gap between students from low- and middle SES backgrounds, Barton (2004) characterizes the problem as follows:

> [Let's take] a malnourished child who entered the world at a below-average birthweight and now has health problems and decaying teeth. Will high standards, test-based accountability, and higher-quality teaching boost this child's achievement enough to eliminate the [achievement] gap? Not likely, although these actions are likely to raise his or her achievement . . . closing the gap must be more than a one-front operation. Educators must hold ourselves responsible and accountable for improving schools when and where we can. At the same time, we must recognize that the achievement gap has deep roots. *Governments, communities, neighborhoods,* and *families* have the responsibility to create conditions that remove barriers to cognitive development and support learning in the home [italics mine]. (p. 13)

One way in which this can be accomplished is through ensuring that teachers of children from low SES homes are well trained for and adequately supported in their work.

Teacher Preparation and Developing Professionalism

Both school and nonschool factors underlie the achievement gap between children from low and those from middle SES families. Conditions that improve learning both in and out of school are inextricably intertwined. Communities with wealthy families that value learning are likely to attract good teachers, have strong schools, and have healthy parent-teacher interactions. Low SES communities are less likely to attract experienced, qualified teachers and also are less likely to attract resources. Frequently, experienced teachers are sent to teach the children of the privileged; the least experienced are sent to teach children living in low SES neighborhoods. Yet professionals who work with students from low SES backgrounds need to be especially well prepared to teach these children.

Unfortunately, research shows that students from low SES and culturally and linguistically diverse groups often attend schools where they are taught by teachers who have minimal preparation and where there is high teacher turnover. Many low SES public schools don't pay their teachers as much as wealthier schools just a few miles away (Reuters, 2011). In California, 43% of teachers in high-risk schools reported that the rate of teacher turnover was a serious problem, compared with 11% of teachers in low-risk schools. In New York, 63% of teachers in high-risk schools reported teacher turnover rate to be a serious problem, in comparison with 17% in low-risk schools (Perkins-Gough, 2004). One study of 46 industrialized countries found that the U.S. ranked number 42 in providing equitable distribution of teachers to different groups of students. Sixty-eight percent of upper income eighth graders in the United States had high-quality math teachers; only 53% of the low SES schools had math teachers who were considered "high quality" (Breaden, 2008).

Teachers need support, including professional development, and time to collaborate with one another. In addition, teachers need adequate monetary compensation for their work. But why would a well-trained teacher take a low salary, teach in a poorly equipped school, and work under considerable pressure attempting to make children from low SES families perform up to standards of No Child Left Behind, especially when parental or home support is limited? Again, teachers need to be paid what they are worth and supported in areas of professional development.

Research suggests that a school's approach to professional development is most effective when it is linked with standards, tied to school improvement, and integrated into teachers' daily work (American Institutes for Research, 2005). Teachers need time to visit each other's classrooms and discuss what they can learn from each other.

Peer coaching can be very useful. Some schools use existing professional development funds to pay teachers a stipend for the time that they spend developing curriculum. Others use these funds to pay for substitutes so that teachers have additional time to share professional knowledge and observe in each others' classrooms.

Staff of successful, high-poverty elementary schools spend a great deal of time collaborating around instructional issues; research shows that scores improve when teachers have weekly planning time together (Picucci, Brownson, Kahlert, & Sobel, 2004). Like students, educators benefit from supportive relationships. Educators feel supported when they are given time to collaborate, provided with ongoing professional development and training, and recognized for their efforts.

> At the school where I worked for some years as an SLP, 9% of the children were White; the rest were children of color, and many came to kindergarten without speaking English. One-third of the students were English language learners, and more than 20 different languages were represented on campus. Sixty percent of the students qualified for a free or reduced-cost lunch program. As might be expected, teaching children from such diverse backgrounds posed many challenges. Fortunately, the school principal furnished a high level of support for the teaching staff. Weekly meetings provided an opportunity for teachers from each grade level to share, on an ongoing basis, what was happening in the classroom and how methods and materials could be improved. Inexperienced and experienced teachers shared ideas while the vice principal and others taught their classes for that hour. This was a very helpful strategy for supporting teachers as they strove to successfully work with the children. On the occasion of a Title One Achievement Award for the school, the principal even took the time to send a thank-you letter to each staff member at home.

As professionals who work with students from low SES backgrounds, teachers and others must hold appropriately high expectations for these students. Unfortunately, low expectations are common—this is a trap to be avoided. Little may be expected of students in high-poverty schools. Students in these schools may get fewer assignments, and the assignments that they do get may be "dumbed down." In some high-poverty urban middle schools, coloring assignments may be given. As described by Haycock (2001), in one urban high school the eleventh grade English teacher assigned students to read the book *To Kill a Mockingbird.* The teacher then asked the students to color a poster about the book afterwards.

Teachers and other professionals who work with students from low SES backgrounds need to be culturally responsive. They need to spend classroom and nonclassroom time developing personal relationships with their students. When these relationships are established, students respond favorably. Many low SES schools recognize that they need to extend services beyond the school day. These extended services help students feel a sense of belonging at the school. Haberman (2005) refers to "star teachers," who develop contacts with their students outside of school. They give significant amounts of time, before and after school, to students who need additional help with coursework. If the students appear in court, the teachers are there. One teacher stayed up all night with a seventh grade girl who was having a baby.

Because I hold down two jobs, travel, and have a 14-year-old son, I don't have a lot of extra time to spend with students outside of paid working hours. Many professionals experience a similar dilemma. However, I have found that being warm, caring, and concerned does not have to take much extra time out of my schedule. Literally, I have found that 5-minute conversations here and there, conversations which show concern and interest, cost me no money and very little time, and reap great dividends. Anecdotally, I have found that when my students feel like I care for them as people, they perform better academically. More is said about this in Chapter 7.

Payne (2003) states that, when students from low SES backgrounds who have made the transition to middle-class status are asked how they did it, most of these students cite relationships: with a coach, teacher, or other role model who took the time to be interested in them as individuals. Many children from low SES families cannot envision what skills and educational attainments are needed for professions such as teacher, dentist, lawyer, or social worker. In addition to serving as mentors and role models themselves, teachers also can find mentors in the community who are members of these professions and can come to schools and talk to children about their paths and how, specifically, they achieved their personal success.

To summarize, meta-analyses of the research identify six school factors associated with student achievement (Barton, 2004; Burke, 2012; Neuman, 2009; Reardon, 2011):

1. *Rigor of the curriculum.* The more appropriately rigorous the curriculum, the higher student achievement will be.
2. *Having experienced teachers.* Low SES and minority students are more likely to be taught by teachers who have three or fewer years of experience. These students need experienced teachers to guide them.
3. *Teacher preparation.* Students in high-poverty schools are much more likely to be taught by "out-of-field" teachers (Barton, 2004, p. 12). Students need teachers with expertise in the subjects that they are teaching.
4. *Class size.* Unfortunately, research indicates that classes with a high percentage of minority students are likely to have 25 or more students. Smaller class sizes are ideal.
5. *School safety.* Research has shown that a positive disciplinary climate is directly linked to higher achievement by students. It is hard for students to learn when they do not feel safe. The number of minority students who fear an attack on the way to school or at school is double that of nonminority students with such concerns. More minority than White students report avoiding going to one or more areas in the school because they feel that it is unsafe.
6. *Technology-assisted learning.* Research shows that although technology has permeated U.S. schools, computers are somewhat less likely to be available to minority than nonminority students. The gap widens in terms of the availability of the Internet in classrooms and becomes even wider for advanced use (e.g., conducting research on the Internet). In 1999, 61% of students in low-minority enrollment schools were assigned research projects utilizing the Internet; in schools with high-minority enrollments, only 31% of students were assigned such projects. Similar discrepancies exist in schools with high numbers of students from low SES backgrounds. Students from the most advantaged backgrounds are almost twice as likely to use the Internet as those from the least advantaged backgrounds (National Center for Education Statistics, 2005).

Obama (2006) stated:

> Sometimes we need both cultural transformation and government action—a change in values and a change in policy—to promote the kind of society we want. The state of our inner-city schools is a case in point. All the money in the world won't boost student achievement if parents make no effort to instill in their children the values of hard work and delayed gratification. But when we as a society pretend that poor children will fulfill their potential in dilapidated, unsafe schools with outdated equipment and teachers who aren't trained in the subjects they teach, we are perpetrating a lie on these children and on ourselves. We are betraying our values. (p. 63)

In addition to helping children from low SES homes fulfill their potential by providing better schools with appropriately trained teachers, we can support policies that integrate schools by students' SES. These policies help all students succeed.

INTEGRATING SCHOOLS BY STUDENTS' SOCIOECONOMIC STATUS

It is common knowledge that students are assigned to public schools based upon zip code/area of residence. Because of this, low SES children get clustered into schools together and often do not mix with middle SES children. This has a negative impact on the low SES students' performance in many areas.

In a recent study, Aikens and Barbarin (2008) used data from a cohort of 17,401 children in a longitudinal study of their performance from kindergarten through third grade. The purpose of the study was to examine the extent to which family, school, and neighborhood factors accounted for the impact of SES on children's early reading. Using hierarchical linear modeling techniques, growth curve models were estimated to depict subjects' reading trajectories from kindergarten through third grade. Family characteristics were the largest contributor to the prediction of initial kindergarten reading disparities. These family characteristics included parental involvement in school, home literacy environment, and parental role strain. However, neighborhood and school conditions contributed more than family characteristics to SES differences in reading learning rates. The relationship between school characteristics and reading outcomes suggested that the makeup of the student population, as indexed by poverty concentration and number of children with reading deficits in the school, was related to reading outcomes.

In sum, this study showed that for low SES kindergarten students, the main predictor of reading success was family factors. However, as students grew older, the main predictors of reading success were related to neighborhood and school conditions. Specifically, low SES students' reading achievement was negatively impacted by the fact that there were large concentrations of these students in certain schools. Having schools with large concentrations of low SES students, many of whom had reading deficits, was shown to correlate positively with negative reading performance outcomes. The greater the number of low-SES students in any given school, the lower the reading scores.

Clearly, it is important to integrate students by SES so that low-SES students will not be clustered in certain schools. A small but growing number of school districts are integrating students by SES. These districts include San Francisco, California; La Crosse, Wisconsin; Cambridge, Massachusetts; and Wake County, North Carolina.

In 2000, the Wake County school board voted that no school should have more than 40% of its students eligible for free or reduced-cost public lunch or have more than 25% of its students performing below grade level. Early results of Wake County's plan indicate that it is raising achievement for all students (Rumberger & Palardy, 2005). What is the basis for these results?

Research indicates that student achievement is driven primarily by the socioeconomic makeup of a school, not by its racial makeup. As stated earlier, schools which have large numbers of low SES children tend to have overall lower achievement scores than schools with more middle SES children. Clustering low SES children in certain schools is a less than optimal practice. The SES of a school is the single most important determinant of academic success (Kahlenberg, 2006).

Rumberger and Palardy (2005) found that a school's overall SES has as much impact on the achievement growth of high school students as did the students' individual SES backgrounds. Scores from the 2000 National Assessment of Educational Progress showed that students from low SES backgrounds attending middle SES schools performed better in math than did middle-class students attending high-poverty schools (National Center for Education Statistics, 2005).

Why is it advantageous for students to avoid high-poverty schools? These schools tend to have low parental involvement, high student mobility, and high teacher turnover. In addition, as noted previously, teachers in low SES schools, on average, have less experience and training than teachers in middle SES schools. In addition, in low SES schools, students are more likely to disparage academic achievement (more is said about this in Chapter 7).

In response to these issues, Wake County redrew school district boundaries and made extensive use of magnet schools with special music and arts programs, foreign language options, and other attractive choices: choices that middle SES parents want. Almost all of the special-theme magnet schools were located in high-poverty areas in Raleigh. At this time, although many of the magnet schools are in "tough neighborhoods," several have waiting lists. Students from low- and middle SES backgrounds are being increasingly integrated as middle SES parents choose magnet schools with desirable programs for their children (Rumberger & Palardy, 2005).

Wake County's students from low SES backgrounds are performing substantially better than those from other urban low SES North Carolina districts with concentrated poverty. On the 2005 High School End-of-Course examinations, 63.8% of the Wake County students passed, compared with 47.8%, 27.9%, and 48.7% of those in neighboring counties. Wake County's students from middle SES backgrounds are achieving at high levels. The results of Wake County's program are consistent with those of national research that finds that students from middle SES backgrounds do well in economically integrated schools, as long as the concentrations of poverty do not reach above 50% (Kahlenberg, 2006; Rumberger & Palardy, 2005).

Cambridge, Massachusetts, has drawn students from private into public schools by making every school a magnet school. The district allows families to choose from among the district's 12 elementary schools, each of which offers a special and distinctive program. Cambridge requires that the percentage of students eligible for reduced-cost or free lunch must fall within a small range of the district-wide average (43%). Parents rank their preferences for which schools they would like their children to attend. The district then assigns students with the overarching goal of achieving economic school integration. More than 90% of students receive one of their first three choices (Fiske, 2002).

When Cambridge first implemented this controlled-choice plan in the early 1980s, the district had a 13% increase in new minority students and a 32% increase in new White students. The proportion of school-aged children in the community attending public (not private) schools rose from 88 to 95%. Kahlenberg (2006) states that if educators are serious about narrowing achievement gaps and raising the performance of students from low SES backgrounds, more districts should consider giving all students the chance to attend majority, middle SES public schools.

My own experience as the parent of an elementary school child bears out the feasibility of attracting middle SES families to low SES schools. It is interesting to look at my own life situation. Mark is the only child of two White, middle SES parents, both of whom have Ph.D.s. The first school my son attended mirrored the White, middle- class lifestyle my husband and I enjoyed. The school building was only 20 to 30 years old and had a modern new computer laboratory, as well as a fairly new multipurpose room. The grounds were well manicured, and the classrooms were clean, bright, and modern. Many of the parents, and children, were expensively and trendily dressed.

By contrast, the elementary school my son transferred to in third grade, where he was very happy with his new classmates and teachers, was built over 100 years ago. The buildings were quite decrepit and expensive to heat and air condition. Carpets were perpetually dirty, despite the custodians' best efforts, and some even had holes in them. In one of the classrooms, despite the school's best efforts at repair, rain literally came through the ceiling.

The school did its best by adding new play equipment to the playground and painting colorful murals on the ancient walls, but this did not compensate for the lack of space for a school library. There was no computer laboratory. The overall SES of the parents at Mark's new school appeared to be lower than that of the parents from his previous school; certainly his new school had more minority students.

> Why would middle-class parents move their child out of a much newer, more modern school into one that was literally falling apart, and in which the overall SES of the parents and children is lower? The answer for my husband and me was the lure of its fine arts program and kindergarten-through-eighth-grade structure. My personal experience is in accord with Kahlenberg (2006), who maintains that middle SES parents can be attracted to schools with students from predominantly low SES backgrounds if the school has a specialty that is attractive: a specialty such as fine arts or a foreign language emphasis.

Successful integration of children from low and middle SES homes into the same school has been well demonstrated in districts such as Wake County and Cambridge. It bears emphasis that the overall improvement in test scores had nothing to do with ethnic background and everything to do with SES. Part of the success of these school districts was related to the provision of supportive programs and relationships.

SCHOOL ENHANCEMENT: PROVIDING SUPPORTIVE PROGRAMS AND RELATIONSHIPS FOR STUDENTS FROM LOW SES BACKGROUNDS

Parallel Education Systems

The importance of supportive programs and relationships for students from low SES backgrounds cannot be overemphasized (Roseberry-McKibbin, 2013). Olszewski-Kubilius and associates (2004) point out that some of the most academically successful groups in the nation have created a network of supplementary opportunities for their children; these can be thought of as a *parallel education system*. The term "parallel education system" is highly accurate: it describes the opportunities given to middle and upper SES children and highlights the utter contrast between them as reflected by the lack of opportunities available to most children from low SES families. Many middle SES parents, for example, enroll their children in after-school art, theater, and sports programs and provide (often expensive) lessons in areas of interest to the child, such as ballet, horseback riding, or karate; tutoring, family trips, and other broadening experiences for children are commonplace in these families as well. Low SES children are not exposed to these same opportunities.

Reardon (2011), in his analysis of the growing achievement gap in the United States between low- and middle/high-SES children, found that a variable strongly related to this gap was the amount of money families spent on their children. He stated that perhaps because of parents' increasing involvement in their children's cognitive development, middle- and high-SES parents in the 21st century invest a great deal more money in their children than parents did even back in the 1970s. Middle- and upper SES parents' provision of a parallel education system for their children is much greater than it was 25 years ago. A factor discussed elsewhere in this book is that many more low SES than middle SES homes are headed by single mothers who cannot afford to provide parallel education for their children. School sites and districts can help to create this parallel education system for their students. At level 2, the district/school site level, professionals are in good position to encourage and provide structures and programs that promote learning for students from low SES backgrounds (Neuman, 2009). One of these programs is all-day kindergartens.

All-Day Kindergartens

The learning gap between children from low- and those from middle-SES homes grows smaller when children are enrolled in all-day kindergarten (Posnick-Goodwin, 2006). In most schools, children attend kindergarten for a half-day (or approximately 3½ hours). Individual schools and school districts with large numbers of students from low SES backgrounds, especially those who have never been to preschool, can consider the possibility of all-day kindergartens. Children who are at risk for educational underachievement should begin kindergarten in the summer before school officially begins. They also should participate in a booster summer program after kindergarten to better prepare them for the requirements of first grade (Takanishi, 2006). Among other things, these programs should incorporate a strong focus on emergent literacy skills.

Schools can help prevent many later problems in children's literacy skills by administering intensive, targeted prevention programs in the early grades, especially kindergarten. If kindergartens last all day, teachers have more time to administer much needed focused literacy programs. This is supported by IDEA 2004 (the 2004 version of the Individuals with Disabilities Education Act), which emphasizes early intervention in early grades to reduce referrals to special education. This early intervention emphasis applies to reading especially.

Clark (2012) summarizes research which consistently documents more positive academic outcomes for all children enrolled in all-day kindergartens. Children who attend all-day kindergarten score higher on standardized tests, have fewer grade retentions, and higher levels of first grade readiness than children who do not attend all-day kindergarten. They also rate higher on teacher observations of social skills.

Parents report that all-day kindergartens benefit their children socially, and that teachers in these programs provide suggestions for home activities more frequently. Teachers surveyed believe that they have more time for individual instruction; they also have more time to get to know children and families, thus enabling them to better meet children's individual needs. Some studies have found that in all-day kindergartens, teachers are able to devote more time to small group instruction and place a greater emphasis on small group activities when compared with half-day programs; half-day programs typically emphasize less individualized, large-group instruction much more (Clark, 2012).

Implementing the Arts

Arts education can have powerful effects on struggling students, especially if they are from low SES backgrounds. Studies have found that gains associated with arts participation are greatest for students at most risk for academic failure: those in the lowest SES quartile (Rabkin & Redmond, 2006). Rabkin and Redmond cited studies showing that integrating the arts into the regular school curriculum was extremely helpful for low-performing students, especially students who were nonproductive, disruptive, and withdrawn (e.g., Ingram & Seashore, 2003).

As an example, art can be integrated into history by having students make a felt quilt with each patch representing a key idea in the Constitution. To help students grasp math concepts, teachers can use music. Students can listen to a simple melody, follow the notes on a musical staff, count the number of times each note occurs, and graph the results.

With educators under so much pressure to have students perform well on standardized tests, the arts often are neglected, much to students' detriment. Many schools align with the dominant education policy in the United States today: this policy assumes that struggling students will not achieve high standards without a relentless, drill-and-kill focus on academic fundamentals, behavioral control, and a strong emphasis on testing. But research has shown that integrating arts into the regular curriculum can help even with standardized test scores.

In one study, a low SES school implemented an arts-integrated approach to the teaching curriculum. The number of students at the school scoring at or above national norms in reading comprehension tripled in 5 years, and 20% more eighth graders than third graders were found to perform academically at or above their grade level. At a more conventional school several blocks away, more third graders than eighth graders were found to be working at grade level, a pattern that is much more typical of students from low SES backgrounds (Weissmann, 2004).

Rabkin and Redmond (2006) state that with effort, even the poorest of schools can integrate arts into the curriculum. Level 1 support is necessary for this to occur, however. As these investigators point out, arts education deserves far more than a meager $35 million line item in a federal education budget of some $70 billion. Integrated arts education should be the target of a healthy proportion of state and local education budgets as well. Why? Because these programs work. (p. 64)

Students from low SES backgrounds need exposure to music, plays, art, and museums (Gustafson, 2002). Because so many of these students are not exposed to the world at large, field trips are extremely important. Teachers and schools need a supportive environment and freedom to take students on field trips where they can learn what their more privileged peers learn from their home environments and from their parents. Students from low SES backgrounds also can benefit from supplemental programs that provide further enrichment.

Providing Supplemental Programs

During the first 18 years of their lives, students spend approximately 20% of their waking hours in school (Neuman, 2009). Neuman points out that students have 185 free days a year. Thus, students' achievement can be raised by making good use of the other 80% of their time; this is most effectively accomplished by working with caregivers and also providing programs outside school (e.g., before and after school, during vacations). Schools can help boost the achievement of inadequately performing students from low SES backgrounds by providing "extras" via funds to extend instruction. For example, Kentucky gives schools money to provide additional instruction before school, after school, and during the summer. Other states have initiated summer programs. Another example, mentioned earlier, is the implementation of all-day kindergarten.

One innovative strategy is for elementary schools to provide prekindergarten experience for children. A free pre-kindergarten program was implemented in the school where I worked as an SLP for some years. One summer, the principal other school personnel looked at the list of children preregistered early for kindergarten. They called the parents of these children and asked if they would be interested in having the children participate in a free "prekindergarten" program. In the principal's words, the parents' response to the proposal was "overwhelming." Using Title 1 funds, a program was created for the looks like there is a spacing issue hereschool year in which 40 children (in four groups of 10) attended school for 20 half-days before they formally began kindergarten. They spent time with a credentialed teacher learning school basics such as classroom routines, classroom behavior expectations, and classroom language. They were introduced to basic concepts such as the alphabet and numbers. Preliminary results indicated that, with use of prekindergarten programs, children were much better prepared for the demands of formal schooling. For these children, school was much less of a "culture shock." They adjusted better to kindergarten and performed better academically than children who did not participate in the program.

In addition to prekindergarten programs, schools also can implement after-school programs. For children from low SES families, after-school programs are an excellent place to spend precious resources that can help boost the skills and abilities of at-risk students. While low SES parents struggle to provide shelter and food for their families, thousands of children are left without an enriching, safe place to be after school gets out. Today, more than 78% of mothers of school-aged children work outside the home; as many as 10 million children ages 6 to 9 years care for themselves (Neuman, 2009). As Neuman states (p. 158), "too many children must fend for themselves in libraries, malls, subway stations, and neighborhood stores, or behind locked doors in housing developments. We need to break this grim cycle by making out-of-school time productive for children."

The few hours between the end of school and when parents get home from work are some of the most underutilized and dangerous in children's lives. The impact on the community is major: Juvenile crime triples when school is over for the day; children have a fourfold greater chance of being the victim of violent crime during after-school hours; children left unsupervised for 11 or more hours per week have twice the risk of substance abuse than those who experience adult supervision; and, unsupervised children are three times more likely to become teen parents (Cain, 2004).

Also of relevance are home and neighborhood resources such as books, libraries, computers, trips to educational places, and so forth. Research has shown that these home and neighborhood resources seem to have the greatest impact on students' achievement when school is not in session, before students enter school, during after-school hours, and during the summer. Neuman (2009) discusses the "summer slide" (p. 36), noting that when schools are open during the regular academic year, students from low and high SES backgrounds make comparable gains in math and reading. During the summer, however, the more privileged students continued to improve academically, whereas the less advantaged students lose ground. Aikens and Barbarin (2008) agree, stating that research converges upon the act that summer experiences are more responsible for the often discussed achievement gap than are experiences during the academic year.

These findings are in keeping with the recognized value of the "parallel education" typical for children of middle- and high-SES families, including summer school or private tutors, as well as parent-child reading experiences and family trips. Students from low SES backgrounds usually do not have any of these advantages. They play with their friends, watch TV, and play computer games during their free time. Schools can help these students by providing summer enrichment programs to help them not lose ground while school is out. Some school districts work with nonprofit organizations to provide summer tutoring, reading, and enrichment programs for low SES students.

It is ideal if extra (e.g., summer and after school) programs can provide a balance of physical activity, socialization, and academic support. Children as young as elementary school age struggle with health issues such as diabetes. The average third grader in urban communities engages in less than 25 minutes of vigorous exercise daily outside of school. Over 65% of urban children do not participate in extracurricular activities that involve any form of physical exercise. Thirty-two percent of students are obese or overweight (Cain, 2004). Children's participation in sports is far more time-consuming and expensive than generally is recognized, and low SES families have difficulty affording to enroll their children in organized sports.

> For example, as noted elsewhere, the cost of my son's karate lessons was approximately $150 a month (to which must be added the gas money to drive him to karate several times a week). This expense is modest, however, in comparison with the cost of participation in a high school soccer program by a colleague's daughter: between $2000 and $3000 a year. The parents of some of Mark's friends pay $6,000 per season for their children to participate in competitive soccer. Low SES parents typically do not have the money for even low-cost programs for their children, so supplemental programs such as after-school and summer programs can provide opportunities for physical activity for these students.

Schools may especially need to offer support to children from homes in which the parents' background differs from that assumed by the school. Even though I am a White, middle-class parent, for example, I grew up in the Philippines, so my scholastic knowledge doesn't include much that would be considered the "basics" in today's schools. As a result, I have experienced some degree of cultural dissonance in helping my son with his homework assignments. For example, in third grade, Mark brought home his social studies book so he could finish an assignment about Pocahontas. I have certainly seen the Disney movie, but growing up in the Philippines, we did not study many of the things (like Pocahontas) that are taught in American schools. Mark is finishing eighth grade now; in the fall, he will be enrolled in a public high school where one of his classes will be Honors Biology. We ordered the textbook on Amazon so that he could study it over the summer; I am studying it with him!

I am increasingly humbled by how much I don't know, and how challenging it is for me to help Mark with his homework sometimes, even though I have a Ph.D. in speech-language pathology. I can talk about Philippine national hero Jose Rizal, describing how he died serving his country; I can sing the Philippine national anthem, and describe the islands and provinces of this lovely archipelago nation. I can explain how to treat a jellyfish sting, and how to dig for oysters in the sand. I can talk about the tides, and how to watch out for undertows. But I am very hard pressed to discuss Pocahontas' marriage to John Rolf, or to know the name of her father. I have limited understanding of American history and politics, and am thankful that I can direct my son to his father when he has questions in these areas. When these kinds of situations occur with my son, I am vividly reminded of how we, as professionals, must not assume that parents have even general knowledge of curriculum content; we may need to provide extra support to students from families in which parental knowledge or background does not match the school's expectations.

Students may need support with homework for other reasons: (1) they don't know how to do it, (2) they don't have time to (e.g., they may need to help families with child care or other tasks), (3) they don't plan, and (4) they don't want to do homework because they do not see that it is meaningful to their lives. Payne (2003) discusses a very successful middle school program in Texas. The last 45 minutes of the school day are scheduled for homework. Students who don't get their homework done must go to the cafeteria, where tutors assist them with their homework. They must stay until the homework is done. A pre-arranged late bus takes the students home.

My son Mark and I currently serve in an after-school support program in our district. Students who live in a low-SES apartment complex usually come home to an empty apartment because their parents are working several jobs (minimum wage) just to pay for rent and food. Through a district-funded program, these students can come to the apartment complex's recreation room and read books, play games, and obtain homework support. It has been very gratifying to assist these students, who are grateful for the extra help that their parents are unable to provide. When we were there last Wednesday, Mark helped some students with math while I worked at another table with several girls (second and third grade). They had math assignments, but didn't seem to know how to do them without my help. When we sat down at the table to actually do the worksheets, the girls did just fine. I realized that what they truly needed and wanted was an interested, caring adult to sit with them and encourage them while they did their homework. The girls didn't mind that I didn't speak fluent Spanish and was a new adult in their world; they were just happy to have me with them (and I loved being there!)

Schools also can support low SES students by giving them a "trip into the future." Several programs that expose low SES students to universities are described later in this chapter. In some schools, during the spring semester, sixth graders are taken to the middle school for a field trip to see what the middle school is like. Each student who transfers from elementary to middle school is allowed to select one friend to be assigned to his homeroom class so that he or she will be guaranteed to see a familiar face on beginning middle school in the fall.

Opportunities for Schools to Connect with Community Resources

As noted at the beginning of the chapter, it takes a village to raise a child. Parents cannot succeed alone in raising children to be successful; neither can schools. At level 2, the school site and school district level, professionals have a number of options. Several of these involve working with local churches, retired persons, other community organizations, and older students.

Members of local religious organizations can be recruited to provide tutoring services to students. (Note: I refer to these as *churches*;

however, we should remember that many places of worship are referred to by labels such as *synagogue, mosque,* and *temple.*) If students speak a language other than English, a church whose members speak this language can be approached. For example, Sacramento, California, has over 100,000 immigrants and refugees from the former Union of Soviet Socialist Republics. Several years ago, in response to my request for assistance on a research project requiring a knowledge of Russian, the pastor of a local Russian church was extremely helpful, spending time translating documents and recruiting church members for the project. The pastor shared that he was very happy for the opportunity to make connections between the church and the wider community, in this case, the university.

Churches have great untapped resources of people who are willing to work with students of all ages. Religious institutions traditionally view opportunities to volunteer as opportunities to "serve" in a general sense. These institutions can be asked to support schools' work with students in two ways. First, congregation members can come to school sites and work with students there—as volunteers in classrooms or as volunteers in after-school programs that provide tutoring services on site. Churches also may be asked to provide after-school programs at the church sites themselves. Clearly, transportation would have to be worked out. In some communities, students can walk to the church.

Even in low-income neighborhoods, churches may be clean and well-maintained buildings, perfect places for students to come after school, where they can be tutored in academic subjects and even engage in safe recreational activities such as basketball. As noted, it is common knowledge that the time period between 3 and 6 in the afternoon constitutes peak hours for juvenile crime as well as experimentation with drugs, alcohol, and cigarettes, hours when many "latchkey kids" are home alone with no adult supervision. Nationally, more than 14 million school-age children (25%) are alone after school each day. Among them are more than 40,000 kindergartners (Neuman, 2009).

Working at school sites with adults or going to after-school programs sponsored by churches would substantially help many students from low SES backgrounds to keep out of trouble and have safe, supportive places to be while their parents work. In these places, they may form those close relationships with adults that can help them rise out of poverty and see a future that is different from the one currently experienced by their parents. The church I attend has several hundred church members who meet with struggling third graders once a week to provide reading tutoring. This is done for free, because the tutoring is viewed as a ministry and thus all tutors work on a volunteer basis.

In addition to seeking extra support from churches, professionals may seek assistance from retired persons, many of whom are healthy, active, and looking for meaning and purpose in their retirement years. For example, a family friend with a doctorate in education is retired from his full-time job, but he tutors children through the Kiwanis club, a community service agency. He loves this work and looks forward to the fulfilling task of helping struggling students succeed academically.

In one example of a successful venture that connects retired persons with low SES students, Tucson, Arizona, has a program called Experience Corps. It is a program of Civic Ventures, a Washington, D.C., nonprofit organization that aims to help children out of poverty by reducing school dropout rates. Experience Corps links adults over 55 years of age with children and youth in their communities. These volunteers read with children, tutor them, help them increase their self-confidence, and help them get on the pathway to a stable, middle-class life. In this nationwide program, 80% of the children who participated increased their reading skills by at least half a grade level (Kornman, 2004).

Volunteers receive 20 hours of training before they meet with students. In addition, they receive ongoing training in child development, lesson planning, and tutoring strategies. Volunteers receive a small stipend for their services, and their skills are evaluated by on-site supervisors. Because today's older Americans are healthier, better educated, and living longer than any group in history, programs like Experience Corps can utilize their time and energy in helping children, particularly those from underprivileged communities.

A number of other service organizations whose members enjoy working with students are are available in most cities: Junior Leagues, Rotary Clubs, Shriners, Scottish Rite Centers, and others. These organizations often are looking for volunteer outreach opportunities. High school students also can be recruited to work with younger students. For example, the state of California has a community service requirement: Students cannot graduate from high school without fulfilling it.

In some elementary schools, students from the local high school help teachers with tasks ranging from xeroxing to grading homework. Their help might be better utilized in working directly with elementary students who are struggling academically. Younger students typically look up to high school students as being "cool"—so high school students, when properly trained, can be extremely influential in the lives of elementary and junior high school students. College students represent another potential source of support for teachers to utilize. College students in programs such as education and speech-language pathology are often looking for local volunteer opportunities in schools that will help them prepare for their professions.

For college students who do volunteer work with children in local schools, college coursework often "comes alive" as they are able to relate information in textbooks and professors' lectures to actual children they are working with. As a professor, I have found that my students who work with children in local schools tend understand course content better because they are actually able to apply it in a "real world" setting. It would be ideal if colleges, elementary schools, junior high schools, and high schools could collaborate to utilize the skills, ingenuity, and volunteer spirit of older students.

To summarize, professionals can tap into many local organizations, both religious and nonreligious, to provide extra support to students from low SES backgrounds who struggle in school (Matsumoto & Brown-Welty, 2009). Again, for students to get out of poverty, they need close personal relationships with mentors, and these mentors can be recruited from local organizations, high schools, and religious institutions (Holcomb-McCoy, 2011.)

Because many low SES students live with so many stressors (described in Chapter 1), school and community programs can help them to learn to become more resilient. *Resilience* refers to achieving positive outcomes despite risk. Resilient people are able to lead more successful lives than expected despite being a greater than average risk for serious problems. A resilient child is able to live with the future in mind, and to look ahead with hope. Resilience is an ecological phenomenon that cannot be developed by the sheer willpower of the at-risk person; it is developed through connections with the environment. The bond between parent and child is the most critical factor in a child's development of resilience. Other sources of building resilience in children include neighborhoods, schools, and the community at large. Environments can provide protection and enhance the possibility of positive outcomes. Because some families may be difficult to reach, schools can provide a buffer for students at risk and contribute to positive development. Perceived connectedness with a school is associated with reduction in violent behaviors, substance abuse, and levels of emotional distress (Brooks, 2006).

An ecological model of resilience building involves surrounding students with a network of nurturing, supportive relationships. This network includes the family, community organizations, neighborhoods, and religious organizations. Supportive networks of relationships can enhance students' academic performance, resilience, self-esteem, and motivation to succeed in school.

Barone (2006) describes teachers who promoted resilience in their students:

> [S]everal teachers did more than teach the curriculum. They found time before, during, and after school to chat, work with students, and as a result build friendships. During class time, they nurtured students as they helped them achieve the high expectations they set . . . they developed personal relationships with students and supported them as they attempted to reach high expectations . . . the intermediate teachers, even though their classes were larger than primary classes, found time to converse with students and support them as individuals in their academic and personal endeavors.

As part of promoting resilience, professionals can work to accurately identify gifts and talents in SES students. If these gifts and talents are recognized and nurtured, students' educational and thus future vocational opportunities will be enhanced.

SERVING GIFTED STUDENTS
FROM LOW SES BACKGROUNDS

Experts have stated that students from low SES backgrounds tend to be underrrepresented in programs for gifted and talented children. Three major barriers exist to these students' being served in gifted programs: (1) difficulty with identification for these programs owing to biased standardized tests, (2) low teacher expectations, and (3) lack of appropriately challenging curricula for these students, many of whom are culturally and linguistically diverse (CLD) (G.A.T.E. Resources, 2012; Kitano, 2003; Olszewski-Kubilius et al., 2004).

Some authors have suggested that the odds are distinctly against enrollment of gifted children of low-income families in appropriate academic development programs:

Things like poor kids and gifted programs just don't go together. . . . I think that people in their heart of hearts really think that when kids are poor, they can't possibly perform at the level of kids that are advantaged because they haven't had certain kinds of advantages in their home. I call them my list of prerequisites to being gifted. You must have two parents; they must be college educated. You must be White. You must be in the suburbs. I know this sounds a little bit facetious, but if you look at the enrollment in gifted programs, it's not facetious. (Swanson, 2006, p. 11)

Chapter 3 addressed the drawbacks of using standardized tests with students from low SES backgrounds, particularly CLD students. In addition to the inherent bias of standardized tests, teachers' low expectations of these students is a key variable in their low performance. Coleman and Southern (2006) state that among the gifted are children with potential who are economically disadvantaged, have a disability, or are limited English-proficient. All are underserved. Many explanations have been offered.

A strong consensus exists that the lack of identification of such children for gifted programs is a problem that lies outside the child, implying that the identification system is the problem. Lohman (2005) suggest that many of the most talented CLD students have not had opportunities to develop high levels of the skills valued in formal schooling. Olszewski-Kubilius and colleagues (2004) point out that, in the twelfth grade, underrepresented minorities typically constitute only 5% of students with the high SAT scores typical for students who gain entrance into the most selective institutions of higher education. Blacks, Native Americans, and Hispanics are underrepresented in advanced placement classes

To address this situation, experts have recommended some specific strategies. One is to use multiple assessment instruments and alternative methods for identifying gifted students from low SES minority backgrounds. These methods can include performance-based assessment measures based on Gardner's theory of multiple intelligences, discussed in Chapter 7 (e.g., Olszewski-Kubilius et al., 2004). Teachers can be trained to look for ways to develop children's identified types of intelligence (e.g., linguistic, musical, mathematical, spatial, interpersonal). Nonverbal ability tests also can be used, although it probably is best for professionals to be trained to look for and cultivate different kinds of intelligences.

Another strategy for identifying and serving gifted students from low SES backgrounds was implemented in South Carolina. Educators of the gifted at three South Carolina elementary schools took a different approach to the issue of underidentification of CLD students from low SES backgrounds. These teachers adopted instruction methods and curricula typically reserved for higher-achieving, gifted students and used them with *all* of their students (Olszewski-Kubilius et al., 2004). The teachers used units developed by the Center for Gifted Education at the College of William and Mary as a starting point.

This project, called Project Breakthrough, focused on several major areas. First, staff demonstrated successfully that using high-end curricula developed for gifted and talented high-achieving students had a positive effect on all students' achievement. Second, the staff all took part in continuing education activities that increased their understanding of how to boost the challenge and rigor of their content and instruction. The results of Project Breakthrough showed that many students showed significant gains in achievement.

As supported by the approach described for Project Breakthrough, teachers need to treat all students as though they are gifted and teach them in ways that challenge them to do and be their best. Another highly recommended approach uses Gardner's theory of multiple intelligences (described in more detail in Chapter 7) as a springboard for helping all students find and develop their strengths.

It is instructive to compare the programs used to identify and support gifted children in two different elementary schools. At one school, serving primarily children of middle SES families, children are identified as qualifying for gifted and talented education (GATE) by use of a paper-and-pencil, standardized intelligence test and by state test achievement scores. Children who are bright, creative, and talented in various ways but whose learning or test-taking ability is challenged by delayed development of visual and fine motor skills, for example, will not qualify for GATE at this school.

At this middle SES school, everyone knows who is a GATE kid and who is not. GATE at this school is a separate, "pull-out" program: As their classmates look on, GATE-enrolled children leave the classroom each Thursday afternoon for a special program for "the smart kids." Large letters on the bulletin board in front of the school announce "GATE Night" for parents of those children who have been identified as qualifying for GATE: the intellectual elite. Parents of GATE children proudly attend this meeting; the rest of the parents stay home, feeling that their children are in some way intellectually inferior. Their children, so obviously excluded from certain activities, may well experience some loss of self-esteem.

At another elementary school, which serves both middle- and low SES families, children are not regarded as "less than" in any way. At this school, everyone is smart. No GATE program per se is in place. Many curricular and extracurricular activities are made available to develop children's intelligences. Those who are budding artists love Art Club but also may excel in (or even just enjoy) other areas. Musically gifted children may join choir. An after-school Spanish club is planned to support multilingualism. This school's philosophy is that every child is gifted; the principal and the teachers subscribe to Gardner's theory of multiple intelligences. According to this school, it is the job of the school and the parents to identify children's gifts and to make GATE-type opportunities available to everyone.

As previously mentioned, Mark will start high school this fall. There are excellent high schools in our district; we are so grateful. The high school we chose, Casa Roble, is a flexible high school that has a broad definition of GATE. A feature we especially appreciate about Casa is that there are classes and educational opportunities for students who are "good with their hands." These students may not excel in academics, but many are gifted in areas such as mechanics and woodworking. Casa recognizes this, and promotes coursework and opportunities that support these students in choosing careers that they can excel in, even if academic courses are not their strong suit.

As another example of an innovative way to serve gifted students from low SES backgrounds, Coleman and Southern (2006) described an acceleration program developed for used with such students. Accelerating Achievement in Math and Science in Urban Schools (AAMSUS) is a research and demonstration grant funded under the Javits Education for Gifted and Talented Program. For participation in the AAMSUS-funded program, the researchers selected 200 fourth-grade children from low SES families in two Ohio cities, Dayton and Toledo. Teachers and parents were actively involved. Teachers nominated children for the AAMSUS-funded program on the basis of standardized tests, curriculum-based assessments, and their own personal recommendations.

On Saturdays, children in the AAMSUS-funded program were transported from their local schools to a high-interest math and science enrichment program at two local universities. The children also received focused instruction during the summer at the university sites. In addition, they participated in a residential program in which they lived on the college campuses for 10 days. They slept in the dorms, ate dorm food, and utilized laboratory and classroom facilities. This program allowed the students to experience life on a college campus (Coleman & Southern, 2006).

Preliminary results of the AAMSUS-funded program showed that many students demonstrated strong evidence of academic achievement; other students did not. Anecdotally, teachers reported that students acted differently at their home school sites. Homework was finished more promptly. Many more conversations about curriculum content were noted; such conversations were rare before the summer program. As Saturday approached, students were excited. Their behavior improved noticeably; they did not want to jeopardize their continuing program participation by misbehaving in school.

Basically, AAMSUS identified children with early potential, measured their strengths and abilities in math and science curricula, and provided accelerative experiences (in-class enrichment, summer college residential programs, and Saturday classes). In addition, AAMSUS built a support network for students that included a cohort, mentors, and trained professionals.

As previously discussed, students from low SES backgrounds can scarcely be expected to thrive without such networks, and most successful academic programs help provide this support. With all low SES CLD gifted students, professionals need to create a multicultural learning environment and make sure that the curriculum reflects a variety of cultures. If professionals provide this type of environment and connect students with role models and mentors, they can and will thrive and succeed, becoming engaged contributors to society (G.A.T.E. Resources, 2012).

It is critical for professionals to be aware that students from low-SES backgrounds, especially CLD students, are regularly underidentified for participation in any type of program for gifted and talented students. Through use of innovative and flexible means of identifying these students, they can be provided with the support and nurture that they deserve, the support so often available only to students from families with more money.

CONCLUSIONS

The tremendous inequalities in schooling opportunities for low- and middle SES students have contributed to a growing achievement gap in our country. There are solutions to this problem at levels 1, 2, and 3. If these solutions are implemented regularly and conscientiously at all levels, we can level the playing field and help all students succeed, not just those who happen to be born in the right zip code.

Rothstein (2004) points out that:

[P]eople are so wedded to the notion that school reform alone is sufficient. . . . For nearly half a century, economists, sociologists, and educators have been aware of the association of social and economic disadvantage with student achievement gaps. Most, however, have avoided the obvious implication of this understanding: Raising the achievement of low-income children requires *ameliorating the social and economic conditions of their lives, not just reforming schools* [italics mine]. (p. 43)

All professionals who work with children need to pull together to reform school practices and to implement laws and policies that will ameliorate the social and economic conditions that keep children from low SES homes from experiencing the future they deserve: a future filled with hope and opportunity.

CHAPTER HIGHLIGHTS

▨ Research over the decades consistently documents the growing achievement gap between minority, low SES students and White, middle SES students. Unfortunately, the dropout rate of the former group is high, with incalculable costs to society.

- Laws have been enacted to try to close the achievement gap; these laws and their attempted enforcement have not had the intended results.
- Schools in low SES areas often attempt to serve students with facilities that are dilapidated, dated, and sometimes downright dangerous. Resources and materials are limited; teachers are often inadequately trained and lack experience.
- We must pay good teachers well for their work. In some countries, the salaries of teachers are equivalent to those of engineers and doctors. Skilled, well-paid teachers in the United States tend to cluster in middle and upper SES schools. We must attract these teachers to serve students in low SES schools and neighborhoods.
- Low SES students tend to respond especially well to teachers who are warm, caring, and willing to establish relationships with them. In these relationships, teachers often serve as mentors who help low SES students dream of a brighter future where they can become educated and productive.
- Meta-analyses of research identify six school factors associated with higher student achievement: (1) rigor of the curriculum, (2) the availability of well-qualified and experienced teachers, (3) small class sizes, (4) safe schools, and (5) technology-assisted learning.
- In the United States, large concentrations of low SES students cluster in schools; this can have deleterious effects on their performance. One way that some states have found of successfully integrating schools by SES is the provision of specialized, attractive programs (e.g., art, music, technology). Housed in magnet schools in low SES areas, these programs often attract middle SES parents who want specialized programs for their children.
- Low SES students benefit from the provision of a parallel education system. Middle SES parents provide this system for their children through enriching experiences and activities outside of school; most low SES parents cannot afford these experiences and activities. Research shows that low SES students benefit greatly from all day kindergarten, implementation of the arts, enriching summer and after-school programs, and connections with community resources (e.g., churches, retired persons).

■ If low SES students receive the benefits of a parallel education system, this can help them develop resilience: the achievement of positive outcomes despite risk. Resilience is developed through connections with the environment.

■ Part of helping low SES students develop resilience is through accurate identification and nurturance of their gifts and talents. Many low SES students, especially if they are culturally and linguistically diverse, are not identified as "gifted" or provided with opportunities for enrichment. These students, when properly identified and nurtured, can be provided with opportunities to develop their talents and prepare to be full contributors to society.

7

Practical Strategies for Enhancing Learning, Motivation, and Self-Esteem in Low SES Students

*It's not that I'm so smart; I just
stay with problems longer.*

Albert Einstein

When Marcos starts kindergarten at age 5, he has never been in a structured setting outside of his home before. Not only does he not speak English; he has no idea why things move along so quickly and are so rigidly scheduled. Just when he is enjoying drawing a picture, suddenly it is time to put the crayons away and go to recess. At recess, finally, he gets to run around and play with his friends. But just as their game of tag is really heating up, the bell rings—and it is time to go back inside.

Later, at lunch in the cafeteria, Marcos eats slowly. He gets a free hot lunch at school each day. He savors his food, appreciating it as he feels the pleasant sensation of a full stomach. But now his teacher is telling the class that it is time to go outside. Marcos really wants his dessert;

he doesn't get treats like pudding at home. He can't have it—lunchtime is over.

In class, the teacher gets ready to teach the class how to do simple addition problems. She explains them verbally and then expects the children to complete a worksheet of problems by themselves—she tells them that they need to work *independently*, whatever that means. Marcos has no idea how to do these problems. No one has shown him exactly how to look at the addition process on the paper so it makes sense, or used anything like beads, chips, or tokens to show how things "add up" in real life.

A wave of shame sweeps through him as he sees most of his classmates doing the problems with ease. The teacher's back is turned. Marcos stealthily glances at the sheet of the girl beside him. He doesn't think he should be copying from her paper, but it is the only way he can hope to get any of the problems correct. The teacher has said that children who get 90% or more of their problems correct will get a lollipop. Marcos wants one. He feels fidgety; he wishes he could get up and walk around instead of just sitting there. School isn't much fun. Marcos gets only 30% of his math problems correct—no lollipop. On his first-trimester report card, the teacher reports to his parents that he has deficiencies in most areas of school and that they need to work harder with him at home.

As previously mentioned, when Mark starts kindergarten at a public school, he has had several years of preschool. He already knows his shapes, colors, and letters of the alphabet. Because he has been at a Montessori preschool, where activities are minimally structured, the relative rigidity of the fundamental school kindergarten is hard for him at first. He eventually adjusts, however; after all, he is accustomed to a time-conscious schedule at home. Although his parents try not to rush him, he is aware of the clock and that there are certain times for everything.

Because of his advanced oral vocabulary and many hours of being read to at home, Mark can readily understand the decontextualized language of the stories in his classroom. He is an active child, however, and sitting a lot in kindergarten is not easy for him. It is made easier by some support at home: His mother, recognizing his need for movement, has provided a miniature trampoline in the living room for him to jump on before he goes to school.

He enjoys "working off steam" in this way, and he knows that when he goes home, he can do it again. Mark has some as yet undiagnosed fine motor and visual motor deficits, but in most areas, he is still able to meet the standards of the kindergarten curriculum.

INTRODUCTION

Most students from low SES backgrounds need extra support to learn optimally at school. Educators and other professionals can provide this support by working to make the physical environment as conducive to learning as possible. They also can use practical strategies to increase whole-brain learning. Some of these strategies involve helping students reduce their stress levels to free up their brains for learning, for taking in information that they are taught. Related strategies address helping students increase their memory skills.

Many young children from low SES homes come to kindergarten with a language information structure that is not adequate to process the language information load of the classroom. For these children, it is extremely important to increase contextual cues to enhance learning. Some students may come from a culture of resistance, where academic success is discouraged. They may display challenges with motivation, self esteem, and the ability to work independently. Direct strategies and activities to help increase these skills are the subject of this chapter.

ENHANCING LEARNING:
OPTIMIZING THE ENVIRONMENT

Professionals who serve the needs of children from low SES homes work in many settings. Some are speech-language pathologists (SLPs) or other special education personnel who work with these students in small therapy rooms. Others teach in traditional classrooms. Whatever the teaching environment, it can be optimized in ways that are especially beneficial to learning for these students.

First, clutter and distractions in the environment can be limited. For students from low SES backgrounds who have challenges with focusing and paying attention, making the classroom relatively simple and clutter-free can be very helpful. In my district, some teachers use the "office," in a quiet corner of the classroom, that has nothing on the walls. This area is similar to a library carrel, where a student can sit and work without the visual stimulation of being able to look around the entire classroom. Maxwell (2010) states that if there are too many visual displays in a classroom, students may have difficulty discerning the most important information that is being conveyed. Put informally, in terms of visual displays in classrooms, less is more.

Next, it is important to optimize the signal-to-noise ratio in the classroom (or therapy room). The teacher's voice needs to stand out above background noise in the classroom. As noted, many children from low SES homes have a history of otitis media, or middle ear infections. These children often have difficulty hearing in noise. Research shows that they and many other children benefit from an increase in loudness of the teacher's voice by approximately 20 decibels (dB). A somewhat louder voice creates a better signal-to-noise ratio for the children, who then pay better attention and learn more (Nelson, Kohnert, Sabur, & Shaw, 2005; Windsor & Kohnert, 2004). More is said about noise in Chapter 8.

In many school rooms, students sit on uncomfortable plastic chairs. Students can be provided with chair cushions to increase comfort. Very active students often learn well if they sit on a large, "bouncy" activity ball, rather than on a traditional chair. In my own clinical experience, a few extremely active students learned best when they were allowed to stand up for most of the day. It is important to prevent such children from disrupting their classmates; nevertheless, this strategy is worth trying.

Of relevance here is Gardner's theory of multiple intelligences, described later in this chapter. Students with strong abilities in kinesthetic intelligence (good athletic skills) often find it quite challenging to sit still for long periods. These students can be given "movement breaks" to help dispel excess energy so that that they can concentrate better.

Jones (2002) states that the peak daily learning time for most students is the period 8 to 10 AM. Professionals may wish to consider teaching more abstract, difficult information during this time slot, using the afternoon hours for less cognitively demanding tasks. Jones also discusses what many early childhood professionals already know: Children's attention spans, up till the age of 7 years, roughly correspond with their chronological age. A 5-year-old, for example, will have an attention span of 5 minutes for a particular task.

Many children have difficulty paying attention in school because they are asked to sit still at their desks and focus for much longer time spans than they are maturationally ready for. Children may be expected to sit and do tasks at their desks for 1 or 2 hours without breaks or being able to get up and move around. Movement breaks can help children to focus much better in class. Music can influence students' moods, create relaxing climates, and even relieve stress. Most teachers who use music choose musical pieces that have a strong, repetitive beat and instruments that lend themselves well to this feature. Classical music often works well.

Table 7–1 lists suggestions for improving the classroom environment according to the age levels of students. Of particular value is keeping a water bottle handy throughout the day. Dehydration is well known to have many negative sequelae: thirst, headaches, impaired digestion, and reduced cognitive functioning. It is important to avoid caffeine-filled sodas, which both contribute to dehydration and increase blood sugar levels (with predictable results). Students need to be strongly encouraged to drink as much plain water as possible to enhance both comfort and school performance.

When students are physically comfortable in their classrooms and therapy rooms, professional can begin to implement practical strategies for whole-brain learning. As discussed in Chapters 4 and 5, specific strategies have been identified to increase the oral and written language skills of students from low SES backgrounds. These strategies can be enhanced by adding others that increase whole-brain learning, the ability to use both the right and the left hemispheres of the brain to promote optimal cognitive and linguistic functioning.

Table 7–1. Suggestions for Improving the Classroom Environment

Kindergarten Through Third Grade

Overall Goal: To create an atmosphere of security, reassurance, and comfort.

- Offer recess 2 to 3 times a day
- Have frequent "stretch" breaks for children to move around
- Lighting should be low and natural; try to avoid artificial light as much as possible
- The teacher manages much of the materials and introduces responsibility slowly
- Have rugs and carpeted areas
- Have a reading center with soft pillows and a rug where students can come to read and relax
- Colors should be bright yet soothing and warm
- Let students keep water bottles at their desks to sip from throughout the day

Fourth Through Sixth Grade

Overall goal: To promote collaboration and outreach, and a team spirit

- Have an average level of lighting
- Provide interesting and flexible, easy-to-move seating arrangements
- Place students with new friends; don't let them choose their partners until the end of 6th grade when their brains are mature enough to handle this better
- Provide dry-erase boards
- Let students keep water bottles at their desks to sip from throughout the day
- Provide structure, but also give students opportunities to do independent work
- To encourage students working together, provide activities that utilize the concept of groups, teams, and partners
- Make sure students get some time to work on computers

Eighth Through Twelfth Grade

Overall goal: To promote planning and organization, ability to speak in front of a group

- Post schedules of activities and check off activities as they are completed

Table 7–1. *continued*

- Model study and organizational skills; demonstrate calendars and even electronic planning devices
- Lighting should be normal to bright
- Include state-of-the-art technology such as the Internet, other computer resources
- Include motivational posters with appropriate role models

Source: Adapted from Jones (2002).

PRACTICAL STRATEGIES FOR ENHANCING WHOLE-BRAIN LEARNING

Reducing Stress

As mentioned in an earlier chapter, Farah, Noble, and Hurt (2005) showed, in a study of poverty and brain development, that children from low SES families who are under stress may have high levels of cortisol, a chemical released by the brain during times of stress. When produced in high quantities, cortisol can alter brain tissue by making it vulnerable to processes that destroy brain cells. Cortisol negatively affects brain cells and pathways, thereby inhibiting learning in students experiencing high levels of stress. Degeneration of brain tissue occurs as well. Blair and colleagues (2011) studied a sample of 1,292 low SES children in a longitudinal research project. They found that high cortisol levels early in life were uniquely associated with executive functioning skills at age 3. Thus, research confirms that low SES children are vulnerable to the effects of stress. Professionals can help these students cope with stress in a variety of ways.

An important stress reliever is aerobic exercise, which stimulates and calms the brain. Physical movement benefits everyone. Professionals who work with students of any background are well advised to provide short breaks for the children to get up, stretch, and move around. A technique called the "cross crawl" (Dennison & Dennison, 1986) is highly recommended: The child stands up, raises the right knee, and touches the left hand to it, and then raises the left knee and touches the right hand to it, continuing until approximately 20 of these sequences have been performed. The goal of the cross crawl exercise is to stimulate both sides of the brain, and it is very effective. This exercise takes only a minute or less. In general, children sit still far too long in classrooms and in therapy sessions. Exercise stimulates oxygen to the brain, helping students learn more efficiently and effectively. Accordingly, it is important that professionals avoid taking away recess or physical education (PE) sessions as a punishment for students.

To reduce stress, students also can be taught to do deep breathing and other relaxation exercises (Holcomb-McCoy, 2011). I have used these with my university students! Deep breathing draws oxygen into the brain, helping students be more alert. It also can help students to relax, especially during stressful times such as during test-taking. Use of calming, soothing music is another way to help relieve stress. Classical music is a popular favorite with many professionals. Some professionals (e.g., Morris, 2011) use "fidget toys," such as small squeezable balls, to allow students to relieve stress by fidgeting and moving around while learning. Children who are very active and have trouble listening (and thus feel stressed) can be given "squishy" balls or other quiet toys to squeeze. This keeps their hands busy and, ironically, can truly help them concentrate better, especially during listening activities. Some readers may remember "worry beads," smooth beads which can be handled to calm one's nerves. Children in situations of stress can benefit from being given the opportunity to make small, repetitive, soothing motor movements.

Students also can be given blocks of time during the day to record their thoughts in a journal. Often, the simple act of writing something down, especially if it is negative, can provide the writer a great sense of relief.

Research has shown that children who go to bed early seem to have healthier cortisol levels than children who stay up late. All educators know that it is very difficult for a tired student to learn optimally. Professionals can provide the relevant information to parents in the hope that they will act on it appropriately (Jones, 2002), although parents operating in survival mode may not implement changes recommended by professionals. In such cases, I talk to the students themselves about the importance of a good night's sleep, despite the counter message of family lifestyles and habits. Unfortunately, I have found so often in my career that low SES children have to parent themselves.

Another self-care issue with these children is nutrition. Lack of structure in the home may be a major factor contributing to a poor diet. Professionals can teach these children about the benefits of adequate protein, for example, and about the importance of drinking lots of water, although implementation of any changes at home may be difficult. It is ideal to point to role models whom the students admire, for example, teachers can post pictures of revered athletes to illustrate the benefits of exercise, eating healthy meals, and getting enough sleep.

Increasing Memory Skills

Because of many of the problems experienced by these students (e.g., high levels of cortisol, lack of sleep, or inadequate nutrition), they may have difficulty remembering information acquired through the usual modes of hearing and seeing. In my own clinical experience, virtually 100% of the students from low SES backgrounds who are referred for speech-language testing have deficient memory skills. Due to many of the factors we have discussed, especially stress, low SES children's memory skills can be negatively impacted (Jensen, 2009). Evans and Schamberg (2009) discuss how childhood poverty and chronic stress can impact low SES students' working memory; this impact can last into adulthood. Thus, all professionals who work with these students should implement strategies to improve memory skills.

To increase memory skills, students can be taught several crucial steps:

1. *Rehearse information*—Say it, see it, repeat it, do it again.
2. *Associate information*—Tie it to something you already know.
3. *Visualize information*—Make a picture in your head.

The work of Nanci Bell (1991) has been very influential for many professionals who work with students exhibiting difficulty with memory. Her program, *Visualize and Verbalize*, helps students create detailed images in their brains to help them recall information. I have used principles of Nanci Bell's program very effectively with my own students to help increase their reading and listening comprehension.

I tell the students that we are going to learn to "make a picture in our brain." I tell them that their brain has a TV in it (I have yet to meet a child who did not know what a TV was). I begin by asking a child to tell me about something in his life that is not present. For example, I may say: "Tell me what your kitchen looks like." The child describes the kitchen. When he has finished the description, I say: "But you are not in your kitchen, are you? How were you able to tell us about it?" At this point, an "aha!" look often comes into the child's eyes. I say: "You were seeing your kitchen as a picture on the TV in your brain, weren't you?" I spend time with all the children having them describe something familiar that is not present in the room. We then move on to more sophisticated activities, and I teach the children to visualize in detail as an adjunct to reading and listening.

Bell (1991) recommends having children begin with the "what" and then go on to create detailed images complete with color, shape, size, mood, background, and other parameters. Research shows conclusively that the more detail that students use in their images, the clearer and stronger the memories are. It also is helpful if images are exaggerated and include movement (Jones, 2002). Jones uses the acronym ACE: association, color, exaggeration.

As an example, the ACE acronym can be used as follows to remember a name. For example, when my son started at a new school, I had so many new names to remember: children, parents, teachers, other school staff. One little boy who I frequently saw in the mornings was named Louis. I used ACE by *associating* him with King Louis, visualizing him with a little gold (*color*) crown dancing wildly (*exaggeration*) on his head. One of the moms I really liked was named Eileen. She had blue eyes and was slender. So I associated her with a blue eye, as in Eileen (*color, association*) and with being *lean*, as in Ei*leen* (*exaggeration*, she is slender, but not super thin).

Jones (2002) suggests other ways in which color can be used in aiding students' recall. She recommends using colors for each subject, for example, blue for math, green for science, red for social studies, yellow for reading, and so on. Folders for each subject can be in the color for the subject. Assignments in various subjects can be written on the whiteboard in the color of pen for that subject. Because many children from low SES homes thrive on structure and routine, this is an excellent strategy for helping them organize their learning and experience predictability.

It is a well-known fact that words set to rhyme or music also are more easily remembered . When possible, teachers can sing with their students, especially younger ones. Songs are available for days of the week, for names of the continents, and other subject matter. Rhyme also is fun, and it helps stimulate memory. Professionals can use music and rhymes, especially for helping students memorize basic facts.

People understand and remember information best when skills and facts are embedded in spatial memory. In other words, memory functions best when supported by touch and physical manipulation, rather than relying on passive intake of information. (Appropriately updated, the old Chinese proverb now reads: "I hear, I forget; I see, I remember; I do, I understand."). Manson (2005) states that students from low SES backgrounds often benefit from *active learning*, in situations in which they actively manipulate objects and materials related to the subject matter.

This researcher discusses a study (Basham, 1994) of fourth grade inner-city students; 83% of them were identified as being "at risk." The students participated in an interdisciplinary, hands-on, 2-week learning unit about the environment. The goal of the study was to determine the effects of active learning on students' attitudes about science and their knowledge of subject matter. Lessons covered a wide range of environmental issues such as deforestation, pollution, Earth appreciation, and recycling. Students engaged in activities with environmental topics including insects, trees, soil water, trash, paper, and recyclable tires. Children were encouraged to discover environmental problems through artwork, experiments, and literature-based activities; they were encouraged to become active participants in solving these problems.

To evaluate the efficacy of this program, attitudes about learning and science were assessed through several means. Nineteen of the students were surveyed before and after the program. In-depth interviews were conducted with seven students. Results of the surveys and interviews showed that positive attitudes toward science and learning about science significantly increased as a result of the active style of instruction and learning. In addition, all students were observed to have learned the subject matter to mastery level.

Haberman (1999) also discusses the success of active, hands-on learning. Students do not learn best by only reading textbooks or watching demonstrations: they need to actually *experience* what they are learning. As Wolfe (2001) says, would you rather go on a cruise to Hawaii or see pictures of someone else's trip there?

This sounds like a pretty silly question, yet we have traditionally structured our students' learning by "showing them pictures." We have placed students at desks, admonished them to be quiet, and limited their study of the curriculum to reading or listening rather than experiencing. Aristotle supposedly said, "What we have to learn to do, we learn by doing." Concrete experience is one of the best ways to make strong, long-lasting neural connections. These experiences engage more of the senses and use multiple pathways to store, and therefore more ways to recall, information (Paul & Norbury, 2012). This is probably why we remember what we have experienced much better than what we have heard or read. True, it is not possible for students to experience everything we want them to learn, but we probably miss many opportunities to engage students in more authentic learning. (p. 188)

When professionals help students from low SES backgrounds with active learning, one way they can do this is to help children, especially young ones, experience contextualized language in settings that make it concrete and real.

CONTEXTUALIZING LANGUAGE FOR
CHILDREN FROM LOW SES BACKGROUNDS

Children from Low SES Families and Language Learning in School

Professionals who work with students from low SES backgrounds in school settings need to be aware of whether learning situations involve concrete versus abstract experience (Kaderavek, 2011; Paul & Norbury, 2012). Wolfe (2001) discusses three levels of learning: (1) concrete experience, (2) representational or symbolic learning, and (3) abstract learning. As an example, beginning with concrete experience, a little girl walking with her mother sees a small, furry, four-legged creature that meows at her. The mother tells her that this is a *cat*. After determining that the cat is friendly, her mother lets her pet the cat, which purrs as the little girl strokes its soft fur. The child stores this multisensory experience in her brain in a physiological connection between neurons. In the future, when she encounters other cats, the word *cat* probably will not be very hard for her to remember, because she has just experienced level 1 learning—a concrete experience.

At level 2, representational or symbolic learning, learning occurs through exposure to symbols or representations such as objects and pictures. Although this is not as effective as concrete experience, it can be considered "second best" as a level of teaching. For example, a child may have never seen a cat. Yet she can be shown pictures of cats and maybe even be presented with various toy cats. This will assist her in learning the word *cat*. It would be ideal if she had hands-on experience with actual cats, but at level 2, at least she is exposed to symbols that help her learn the word.

At level 3, abstract learning, only abstract information is used: usually, this information comes in the form of words and numbers. For example, a child may see the word C-A-T printed on a page: she is reading about it. The teacher says "cat," and she hears the word. But perhaps she has never seen a real cat or even been exposed to pictures of cats or toy cats. It will be quite difficult for her to learn the word because she has not experienced the first two levels of learning.

As discussed elsewhere, this is a major reason why students from low SES backgrounds have so much difficulty in school. Language is a system of symbols used to represent concepts that are formed through exposure and experience (Bloom & Lahey, 1978). If students have had little exposure to various experiences, they do not bring a "memory bank" of experiences to school with them. Successful teaching, of course, utilizes things that learners already know and builds on that store of information. Children from low SES homes often have very low stores of information, so teaching must occur through utilizing levels 1 and 2 as much as possible before moving to level 3: abstract learning.

As a related consideration, Weiner (2001) notes that schools expect kindergartners to come to school able to use language to learn about things they have not directly experienced. They need to be able to learn by discussing a variety of topics with others. Many children from low SES homes, however, come to school with their language levels not matching the level expected even in kindergarten. Their language information structure (LIS) is not on par with the language information load (LIL). For these children, classroom instruction will be, to put it informally, "way over their heads." These children frequently have had much less experience with oral and literate language than their more privileged counterparts, yet the school curriculum is based on the assumption that children have acquired all of this experience in the home, before entering kindergarten. When the LIL of the classroom exceeds children's LIS, content learning is impaired, and the level of the LIS increases very slowly.

As discussed earlier, many schools, in their attempts to raise standardized test scores, have pushed standards down so that younger and younger children are expected to know more and more. Weiner (2001) accurately states that the people who write commercial school curriculum materials and state standards for content areas, and develop educational assessments, often base their ideas on their own middle-class children or on the children of middle class friends. This researcher goes on to say that well-meaning policy makers write objectives not attainable by a kindergartner from a low SES home: "Freed from the weighty anchor of reality, individuals may fantasize freely about what young children could learn or what they should learn" (Weiner, 2001, p. 10). My own professional experience unfortunately bears out the truth of this observation this is so true. Sometimes, I think to myself, perhaps too cynically, that I would like to see these policy makers come to my school for a month or two and teach in one of our classrooms. After this hands-on experience with actual low SES children, I would be very interested to see if their academic and curricular goals were quite so lofty. Students from low SES backgrounds often are not prepared, academically or psychologically, for the rigorous demands of school when they enter kindergarten.

For example, in many California kindergartens, children need to read and solve story problems, make and use graphs, and understand mathematical set theory. Weiner (2001 points out that to decision makers, "abstract" means "high standards," and "concrete" means "watered down." In actuality, if ideas are presented concretely first, then children will understand them abstractly later. Weiner stresses that children from low SES homes need more contextualized language, direct hands-on experiences with objects, opportunities for cooperative learning, opportunities for individual exploration, and enhanced one-to-one conversational opportunities.

A majority of classroom activities, even in kindergarten, rely on students' skill with decontextualized language (Turnbull & Justice, 2012). Many children from low SES families come from homes in which language is highly context-dependent. Listeners need a shared experience because the casual register of language used does not provide all the necessary information. The contextualized language of casual register depends heavily on nonverbal supports and shared meanings between listeners and speakers. Children from environments where casual register is used struggle in the classroom because the language supposedly provides all of the information, with little if any context. The language of the classroom is highly abstract.

By contrast, children from middle SES homes come to school with the ability to understand and use language removed from actual actions and objects. They usually can use language to talk about things that are not physically present in the classroom. Typical classroom interactions depend very heavily on these skills, which grow out of literally thousands of conversations early in childhood in which the child leads and the adult scaffolds the communication.

As we discussed in detail in Chapter 4, children from low SES families experience fewer of these conversational opportunities at home. When they enter kindergarten, they can talk about actions and objects that are physically present in their environment, but they are challenged to use language to talk about things that are not physically present. Thus, the LIS of these children is not equipped to meet the demands of the classroom, even at kindergarten level.

Unfortunately, a vicious cycle develops: Children from low SES families do not have the language skills to meet classroom demands. When they go home at night, they may not learn any more language skills. Thus, at school, these children are consistently asked to do things they cannot do.

Children from poverty homes, in order to learn, need real-world experiences with real-world objects, meaningful tasks, opportunities to make activity-based discoveries, and individualized pursuits that allow them to engage in learning. Instead, the current school curricula encourage contrived tasks, requests to parrot back unconnected pieces of information, admonitions to remain silent, and artificial activities with abstract drawings. According to Weiner (2001), children from more privileged homes are able to bear up under these conditions; children from poverty homes "stumble on the first day" (2001, p. ix).

A basic tenet of teaching at the elementary school where I worked for some years as an SLP was to provide students with opportunities to *practice language*. The principal encouraged teachers to increase children's language experiences as much as possible, in both teacher-student and student-peer conversations. His premise was that many children from low SES homes come to school without a basic language foundation, and this is the heart of the challenges they experience in school. Thus, he encouraged teachers to attempt to draw students out and help them elaborate on topics, rather than just giving brief answers and then moving on to the next student. He helped teachers avoid what he called a "one-way dialogue," in which the teacher talks and students sit passively; again, practicing language, speaking and listening, as well as reading and writing, as much as possible was the goal.

Students from low SES homes learn best from hands-on activities that are relevant for them. Professionals use many types of hands-on manipulatives to provide multisensory learning for children. Objects like buttons, chips, noodles, straws, paper clips, and others can be placed in containers for use in various activities. They can be especially helpful for learning in math.

In point of fact, relevance is a factor in any learning experience, as borne out by my own observations of a child from a middle SES family: my son. He had always dreaded doing math worksheets for school. But, in preparation for a longed-for trip to Disney World, he willingly and competently performed frequent computations to determine how much he had saved from his allowance, and earned from extra chores, for his spending money, as he excitedly counted and sorted his collection of coins and $1 and $5 bills. He was fully engaged in this relevant, fun, and hands-on math learning experience.

Increasing Contextual Cues to Enhance Learning

Professionals can change the way they speak with young students especially. As noted by Hart and Risley (1995), young children from low SES backgrounds are likely to have much less experience with conversations, the interchange of speaking and listening, than are those from middle SES backgrounds. Thus, especially in kindergarten and the preschool years, specific modifications in how teachers and other professionals speak with these children are recommended, especially in group settings such as the classroom (Davis & Banks, 2012; Paul & Norbury, 2012; Roseberry-McKibbin, 2008; van Broekhuizen, 2006). To enhance learning, linguistic contextual cues can be increased in several ways:

- *Slow down rate of speech.* Pause frequently, lengthening the pauses between sentence boundaries (wherever a period, question mark, or comma would appear if speech was written down).
- *Rephrase and restate information.* For example, the teacher could say: "Water is good for our bodies and brains. We need

to drink at least 8 glasses of water a day to help our bodies and brains perform at their best. To help our bodies and brains feel good and perform well, we need to drink at least 8 glasses of water a day."

- *Use short sentences; reduce sentence length and complexity.* Ideally, professionals should use sentences that are just slightly longer and more complex than the child is capable of producing.
- *Use visuals to accompany everything spoken.* For example, write or draw something; use of transparencies can be very effective. Today's SmartBoards help enhance visual learning for students. If the classroom is equipped with iPads for students, these can be quite helpful to visually enhance lessons.
- *Bring props for more hands-on learning.* Many students learn optimally when they are able to manipulate actual objects.
- *Use preparatory sets.* Make sure students know in advance what is going to happen. For instance, teachers can begin the day by reviewing the daily schedule, which has been written in advance on the whiteboard or SmartBoard. They can go over the planned activities with the class and erase or cross out each activity as it is completed.

Because many children from low SES homes find it challenging to adjust to the structure and routine of school, use of preparatory sets is very helpful. A sample preparatory set follows: "We are going to do math now. We will open our books and do the problems from page 60. So—please open your math books and do the problems on page 60." When teachers and other professionals use preparatory sets, students know what to expect.

Owens (2012) states that there may be a relationship between stored word knowledge and comprehension of discourse. The more words children have stored in their knowledge bank, the easier it is to comprehend the discourse of the classroom. The language experiences of young children before kindergarten can be likened to deposits in a bank account. More privileged children have a great deal of linguistic "money in the bank" (a more erudite description, from Weiner, is "appropriate stored context from previous positive language experiences" [2001, p. 101]). Because most children from middle SES homes have a lot of linguistic money in the bank, when academic withdrawals (demands) are made, plenty of money is available for those withdrawals. Children from low SES homes have much less linguistic money in the bank. Thus, when they arrive in kindergarten and academic demands are made, they have much smaller linguistic reserves on which to draw. Academic demands, or withdrawals, on these low reserves create deficits, including immediate learning problems in the classroom. To prevent such problems, these children need context-based conversations in order to learn at maximum capacity (Paul & Norbury, 2012).

It is easy to think that when children from low SES homes arrive in kindergarten, their academic fate has already been determined. How can school professionals hope to make up for the vast discrepancy between the prekindergarten linguistic experiences of children from middle- and those of children from low SES backgrounds? How can a major infusion of linguistic "cash" be deposited into the mind banks of these children when they arrive in school?

Researchers discuss ways in which these aims can be achieved; these strategies are summarized in Table 7–2. Weiner points out the importance of engaging the child in "natural" conversations:

> Increasing classroom conversations and conversation-like experiences allows schools to continue the language development process where the homes have left off. Conversations are dialogues rather than narratives. They take place between two people . . . The lower a child's language level, the more the child needs to control the topic of conversation. (p. 36)

The parallel nature of these strategies and those aimed at increasing early language skills reflects the fact that most children from low SES families need conversational interactions that compensate for the deficiency of linguistic experiences in the home in comparison with more privileged children.

Application of the suggested strategies may seem almost too easy, surely, increasing the language skills of low SES kindergarten children must require more complex interventions than just talking with them. It really is that simple, however. Early literacy strategies are discussed elsewhere in this book; here, it is enough to say that holding as many conversations with children as possible helps to contextualize the school experience for them, thereby scaffolding academic information so that it becomes comprehensible to them. In addition, this approach obviously serves to increase their oral language skills.

Table 7–2. Increasing Children's Conversational Experiences

☑ Look for chances to talk one-on-one with children. For example, talk with children while distributing materials or carrying out routines (e.g., "Here are 4 crayons: red, blue, green, yellow. The yellow one is the shortest one."

☑ Use transition times to comment on positive student action (e.g., "Thank you for cleaning up your desk before we go out to recess."

☑ Talk to individual students as they complete their work (e.g., "You found two of the missing pictures already—nice job.").

☑ Instead of letting children work silently, talk them through lessons (e.g., "We are looking at pictures of things that begin with /b/. Oh, look! You found a *ball*. Here is another thing that begins with /b/. It's a *baby*."

☑ Use information talk instead of questions. Young low-SES children may become anxious under repeated questioning. We can "pour words" into children's actions so that they can have opportunities to hear how language works in specific situations.

☑ Allow children to respond nonverbally if they do not want to speak. For example, create conversational turns by saying things like "If the sun is shining, clap your hands." "If it is recess time, stand up."

☑ Bring in volunteers to have conversations with children about their interests or about what they are doing in school.

☑ Increase child-to-child conversations. Children can work on projects together; cooperative learning activities work well here.

☑ Respond in ways that promote continued talk. For example:

> KATIE: My mommy and daddy and I went to the store.
> PROFESSIONAL: That sounds like fun. Tell us about some of the things you bought.

An example of a way to discourage continued talk would be:

> KATIE: My mommy and daddy and I went to the store.
> PROFESSIONAL: That's nice. Hope you got a lot of good food.

☑ Provide opportunities for children to use language and interact during the learning process. For example, if the class is learning about the ocean, children who have been to the ocean can be encouraged to share these experiences with the class. When children are learning new concepts in a subject like math, they can be encouraged to rehearse their strategies out loud. My son's kindergarten teacher always asked for volunteers to come and read sentences on the whiteboard; these sentences were related to the theme for the month (e.g., the ocean or the solar system).

continues

Table 7–2. *continued*

☑ Give all students opportunities to practice various forms of language. For example, students need to gain facility with making requests, negotiating, problem-solving, explaining concepts to others, and so forth. Students need many opportunities to practice these kinds of language acts in the classroom setting (Brice & Montgomery, 1996).

☑ Arrange the physical setting of the classroom so that it promotes talking and interaction. Individual desks and carrels do help students focus for certain tasks, but they discourage interaction. For purposes of enhancing students' interaction with one another, teachers can provide learning centers, interactive classroom displays, and large tables for group work.

Source: Adapted from Kaderavek, 2011; Paul and Norbury, 2012; Roseberry-McKibbin, 2013; Weiner, 2001.

When teaching about particular topics, professionals can contextualize language by identifying the key concepts and vocabulary needed to understand the lesson. Then the vocabulary with which the students may be unfamiliar can be introduced, using objects, gestures, and other visual aids to ensure that learning of key vocabulary words is accomplished before the main lesson is started.

Professionals need to provide instruction not through language alone but with the assistance of gestures, visual aids, body language, facial expressions, demonstrations, and hands-on experiences. Concrete and immediate referents should be provided to support new concepts being taught. Conversational interaction that is interesting and relevant to students also should be provided (ERIC Clearinghouse on Urban Education, 2006). An example of such interaction is presented in Table 7–3.

Weiner (2001) has written an excellent and detailed description of CurricuLanguage, a method for very gradually building LIS for children from low SES homes so that they match the language of the classroom. CurricuLanguage uses the principles of beginning with highly contextualized language and gradually scaffolding learning so that low SES children are able to successfully learn and rely on increasingly decontextualized language. A major premise of CurricuLanguage is to build language skills and content knowledge at the same time. For readers familiar with the concept of sheltered English for students who speak a language other than English, CurricuLanguage

Table 7–3. Context-Embedded Strategies for Teaching About the Moon

1. *Professional brainstorms with students about what they already know* about the moon (building on children's previous knowledge). For example, the professional says "What do you know about the moon?" Students might answer ""It is up in the sky" "It gets fat and then gets skinny" "It's cold." (or, my son's statement when he was 4 years old "It's made of vanilla ice cream").

2. *Professional uses visuals to focus on the topic.* For example, the professional might use a PowerPoint presentation to show the first landing on the moon and ask students to describe what they see.

3. *Professional provides hands-on experiences.* For example, using a projector or lamp (the sun) and a tennis ball (the moon), the professional demonstrates how the shape of the moon appears to change. The students sit in a circle and help move the "moon" around the circle in the light of the "sun." The professional might also have the students jump two or three times to demonstrate the effects of gravity. Why do we fall? What happens when we drop things? We can discuss the gravity of the moon and how it affects the tides.

4. *Professional has students record experiences in their notebooks.*

5. *Professional reviews test vocabulary and concepts with games and worksheets.*

Source: Adapted from ERIC Clearinghouse on Urban Education, 2006; Roseberry-McKibbin, 2008; van Broekhuizen, 2006.

utilizes many of the same methods and principles: teaching content areas through the use of highly contextualized language in order to build both language skills and content knowledge.

Language skills and content knowledge are important for older as well as younger students from low SES backgrounds. These students also may need academic, abstract information to be contextualized. Fisher, Frey, and Williams (2002) are faculty members at Herbert Hoover High School in San Diego, California. Hoover's achievement scores were the lowest in the county and among the lowest in the state. Teacher turnover was high, and morale was low. One hundred percent of the students qualified for free/reduced cost lunch, 96% were members of minority groups, and 46% were English language learners.

Educators at Hoover, discouraged by year after year of low performance, implemented school-wide what they called "seven defensible strategies." Subsequently, over a period of several years, scores on formal state standardized tests for the school increased dramatically. For example, reading achievement scores went up two grade levels. State accountability targets were met for the first time in a decade. In 2001, 40 seniors from Hoover were admitted to California universities, including 12 students who were admitted into the prestigious and internationally known University of California, Berkeley. Hoover's "seven defensible strategies" are explained in Table 7–4, and supplemented by several other sources that also have documented the success of these strategies (for example, Table 7–5). Of note, Hoover's strategies emphasize the con-

Table 7–4. Seven Defensible Strategies

Name of Strategy	Description
1. Read alouds	Teachers read aloud to their students for at least 5 minutes a day; students may follow along or just listen.
2. K-W-L charts	Know-Want to Know-Learn charts hook students into learning by asking first, "What do you know about this subject?" Then they are asked, "What do you want to know?" And finally, at the end of the unit, "What have you learned?" K-W-L charts help students organize their inquiries (see Table 7–5 for a sample K-W-L chart)
3. Graphic organizers	These provide students with visual information that complements class discussion or text
4. Vocabulary instruction	Teachers focus on "transportable vocabulary;" skills that students can use across content areas
5. Writing to learn	Writing-to-learn strategies are used at the beginning, middle, or end of class to help students inquire, reflect upon, or clarify content.
6. Structured note-taking	Students draw a line about two inches from the left side of the paper, log main ideas and key words to the left, and details to the right of the line. They write a brief summary of the lesson at the bottom of the page.
7. Reciprocal teaching	This allows students to become the instructors of the content they are studying. They work in groups of four and read a passage together, following a protocol for questioning, clarifying, predicting, and summarizing.

Source: Adapted from Fisher, Frey, and Williams, 2002; Roseberry-McKibbin, 2001, 2007.

textualization of language. These strategies use multiple modalities and build on students' prior learning experiences to teach new information.

One of the strategies used at Hoover, as seen in Table 7–4, is structured note-taking. Note-taking is a very important skill as these students get older. Table 7–6 describes strategies that can be used to help students take notes in an active manner.

Table 7–5. Sample K-W-L Chart

Content area: **Geography**		
What I Know	**What I Want to Know**	**What I Learned**
San Diego is in southern California	What are the names of all the continents?	(fill in answers in this column)
There are 7 continents in the world	Which is the smallest continent?	
We live in North America	Which is the largest continent?	

Table 7–6. Strategies for Active Note-Taking

Allow students to use a variety of writing instruments. Some may prefer pencils, others pens. Allowing students to choose their writing instruments heightens their interest in the writing process as well as in the information they are hearing.

Encourage students to use Highlighter pens when reviewing notes. Teach them to only highlight *key* words and phrases, not whole sentences, as this will aid in review later on.

Have students review their notes within 8 hours of actually taking the notes. They will retain the information better that way.

Encourage students to re-write their notes by hand. Although taking notes on laptop computers is becoming more popular, typing does not aid in recollection as well as handwriting does.

Have students make flashcards from key concepts written down in note-taking. They can carry these flashcards with them and review the flashcards when they have downtime (e.g., standing in line at the grocery store).

Encourage students to explain the notes to another person. Talking about the notes is very helpful for retaining information.

Source: Adapted from Jones, 2002; Roseberry-McKibbin, 2008; Wolfe, 2001.

In summary, when working with students from low SES backgrounds, professionals need to keep in mind the overarching principle that these children bring much less language experience to school with them. Thus, to help these students succeed, it is important to ensure that the language of the classroom is contextualized as much as possible. This strategy also helps students develop their skills in executive functioning.

DEALING CONSTRUCTIVELY WITH STUDENTS FROM THE CULTURE OF RESISTANCE

Some researchers (e.g., Bennett, 1995; Ogbu, 1997) have suggested that students from low SES backgrounds may become members of a *resistance culture*. Members of this resistance culture believe that success in school means that the student is selling out and trying to act "middle class" (Woolfolk, 2008). If these students want to maintain their identity and status within their groups, they have to reject habits and behaviors that lead to success in school: attending class, cooperating, doing homework, and studying (Neuman, 2009). Participation in a resistance culture has been associated with White, Hispanic, and African American students from low SES backgrounds in the United States, as well as with less-privileged White students in England and students from low SES backgrounds in Papua New Guinea (Ogbu, 1997; Woolfolk Hoy, Demerath, & Pape, 2002).

Last week, one of my African American seniors, Takissha, came to the course final. Ordinarily poised, composed, and prepared, this single mother of four visibly struggled to contain her tears so that she could focus on the test. After she was finished, I followed her out of the classroom and into the hallway. I told her that if she wanted to be left alone, no problem; however, if she wanted to talk, I was there and willing to listen. The classroom door opened and Jonda, another African American senior, came over to us because she was finished with the final. Takissha explained that many of her friends from the African American community, who she had known for 20 or so years, refused to come to her graduation ceremony (where she would receive her Bachelor's degree). She wept as she explained to Jonda and me that her friends had not supported her decision to further her education by attending college. Her family tried to understand and be supportive, but Takissha was the first in her family to graduate from college and was unable to impress upon her family and friends the significance of her hard work. She was devastated at the lack of support from her community.

Jonda put her arms around Takissha. With wet eyes, she described her own personal experience of being rejected by both family and peers for her own attempts to attend college and receive a higher education. She described incident after incident of rejection, misunderstanding, and hardship as she worked to pursue a higher education. Jonda and I encouraged Takissha with what we hoped were words of comfort, stressing that we were her new friends and community, and that we would be there for her.

I will never forget standing in that university hallway, watching two bright, successful African American women crying as they described the incredible obstacles they had had to overcome in order to graduate from college. For so many of my college students, family support is assumed and expected—emotional, financial, physical. But not only did Takissha and Jonda not have support; instead, they had to battle the negativity, slurs, criticism, and rejection that accompanied their attempts to get college degrees. Watching them, I was so moved by all the obstacles they had overcome. At graduation, sitting several rows behind them, I was overwhelmed with admiration and respect for these two women who had fought so hard to obtain an education in the face of substantial barriers and without the support network that most of us take for granted.

If students from low SES backgrounds in the United States are members of involuntary minority groups, they may be especially at risk for membership in a resistance culture. A large body of ethnographic research suggests that minority success in education may, to a large degree, depend on the nature of the minority group (Holt & Smith, 2005). Involuntary minorities who have a history of discrimination and suppression may be less likely to buy into majority group cultural practices that value education and uphold educational attainment as a route to personal and career success (Ogbu, 1995; Olszewski-Kubilius et al., 2004). Research has suggested that African American urban youth experience feelings of alienation in the school community and do not regard education as being rewarding; these students are especially vulnerable to emotional detachment from school (Holcomb-McCoy, 2011; Talbert-Johnson, 2004).

By contrast, voluntary minorities who have immigrated to the United States to improve the quality of their lives have not experienced suppression and discrimination to the degree that involuntary minorities have. Ogbu (1995) states that these voluntary minorities are more likely to adopt majority cultural values, especially regarding the importance of education. Thus, when considering whether students from low SES backgrounds are part of a resistance culture, educators also must determine if they are members of an involuntary minority group.

Coleman and Southern (2006) expand on this theme, stating that for many students from low SES backgrounds, being academically successful is not valued by students' peer groups and is even viewed as a betrayal of the student's roots. These attitudes are present throughout elementary school, and once having reached middle school and high school, it is extremely challenging for a student to make a personal choice to be an academic achiever.

Payne (2003) discusses the fact that for persons in poverty to get out of poverty, they usually have to suspend their relationships with members of their communities and undergo some uncomfortable, unfamiliar changes. For students who are members of a resistance culture, a great deal of internal fortitude is required to suspend familiar relationships with other members of the resistance culture and attempt to succeed despite considerable pressure to the contrary. Persons who want to rise above generational poverty may need to face substantial resistance from those closest to them: friends and family members whom they love. It is in circumstances such as this that educators and other professionals can provide the relationships and role models to give these students the support that they need.

As noted, Payne (2003) discusses the importance of role models for students from low SES backgrounds who desire to move into the middle class. She and other experts believe that role models provide, among other things, emotional resources for students (Maxwell, 2010; Reynolds & Fish, 2010; Roseberry-McKibbin, 2013). Emotional resources dictate behavior; eventually, they dictate achievement. Payne states:

> Emotional resources provide the stamina to withstand difficult and uncomfortable emotional situations and feelings. Emotional resources are the most important of all . . . because, when present, they allow the individual not to return to old habit patterns. In order to move from poverty to middle class or middle class to wealth, an individual must suspend his/her "emotional memory bank" because the situations and hidden rules are so unlike what he/she has experienced previously. Therefore, a certain level of persistence and an ability to stay with the situation until it can be learned . . . are necessary. This persistence (i.e., staying with the situation) is proof that emotional resources are present. Emotional resources come, at least in part, from role models. . . . It is largely from role models that the person learns how to live life emotionally. (pp. 17–18)

According to Payne and others, the role models provided by school personnel constitute the greatest free supply of emotional resources for children from low SES homes. As we said in chapter 6, a major hope for children living in poverty is the availability of role models, usually professionals in public schools, who are willing to spend time with them and mentor, nurture, and support them as they attempt to make the transition from poverty to middle class circumstances (Davis & Banks, 2012; Reynolds & Fish, 2010). If students feel that teachers don't care about them, they may cut classes or skip school more often (Maxwell, 2010). Reynolds and Fish state that an irony of our current education system is that the older students get, the less they rely on their families and the more they rely on environmental role models. However, during middle school and high school, classes become larger and teachers become more impersonal. To offer more support during this period, Reynolds and Fish recommend that middle and high schools adopt a model of personal and academic advising similar to that of but more intense than the model used in colleges and universities. In some schools, counselors may be able to fill this role. However, any professional in a school can become an encourager, mentor, and friend to an at-risk low SES student.

Several years ago, in my junior Language Science and Development class, I noticed a very quiet student who always sat in the back near the door. She was clearly a re-entry student of color, and I observed that she sometimes looked uncomfortable in a class full of White, 21-year-old middle SES young ladies. Though her clothes were neat and clean, they were not fashionable or new.

One day this student came to my office for a meeting, and her story poured out. She was Alethea Chamberlain, an American Indian of the Linan Apache tribe. She had been a full-time, at-home mom for some years, but now her husband had lost his job in the recession and she wanted to get an education so that she could provide for her family. "I feel so fat and self-conscious," she told me. "All these skinny White girls and their nice clothes make me feel so uncomfortable." Her father was deceased, and her mother did not live nearby. She had been raised in intense poverty, and college was challenging for her on multiple fronts.

Immediately I told Alethea how few American Indian SLPs there were in our country, and shared how very glad I was that she was in the major. I congratulated her for her early test scores, noting that she was doing so well in the class and that I was encouraged by her progress. I told her that though today's 15-minute appointment was brief, I wanted to talk to her more and get to know her better. I encouraged her to come back and see me again. She did so, and I could see that she was feeling supported by our discussions.

In October of that semester, she was diagnosed with a glioblastoma: a malignant brain tumor that tends to quickly kill its victims. After I recovered from my shock, I called her often and met with her. After her surgery, I visited her in the hospital; we even went wig shopping together when her hair fell out. I brought Mark to visit her at her home. With support, encouragement, and considerable direction on my part, Alethea applied for and won an ASHA (American Speech and Hearing Association) Student Minority Leadership Award—complete with an all-expenses paid trip to ASHA's 2008 convention in Chicago.

I will never forget the moment I saw Alethea at the ASHA convention—professionally dressed, confident, engaged, meeting with leaders in the profession, and even talking with universities about possible Ph.D. scholarships. One university offered her a fully paid Master's and Ph.D. scholarship if she would conduct research in the area of communication disorders in the American Indian population.

I thought back to the shy, quiet junior that had been in the back corner of my classroom just one year ago. How very different she looked a year later, and how overjoyed I felt at the privilege of being a steppingstone in the career path of this bright, highly deserving student. I was forcibly reminded that although I had not spent any money on Alethea, what I was privileged to invest was time, support, friendship, and encouragement; to show her in multiple ways that she was not alone, that she had what it took to succeed; that our profession needed her.

In September of 2011, Alethea died after a long and courageous battle with brain cancer. She is forever remembered and loved by friends, family, faculty, and fellow students. She embodied my belief that truly, the presence of caring mentors who are willing to invest time and energy can be a catalyst for growth, change, and success. I shall always miss Alethea; she was taken way too soon. But she lives on in my heart, inspiring me to move forward and carry on my mission of believing in, encouraging, and investing in students with potential; students who can and do succeed if a mentor is willing to provide the support, encouragement, direction, and love that they need.

As mentioned earlier, such transitions may be difficult because of resistance from members of the student's families or cultural group in general.

I will never forget David, a Mexican SLP living in Alaska, who I met at a conference. He told me that when he was in college, another Mexican man beat him up for going to college and trying to be "better than everyone else." An African American student, Denae, was the first member of her family to go to college. In a moving presentation to my multicultural class, Denae talked about the discrimination and verbal and emotional abuse she had received from her family for going to college because they felt that she was trying to be "better" than they were—to rise above "her place" in the world. Denae's mother had been a prostitute; Denae herself was an unwed mother with a little girl. Denae's fellow students, mostly White women from middle and upper SES homes, were shocked to learn that not only was Denae not encouraged to go to college, but actually was persecuted for it.

As uncomfortable as these stories are to read, especially for persons from middle SES backgrounds, it is important to recognize the types of pressures experienced by some students from low SES families as they try to rise out of generational poverty by obtaining further education. This realization can motivate professionals to include emotionally supporting and mentoring these students as part of their practice.

For many professionals who work with students from low SES backgrounds, it is easy to forget the basic and the obvious: caring about students personally and serving as role models and mentors. Miller (2006) interviewed many educators who work with less privileged adolescent students. She found that successful educators emphasized the personal connection they made with their students. For example, these educators helped young people to feel cared about by calling them by name. Miller states:

> They [educators] act as role models, pushing students to identify short-term and long-term goals and then inspiring them to go the distance to achieve them. . . . Whether role models work one-on-one with a few stu- dents or inspire an entire community, they can wield enormous

power in helping kids set goals . . . forging personal relationships with students is a priority. . . . Students know that at least one adult will ask them how they're doing every day. (p. 50)

In addition to providing support themselves, professionals also can recruit peer mentors as stated previously (Davis & Banks, 2012; Paul & Norbury, 2012). As described in Chapter 6, Olszewski-Kubilius and her associates (2004) conducted an extensive research project in which they worked with culturally and linguistically diverse (CLD) gifted elementary and middle school students from low SES backgrounds. Project EXCITE was a collaborative program of a university-based gifted center and local high school districts designed to train and prepare gifted CLD students in elementary and middle schools for advanced tracks in science and math in high school. Acknowledging the culture of resistance, these researchers recruited successful high school and college CLD students to serve as role models, helping the younger students visualize the path that they were expected to prepare for and eventually take. The older CLD students tutored students, served as teaching assistants for after-school sessions, and spoke to parents and students about their experiences of achieving in high school.

Olszewski-Kubilius and associates (2004) also grouped Project EXCITE students within their homerooms to provide peer support. For example, they gathered sixth graders taking pre-algebra together into a support group in their middle schools. Finally, these researchers had Project EXCITE students spend time on college campuses, broadening their exposure to and experience with an international group of older, successful CLD students. Results of the Project EXCITE program to date have shown that most of its students were retained in the program, earning high grades in science and math at school. An important finding was a 300% increase in CLD students qualifying for an advanced math class in sixth grade after 2 years of involvement in the program. The researchers stated that among the most potent variables contributing to the success of this project were the provision of older CLD role models and clustering gifted students with their CLD peers in order to provide support against the perception that they were "acting White" (p. 154). Peer relationships were carefully monitored by Project EXCITE staff, and families were always included as much as possible.

Such data-based research projects show that students who experience pressure in a culture of resistance can be supported and encouraged to achieve their potential. Although many schools may not be equipped to carry out a project as large as Project EXCITE, the principles of this successful program can be applied in many school settings.

Other researchers (e.g., Gandara, 2004; Kitano, 2003) cite the success of programs that utilize older CLD students from younger students' cultures to serve as role models, to encourage the younger students' academic and life success. Gandara (2004) describes the Puente Project, which, among other things, utilizes older Hispanic students from California colleges as role models to work with Hispanic high school students, encouraging them to prepare to enter 4-year colleges. Students also are kept together in cohorts; school friendships are an important variable in student engagement, and they reduce the likelihood that students will drop out of school.

Many Puente students indicated that they associated with other Puente students; in addition, Puente students were less likely than non-Puente students to drop out of high school. This program has been very successful; 43% of Hispanic high school students who participated in the Puente Project attended 4-year colleges, in contrast with 24% of high school Hispanic students who were not involved in the Puente Project.

Holcomb-McCoy (2011) discusses the fact that African American students who transition from junior high to high school may experience racial stereotyping and low expectations on the part of school personnel. Holcomb-McCoy states that these students frequently lack positive role models from their communities. She recommends that high schools specifically set up opportunities for African American students and their parents to meet with mentors who understand Black community challenges, racial identity development, and other factors that might hinder students' success in school. She suggests that to locate mentors, educators can contact Black churches, local universities, fraternities and sororities, corporations, and college sports teams. She states that successful older students can be especially valuable as mentors.

Taken together, the results of these research projects and expert experiences point to the following recommendations: (1) Place younger low SES students with older successful role models, preferably those of the same CLD background; (2) have those role models speak with parents as well as students, encouraging the parents to support their children in pursuit of higher education, and (3) prevent as much as possible influences of the resistance culture by keeping students together in supportive peer groups.

ENHANCING SELF-ESTEEM AND MOTIVATION: PROVIDING APPROPRIATE LEARNING INCENTIVES

If they do not receive substantial support from their schools and communities, students from low SES backgrounds may become victims of learned helplessness. Students who fail continually may come to believe that succeeding in school is impossible. As Neuman (2009, p. 71) states, "children whose memories are storehouses of deprivation and denial are robbed of the ability to dream about a better future." Because they are surrounded by family members and neighbors who never finished school, dropping out seems normal (Woolfolk, 2008). In chapter 6, we talked about the high personal and societal cost of dropping out of school. Jobs available to those without high school diplomas scarcely pay a living wage. If the head of a family of three works full time for minimum wage, the family's overall income will still fall below the poverty line. Children from low SES homes, especially if they encounter racial discrimination in addition to poverty, often become convinced that they cannot advance in the mainstream by doing well in school.

Rothstein (2006) notes that students from low SES backgrounds may not go to college because they don't experience significant peer, parental, or community pressure to take college-preparatory courses or get the grades required for college. Even if lower-SES parents say that they expect their children to get good grades, they are less likely than middle SES parents to enforce these expectations. Educators, including counselors, can stress to less advantaged children the importance of doing well in school, but these exhortations compete with self-image, formed early in life, and reinforced daily by peers, caregivers in the home, and the wider community. Low SES students in these circumstances need additional reinforcement in the school setting.

As noted earlier, research has found that low SES children hear many more discouraging remarks than children from middle SES homes. It is quite challenging for professionals in a school situation to overcome some years of negative talk in students' homes. Words and thoughts determine feelings and actions, however, and professionals can teach children from low SES homes to use different words, in the hope that eventually their thoughts, feelings, and actions will change for the better. For example, in my son's karate dojo, one instructor stressed that "we don't say that something is *hard*—we say that it is a *challenge*." The children were quick to grasp this difference and enjoy its application in their karate practice—and presumably in other experiences as well.

Experts (Nelson, 2010; Paul & Norbury, 2012) have discussed the concept of executive functioning (EF): the ability to plan and evaluate one's performance when engaging in goal-directed behavior. Executive functioning can be divided into two basic areas (informally, I call them the *head* and the *heart*): (a) goal-oriented planning and self-monitoring behaviors such as organization and time management (the head), and (b) personal efficacy behaviors such as perseverance in the face of difficulty and the use of positive self-talk when things are challenging (the heart). In Chapter 8, we discuss the area of EF involving goal-oriented planning and self-monitoring behaviors. Here, we discuss personal efficacy behaviors, or the heart of EF, and how we as professionals might help low SES students to implement these.

Ackerman and Brown (2010) state that academic success relies, among other things, on perseverance in the face of challenge. Children from highly stressful low SES homes may have a sense of learned helplessness; they give up early when presented with challenges. Ackerman and Brown comment that in stressful environments where there is a high degree of chaos (discussed further in Chapter 8), disorganization, and unpredictability, children may learn that persistent efforts in the face of challenge are not rewarded.

Although we as educators can rarely directly influence students' home environments, we can be sure that our own interactions with them in educational settings emphasize that perseverance in the face of challenges brings rewards. We can teach students to reinforce themselves, to use positive self-talk (Holcomb-McCoy, 2011; Kaderavek, 2011). A highly successful strategy that I have used in my own work as an SLP with students from low SES homes is a brief exercise in self-talk. Some of my children exhibited some behavior problems related to home environment issues. So, whenever they came for speech- language therapy, I led the following ritual: They all held hands and said in unison: "I am here because I'm special. I will work hard and do my very best. I am successful. So let it happen today!"

The children enjoyed this ritual, and their behavior improved: anecdotal evidence of the benefits of positive self-talk.

Payne (2003) emphasizes the importance of positive self-talk for children from low SES homes. My own experience both as a parent and as an SLP supports this assertion. Children can be taught to frame experiences positively: "It's not a test, it's a game—I'm going to show that I can't be tricked by the people who made up the test questions." "The teachers are not trying to make me miserable; they are trying to help me learn a lot so I can grow up to get a good job, live in a nice house, and take fun vacations." If professionals can help students to learn positive self-talk, much better academic and overall educational results can be obtained. The benefits of this strategy no doubt relate to relief of stress that can impair brain function.

In order to have good self-esteem and persevere in the face of challenges, students not only need to learn and use positive self-talk but also need to have an emotionally safe classroom environment in which they have the sense that the classroom is a "family" (Landsman, 2006). Classroom environments can be made more friendly to children and enhance their self-esteem by using special entry and exit activities.

In the morning, the teacher can stand in the doorway and welcome students as they come in, shaking their hands, making eye contact, and calling them by name. This activity serves several purposes. First, it provides tactile contact, which can make many students feel more positive about the teacher and the classroom. Second, it helps students learn how to appropriately greet people. As the saying goes, we never get a second chance to make a good first impression; these students need to learn how to shake someone's hand, look the person directly in the eye, and greet the person (as expected in job interviews they will experience as adults).

At the end of the day, a designated student can stand at the door, say goodbye to each classmate (using the classmate's name), and shake the person's hand. This student can be the "celebrity of the day," "star of the week," or whomever the teacher designates. Classroom entry and exit procedures such as these can help students to bond with each other and the teacher and, as stated, to learn good manners that will be helpful to them as children and as adults later on. Teachers (at least at the elementary level) can develop a team spirit among students by using the term "friends." For example, the teacher can say: "OK, friends, let's line up for lunch."

Every experienced professional knows that in terms of encouraging students, "catching them being good" is far more effective than being punitive. Punishment does have its place when students are being deliberately defiant or disruptive, but reinforcement of good behavior generally is far more effective, as shown in the following real-life case example. I have had a great deal of success "catching kids being good."

Johnny was a low SES boy on my speech caseload. He could accurately be described as a "poor sport." Whenever another child won a game, Johnny reacted badly, pouting and whining. One day, when he lost a game, he did not pout or whine. I immediately recognized this as a "teaching moment." I jumped all over this. I gave him a big smile and said: "Wow, Johnny, you are being such a good sport! I am so proud of you! I don't hear any complaining! You will get an extra sticker today." He was very surprised. I then further shaped his behavior, teaching him how to be a graceful winner and congratulate the other child. I helped Johnny understand that it was OK to be mad inside when you lose, but in order to be a good friend, you must at least say, "Nice game" or "Good job" to the winner. Johnny's sportsmanship skills improved immensely. This improvement had a very positive effect on his school interactions overall, presumably based on increased confidence and self-esteem. I think that "catching him being good" and shaping his behavior from there was much more effective than punishing him for being a poor sport. Johnny needed to be encouraged and, fortunately, I was grateful to be there to do just that—"catch him being good"—and to encourage him.

Jones (2002) describes an excellent idea for helping younger students in a classroom setting encourage each other. The teacher can cut out large cardboard "hands" and staple them to tongue depressors or similar "handles." Each student keeps a "hand" on his or her desk. When a classmate has done something special or done an especially good job on a task, the teacher says to the class: "Let's all give Kira a wave for her great work on that poem." Students pull out their hands and wave at the student who is being honored.

At one elementary school, a classroom teacher used a behavior management system that gave students "good checks" and "bad checks." Every child's name was up on the whiteboard in the front of the classroom. Students who got a certain number of good checks for the day received a reward. Several children routinely got "bad checks" next to their names, for all to see; these children, for various reasons, had difficulty conforming to the rigidity of the classroom routine. The students who got the most "good checks" tended to be well-behaved, very quiet girls who were good at completing worksheets. As might be expected, the few children with many bad checks had very low self-esteem and did not enjoy school, which could have been avoided with a different and more positive behavior management system.

In addition to enhancing low SES students' self-esteem by helping them learn to use positive self-talk and having supportive activities in the classroom, professionals can do much to support them in terms of physical appearance. In interactions with others, outward appearance does count, and in many children from low SES homes, self-esteem is negatively affected by their physical appearance. Many of these students wear shabby or ill-fitting clothing and may even be unwashed. Other children and even teachers may assume that these students are not bright and successful.

In the school where I worked for some years, the children wore uniforms. As noted earlier, 91% of these children were from CLD backgrounds, and many were on welfare. Even with the uniform, the effects of poverty were still evident. Some children's uniforms were clean and fresh, and their shoes, jackets, and jewelry spoke of more money in the home. Other children's uniforms were worn-looking, dirty, and rumpled; their jackets were dingy and their shoes were cheap. Although school uniforms can be very helpful in addressing self-esteem issues related to appearance, a uniform cannot entirely conceal a child's low SES status.

Middle class parents can afford to provide their children with attractive, fashionable, good-quality clothing and student gear. Status symbols such as jackets, shoes, and backpacks affect children's perceptions of one another. Many children from low SES homes, however, already are perceived by classmates and teachers alike as "different" in a negative way, even before they speak or write a sentence, because their families cannot afford these status symbols.

Lyon (2006), a professor at Saint Ambrose University in Davenport, Iowa, gave her college students (teacher education majors) an innovative assignment: they were to go out and purchase new school supplies and spend only $6.00. The assignment yielded some interesting themes for these college students from middle SES backgrounds. First, they discussed how time consuming it was to "pinch pennies" because they had to spend so much time searching for the best deals; they could not just walk into a store closest to their homes and select whatever was available.

Second, most of the students expressed feelings of disgrace and shame after trying to purchase necessary supplies with just $6.00. One student talked about how other parents and children around her were reaching for fancy materials, but on her strict budget, she could not afford any of these. Third, students realized why children are teased and have low self-esteem: partly because their parents cannot afford the best in supplies, the status symbols that children scrutinize in one another. Lyon's students concluded that trying to buy school supplies on such a limited budget was frustrating, time-consuming, and embarrassing.

Schools can address the situation of students' school supplies, cleanliness, and clothing by raising funds to provide shower facilities for students who need them. Professionals who travel can collect (*collect*, not steal) those little hotel-size soaps, shampoos, and bottles of moisture lotion for their students.

In schools that require uniforms, a supply of clean uniforms can be kept available for children whose homes do not have laundry facilities. Some schools have washers and dryers to help students have clean clothes. I and some of my colleagues have sometimes brought jackets and other clothing for students who did not have appropriate wraps for cold weather. Professionals can initiate clothing drives to help collect appropriate clothes for students, especially in colder weather.

When students are provided with rewards for good work, these rewards can consist of personal hygiene items, "cool" stickers, and trendy, desirable prizes such as snazzy pencils or erasers, popular movie-themed notebooks, colored markers, and other necessary school supplies. Although the provision of clean clothes, showers, personal hygiene items, and school supplies is outside the traditional role of the school, these essentials can help students have better self-esteem and, ultimately, better motivation to succeed in school. When students are motivated, they will be in a better position to increase their independence and ability to direct their learning in the classroom.

INCREASING STUDENT INDEPENDENCE AND SELF-DIRECTION

Basic Principles

As discussed previously, the United States has one of highest high school dropout rates in the industrialized world. By their senior year, American high school students score lower on science and math tests than most of their foreign peers. One reason for this lack of academic success relates to student motivation.

Ultimately, to be successful in school, students need to see the benefits of education for themselves. Many schools, especially those that serve low SES students, rely heavily on extrinsic rewards (Ginsberg, 2004). Haberman (2005) notes that, although it is true that young children from low SES families need structure and extrinsic rewards, these children will get older, bigger, and harder to motivate with extrinsic rewards. Children in kindergarten do indeed need teachers who put some consistent structure into their lives: something they can readily depend on. This is where learning in school starts, with where the learners are, but it is not where it should end. Haberman states that the goal of school is to develop internal motivation: to help children develop into people who will be committed to lifelong learning, even when no one is around to control and supervise them. He emphasizes that the danger of getting short-term achievement results from directing, telling, and mandating student behavior is that the long-term goal of making students into critical thinking, independent learners is lost.

Some researchers believe that, to increase students' motivation and ultimately their performance, teachers should use simple directives, rote learning, and rigidly programmed methods of instruction when they work with students from low SES backgrounds or students of color. Lumping all these low SES students together as a group and using packaged methods of teaching is worrisome. Interacting with students in a programmed way denies them the challenging classrooms that teachers want to provide, in which exploration, critical thinking, and the development of multiple intelligences are encouraged. Rigidly prescribed, programmed methods of instruction would never be accepted by many middle SES parents, who want holistic approaches and challenging curricula for their children. Treating students from low SES backgrounds as though they need rote learning at the expense of critical thinking and problem solving is a great disservice (Landsman, 2006).

Wilcox (1982) observed a first grade teacher who worked with students from low SES backgrounds and used explicit, direct instructions to control their behaviors (e.g., "You need to do the assignment. Sit down and get to work"). There was no expectation that the students would exercise self-control. By contrast, a first grade teacher of middle class students used suggestions and indirect statements to encourage self-regulation and self-control (e.g., "You have 10 minutes. Use your time wisely"). Both of these teachers used strategies that were effective in their classrooms. As suggested by this Wilcox,, however, perhaps the less advantaged students were being trained to "stay in their place." She speculated that if these students weren't encouraged to develop self-regulatory abilities, then later in life they would not be able to access professional positions requiring independent, self-directed achievement.

Kozol (2005) visited more than 60 schools that served primarily children of color from low SES homes. He observed that many inner city schools have embraced a pedagogy of "direct command and absolute control . . . approaches [which are] commonly employed in penal institutions and drug-rehabilitation programs, as a way of altering the attitudes and learning styles of black and Hispanic children" (p. 266). For example, in many schools, silent lunches have been instituted in the cafeteria. On days when children misbehave, there are silent recesses as well. In Kozol's study, one teacher stated: "If we were not a segregated school, if there were middle class white children here, the parents would rebel at this curriculum, and they would stop it cold—like that!" (p. 271). Kozol refers to the "intellectual straitjacket" used to control the behavior of poor children.

In a related vein, Haberman (2005) describes the goals of many high-poverty schools for their students: Get a job and stay out of jail. Professionals who believe that their students are future menials, adults who will perform only in low-level occupations, often deliver a watered-down curriculum in which students are not expected to learn advanced content. Low expectations become a self-fulfilling prophecy.

Brazilian educator Paulo Friere (1970, 1995) calls this phenomenon "the pedagogy of the oppressed." Friere argues for a system of education that emphasizes learning as an act of culture and freedom. He discusses the concept of "banking education," in which passive learners have preselected knowledge deposited into their minds. He also refers to the "culture of silence," in which people who are dominated lose the means by which they can critically respond to the culture that is forced onto them by the dominant culture.

To truly implement the increase student self-direction, independence, and motivation to succeed, teachers need a pedagogy that puts students' voices at the center of learning, that provides time to listen to and guide students, as well as a safe place in which students' issues can be respectfully explored. One high school teacher in Minneapolis realized that many of his students from low SES backgrounds had little control over their lives (especially if they were homeless). He created a classroom in which students could experience being in control. Students were allowed to write papers on any topic connected to their own personal interest (Landsman, 2006).

Unfortunately, as previously discussed in relation to Hart and Risley's (1995) research, controlled and rigid programming in schools for students from low SES backgrounds is reflective of the ways in which their caregivers have interacted with them in their homes since infancy. Professionals in schools have to work hard to overcome this. Covington and Teel (1996) point out that the ultimate goal of educators is to help students choose activities that they are interested in, and to let them participate in choosing their own rewards. One way to do this is by implementing the equity game.

Implementing the Equity Game

We have stated that according to statistics, among industrialized nations, American schools are near the bottom of the achievement ladder. This finding has led to many calls for the adoption by American schools of rigorous standards and for accountability of both students and teachers for meeting these standards. The mandates of No Child Left Behind (2002) have demanded that schools be held accountable for student achievement.

However, in addition to calling for higher standards, it is critically important that American schools address the issue of student motivation as demonstrated by independent behavior and self-direction. Schools can raise standards as high as they want to, but this will not help students from low SES backgrounds see the relevance of school to their daily lives (Holcomb-McCoy, 2011). One factor is the culture of resistance. Some students want to defy the system; others merely try to "fly under the radar" to avoid failure by not participating at all. How can professionals help these students become self-directed, independent learners? How can meaningful learning incentives be provided for them? Two basic ways are (a) emphasizing effort over ability, and (b) teaching through multiple intelligences.

Emphasizing Effort Over Ability

We said earlier that students from highly stressful homes marked by unpredictability and disorganization may have a sense of learned helplessness because at home, persistent efforts in the face of challenge are not rewarded. These students may not believe that their efforts will "pay off" in terms of many situations, especially situations where they need to learn new material.

Nelson (2010) discusses the fact that students who see their intellectual capacity as static and unchangeable are less likely to expend effort than those who view their intellectual capacity as being dynamic and capable of change. Put differently, if students believe that they are born with a certain amount of intelligence (or lack thereof) and that nothing can be done to change this, they will probably not be motivated to work hard. Why bother? However, in many classrooms, teaching practices turn school into an *ability game*: characterized by belief that some students are born with more ability than others, and that this is not necessarily subject to modification. This outlook promotes motivation to perform based not necessarily on the desire to learn, but on the drive to outperform others, in an attempt to bolster one's reputation for ability. In the ability game, motives to achieve rise out of a fear that others will do better. In the ability game, students' innate ability, rather than hard work, is emphasized.

Instead of promoting the ability game, schools can motivate students by promoting the *equity game*: characterized by a learning environment in which students are not caught up in comparing themselves with others, and in which students can experience the excitement of intellectual discovery, can engage in creative problem-solving, and experience the satisfaction of self-improvement. Two major aspects of the equity game are: (1) the ability to express oneself through different modalities, and (2) motivation to excel for pride in one's own accomplishments, not motivation to outshine others (Covington & Teel, 1996). An example of the second aspect follows.

As noted, most schools work hard to boost students' achievements in reading. Different schools may use various methods to implement this intervention. The teacher at one predominantly middle SES school used the ability game when she instituted a contest to see which child could read the most books each month. The parents wrote down the titles of all books and signed the book sheet(s). The child who had read the most books at the end of the month was awarded the "Book Nook Lion." This stuffed animal became the hotly competed for prize among the children, because winning it meant that they would be honored in front of the group and get their own personal stuffed lion to take home. As might be expected, the students with better reading skills and parents with time on their hands typically were the winners of a Book Nook Lion every month. Children from low SES homes, however, tended to have less well-developed reading skills. Most of them were from homes with several siblings, and their parents often did not have time to read to them or otherwise provide literacy support; such children never got a Book Nook Lion at all. This is a prime example of the ability game at its dubious best.

By contrast, at another elementary school a computer program called Accelerated Reader is used. Children read books that are assigned by specific grade level. When they have finished reading a book, they take an individual computer multiple choice quiz to assess their comprehension of the material. If they score below 50% on any quiz, they must re-read the book and re-take the quiz. Children each have their own individual profile that details the number of points they have earned based on the level and quantity of books they have read. The point total also reflects the percentage of accuracy they have gotten on each computer quiz. Children compete with themselves, not with one another. This is an excellent example of the equity game; when children do well, they feel the satisfaction of self-improvement.

Another example of the equity game is seen in my son's karate class. Clearly, some children are more athletic than others. Students are not rewarded for intrinsic athletic skill, however, as they are in team sports such as baseball and basketball. In the karate class, children are awarded little cloth stars to sew onto their uniforms for achievement in various areas. For example, they receive a silver star each quarter for good attendance; they receive a red star if they bring a friend, a light blue star for community service, a dark blue star for reading 10 books; a gold star for maintaining a B average in school, and a green star for doing a certain amount of set exercises at home.

Children who are not as athletically gifted as their classmates can still earn a lot of stars if they are willing to work for them: to pick up trash in the community park, to read a lot of books, to not skip classes, to do pushups at home at night. This system is embraced by parents because the child's willingness to work hard is what matters and what is rewarded. Thus, children compete with themselves, not with other children, and learn to feel the pride of individual achievement.

In the ability game, however, students whose abilities lag behind those of their peers may react in one of several ways. They may not participate, generating a pattern of nonperformance. They may procrastinate, or may set impossibly high goals. In short, these students, many of whom are from low SES homes, often will become chronic academic underachievers.

In classrooms that promote the equity game, rules establish a level playing field so that all students can strive to do better and feel successful in school, no matter how well or poorly their peers are doing. In the equity game, students feel proud, not necessarily over "winning," but over persistence, improvement, and the quality of their efforts. Research supports the efficacy of this method.

Dweck (2007) studied the effects of using praise for ability versus emphasis on effort with groups of low SES students in New York schools. She found that if students were praised for being intelligent, their performance did not improve; in fact, they became more anxious. However, if students were praised for *effort*, they performed better. In one study, two groups of fifth graders were tested on difficult math problems. Everyone failed. Group A, praised for their effort on the first test, simply assumed that they hadn't focused hard enough on the test. They became very involved in using strategies to help them to succeed the next time. However, those praised for their intelligence were miserable: they assumed that their failure meant that they really were not as smart as they had been told.

Having artificially introduced a round of failure, Dweck then gave all the fifth graders a final test that was of the same level of difficulty as the first round. Those who had been praised for their intelligence/innate ability did about 20% worse than they did the first round. Those praised for their effort raised their scores by about 30%. What was the difference?

Dweck stated that emphasizing effort gave the students a variable that they could control. They came to see themselves as being in control of their success. Emphasizing innate ability, or natural intelligence, took the task out of the children's control and did not provide a good recipe for responding to failure.

In another experiment, Blackwell, Trzesniewski, and Dweck, (2007) studied several hundred low SES students at Life Sciences Secondary School in East Harlem, New York. There was a semester-long intervention conducted to improve the students' math scores. The students were split into experimental and control groups. The control group received instruction in study skills. The experimental group also received instruction in study skills, but in addition, there was a special module on how intelligence is not innate. This special module consisted of two extra lessons, a total of 50 minutes spent not teaching math, but that the brain is like a muscle; giving it a harder workout makes you smarter. The students read aloud an essay about how the brain grows new neurons when challenged. The students saw pictures of the brain and acted out skits.

After the intervention was concluded, the students in the experimental group improved their study habits and grades to a significantly greater extent than the controls. The only difference between the experimental and the control group was the special, 50-minute module which explained that working the brain harder makes it smarter; that effort pays.

Utilizing Multiple Intelligences

In addition to emphasizing effort over ability, the equity game involves, overall, rewarding students' expression of their thoughts and ideas through any of a number of modes of expression. These modes of expression can include written/verbal (e.g., an essay or speech), bodily/kinesthetic (e.g., pantomime), visual (e.g., creating a diagram or drawing a picture), and spatial (e.g., devising a time line). In this context, *equity* means honoring many types of ability, not just ability defined by abstract and verbal reasoning.

This important concept can be viewed through the lens of Gardner's theory of multiple intelligences (Armstrong, 2011; Gardner, 1993). Gardner divided general intelligence into eight components. His premise was that each person possesses all eight intelligences; however, people tend to be dominant in one or two areas of intelligence. These eight intelligences are as follows:

1. *Logical-mathematical ability:* the ability to reason in a logical fashion and think in terms of quantitative relationships and numbers (e.g., mathematicians)
2. *Linguistic ability:* the capacity to represent one's thoughts and ideas in words in either spoken or written form (e.g., authors, teachers)
3. *Musical ability:* the ability to think in musical forms; sensitivity to pitch, rhythm, and musical tones (e.g., musicians)
4. *Bodily-kinesthetic ability:* the capacity for expressing ideas, thoughts, and feelings through bodily movements and gestures, and the possession of speed, coordination, and dexterity (e.g., athletes, dancers)
5. *Spatial ability:* the ability to think in spatial or visual terms (e.g., chess players, pilots)
6. *Intrapersonal ability:* A highly developed sensitivity to one's own feelings and thoughts as well as the ability to make realistic judgments about one's particular strengths and weaknesses for purposes of self-discovery (e.g., those who write their own autobiographies, those who love to journal)
7. *Interpersonal ability:* the ability to detect emotions, moods, and motives of others and act on this information to influence individuals and groups (e.g., salespeople, ministers, counselors)
8. *Naturalist intelligence:* nature smart; the ability to learn through exposure to and interaction with nature (e.g. game wardens, park rangers)

American schools tend to reward linguistic and mathematical-logical ability. Armstrong (2011) notes that we esteem the highly logical and articulate people in our culture; students are not reinforced for gifts in other areas. As stated before, regular art, performing arts, and music often are set aside or totally eliminated as schools frantically race to keep up with the mandates of No Child Left Behind (2002). Music, art, and physical education may be dropped completely and replaced by repeated drills in math, reading, and spelling. Instead of going to recess, children stay inside and fill out worksheets.

In today's headlong rush to prepare children to fill out standardized scantron state and federally mandated tests, multiple intelligences are ignored and often completely overlooked. This especially penalizes students from low SES backgrounds, who, as we have pointed out, often are behind their more privileged age peers in linguistic skills before they even reach kindergarten. Moreover, as noted earlier in this chapter, research shows that, often, low SES students do well in art: an area that has increasingly fallen victim to the higher, stakes-driven priorities of reading, writing, and math.

In order to motivate students from low SES backgrounds (and indeed, all students) to learn, schools must do their best to let go of practices based on the ability game, which often rely exclusively on linguistic and mathematical means of expression, and incorporate practices based on the equity game. In the equity game, students are matched with preferred rewards and allowed to express themselves through different modes. They are allowed various forms of expression. Curiosity is rewarded. Table 7–7 is one example of a checklist of ways students can express themselves in a variety of modalities to demonstrate knowledge in subject areas.

Table 7–7. Examples of Assignments Using Multiple Abilities

1. Draw a picture, mural, or poster
2. Make a sculpture or plaster figure
3. Invent a game
4. Create a PowerPoint presentation
5. Create an experiment
6. Do a dance
7. Do a pantomime or skit
8. Write a story
9. Write a song
10. Bake something
11. Write a poem
12. Take pictures with a digital camera or camcorder
13. Make a chart with numbers
14. Think up an advertisement to sell an idea
15. Make a speech to the class
16. Make a scrapbook
17. Do a puppet show
18. Make a map

Source: Adapted from Armstrong, 2011; Covington and Teel, 1996.

In summary, in the ability game, students work to outperform others. This puts students from low SES backgrounds at a great disadvantage. In the equity game, students are able to express themselves through different modalities. Most of all, they are motivated to excel in order promote pride in their own accomplishments and efforts: not to compare themselves with others.

CONCLUSIONS

Success in teaching students from low SES backgrounds requires an appreciation of some basic principles of learning coupled with awareness of the specific vulnerabilities of these children. When professionals incorporate practical strategies that enhance learning, students will experience greater academic success. A large part of this is helping students be motivated, self-directed learners who use their unique and individual gifts to create enriching lives for themselves. To truly narrow the achievement gap between SES students from low- and those from middle SES backgrounds, professionals must enhance their learning opportunities in educational settings as much as possible. As Payne (2003) says, about the only way out of generational poverty is through education, and professionals who work with children have the opportunity to provide that education for the next generation.

CHAPTER HIGHLIGHTS

- Low SES students often benefit when professionals incorporate strategies for optimizing the learning environment. These strategies include limiting clutter and distraction, decreasing extraneous noise, giving students movement breaks, teaching important content information in the morning, and helping students remain hydrated.
- Students need to be taught in ways that engage the whole brain, not just the left side of brain, as is typical in many American schools. Whole-brain learning ultimately is more successful for these students, especially if they come from

homes where oral and literate language development has not been emphasized.

▢ Because so many low SES students have memory challenges, we can incorporate specific strategies to encourage memorization of important information. These strategies include visualization; using association, color, and exaggeration; and promotion of active, hands-on learning.

▢ Students from low SES backgrounds have less overall experience with language and use language in casual register. They often flounder in situations such as classrooms and therapy rooms where language is formal and highly decontextualized. It is important for professionals to work hard to contextualize language and academic content as much as possible; this is especially important with young children during their early school experiences.

▢ Some low SES students may come from a culture of resistance, where those close to them discourage academic achievement as an act of betrayal to their roots. In order for these students to succeed academically and eventually vocationally, they need a strong support system of education personnel and mentors to provide the emotional resources to succeed. These mentors can include teachers and other school personnel; peer mentors are often very successful.

▢ Low SES students may demonstrate learned helplessness because of prior and current overwhelming life circumstances. A big part of professionals' job is to help these students learn that at least at school, persevering in the face of challenges brings concrete rewards. Professionals can help increase students' executive functioning skills in the area use of self-efficacy behaviors such as perseverance and positive self-talk.

▢ Because the self-esteem of many low SES students is lowered by challenges with personal appearance, schools can provide resources. These resources include laundry facilities, soap, shampoo, and clean clothes. Rewards can come in the form of bright, attractive school supplies that low SES families might not be able to afford.

▢ As much as possible, professionals need to increase students' motivation to succeed; implementing the equity game is very helpful. In the equity game, students' own actions and perseverance toward goals are encouraged; references to innate ability are discouraged.

If professionals define intelligence flexibly, they can promote and reward students' expression in a variety of modalities. For example, some students have very high musical ability; others excel in linguistic ability; some have excellent spatial skills.

8

Poverty and Highly Mobile Populations: Mitigating the Impact of High Mobility and Chaos

If there is a poor man with you, one of your brothers
. . . you shall not harden your heart, nor close your
hand from your poor brother; but you shall freely
open your hand to him, and shall generously lend
him sufficient for his need in whatever he lacks . . .
for the poor will never cease to be in the land . . .

Deuteronomy 15:7–8, 11a

It is the month of October. Both Marcos and Mark have October birthdays. Marcos' mother would like to have a lovely party for her son, but she and her husband don't have any extra money. Besides, they need to move again. They are migrant agricultural workers and typically need to move three or four times each year. Marcos' mother is sad for her son. He has made several friends at his new school. They seem like nice boys, and Marcos' mother wishes he did not have to leave these new friends.

Marcos' mother realizes that she needs to notify the school of their impending move. She hates to do this; Marcos is in the process of getting assessed for some special education support from the school's resource specialist. The speech-language pathologist (SLP), whose own child has had challenges similar to those experienced by Marcos, has pushed hard for Marcos to get extra support for reading and just generally has "gone to bat" for Marcos. Although the SLP is a middle SES White woman who speaks very little Spanish, she seems to know what Marcos and his family are going through, and Marcos' mother has felt a real bond with her because they both have boys around the same age who struggle in school. Marcos' mother is especially sad to say goodbye to this new ally.

When Marcos and his family move to a new area with a different school, the special education referral process will start all over again. Marcos' mother has been told that from the time of referral for special education assessment, school personnel have 60 days to act on this referral. By that time, the family may have to move again. Marcos' mother longs to stay in one place where her child can get some help, but it is not possible. She wonders if Marcos will ever catch up. She and her husband moved to California from Mexico to pursue a better life for their children. So far, their life in California is not much better than the one they had in Mexico.

For Mark's birthday, his mother has rented the karate dojo where he takes lessons to give a big party. She has invited old friends and new ones: friends from Mark's preschool days, friends from the school he attended from kindergarten through second grade, and friends from Sunday school, in addition to friends from karate and from his current elementary school.

The party is a huge success. About 30 children and many parents are there, and Mark is showered with "cool" birthday gifts. The children are served pizza, cake, and ice cream. As the party winds down, everyone thanks Mark and his parents for how much fun they had. New and old friendships have been reinforced, and Mark has had a truly memorable time — which his parents recorded on camera for the family to enjoy later. On the short drive home after the party, Mark reminds his parents that they need to go shopping for his Halloween costume.

A week or so after Mark's birthday party, his mother runs into his school principal in the school hallway. The principal remarks on how well Mark is doing, praises him as an especially likable and engaging child, and reports that his classroom teacher is really proud of his progress. Things are going well for Mark!

INTRODUCTION

This chapter addresses the characteristics and needs of low SES students who are especially vulnerable to high mobility and resulting chaos and its impacts. The two specific populations of interest are migrant students and homeless students. Their issues are very similar, and they are often vulnerable to deficits in executive functioning (EF) in the areas of planning and organization. These deficits especially involve application of problem-solving processes at the outset of a novel, non-automatic task. These deficits are described, and specific remediation strategies are explained.

CHAOS: DEFINITION, CHARACTERISTICS, AND IMPACT ON STUDENTS

In Chapter 1, we introduced the construct of chaos. Here, this construct is expanded upon and explained in more detail as it relates to highly mobile low SES children. When students are highly mobile, they often experience substantial chaos in their lives. Brooks-Gunn, Johnson, and Leventhal (2010) explain two major categories of chaos: *disorder* and *turbulence*. Disorder involves three areas: (1) noise and confusion, (2) crowding and density, and (3) clutter and messiness. Turbulence involves: (1) low supervision and monitoring, (2) fluidity and instability of residents of a home, and (3) lack of predictability and routines (Table 8–1). Children from environments characterized by disorder, turbulence, or both are at risk in a number of areas. For example, they often demonstrate behavioral problems and difficulty

Table 8–1. Constructs of Chaos

Disorder	Turbulence
1. Noise and Confusion • TV on • Ambient environmental noise • Many individuals living in a small space	1. Low Supervision and Monitoring • Latchkey kids • Children unsupervised in public places such as malls, parks
2. Clutter and Messiness • Number of items lying about that are not put away • Neighborhood clutter (e.g., trash, drug paraphernalia, broken windows)	2. Fluidity and Instability of Residents • Moving from living unit to living unit • Frequent changes in household residents
3. Crowding and Density • Number of household members • Number of people sharing a room	3. Lack of Predictability and Routines • No regular bedtime • Few—no family meals together • Lack of predictable, structured routines such as getting ready for school in the same manner each day

Source: Based on Ackerman and Brown, 2010; Fiese and Winter, 2010; Lichter and Wethington, 2010; Vernon-Feagans et al., 2011; Wachs and Evans, 2010.

with social skills (Evans et al., 2010; Fiese & Winter, 2010). If chaos is experienced both at home and at school, the risk is cumulative (Maxwell, 2010).

Characteristics and Impact of Disorder

In terms of the first area of disorder, noise and confusion, many low SES homes and some homeless shelters are near major areas of transportation (e.g., freeways, airports). Noise interferes with relaxation and sleep, and elevates physiological arousal. It disrupts concentration and attention, and can make people feel irritable and hostile

(Evans et al., 2010). The household may contain a high number of people. In many homes, the TV is on a great deal.

Christakis and colleagues (2009), mentioned in Chapter 1, conducted a study of the impact of TV on parent-child interactions. Each hour of audible TV was associated with significant reductions in child vocalizations, vocalization duration, and conversational turns. Each hour of TV was also associated with significant reductions in adult male and female word count. In sum, TV and its noise were significantly associated with reduced child and adult vocalizations and interactions.

In Chapter 1 we discussed the research of Vernon-Feagans et al. (2011), who studied the impact of household chaos, especially including high levels of noise, on children's developing language. They concluded that in terms of language development, early word learning is faster and more efficient when children are engaged in joint attention activities with caregivers. It is hard for these joint attention activities to occur effectively in the presence of constant noise. The combination of high levels of noise and crowding is deleterious to children's developing language, especially in the early years. High levels of noise have been associated with poorer attention, memory, reading, and overall language and academic achievement (e.g., Riley & McGregor, 2012). According to Evans and Hygge (2007), reading deficits are the most robust adverse developmental outcome associated with chronic noise.

Crowding and density, the second area under the category of disorder, are defined by the number of household members or the number of people per room in a household. From a neighborhood perspective, crowding is often measured by the number of housing units, individuals, or households per census block group or tract (Brooks-Gunn et al., 2010). Because crowded environments are often overstimulating, confusing, and unpredictable, children's development of social interaction skills is compromised (Evans et al., 2010). The combination of crowding and noise can be especially deleterious to parent-child relationships, as parents in these conditions tend to be less patient with and responsive to their children; they are less likely to verbally engage with their children (Evans et al., 2010). There may be less parental warmth and harsher, more hostile interactions between parents and children.

The third area under the category of disorder, clutter and messiness, is more challenging to define and operationalize. Clutter and messiness can refer to individual living units or to entire neighborhoods. For example, in homes as individual dwelling units, clutter can refer to the number of items lying about in plain sight that are not put away. In neighborhoods, the presence of trash, broken windows, graffiti, shards of glass, empty alcohol bottles, and drug paraphernalia all contribute to clutter and messiness. If children come from cluttered and messy homes and neighborhoods, they may have difficulty keeping their things neat and ordered at school in accordance with teachers' expectations.

When a child lives with a high level of disorder, externalizing behavior and attention problems can result. There are links to disorder and lower linguistic and cognitive measures, including lower expressive vocabulary skills (Brooks-Gunn et al., 2010). Household confusion has been associated with lower early reading abilities (Johnson, Martin, Brooks-Gunn, & Petrill, 2008).

Characteristics and Impact of Turbulence

In terms of the category of turbulence, first, children may experience the aspect of low supervision and monitoring. For example, many children come home to an empty living unit after school because their parents are working. They may spend a great deal of unsupervised time in malls, stores, and parks.

Second, fluidity and instability in a child's life also contribute to chaos. Fluidity and instability can involve moving from one residence to another. They can also involve a "revolving door" of individuals who live in the home. For example, if a single mother is involved in serial monogamous relationships with live-in boyfriends, this situation contributes to fluidity and instability for the child. According to Lichter and Wethington (2010), recent estimates suggest that approximately 25 to 35% of American children will live with cohabiting parents during childhood. The instability of cohabiting unions can lead to elevated levels of instability in children's lives. Evans et al. (2010) state that changes in household composition can be highly disruptive, especially to young children who form attachments to parental partners. In an earlier chapter, I talked about LaVera T., who lived in a home with a father, three mothers, and 12 children.

If turbulence is present to a great degree in a child's life, especially in the area of fluidity and instability, there may be greater levels of juvenile delinquency, crime, and child maltreatment (Coulton, Crampton, Irwin, Spilsjury, & Korbin, 2007). The domestic partners of parents may not have the patience, with children, that would be shown by the children's biological parents. In these cases especially, maltreatment can result. Child abuse is more prevalent in single-parent than in two-parent families.

A third aspect of the category of turbulence is lack of predictability and routines. Routines occur repeatedly over time, and they convey what needs to be done by whom. Highly mobile low SES families are constantly subject to disruptions in routine, especially if they are homeless. Even if they are housed, lower-wage workers have more change and less regular schedules than workers who are paid more; these workers are also more likely to work during the evening or at night (Evans et al., 2010). For these workers and their children, establishing routines is challenging indeed.

The lack of predictable routines has a great deal of impact of many areas of a child's life: executive functioning skills (discussed later), language, cognition, and others. According to experts (e.g., Brooks-Gunn et al., 2010; Vernon-Feagans et al., 2011), lack of predictability and routines specifically impacts children's social skills especially. Weisner (2010) explains how social exchanges are "unpredictable, brief, and few" (p. 213). Basically, children are not able to engage in long, extended exchanges with others: types of exchanges that promote higher order social skills and even narrative skills. Children who live with lack of predictable routines may have difficulty with comprehending temporal sequences as well as cause and effect relationships (Evans et al., 2010). In addition, these children may have more difficulty following school classroom routines (Roseberry-McKibbin, 2013).

When students enter school in kindergarten, and every year after that, they need to learn and follow classroom social routines or scripts (Brinton & Fujiki, 2011; Westby, 2006). Middle class parents build routines in their children's worlds: going grocery shopping, attending church, eating out at restaurants, visiting the local library, attending team sports practices, and others. These highly familiar events and the verbal rituals that accompany them become internalized over time. Along with this internalization, a set of oral language scripts develops: these scripts are predictable language sequences that condition children to know how to act and to expect what is next. Because low SES children often are not exposed to these routines in their everyday lives, they may come to school without a basic oral script set. When children have lived with casual, informal, unpredictable, continuously shifting schedules, the order, regimentation and time-slottedness of school can be a great shock to them (Geiss, 2011; Neuman, 2009).

Wachs and Evans (2010) comment that routine tasks of daily living provide security and identity for children. Without the ability to sustain meaningful daily tasks and activities in a regular manner, children cannot acquire a sense of continuity, order, and purpose in life.

Chaos: General Impact on American Children

When we think of chaos, we think of its impact on migrant and homeless students. Migrant and homeless students are frequently subjected to severe chaos. However, since the Great Recession, traditionally "middle SES" students are also now more subject to the impact of chaos. These students experience mild-moderate chaos; chaos is not experienced to the degree or depth that it is by migrant and homeless students. Nevertheless, since the Great Recession began in 2007, chaos is present to a greater degree in middle SES communities than it has been in the past.

We all know how deeply home foreclosures and job losses have impacted American families. My husband and son and I personally know families, whose children are friends of Mark's, who have lost their homes to foreclosures and have been forced to move to smaller homes in less traditional neighborhoods. Along with this, middle SES traditional full-time at-home mothers have been obligated to enter the work force when their husbands have been laid off from their jobs. This phenomenon has contributed to chaos, even in the lives of traditionally middle SES students from relatively stable homes. Many of these children are physiologically and environmentally vulnerable to difficulties with EF. Although formerly middle SES students are not as vulnerable to EF deficits as migrant and homeless children, they may still demonstrate the impact of mild-moderate chaos in their lives. It is important for us as professionals to account for this when we work with students.

As we enter into the middle of the second decade of the 21st century, I think it is safe for us as professionals to assume that many of the students we work with in the schools will have experienced some degree of chaos in their lives. We can plan our interactions and teaching methods with students accordingly, implementing some of the suggestions in the last section of this chapter.

Chelsea M. is a personal friend of mine—her son is in Mark's class at school. Chelsea finished high school and attended college for 1 to 2 years. She met and married an attractive man with a stable job. When Chelsea became pregnant with the first of their three boys, she stopped going to college and did not get her degree. She stayed at home with her son, homeschooling him, and then two more babies came along. She homeschooled them also while her husband worked full time outside the home. Money was tight, but the family was happy. Chelsea was fulfilling her lifelong dream and expectation that she would get married, have children, and stay at home to raise them.

But then one fateful day, disaster struck: her husband was laid off from his job. Chelsea had been a happy, full-time, at-home mom, actively involved in homeschooling her three boys and then volunteering for many hours at the public school when they transferred there. Chelsea was the mom you always saw on the field trips, at yard duty, and on the PTA board.

The family's life turned upside down. Chelsea obtained a full-time paying job outside the home, but because she did not have a college degree, the job paid very little. She was forced to work long hours for very little money per hour, but at least the family (unlike thousands of others) did not lose their home. In a touching conversation, an exhausted Chelsea sadly confided to me that she missed her children so much. "I never see them," she said. The shock and trauma of going from a full time, at-home mom involved in her children's lives to a mom who worked outside the home was overwhelming. The household became much more chaotic; Chelsea was not around to drive her sons to their sports practices, do homework with them, or "hold down the fort" like she used to. Her husband eventually found another job, but it paid a low hourly wage. The expected, middle class dream was a thing of the past as the family struggled to cope with their new, unwanted circumstances.

HIGH MOBILITY AND CHAOS: SPECIFIC IMPACTS ON SCHOOLS AND CLASSROOMS

Although individual students are impacted by chaos and high mobility, classrooms and schools as institutions are impacted as well. In a given school year, homeless students may attend 3 to 4 different schools (Murphy, 2011). High mobility diminishes students' chances of graduating from high school; highly mobile students often earn significantly lower standardized test scores than those typical for their less mobile peers. These low scores and reduced high school graduation rates can hurt the scores and ratings of schools, who are under substantial pressure to perform at the highest possible level.

Excessive mobility also is a burden at the school site and district levels. Administrators and office staff need to obtain curriculum and health records for newly arriving registrants. They also must transfer records of students who leave, often not knowing where these students are going. Allocating time and resources to these tasks reduces overall per-pupil resources, slows school improvements, and impedes efforts to build community (Hartman, 2006). Excessive mobility often hurts stable students too: It slows down the pace of the curriculum, because teachers have to review more. A higher incidence of emotional disturbances in these children may be rooted in the frequent and sudden disappearance of classmates and friends (Murphy, 2011).

In terms of the impact of chaos on schools, research has linked child outcomes with crowding and noise levels in classrooms. First, teachers in crowded, noisy classrooms are obliged to spend more time disciplining children and less time teaching content. These teachers may be more likely to feel annoyed, tired, and impatient; this can reduce their teaching effectiveness in comparison to that of teachers who serve in quieter schools (Evans & Hygge, 2007). If classrooms are crowded, students may experience cognitive overload and become disruptive; research shows that high classroom density is associated with lower reading scores. Crowdedness in classrooms can also lead to social interaction problems, especially because privacy cannot be obtained when desired. Thus, children may psychologically withdraw, reducing their social interaction with others. Reducing children's chronic exposure to classroom overcrowding benefits their academic achievement and cognitive development; this is especially true for minority students (Maxwell, 2010).

If students are in a chaotic classroom that is crowded and noisy, it is more difficult for them to engage socially. Healthy engagement with the environment involves sustained and progressively more complex interactions with others. These interactions may occur less frequently in chaotic classrooms, especially because group activities are limited; teachers prefer to have students engage in quiet paper-pencil activities such as worksheets or in computer-aided instruction (Maxwell, 2010).

As we said in Chapter 7, noise can interfere with students' comprehension of classroom material being taught (Roseberry-McKibbin, 2008). It can also interfere with their ability to think, especially when completing work requiring higher levels of thinking (Maxwell, 2010). Riley and McGregor (2012), in a study on the impact of noise on typically-developing children, concluded that noise limits expressive vocabulary growth in children, reducing the quality of word form representation in their lexicons. Noise in a school also interferes with attention and memory, making it difficult to focus on tasks. Children may learn to tune out the noise; unfortunately, along with this, they may also tune out content that the teacher is trying to teach them.

SPECIAL CONSIDERATIONS IN SERVING MIGRANT STUDENTS

Migrant workers in the United States seek temporary or seasonal work in fishing, agriculture, or related industries such as food processing. They follow the growing seasons across the country. Many migrant workers have an average income below the national poverty line (Castillo, 2012). According to the U.S. Department of Agriculture (2012), 32% of migrant workers have less than a 9th grade education compared to 3% of the American workforce as a whole. They are at a disadvantage due to limited English language skills as well as low levels of education.

Children of migrant agricultural workers frequently experience discrimination, health problems, poverty, and language barriers. They may have asthma, middle ear infections, and anemia. Their high mobility often greatly affects their educational attainment. Many of these children attend up to six or seven schools a year. They have to constantly adapt to new curricula and new procedures. They have to continuously establish social ties and adjust to new school cultures. Many migrant students drop out of school in their teens (Castillo, 2012).

A very frequent problem for these children is the lack of consistent classroom structure that supports learning to read. High mobility means that migrant students often receive very fragmented reading instruction. When their reading skills are depressed, their academic performance overall is negatively affected (Jachman, 2006). Children of migrant workers are especially vulnerable if they have special education needs. They often have limited access to special education services because they are never in one place long enough to be assessed and begin intervention (Hardman et al., 2011).

SLPs, teachers, and other professionals who work with children from migrant families often cannot follow through on planned services for these children because the family moves on and the children no longer attend the school. I cannot tell you how many times I have gone to assess a migrant or homeless child who was referred for speech-language testing only to find out that he or she was no longer at the school. Even more frustrating have been the experiences where I have assessed a child, completed all paperwork for him to begin speech-language therapy, and then been told that he and his family are no longer at the school. All my hours of assessment and paperwork feel like they have been in vain. That is not quite accurate, as I can do my best to send the paperwork to the child's new school, wherever that may be. I always am concerned about highly mobile children "falling through the cracks" because paperwork transfer is often slow and cumbersome. However, we all as professionals must do our best to try facilitate the paperwork process for students who move often. Today, electronic tracking systems have been helpful in expediting transfer of information between school districts.

The following case example, based on a real-life situation, illustrates some of the difficulties in providing needed services to children of highly mobile families.

> Joel was a likable sixth grade Mexican student with a pleasant, easy-going manner who was referred to me for evaluation for his "stuttering." In fact, Joel didn't stutter, but the classroom teacher reported that his reading and writing skills were commensurate with those of a first grader. I saw problems with his fine and visual motor skills. His oral language was very limited, even in Spanish. I wondered why

he had not been referred to special education before. I was especially concerned because he was going to be entering junior high school in a few months.

When I expressed concerns to Joel's classroom teacher, he shrugged and said that the family was always moving—plus, Joel spoke Spanish as his dominant language. School personnel had assumed that his family's high mobility rate and Spanish-speaking background were the cause of his low scores. The need for extra support services had never been considered.

I took the time to prepare a long, detailed report about Joel's written and oral language skills and the need for a comprehensive psychoeducational evaluation before junior high school. I wanted to be sure that Joel would receive the help he needed to succeed in school. When I saw Joel for a last assessment session to wrap up a few loose ends, he shared that his family was going back to Mexico the next day—for 3 or 4 months. Unfortunately, I was never able to find out what became of Joel. At least my report was in his cumulative file so that it would follow him to junior high school.

The special needs of children from migrant agricultural families often are overlooked by educators, especially if these families do not speak English (as in the example of Joel). It is easy to disregard the learning difficulties experienced by these children by ascribing them to irregular school attendance, limited English skills, or both. In point of fact, these children often are barely recognized as legitimate members of the student population as they move from school to school. Nevertheless, so long as these children are in school, teachers and other professionals need to do their best to provide genuine learning experiences and to give them a sense of stability. Some educators have not infrequently worked with students who, by first or second grade, have been to three or four different schools. This is especially true with children of migrant agricultural workers.

In addition to the issue of sporadic schooling for their children, migrant workers and their families often are socially and physically isolated from the larger community. Children may not always receive the language stimulation they need because of this isolation, in addition to the fact that hard physical labor makes their parents too tired to spend much time with them at the end of a day. For example, if parents spend 8 hours a day in 100-degree heat picking strawberries, they will have little energy left over for their children when they get home. In addition, many children in migrant families work alongside their parents in the fields and consequently are fatigued themselves. I have had conversations with students and colleagues who grew up as children of migrant agricultural workers in California. Some of them worked alongside their parents in the fields, in 100+ degree heat, when they were as young as 8 years old.

Both children and parents may have little or no food to eat. Lack of food and basic health care are major issues for these families. To provide health support for migrant families, for a number of years a large annual health fair, called *Su Salud* ("Your Health"), was held in central California. The health fair provided free medical services, including screening, for these families. Some professionals like me who volunteered at Su Salud to provide free speech and hearing screenings interacted with families who had not eaten for several days. It was distressing to consider the value of recommending language stimulation activities in the home for families who did not have even the basics of life such as food and health care.

One year some colleagues and I conducted a survey of 254 migrant Hispanic families at Su Salud. We found that greater than 90% of these families had no health insurance at all. Professionals must be particularly aware of health insurance needs in these types of families and, as previously stated, should have available a list of affordable and accessible health care services to share with the families.

Schools are in a position to provide strong support for migrant families. As a model of community support for such families, several schools in Morse, Texas, with large numbers of migrant students have networks of support and information that are immediately available to families and allow them to tap into available resources. These resources include both education and health services, important for families in hazardous farm-working occupations (Jachman, 2006).

To support the children in these migrant families, teachers in Morse schools have successfully focused on early balanced literacy instruction. Strategies include explicit instruction in phonemic awareness, fluency, vocabulary, phonics, and comprehension—all integrated into meaningful interactions with print. Both group and independent activities are provided. Guided work occurs in small groups of students with similar reading levels. Group composition is fluid and depends on each child's changing needs.

In these Morse schools, children from migrant families have benefited from the use of Accelerated Reader (Accelerated Reader Enterprises, 2006), a previously mentioned commercially produced reading program that includes regular computerized assessments and allows students to select books within their reading level (Jachman, 2006). Payne (2003) has identified Accelerated Reader as a program that can be beneficial to students from low SES backgrounds.

In the Accelerated Reader program, at the beginning of the year, each child is assessed for reading comprehension and fluency. Parents are given a printout of their child's current reading level, with specific suggestions as to how they can appropriately challenge their child at home. Each week, the class is given whole-group reading instruction. In addition, six different reading groups determined by reading level meet each week, and students are instructed at the appropriate level. The children select books provided for their developmental reading level, and are encouraged to read each night at home. When a child finishes a book, the next day in class the child takes a 10-question, multiple-choice computerized test to assess comprehension. A printout of the results gives immediate feedback about the child's reading accuracy. Children can be taught to review what they have read, supported by their parents, to enhance comprehension.

In addition to providing efficacious academic programs for students from migrant families, schools can work at the district level to create an atmosphere and culture sensitive to the needs of highly mobile students and their families (Castillo, 2012). This effort entails providing extra attention and help, involving parents, connecting with school counselors, and assessing students with special needs. In addition, teachers can assign a "student ambassador" to a new child; the student ambassador's job is to be a "buddy" and help the new child negotiate those first few weeks in the new school.

Schools can improve record keeping on student mobility. They also can focus on creating school communities that parents and students value and enjoy and could serve as an inducement to stay if possible. Schools also should offer transportation assistance, especially to migrant students who live in remote locations.

SERVING STUDENTS WHO ARE HOMELESS

Introduction and Demographic Data

The federal definition of homelessness used by all United States public schools includes children and youth who lack a regular, fixed, and adequate nighttime residence. This definition specifically includes children and youth living in cars, shelters, transitional housing, motels, campgrounds, and sharing temporary housing with others. Homelessness is caused by people's inability to pay for housing; it is impacted by both income and the affordability of available housing (National Alliance to End Homelessness, 2012).

Basically, displaced individuals can be divided into three groups: (1) single adults, (2) families with children, and (3) unaccompanied youth. Families with children represent the fastest growing category of the homeless population (Murphy, 2011). Thirty-nine percent, or 1.37 million, of homeless people are children younger than 18 years of age. It is estimated that between 25–40% of homeless children are under the age of 5 (Perlman & Fantuzzo, 2010). Approximately 47% of children in homeless families are African American, even though African Americans make up only 15% of the U.S. total population (Child Trends Databank, 2012).

Unaccompanied youth are persons under the age of 18. They may be *runaways* who have left home without parental permission. They may be *throwaways*, or young persons who have been told by a parent or guardian to leave and who are not permitted to return home (Murphy, 2011). Unaccompanied youth may also be *system youth*, or those who live in situations such as foster homes or in juvenile justice facilities. It is estimated that currently, there are approximately 1.5 to 2 million unaccompanied youth in the United States.

According to the most recent federal data, in the 2008–2009 school year, there were 954,914 homeless children and youth enrolled in public schools. This enrollment represented a 20% increase from the 2007–2008 school year, and a 41% increase from the 2006–2007 school year. It is estimated that African American students are disproportionately represented in these figures (National Association for the Education of Homeless Children and Youth; NAEHCY, 2011).

Of the population of homeless adults, 30% have substance abuse problems, 22% are disabled or have serious mental illness, and 46%

have chronic health problems such as high blood pressure. Fifty-five percent have no health insurance (as compared with 16% of the general population). Two aspects of the job market that are integral to an explanation of the increase in homelessness in recent years are: (1) dwindling job opportunities for those on the low end of the employment spectrum in terms of education, wages, and skills and (2) decreases in the purchasing power of low wages.

Homeless people report that the lack of affordable housing is the number one reason for becoming homeless and a lack of adequate pay as the number two reason for becoming homeless. Many homeless people hold down jobs, but they don't earn enough money to pay for both food and rent (Child Trends Databank, 2012). In every county and state within the United States, the full-time minimum wage worker cannot afford the fair market rent for housing (NAEHCY, 2011).

Certain populations are more vulnerable to homelessness than others. A person released from prison has a 1 in 13 chance of becoming homeless; the young adult who has aged out of foster care has a 1 in 11 chance of becoming homeless (National Alliance to End Homelessness, 2012). According to the National Coalition for the Homeless (2006), people with disabilities and those who are chronically ill have a greatly increased risk of becoming homeless. A disabled person with no close friends or relatives risks dying of exposure if he or she is unable to find a cot in a shelter.

> My son Mark and I have been privileged to work on the streets with members of the homeless community, through our church's ministry, for the last several years. On one Saturday morning a month, we and other church members drive to a homeless shelter where we give out food, clothing, toiletries, Bibles, shoes, and coats. I often pick up trash, which is very plentiful in the area. Trash cans are scarce because authorities are afraid homeless persons will build fires in them.
>
> One day Mark and I were preparing to go home after a morning of serving food and talking and praying with some members of the homeless community. The day was getting hot, and we looked forward to driving back to our comfortable, air conditioned home for lunch. Teresa and

Gwen, two of the women we had interacted with, were waiting for the bus to come and bring them back to their "hotel," a temporary housing unit downtown. Because they had so many bags of clothes that they had gathered that day from our church's pile, they were not sure they could manage to get all their new "stuff" back to where they were staying. They asked me if I would be willing to give them a ride so they could safely bring all their bags back to their place.

I want to note here that homeless men have asked me for rides, and I have always politely declined. But these two women moved me so much. I was not proud of myself as thoughts chased through my mind about actually having them in my car. Did they have lice . . . ? Because they did not have the opportunity for regular showers and clothes-washing, would a pungent odor linger in the upholstery of my car, requiring substantial cleaning later . . . ? Swallowing hard and putting a smile on my face, I said that, of course, I would be happy to bring them home.

On the way, Gwen's story came out. She had been severely beaten several years ago, and sustained substantial traumatic brain injury (TBI). Her medications were so potent that she was sleepy most of the time, and was unable to hold down a paying job any more. Mark and I continued to talk with her and Teresa, and we finally reached their destination. The two women got out, thanking us profusely for the ride.

This last Easter, Mark and I went to a church service in the new chapel next to the homeless shelter. We served food and helped give out sleeping bags. During the service, I sat by a man with tears running down his face. I asked him if he would like to talk about it or be left alone. He said he was having some problems with some of the other homeless men in the shelter, and that he would like me to pray with him. I did, and was thankful for the opportunity to be by his side to provide support, however, briefly.

I had a long conversation (in sign language) with David, a deaf homeless man whose wife had killed their three sons in his presence. He told me that he had lost his mind, but with help, was putting his life back together. We served a woman who had a black eye and cuts and bruises; she said she had been jumped and beaten the night before inside the shelter. An articulate and refined gentleman at the Christmas lunch told me that he and his wife had a nice house in Washington. But she had a stroke; after insurance ran out, they could not pay medical expenses and lost their home. A woman who could have been my sister came to the clothes pile, looking for something to wear. As we talked, she apologized in case she smelled bad. She and her family had been foreclosed on; she had not changed clothes in six days. A woman cried when she saw Mark (he was 11 at the time) and asked if she could hug him. Sobbing, she explained that she had lost her 6 children due to substance abuse problems. She had not hugged a child in a very long time.

A statistic of almost tragic significance is that in a recent survey, 44% of homeless persons reported that they had worked in the past week. Professionals need to remember that

> homelessness is not a product of a moral deficit of an individual but rather a result of complex, sociopolitical issues for which the community at large is responsible. In addition, single adults who are homeless usually possess a number of strengths, including being well-groomed, having at least a GED, and having a history of employment. (Baggerly & Zalaquett, 2006, p. 164)

Specific Characteristics and Needs of Homeless Students and Their Families

Homeless students and families have many needs to be met, including access to education in public schools. It is problematic for homeless children and youth to attend school for a number of reasons. First, their high mobility makes consistent school attendance a challenge as we have said before. Second, enrollment is difficult because schools require documentation: proof of residency, legal guardianship, immunization records, birth certificates, school records). Most homeless families are challenged to provide this documentation, and thus students cannot enroll in and attend school (NAEHCY, 2011). Technically, however, these students should be able to attend school via the provisions of the McKinney-Vento Act.

The McKinney-Vento Act, passed in 1987 and reauthorized as part of No Child Left Behind in 2001, requires that state and local educational agencies provide homeless students with access to school as well as support for their attendance and success. Key provisions of the Act include:

1. Homeless students can remain in one school, even if their temporary living situation is located in another school district or attendance area, if that is in their best interests. Schools must provide transportation.
2. Homeless children and youth can enroll in school and begin attending immediately, even if they cannot produce normally required documents (as listed above)
3. Every school district must designate a liaison between the district and the homeless community to ensure that the Act is implemented.
4. Every state must designate a state coordinator to ensure that the Act is implemented in the state
5. Both state coordinators and homeless liaisons must collaborate with other agencies serving homeless children, youth, and families to enhance educational attendance and success
6. School districts and state departments of education must review and revise their policies and practices to eliminate barriers to the enrollment of and retention in school of homeless children and youth

Despite the provisions of the McKinney-Vento Act, parents who are homeless may not have the resources to shield children from the chaos in their lives. These children lack consistent school records, often have guardianship problems, and lack resources such as school supplies and clothing. They usually have inconsistent school attendance (Maxwell, 2010). Accordingly, their academic skills will suffer because they are not consistently in the classroom. They are more likely to be labeled as having below average intelligence and often perform poorly on standardized tests of math and reading (Perlman &

Fantuzzo, 2010). They are twice as likely as housed children to have a learning disability, repeat a grade, or to be suspended from school (American Psychological Association, 2012).

One problem for homeless students with disabilities is that they have a great deal of difficulty accessing special education programs (Murphy, 2011). I have frequently been in situations where I was unable to obtain a parent or guardian signature for a speech-language evaluation, let alone for an individualized education plan that would enable a child to access therapy. For both migrant and homeless students, even if special education paperwork is completed, they may move before therapy begins. Again, as a professional who provides special education services, one of my biggest barriers to providing these services to homeless students is that I am unable to obtain parent signatures that I legally must have before I provide any assessment or treatment services at all.

Students who move frequently may be reluctant to establish new friendships or rely on adults for support and guidance; they know that they will soon have to break those ties and start over again (Evans et al., 2010). Homeless children may feel frustrated about a lack of opportunities for play and social interaction with other students at the school, knowing that they will need to change schools again soon (Swick, 2010). It is estimated that each time a child changes schools, he is set back an average of four to six months (National Center for Homeless Education, 2006).

Homelessness correlates with being retained in school. Studies affirm a strong relationship between grade retention and dropping out of school. By one estimate, a student who is retained one time faces a 40% increase in the likelihood of dropping out of school. If that student is retained twice, the likelihood of dropping out increases to 90%. Less a than quarter of homeless children in the United States complete high school (National Center on Family Homelessness, 2009).

Many homeless students are hungry, and this impacts learning. They frequently experience physical health problems, developmental delays, and emotional and behavioral disorders. Cutuli, Wiik, Herbers, Gunnar, and Masten (2009) studied 66 children between 4 to 7 years of age who were staying in an emergency shelter for families. Adversities that reflected negative life events in families predicted higher levels of cortisol in children. Chronic activation of physiological stress response systems can be detrimental at many levels, and is linked to a variety of poor mental and physical health outcomes.

These problems often are compounded by family circumstances such as substance abuse, domestic violence, financial problems, and parental distress (Cutuli et al., 2009; Gerwirtz, Hart-Shegos, & Medhanie, 2008; Murphy, 2011). In one study, the intensity of mental health symptom distress experienced by mothers was significantly higher in the subgroup of homeless children that performed more poorly on outcome measures of behavior, adaptive functioning, and achievement (Huntington, Buckner, & Bassuk, 2008).

A quarter of homeless children have witnessed violence, and 22% have been separated from their families. Homeless families must sometimes break up to receive emergency shelter; for young children, separation from their mothers is highly stressful. Often, this separation occurs because mothers are in substance abuse treatment (Shinn et al., 2008). A significant percentage of homeless mothers have experienced violence during their childhood (Swick, 2010).

By one estimate, 50 to 75% of homeless families have experienced some form of serious violence. Exposure to violence can cause a number of psychological sequelae for homeless students; these sequelae include depression, anxiety, withdrawal, acting out, and aggression (Yu, North, LaVesser, Osborne, & Spitznagel, 2007). One in five homeless preschoolers has emotional problems that necessitate professional care (American Psychological Association, 2012). Emotional problems can impact children throughout their lives. Child abuse and significant separation from primary caregivers is associated with homelessness rates in adulthood that are 26 times higher than rates in the general population (Herman, Susser, Struening, & Link, 1997).

Most homeless parents experience some basic and essential needs (Shinn et al., 2008; Swick, 2010): supportive, responsible, caring helpers, adequate housing, high quality child care, educational opportunities, transportation, and parenting education and resources. A major barrier for homeless parents who seek education and employment is that they do not have child care for their young children. Shelter care often is not ideal.

A problem is that emergency shelters in urban and suburban areas often cannot keep up with the demands for shelter, and turn away requests. Many shelters do not allow unaccompanied minors or families with adolescent boys (NAEHCY, 2011). Some rural and suburban areas may not have shelters at all. In the 2007–2008 school year, only 22% of homeless students lived in shelters. Sixty-five percent lived doubled up with friends or other family members, 7% lived in motels, and the remainder lived in unsheltered locations (e.g., in cars, under bridges) (NAEHCY, 2011).

A problem for toddlers who are homeless is that if they are in shelters, their freedom to explore and learn about their worlds is restricted. There may be a paucity of developmentally appropriate toys and books. Even if toys and books are provided, parents may be too stressed to play with or read to their children. These factors can limit toddlers' language development. Cognitive development can be impacted; for example, it has been found that homeless children who attend Head Start programs have less conventional time knowledge than their housed peers (Shinn et al., 2008).

I mentioned earlier in the book that I collect gently-used children's books to give to low SES children in various areas of our city. I will never forget bringing boxes of books to our local crisis nursery. One of the workers showed me around and explained how children came there. Children between the ages of birth and 5 years old could stay at the crisis nursery for 1 to 2 weeks if their parents were arrested, incarcerated, strung out on drugs, and other extreme circumstances. The worker explained to me that the children loved coming to the nursery, where they had good food, a soft bed, and clean clothes. Often, when their parents came for them, they did not want to leave. I saw half a dozen of them napping: three-and four-year olds, sleeping peacefully under soft quilts in an attractive, quiet room. I was so moved, knowing that this oasis would end soon for them all. I wondered how many of them would be back—and how soon.

Practical Strategies for Supporting Homeless Students and Families

Supporting homeless students and their families is a monumental task that educators cannot undertake alone. We need support from law and policy makers, communities, and governing bodies at all levels of our society. But as individuals, we want to make a difference, however small. What are some ways that we can do this?

School counselors can play a pivotal role in supporting homeless students. Some schools provide parent training, after-school tutoring at homeless shelters, clothing and school supplies, and places in the community where students can play with their friends. As mentioned elsewhere in this book, some schools provide meals, showers, clean clothes, and extended after-school activities. Teachers can open their classrooms to students before school, after school, and during lunch-time for informal, supportive conversations.

In some schools, teachers keep granola bars in their desks for children who are so hungry that they fall asleep in class. Some teach-ers let students leave their materials in the classroom where they won't get stolen; others keep basic toiletries in their rooms for stu-dents who do not have personal hygiene items at home. In some schools, teachers provide school supplies for students, rather than asking them to purchase their own (which many can't afford). These teachers solicit donations from local businesses and community ser-vices. Each Christmas, *all* students are given bags filled with practical items and gift cards to restaurants and grocery stores; no student is singled out as "needy." These types of supports are especially impor-tant for homeless students.

We can also provide support for caregivers; more is said about this in Chapter 9. In this section, meeting the needs of homeless children and mothers will specifically be addressed in terms of research stud-ies that support effective methods of intervention for this population.

Among homeless preschool children, language delays are com-mon. This deficit may be due in part to restricted mother-child inter-actions secondary to the stress of homelessness. As stated, homeless single mothers often have histories of violent victimization; over one-third have post-traumatic stress disorder, and over half experience major depression while homeless. It is estimated that 41% are depen-dent on drugs and alcohol (American Psychological Association, 2012). A mother's emotional distress is a major predictor of her children's well-being across a number of domains (Huntington et al., 2008).

A study conducted by O'Neil-Pirrozi (2003) found that home-less children and their caretakers (usually their mothers) experience stressors such as compromised physical health (e.g., asthma and ear infections in children), depression, loss of privacy, and lack of a daily routine. In these circumstances, it is challenging for mothers to provide adequate language stimulation for their children. O'Neil-Pirozzi examined the language characteristics of 25 homeless mothers and their preschool children to ascertain whether or not a correlation existed between language deficits in mothers and language deficits in children. She found that 60% of the mothers had language deficits and 69% of the children were identified as having language deficits.

O'Neil-Pirozzi (2003) also found that at the time of the study, 62% of the children were receiving no academic instruction and 60% of the mothers suffered from physical and mental health problems, including depression. As noted, maternal depression has been associated with lower quality of mother-child interactions, lower cognitive abilities in infancy, and more negative maternal views of children.

O'Neil-Pirozzi (2003) recommended that SLPs and other professionals support homeless parents and their children by supporting and facilitating children's involvement in extant, affordable educational programs supported at the federal, state, local, or private-sector level. She emphasized that some evidence supports the cognitive and academic benefits of these kinds of programs, especially for preschoolers from low SES families. Many of these programs have a strong family-centered focus. O'Neil-Pirozzi addressed the fact that speech-language pathologists (SLPs) can train others to provide ideal types of language stimulation activities for children from low SES homes. She pointed out that SLPs are well positioned to counsel educational programs about the negative impact of language delays in homeless children; they can provide inservice training for staff of these programs in how to provide language stimulation to homeless children, and how to help mothers learn to provide language stimulation themselves.

Results of a subsequent study by O'Neil-Pirozzi (2006) showed that regardless of educational level, homeless mothers used fewer facilitating language utterances across various contexts (e.g., playing games, reading books). Professionals need to be especially aware of the need for supporting homeless children and their families in all areas, including training caregivers to facilitate their children's language development, even in their environmental circumstances.

O'Neil-Pirrozi (2009) conducted an exploratory study to examine the feasibility of homeless parents' participation in an intervention to increase use of facilitating language strategies during interactions with their preschool children while they were residing in family homeless shelters. The study looked at the impact of the intervention on parents' use of facilitating language strategies, regardless of their performance on a test of single-word receptive vocabulary skills.

In the study, using a prospective pretest/posttest comparison group design, 12 parents were randomly assigned to a 4-session experimental group training which emphasized the use of facilitating language utterances with children (this followed vocabulary testing). Four parents were randomly assigned to a control group intervention.

The results of O'Neil-Pirrozi's (2009) study showed that even experimental group parents with poor receptive vocabulary test scores demonstrated high use of facilitating language utterances with their children before the intervention. After the intervention, the experimental group increased use of facilitating language utterances when they interacted with their children. O'Neil-Pirrozi concluded that it was feasible for parents, even those living in a homeless shelter, to participate in and benefit from a brief language-based group intervention.

This study is very important, because it is one of the first of its kind to actually demonstrate the results of direct work with homeless families in shelters where they were living. There were several key ingredients that made this research project successful, and they are described here in detail.

First, the parents in the experimental group were provided with training focused on dialogic reading strategies, which encouraged children's participation in joint book reading activities, and caregiver use of facilitating language utterances such as expansions, recasts, open-ended questions, and repetition. The 12 parents in the experimental group each completed four 90-minute small group sessions which were held weekly over the course of 4 weeks. Each group consisted of 3 to 6 participants, and sessions occurred at a time mutually agreed upon by the participants. The intervention focused on parents' use of types of facilitating language utterances during interactions with their children in different contexts.

The first intervention session focused on normal language development, and participants were encouraged to discuss their observations of their preschool children's language functioning. During session 2, information focused on parent comprehension and use of three facilitating types of language utterances: expansion, modeling, and closure (e.g., encouraging a child to fill in a predictable word or phrase). During session 3, there was a focus on parent understanding and use of several other types of facilitating language techniques: recasting, predicting what will happen next, and open-ended questions. Session 4 focused on discussion of relevant topics that the group requested during the first three sessions, and on potential for lifelong language development.

During several of the sessions, parents practiced using the techniques with their children. At the end of sessions 1–3, participants were given two age-appropriate children's books. Parents were also given a weekly log to document practice with joint book reading and the language facilitating techniques they were learning. During the subsequent session, the parents were asked to return the weekly log to the facilitator. During the sessions, when the parents were not practicing with their children, the children were cared for in another room. Light refreshments were served. Parents were given a gift card to a local supermarket following their participation in the study.

Results of the study showed that 91% of the experimental group parents attended all four weekly group training sessions. They completed 79% of between-program session practice assignments. Results of the study showed that the experimental group generated a significantly higher percentage of facilitating language utterances during interactions with their preschool children; they increased their use of facilitating language utterances to a greater extent than the control group. O'Neil-Pirozzi concluded that this study provided initial evidence that parents who are homeless may benefit from a four-session group training program that emphasizes preschool children's language development and that these parents may learn to increase their use of facilitating language utterances to their young children. Again, this is the first study of its kind to specifically teach language facilitating techniques to parents who were homeless in the environment of the homeless shelter.

Roberts and Kaiser (2011) conducted a meta-analysis of the effectiveness of parent-implemented language interventions. Although this meta-analysis did not focus on the homeless population, the results of the meta-analysis were similar to the findings of O'Neil-Pirozzi (2009): providing training to parents as little as once a week can provide benefits. Roberts and Kaiser emphasized that research findings converge upon the fact that teaching parents to use extensions is very useful as we have said before; extensions are easy to teach, and their use directly and positively impacts children's morphosyntactic skills. Extensions can be used by early childhood personnel as well as by parents.

We discussed extensions in Chapter 4; because they have been repeatedly shown to be so successful in increasing children's language skills, we briefly review the concept here. Extensions add both semantic and grammatical information to a child's utterance. For example, if the child says, "drink milk," the adult says something like, "Yes, you will drink the cold milk because you are thirsty." Adding new semantic and grammatical information is an excellent, proven, very easy way to stimulate children's language development.

Because many homeless preschool children lack quality experiences in their early learning environments, they need high quality early childhood environments; it is in these environments that the children are most likely to gain the support they need to develop healthy lives. As Swick (2010, p. 300) says, "In high quality preschool, the whole family is energized."

As one example of a high quality preschool, a unique program was implemented in New York. In in New York City, 51% of homeless children are under the age of 5 years; 41% of them do not receive preschool experience. Homes for the Homeless has begun an initiative that focuses on literacy for these children. This agency operates onsite Jump Start Child Development Centers that provide children ages 3 to 5 years with a nurturing and stable environment as a foundation for building strong literacy achievement. In these centers, children are taught preliteracy and literacy skills by literacy specialists. The literacy specialists also hold workshops to teach parents how to support early childhood literacy and about age-appropriate child development milestones and accompanying expectations (Homes for the Homeless: The Institute for Children and Poverty, 2005).

According to Geiss (2011), there are specific constructive things that professionals can do to support homeless students. We can highlight literacy achievement for these students, as statistics indicate that they tend to have specific deficits in reading. We can provide access to materials that the students can take home and keep (e.g., my children's book drive). We can help children feel safe at school through providing a safe, organized, quiet classroom or therapy room with consistent routine and structure.

Geiss (2011) and other experts believe that teaching vocabulary to homeless students should be a strong focus of regular and special education intervention. We discussed strategies for building vocabulary in other chapters, and I agree that vocabulary should be a strong focus for professionals as they work with students who are highly mobile.

It is clear that highly mobile students are vulnerable to a host of challenges. With focused support in all areas (e.g., academic skills, health), these students and their families can be provided with hope, special services, and practical help that meets their needs as people who are struggling to survive in today's society.

INCREASING EXECUTIVE FUNCTIONING SKILLS IN HIGHLY MOBILE STUDENTS IMPACTED BY CHAOS

Definition and Basic Facts

Research has suggested that students from low SES backgrounds may be vulnerable to difficulties with *executive functioning* (EF): this is especially true if they come from backgrounds where high mobility and resulting chaos are present. Being exposed to chaotic conditions where there is a lack of routine is especially detrimental to EF skills (Evans et al., 2010). As we said in Chapter 7, experts have discussed the concept of EF: the ability to plan and evaluate one's performance when engaging in goal-directed behavior (Nelson, 2010; Paul & Norbury, 2012). We said that EF can be divided into two basic areas: a) goal-oriented planning and self-monitoring behaviors such as organization and time management, and b) personal efficacy behaviors such as perseverance in the face of difficulty and the use of positive self-talk when things are challenging. In Chapter 7, we discussed specific strategies for increasing personal efficacy behaviors. In this chapter, we discuss goal-oriented planning and self-monitoring behaviors: the problem-solving processes that are utilized at the outset of a novel, nonautomatic task.

Goal-directed behavior is important for success in life activities. In this goal-oriented behavior, the role of EF is like that of an air traffic controller in coordinating and monitoring all relevant activities, or that of a maestro in conducting an orchestra. Executive functions are used to define the problem at hand, requiring that the person stop and think before acting. EF is critical in terms of thinking of the future, especially regarding the consequences of personal choices (Kaufman, 2010).

Fundamentally, executive functions are enlisted in setting specific goals and then determining what is necessary to attain those goals. For example, a person who wants a good job that pays decently sets a goal to find that job. Then, the person thinks about what is necessary to obtain that job. Does the person have the skills needed? If so, what jobs are available that enlist those skills? How does the person find these jobs? And so on. Components of EF include inhibiting actions, attending selectively, demonstrating emotional control, restraining and delaying responses, setting goals, planning for the future, organizing, and shifting flexibly between activities

A relationship among attention, executive functions, and working memory has been described (Ackerman & Brown, 2010). Executive functions are utilized in such tasks as developing plans for future actions, holding those action sequences and plans in working memory until they are executed, and inhibiting actions that are not relevant. Thus, as noted, executive functions are foundational to setting and achieving future goals. EFs represent core aspects of readiness to learn and cooperate in school; they predict a variety of achievements involving math and literacy (Ackerman & Brown, 2010).

Of relevance here is the previously mentioned research of Farah and colleagues (2005). In an initial study, these investigators examined the neurocognitive performance of 60 African American children, 30 from low- and 30 from middle SES homes, enrolled in Philadelphia public school kindergartens. The children were tested on a battery of tasks adapted from the cognitive neuroscience literature; the tasks were designed to assess the functioning of five key neurocognitive systems.

Farah and colleagues (2005) found, first of all, that the more advantaged children performed better on the test battery as a whole. There were large and significant differences between low- and mid-SES children on tasks designed to tap skills in: (1) the left/perisylvian language system and (2) the prefrontal executive system. The left/ perisylvian language system encompasses semantic, syntactic, and phonological aspects of language. The prefrontal executive system enables cognitive control: flexibility in responding in situations where the appropriate response may not be the most attractive or the most routine one. This system also requires maintenance or updating of information regarding recent events.

Subsequent studies showed that, in comparison with more privileged students, those from low SES backgrounds had significant difficulties in areas of the brain that controlled working memory, which had a negative impact on their EF skills. According to Farah and colleagues (2005), for children from low SES homes, brain disparities in the areas of language, memory, and cognitive control affect their life paths. Language and memory deficits have a negative impact on acquisition of academic skills and, eventually, the ability to pursue higher education and a good job. Lack of cognitive control may negatively impact self-regulation and problem-solving ability. This can result in behavior problems and perhaps even in criminal behavior.

In addition to having difficulties with areas of the brain that control working memory, low SES students who are highly mobile may be subjected to a great deal of screen time (e.g., TVs, computers). We said previously that when environmental conditions are unsafe or hazardous, children often are kept indoors in front of screens, especially computer screens. Computer use can impair EF skills because general browsing encourages the use of multitasking and continuous partial attention. Playing computer games can impair the development of the frontal lobe of the brain, the part of the brain that inhibits anti-social behavior. Children become wired for high speed stimulation; it is difficult for them to think, plan, and reflect when they have been exposed to a great deal of screen time, especially computer time (Morris, 2011; Westby, 2011).

It is not only low SES students who have become accustomed to screen time. Last weekend, my husband and Mark and I went to a graduation party in a nice, upper-middle class home in our city. The older sister of Mark's friend had graduated from high school, and their mother had invited a large crowd to their home. The food was delicious, the crowd large. Mrs. X. had filled water balloons, which were in a bucket in the back yard, so the children and teens could play a water balloon game on this hot June evening. After dinner was over and I had helped Mrs. X clear the table, I went out to the back yard to pick up any trash left out on the lawn. The bucket of water balloons was almost two-thirds full; probably one-half dozen had actually been thrown or used. Going upstairs to look for Mark, I discovered that in each bedroom of the house was a teenager playing a computer game or using an iPhone. Mark's friend was glued to his computer, completely ignoring Mark (who he had not seen for a long time). I reflected on the bucket with so many water balloons just sitting there, unused, while electronic devices mesmerized the teens at the party. I was pleasantly surprised to find that in the front driveway, some of them were actually talking with each other—holding conversations!

To reiterate and summarize, many students from low SES backgrounds do not possess optimal EF skills. They may live for the present, with little or no planning for the future. In addition, the research of Farah and colleagues (2005) shows that these children, because of difficulties with key neurocognitive systems, have difficulties with working memory (needed for competent use of executive functions) and cognitive control (also needed for competent use of executive functions). If less privileged children have intrinsic neurocognitive deficits and extrinsic value systems that do not include planning for the future, their academic, linguistic, and career paths probably will be negatively affected. In schools, professionals need to help these students develop their skills in EF.

Practical Strategies for Increasing the Executive Functioning Skills of Highly Mobile Students

General Strategies

Some factors that can impair EF, and which tend to be very prevalent in the lives of children from highly mobile low SES families, are dehydration, inactivity, sleep deprivation, and anxiety. Educators probably cannot do much about sleep deprivation (except exhort students to go to bed early), but they can make a positive difference in the areas of activity, lowering of anxiety levels, and dehydration, as discussed in Chapter 7. We also said that incorporating physical movement into learning, reducing stress, and encouraging increased water intake are all practical, simple strategies that are available to even the busiest professional on a limited budget. One way professionals can help reduce students' stress is to allow them to talk about their feelings and concerns (Geiss, 2011). In addition, as educators, we can work with students to help build routines into their school days. Even if these students have chaotic home lives, the presence of structure and routines in school can help offset the presence of home chaos and disorganization.

Developing a Sense of Structure, Routine, and Time Concepts

Highly mobile students from low SES homes often experience a lack of external structure and routine as we have said. In homes where parents (often single mothers) struggle to keep food in the refrigerator and steer clear of gang violence, time is rarely referenced. Sometimes parents don't even make sequential statements such as "Put on your socks first, then your shoes." Daily routines, such as departure of the parent for work, often are nonexistent, especially for families that receive Aid to Families with Dependent Children.

When these children enter kindergarten, school is a culture shock. They are mystified by a world that features time slots for everything, in which the day is carefully divided into time for listening, reading, writing, recess, and lunch. Children from middle SES homes fit easily into this regimen; the parents in these families frequently reference time and the clock. For example, even when my Mark was four years old, I'd say things like, "OK, we need to eat breakfast now so we can be at Montessori by 8:45. I will pick you up at 3:00 this afternoon for your horseback riding lesson at 3:30. After your lesson, we will come home and do homework. After homework, we'll eat dinner and then read a story before bed."

Middle SES families with several children may be even more structured and time-conscious. With several children participating in sports and other activities that require several practices a week and games on the weekends, most of these parents and their children are all too acutely aware of time, and many tend to rush around. Ironically, these children are well suited to school life, where rushing around and fulfilling rigid, time-slotted schedules are emphasized.

As an example, the children who attended Mark's kindergarten were expected to wait outside until the second bell rang: not the first bell, the *second* bell. Then they entered the classroom, where the first thing they had to do was put their homework into the specified "Homework Tub." The second thing they had to do was put their library books (which had to be in the *correct* Ziplock bag, not one that a harassed parent substituted for the lost original from the teacher) on the parent volunteer table. Third, they had to go to their desks and take out their writing practice. Such complex, relatively sophisticated regimens for kindergartners are not unusual.

Children from low SES, unstructured homes may have difficulty adapting to routines such as these when they arrive at school with its structure and rigid time slots. Some of these children, feeling powerless, may rebel at the rigidity of the school system in comparison with the homes in which they are being raised. However, to be successful in society, people need to be able to operate in structured environments.

In order for children to develop internal structure, they must experience external structure until they can create their own structure. Many times, children from chaotic environments are comforted by structure, repetition, and predictability of routines. These routines can guide children along the path to creating internal structure so they will not continually rely on outside forces to do so.

Neuman (2009) discusses helping these children through repeated exposures to controllable challenges. Mastery comes through repetition. Professionals can give children challenges which can be accomplished; as children master each challenge, their self-confidence and ability to rely on their own internal structure grow.

To help create internal structure, professionals can also give students choices: "You have 5 minutes. If you choose to finish your paper, you may go to the reading corner and pick a book. If you choose not to finish your paper, you may not go to the reading corner." In this way, students see that they indeed have control over their actions and that their own choices create consequences. This helps create the internal structure students will eventually need if they want to be professionally successful adults. Internal structure relies in part on the ability to implement and experience delayed gratification (Ackerman & Brown, 2010).

Unfortunately, Americans tend to have much difficulty with delayed gratification. For low SES communities, this may be a reflection of the culture of poverty (Payne, 2003), in which the point of life is enjoying and having fun today because the future is uncertain, if there is a future. For children from these communities especially, delayed gratification must be a value that is taught, stressed, and modeled.

In my experience, however, it is not just students from low SES backgrounds who have difficulty with delayed gratification. In the United States today, everything is to be had in an instant. Faster is better. Waiting is bad. The grocery store one mile from our house has signs all over: *Get in. Get out. Get on with it.* No one wants to wait. We want it now. In one true recent situation, a 19-year-old friend of my sister's (who lives at home with his upper-middle SES parents and works part-time at Starbucks) was trying to persuade his parents to buy him a $1,000 cappuccino maker (this was in September). When told that this particular cappuccino maker went on sale for half-price in December, he responded that he did not want to wait that long; he wanted the cappuccino maker right now. Sadly, his attitude is not that rare. Many young Americans display that attitude of, "I want it, and

I want it now." It is up to today's professionals to help them see that, TV commercials and computer games notwithstanding, most people have to work hard and patiently until success eventually comes, and that success is well worth the wait and the effort.

Most middle-class professionals did not consciously think about attending college as practicing delayed gratification. But that is what college is: sacrificing years of life and thousands of dollars so that the future will hold a good job and the resulting material comforts. A colleague who worked at a low SES middle school had pictures on her wall of mansions with expensive cars in the garages. She talked with her students about how they could aspire to this type of "good life": through higher education, delayed gratification, and hard work. Although some professionals might differ with her methods, her idea was sound: to show students that rising out of poverty into a better life is accomplished only through sacrifices, delayed gratification, and persistence in pursuance of personal goals. In Chapter 1, we noted that Payne (2003) discusses the importance, in low SES communities, of entertainment and living for the present moment. I believe that for children from these communities especially, delayed gratification must be a value that is taught, stressed, and modeled.

Delayed gratification is related to students' ability to inhibit their immediate responses to stimuli, thereby allowing themselves time to plan and organize and set goals. They need to learn to pause for self-reflection and analysis. They need to take charge of their own learning, organize their materials, attend to task, do independent seat work, manage their time, prioritize, and plan ahead (Haynes & Pindzola, 2012; Ziolkowski & Goldstein, 2011). Executive control and self-regulated "thinking language" grow out of scaffolding and social support from attentive, supportive people in the child's environment. These people can give students the confidence they need and the tools to eventually internalize orders and directions they hear in their environments and make these into self-talk that they use to direct themselves (Nelson, 2010). As one little boy said to me, "I need to listen to the guy in my head." Using calendars and other planning devices can be immensely helpful; these are not often used in the environments of highly mobile students.

Geiss (2011) discusses the fact that homeless students may have poor attention spans or disengagement and also have difficulty with transitions. She recommends teaching positive alternative coping strategies. She also recommends that professionals define transition times and activities for students during the day. I agree with this; while professionals want to give students autonomy, many (especially those who are highly mobile) need the structure of a consistent schedule that is verbally reiterated each day. For example, when students come into a speech and language therapy room, the clinician can always begin with the same verbal routine and announce transitions into different activities as the session proceeds. Classroom teachers can have daily schedules posted visually on whiteboards or smartboards and can introduce the day by reviewing the schedule for the day before any activities commence. As each activity is finished, the teacher can "erase" it from the board and state that the next activity is about to happen. Although students from structured homes don't need this as much, I believe that it is critical for highly mobile students who have experienced lack of structure, routine, and predictability in their lives.

As a 23-year-old beginning speech-language pathologist, I worked in a very low-income school with many low SES and highly mobile children. Although I made a great many mistakes my first year, I clearly remember how much the children loved coming to speech. Having been raised in Southeast Asia, I was very strict. Students had to raise their hands to share, no matter how small the group. We always began each therapy session with the same positive affirmation. No chaos was allowed, and only one person spoke at a time. A good attitude, with no whining, was expected. My rules were ironclad. The more experienced SLPs who supervised me that year told me I was "rigid." I'm sure they were right; the irony was, my rigidity was very effective with my students. They knew I loved them and cared about them as individuals; this was expressed often. But I think that they greatly needed the structure I provided, and benefitted greatly from it. I actually had students try to fake a speech sound disorder so they could qualify for my services!

Incidentally, stung by the label of "rigid," I asked some of my experienced colleagues if I could come and observe them doing therapy: my goal was to watch, learn, and improve my skills. During these observations, I was amazed to see children being allowed to interrupt, lie on the table, elbow each other, and just generally cause chaos. I wondered if perhaps, even with my lack of experience, I was instinctively providing the structure and firmness that my students so desperately needed, and wanted.

Learning Classroom Routines and Scripts

Highly mobile low SES children also may need help in learning classroom *scripts*, or common routines that are expected of them. For example, children may need to be explicitly instructed about how to line up, how to wash their hands, sit in a circle in their own space, and how to walk quietly to the cafeteria for lunch (Roseberry-McKibbin, 2013). Westby (2006) pointed out that success in school typically is reflected as academic competence. She asserted that in addition to becoming academically competent, students need to know how to "do school"—to follow classroom rules and negotiate appropriately with teachers and peers, demonstrating independence and self-control.

As discussed earlier, many children from low SES families come from homes where they are socialized to interdependent behavior and external control of behavior by authority, rather than to self-regulation and independent, internalized self-control. In order to succeed in school, these students need to be guided in carefully scaffolded activities and lessons where they are gradually taught to be independent and have internalized self-control. It is best if teachers can help children achieve an environment that has structure so that children know what to expect, but to simultaneously leave room for the development of individual autonomy (Maxwell, 2010). Teachers can use various types of scripts to accomplish this. Table 8–2 presents a specific example.

Self-Reflection and Planning: Taking Responsibility for Choices and Consequences

Due to their previously discussed sense of learned helplessness, some highly mobile SES students may have difficulty planning, engaging in self-reflection, and taking responsibility for their choices and consequences. Earlier we said that if children come from chaotic environments, they may have learned that perseverance and planning do not pay off. Thus, we as professionals want to help these children learn

Table 8–2. Changes in Teacher Scripts from Beginning to End of the Year

Early In Year	Later in Year
Teacher tells class when it is time for an activity	Teacher sets play clock to cue children that they are to begin activity
Children work together as partners; class problem-solves with teacher	Class works together as a large group to problem-solve
Teacher repeats directions and rules	Teacher states directions and rules once, then says, "If you don't know, ask a friend"
Teacher puts notes on board for children to finish work	Teacher uses fewer of these notes
Teacher reminds children each Monday that homework packet is due Thursday	Teacher stops reminding children of Thursday deadline; children expected to remember on their own
Teacher models each activity for children	Teacher models fewer activities
All activities are preset and structured by the teacher	Class votes on some activities
Children are to raise their hands to answer, but calling out is accepted and not punished	Calling out is not accepted; it is penalized

Source: Adapted from Westby, 1997, 2006.

that at least in school, perseverance, planning, and taking responsibility are rewarded with good consequences. What are some specific strategies that professionals can use to teach students to self-reflect, plan, and take responsibility for their choices? Singer and Bashir (1999) suggest the following:

Teach students to ask:

■ What is the problem I am having right now? (take time to analyze the problem)

▓ Why am I having this problem? (identifying cause)
▓ What can I do about it? (behavioral adjustment)

Teach students to:

▓ Inhibit their immediate responses, thereby allowing themselves time to plan and organize and set goals.
▓ Pause for self-reflection.

Table 8–3 provides a sample daily goal sheet that can be used with students from low SES backgrounds who have difficulties with monitoring their own behavior and engaging in self-evaluation. Zero points means that they did not do well with the task or activity. One point means that they made a good effort but improvement could be made, and two points means that they did very well.

Table 8–3. Sample Daily Goal Sheet

Task/Activity	Points Earned (0, 1, 2)
Sat in my chair	_____
Did my best to pay attention	_____
Listened and followed directions	_____
Kept my hands and feet to myself	_____
Was kind and polite to others	_____
Controlled my temper	_____
Raised my hand when I wanted to speak	_____
Made my best effort	_____
Put my things in my backpack without being reminded	_____
Cleaned the top of my desk without being reminded	_____

Rewards can be given at the end of each day, week, or month for accumulating a certain number of points. Students also can be trained to think about the consequences of their behavior and to plan alternatives for the next time (Table 8–4). Table 8–5 has additional strategies for improving students' overall EF skills, including memory and attention to task.

Lack of planning skills can be overcome through systematic skill training that helps students assume responsibility for their own learning. Professionals can make work contracts with students to increase the students' ability to plan ahead. One way teachers can reward the

Table 8–4. Tracking Consequences of Choices: My Choice Chart

Student name: _____ Date: _____	
The choice I made was:	The consequence of my choice was:
_____	_____
_____	_____
_____	_____
Next time, I could choose to:	The consequence of that choice would be:
_____	_____
_____	_____
_____	_____
Next time, I could also choose to:	The consequence of that choice would be:
_____	_____
_____	_____
_____	_____
I will remember that each choice I make leads to a consequence. I will try to make good choices so that I can experience good consequences!	

Table 8–5. Improving Executive Functioning: Strategies for Working Successfully with Low-SES Students in the School Context

---

If the students are not persistent and have difficulty persevering in tasks

---

- Support them with encouragement and reinforcement
- Reward small steps with verbal and token reinforcers; do not make them wait too long for token reinforcers; remember, delayed gratification may be a difficult concept
- Do not tell students in advance that something will be "hard." Frame the task(s) positively.
- Let students experience success with easy tasks, and gradually introduce them to more challenging tasks. Point out successes and celebrate them.
- Directly teach students ways to handle frustration. For example, they might be allowed to take a short walk, write in a journal, and/or share their feelings verbally in an appropriate manner.
- Do not give in to students' pleas to get out of doing tasks. Tell them you know they can do it; when they do, praise them ("You showed perseverance! You did it!")
- Teach students terms such as *persistence* and *perseverance*. Even young students can understand these terms. Use the terms as often as you need to.

If the students are quite active

- Allow them to take physical movement breaks when necessary. These breaks can consist of merely stretching or even things like errands (e.g., bringing the attendance sheet to the principal's office).
- Be flexible by allowing them (if possible) to stand up and move around while they listen.
- Relatedly, give them quiet "squeeze" toys such as balls to squeeze while they listen. Though this might appear counterproductive, it can actually be quite helpful.
- Reinforce sitting and focusing—happy face charts and tokens work well.
- Provide students with uncluttered areas and spacing between desks.
- Post picture and word reminders of classroom rules; review these frequently.
- Divide content into short segments, including hands-on practice and opportunities for exploration as much as possible.
- Allow them to have water bottles at their desks that they can sip from throughout the day. Train students to use deep breathing to relax.

continues

Table 8–5. *continued*

If students are distractible and have difficulty paying attention

---

- Discuss what *paying attention* means. Teach students to pay attention with their eyes, ears, and brain. Show them the advantages of working efficiently without goofing around (e.g., if they finish tasks within a certain time period, there is a reward)

- Keep external distractions to a minimum. "Beat the environment at its own game" by reducing visual and auditory distractions as much as possible.

- Visually monitor children's eye contact with assigned tasks. Make sure they keep their eyes on their work.

- Use special attention strategies; for example, use colored highlighter pens and colored pencils to make work more interesting and visually arresting.

- Use color as an organizing aid. For example, social studies materials are blue; math materials are yellow. For color-blind students, shapes can be used as an accompaniment (e.g., math materials are a yellow diamond; social studies materials are a blue square).

- Have a predictable routine. Review this routine at the beginning of each day as a "preview" to the day's activities. Check off each activity as it is accomplished. Because so many low-SES students are from unstructured homes, this is most helpful.

- Present information more than once, using a variety of modalities (auditory, visual, kinesthetic)

- Only provide students with the specific items needed to complete the designated steps of a task. Do not allow distracting, irrelevant items to be part of an activity.

---

ability to plan ahead is to have students fill out a contingency plan, or work contract like that shown in Tables 8–6 and 8–7.

These contracts include a clear statement of what the student is to do, the time at which the work is to be completed, and the stated reward for completing the work. Rewards are contingent on successful completion of the work. Contingency plans are noncompetitive; students' success or failure depends solely on their plans and actions. If an assignment is not done well, and points are removed, students may re-do the assignments according to teacher feedback until the quality of the work reaches an acceptable level.

Table 8–6. Sample Work Plan Contract

WORK PLAN CONTRACT

Student name: _____ Date: _____

Teacher name: _____

For this assignment, I will do the following:

_____

_____

_____

This assignment will be turned in by:

_____

If I complete this assignment according to the steps outlined in this contract, I will receive a grade of _____.

I will do the following to complete this assignment on a daily basis:

Day One   (Date: _____) _____

Day Two   (Date: _____) _____

Day Three   (Date: _____) _____

Day Four   (Date: _____) _____

Day Five   (Date: _____) _____

I agree that I am responsible for getting this work done at the times assigned above. If I do not complete this work according to the above timelines, I will either (1) accept a lower grade or (2) re-do the assignment for a higher grade.

_____   _____
Student Signature   Teacher Signature

Adapted from Covington, S., and Teel, K. M. (1996).

Table 8–7. Work Plan Contract: Example

WORK PLAN CONTRACT

Student name: Kevin Barnes   Date: 10/19/13

Teacher name: Ms. Johnson

For this assignment, I will do the following:

I will write a 3-page paper on why smoking is bad for a person's health and why we should not smoke.

This assignment will be turned in by: 10/25/13

If I complete this assignment according to the steps outlined in this contract, I will receive a grade of 20/20 points; 100%, or A

I will do the following to complete this assignment on a daily basis:

Day One   (Date: 10/20/13) Download information from the Internet on smoking and its effect on people's health

Day Two   (Date: 10/21/13) Write an outline of my paper

Day Three   (Date: 10/22/13) Write the first page of my paper, that talks about what is in tobacco

Day Four   (Date: 10/23/13) Write the second page of my paper, that talks about how smoking affects a person's body and brain

Day Five   (Date: 10/24/13) Write the third page of my paper, that talks about why it is so hard to quit smoking

Day Six   (Date: 10/25/13) Read over my paper for mistakes; edit and print it

I agree that I am responsible for getting this work done at the times assigned above. If I do not complete this work according to the above time lines, I will either (1) accept a lower grade or (2) re-do the assignment for a higher grade.

Kevin Barnes   *Cathy Johnson*
_____   _____
Student Signature   Teacher Signature

One example of a contingency plan is the "Fall Packet" that a local third grade classroom implements in the month of October. The Fall Packet is an assignment, completed by a contract, whereby each student needs to earn 10 points total and turn in the packet by the end of that month. The program includes one mandatory writing assignment. The rest of the points may be earned through each student's choosing of other tasks that he or she would like to do.

For example, a child may earn 2 points by helping Dad bake pumpkin pies and bringing them in to share with the class. The child may earn 1 point for writing a Halloween song to a familiar tune and singing it to the class. One point may be earned for making a Halloween mask; 3 points can be earned for researching the history of Halloween and writing a one-page essay about it. Two points may be gained for completing Halloween word searches. Finally, a child who works ahead can have two or even three nights in a row completely homework-free (the reward for planning and working in advance).

All children who complete the assignment will earn 10 points. They all will probably choose a unique way of doing it, choosing tasks at which they are most proficient (e.g., singing, writing, drawing, cooking). They will learn, the easy or hard way, the benefits of planning and the negative consequences of procrastination (e.g., staying up till midnight the night before the packet is due).

Two especially valuable aspects of the Fall Packet are that: (1) children can choose tasks in accordance with their areas of skill and interest and (2) it incorporates contingency planning: a work contract. Children become aware that they have some choices. Their success will remain primarily in their own hands: they will need to plan ahead and work in a timely fashion. Again, the emphasis is on the pride of individual accomplishment, not on earning the teacher's praise or outdoing classmates.

A twist on this approach is "plan-do-review." For any project, students must include a rationale: why are they doing it? How will they achieve it? When they achieve their plan or goal, they must list the steps they took to achieve it. This can occur on a weekly, monthly, or annual basis. It is tremendously helpful for highly mobile children from low SES homes to "get the big picture" through this sort of planning.

For example, the class can make an annual goal of helping clean up the environment. The children can create monthly, weekly, and even daily quotas for meeting this big goal. Every day, each student can pick up one piece of trash at the school site. A recycling can may be placed in the classroom, and the number of recyclable cans and bottles it contains can be counted each week. Each month, the children can document their progress in picking up trash and recycling, and so forth.

It is ideal if students can choose their own rewards. Tokens are one viable system: students earn tokens to get preferred prizes. With another type of reward system, the Premack principle, students are given the chance to complete one task so they may select another that is pleasurable to them. For example, the teacher may say: "If you finish this sheet of subtraction problems, you can go to the reading corner and choose a book." No tokens are necessary; students receive a reward that is geared to their interests.

CONCLUSIONS

Low SES students who are highly mobile are vulnerable to a host of issues including chaos, which involves conditions of disorder and turbulence in their lives. Chaos is linked to many negative outcomes, including language deficits, emotional problems, and academic failure. Highly mobile students from backgrounds characterized by chaos will often need specific instruction and coaching in strategies for effective executive functioning. Although meeting the vast needs of highly-mobile students and their families can seem like a daunting task, research-based programs and strategies can create opportunities that will increase students' chances of achieving personal success in a society where equal access has become much more challenging to come by. Although professionals cannot control the circumstances of students' personal lives outside of school, they can create welcoming, structured, positive situations and interactions that help students understand that somewhere in their chaotic worlds, support and success can occur.

CHAPTER HIGHLIGHTS

■ Low SES students who are highly mobile generally include homeless students and those from migrant worker families. Their lives are often characterized by chaos.

- Social scientists explain two major categories under the construct of chaos: disorder and turbulence. Disorder involves 3 areas: (1) noise and confusion, (2) crowding and density, and (3) clutter and messiness. Turbulence involves: (1) low supervision and monitoring, (2) fluidity and instability of residents of a home, and (3) lack of predictability and routine. When children experience disorder and turbulence in their lives, the sequelae are numerous. Many of these children have difficulties with language and cognitive development.

- After the Great Recession which began in 2007, more traditional middle SES children began to experience mild-moderate chaos in their lives due to home foreclosures and more at-home mothers joining the workforce. Although these middle SES children were not impacted to the extent that highly mobile children were and are, they may exhibit mild-moderate difficulties that reflect the chaos to which they have been exposed.

- Schools and classrooms are impacted when highly mobile students come and go from school campuses. Schools may experience overall lower test scores, threatening school stability. Teachers and classmates are impacted by high turnover rates of students in classrooms.

- When classrooms are crowded, they are often noisy and chaotic. This can lead to social interaction problems among students, reduced learning, and teacher stress.

- Migrant students are usually the children of seasonal agricultural workers. Their educational attainment is often negatively impacted by their high mobility; some families move 6 to 7 times a year. It is difficult for these students to access special education services. Schools can provide special adjunct programs to support migrant parents and their children.

- The homeless population of the United States has grown, and many more school-aged children have become homeless since the Great Recession. Many people are homeless because even if they work, they do not earn enough money to afford both shelter and food.

- The McKinney-Vento Act technically mandates that school districts make adequate provisions for homeless children. Despite the Act and its intent, homeless students still face many challenges. A high number drop out of school.

- The research of O'Neil-Pirrozi has found that many homeless mothers suffer from depression as well as language deficits; the children do also. She has found that careful, thoughtful provision of education for parents in homeless shelters is possible. This education is effective in helping parents carry out language stimulation activities with their children.

- Highly mobile students are vulnerable to executive functioning deficits, especially having difficulty with goal-directed planning behavior. These deficits are related, in part, to difficulties with working memory.

- Professionals can implement practical strategies to support highly mobile students with executive functioning deficits. These strategies include: (1) helping students develop a sense of structure, routine, and time concepts, (2) giving students choices and allowing them to experience consequences, (3) teaching delayed gratification, and (4) implementing work contracts that allow students to have control of their experiences.

9

Considerations in Working with Families of Students from Low SES Backgrounds

Once social change begins, it cannot be reversed.
You cannot un-educate the person who has
learned to read. You cannot humiliate the
person who feels pride. You cannot oppress
the people who are not afraid any more.

Cesar Chavez

Marcos is struggling mightily in second grade. He should be reading 90 to 110 words per minute; instead, he reads 5 words per minute. When I bring him into my speech room for testing, he tells me: "I can't read—but I'm trying to learn." At one point when he is particularly frustrated with his own lack of progress, he bursts out: "I know I'm stupid!" He looks sad; his lack of self-esteem is reflected in his downcast eyes and sagging shoulders. Marcos has great difficulty with a rapid automatic naming task I give him; success on this type of task is closely related to reading skill. On a simple writing task, Marcos cannot even spell basic words. Nevertheless, the school intervention team is reluctant to formally evaluate Marcos because he speaks Spanish as his primary language and has environmental issues.

I want to call Marcos' mother, but she speaks only Spanish, and I am not fluent enough to have a conversation with her. I need to enlist the services of a Spanish-speaking interpreter—when will I find the time to do that? I make a mental note to call the district office and ask for a Spanish-speaking interpreter whenever I can get a moment to fit it in. This means that I probably will have to skip lunch—or at least eat it very quickly. In the meantime, I advocate to my utmost skill for Marcos, practically begging for a formal assessment of his written language skills to be conducted by another specialist at the school so that he can receive appropriate intervention. On hearing that he may be "given another year to develop," I sigh with discouragement. Marcos' classroom teacher is discouraged as well. I know that she and I have to dig deep, fight hard for Marcos so that he won't just fall by the wayside. Now to find—or create—the extra time in my busy schedule to push for extra services for one little boy.

In the meantime, Marcos' mother knows that her child is having difficulties. She is deeply distressed by his tears at homework time and dreads getting yet another note from the school about Marcos' "deficiencies." She knows that he is being considered for retention in second grade. She struggles with self-doubt and despair. What can she do for her son? She works and cannot get to the school during school hours; even if she could get there, she doesn't speak English. Most of the teachers at school are White and well educated; she is intimidated by them. In the evenings, Marcos' mother comforts him as best she can; later, she cries herself to sleep yet again. She doesn't know where to turn, and she is afraid that Marcos may become a "bad boy" because he is experiencing so much failure in school. She already sees signs of rebellion and anger, and he is only 8 years old.

Mark has struggled with reading too. But after 1½ years of weekly vision therapy to develop his visual motor skills and 2 years of weekly occupational therapy to develop his overall coordination and fine motor skills, paid for by his mother, he has made excellent progress: He scores in the Advanced/Superior range on state standardized testing at the end of second grade. His mother has worked with him diligently every night. She, herself, is in the speech-language therapy field, and Mark's developmental optometrist and occupational therapist had put him at the top of their waiting lists at her request.

Mark is now happy and confident in school. But Mark's parents want more for their son. They agree with each other that all of his aptitudes and talents would be best developed by enrolling him in a different school—one with excellent programs in art and music.

Mark's mother visits the principal at the prospective school on several occasions. She brings her considerable interpersonal and professional skills to bear in these interviews. At the first meeting, when Mark's mother presents her business card to the principal, it shows that she is a university professor with a Ph.D. The principal is friendly and encouraging. Although there is a lengthy waiting list for enrollment in the school, says the principal, Mark has a good chance of acceptance.

So Mark's mother drives the 30 miles to the district headquarters to apply for Mark's enrollment in the coming year. A few months later a letter from the school acceptance committee arrives stating that Mark has not been accepted for that year but he is still on the waiting list. Mark's mother is deeply disappointed; she knows that this school would be an excellent place for her child. So Mark's mother once again visits the school principal to plead her son's case: Can the committee reconsider? The principal agrees to resubmit Mark's application with her own comments. Several weeks later, his parents are thrilled to learn that a space has been created for Mark at the school. Mark and his mother come by the school with roses for the principal, who welcomes him with a hug.

In his new school, Mark joyfully enters an atmosphere more geared to his individual strengths, needs, and intellectual gifts. Thanks to all of the after-school interventions in the previous couple of years, he begins his third grade year with reading skills at the 3.4 grade level (third grade, 4 months). Mark's parents work hard at home with their son on the Accelerated Reader program used at his new school. At the end of the first trimester of third grade, Mark's reading score is at the 5.1 level (fifth grade, 1 month): almost 2 years of growth in one trimester! He is finally "taking off" academically.

Like Marcos' mother, Mark's mother has also experienced frustration and deep distress over her son's difficulties in school; she has cried herself to sleep for the last several years too. She too has received deficiency notices from the previous school about her son's reading, and has been castigated for his lack of attention to task in the classroom. She too has dreaded opening her son's homework folder and finding a teacher's note emphasizing that he needs more help at home. But now, several years and thousands of dollars of special intervention later, Mark's mother sleeps well. She feels at peace inside, knowing that though the road has been long, expensive, and sometimes highly stressful, her child has finally landed on his feet and is well on his way to academic and social success.

Mark has been accepted into the after-school club (Discovery Club) at his new school; they are studying one country a month. In October, it's Germany. Because she has studied German and visited Germany, Mark's mother gives a guest lecture to the children. Mark's mother volunteers in the classroom and also at special school events. Her flexible work schedule allows her to be a truly "involved mom." Already, after 2 months at his new school, Mark has been invited to several birthday parties and has attended play dates with his new friends.

INTRODUCTION

Professionals in the United States are working with increasing numbers of low SES students who are culturally and linguistically diverse (CLD). Many of these students are English Language Learners (ELLS). In the last chapter, we discussed the unique needs of homeless and migrant students. In this chapter, we consider the following topics: special issues experienced by CLD students and their families, overall possible value conflicts between low SES families and middle SES professionals, and facilitating foundational support services for low SES families. We focus on supporting caregivers as they attempt to meet their children's needs in an environment filled with challenges and barriers.

LOW SES FAMILIES: CULTURAL AND SOCIAL CAPITAL

The vast discrepancy between middle SES lifestyles and those of most low SES families, especially those who do not speak English, often is dismaying for professionals who work with less advantaged children. My son is happy and thriving, mostly because of the benefits I am so blessed with, but what about children whose parents don't have advanced academic degrees, professional-looking clothing, business cards, and reliable cars? What about children whose parents lack the resources to establish personal relationships with people in positions of relative power that can be used to get the best for their children? The lack of such resources in low SES families usually is associated with limited opportunities for their children. My joy at my son's happiness is equaled by my sorrow over low SES parents' lack of the very same qualities and life circumstances I possess: the social and cultural capital to obtain the very best possible education for my child.

Severely strained psychological and financial resources may adversely affect a family's ability to work with school personnel, and professionals must be aware of this possibility. According to various experts (e.g., Hale, 2004; Lee & Bowen, 2006; Neuman, 2009), many low SES families, especially those who are CLD, lack the social and cultural capital of White, mainstream, educated families. *Social capital* consists of social connections and networks, and involves trust and reciprocity (Dunn, Schaefer-McDaniel, & Ramsay, 2010). Parent involvement in their children's schooling has been conceptualized as a form of social capital (Yan & Lin, 2005). *Cultural capital* has been defined as follows:

> [T]he advantage gained by middle-class, educated European American parents from knowing, preferring, and experiencing a lifestyle congruent with the culture that is dominant in most American schools. Advantage accrues from enacting the types of involvement most valued by the school. . . . Advantage also accrues from having family and work situations that permit involvement at the school . . . In contrast, some working-class or low-income parents may be less able to visit the school for conferences, volunteering, or other activities as a result of inflexible work schedules, lack of child care, or lack of transportation . . . parents who are less able to visit the school are less likely to gain the social, informational, and material rewards gained by parents who enact the school involvement roles valued . . . by school staff . . . parents who are not able to be present at the school may be viewed as uncaring, an attitude that may have negative ramifications for their children. (Lee & Bowen, 2006, p. 198)

As exemplified in the case study presented at the beginning of this chapter, affluent White parents tend to possess the most social and cultural capital, whereas many low SES parents, especially if they are CLD, possess very little. The availability of cultural and social capital magnifies the effects of parents' involvement on their children's school achievement. Parents who cannot visit the school for events and activities may not know how to best help their children with homework. Research shows that children of parents who are more involved in school activities perform better in school (Yan & Lin, 2005).

As an example, I recently attended a week-long professional conference, and consequently my husband took over my usual "mom" duties of driving our son to school. When I brought Mark to school the following week, another mom told me in a "word of mouth" way that the deadline for class's fall contract had been moved up by a week. Without this "moms' grapevine," I never would have known about the change in the deadline date. The moms' grapevine has proved its worth on a number of other occasions as well, to alert parents to crucial information about school happenings. I have had so many experiences like this, where I and my child would have not known about changes in deadlines, special projects, and other school occurrences unless I had physically been on the campus picking Mark up from school or dropping him off. Some parents must wonder if schools assume that there is a full-time, stay-at-home mom in every family who speaks fluent English and is able to physically be at the school site regularly to volunteer, chat with other mothers, and be in position to pick up critical information through the moms' grapevine. The moms' grapevine is a perfect example of social capital.

As noted, many low SES, CLD families lack social and cultural capital necessary for helping their children succeed in school. Most middle-class White parents are fairly well equipped to advocate on behalf of their children like I advocated for Mark in the situation described at the beginning of this chapter. They know how school bureaucracies work and have easy access to people in key decision-making roles. Parents' ability to speak English as well as their educational and SES status are closely related to the possession of social and cultural capital. Statistics show that 1% of White parents and 5% of black parents do not have high school diplomas, as compared with 27% of Mexican American parents (Gandara, 2004). To summarize, White middle-class parents know how to "work the system"; low SES, CLD parents, if they lack formal educational background, often are "outside the loop."

In the saga of Marcos and Mark outlined in the chapter case studies, Marcos' mother has minimal, if any, social and cultural capital. She is a migrant field worker; she doesn't speak English; she certainly does not know how to work the system. She does not even own a car to drive to the school. Mark's mother, on the other hand, is a highly educated, White, middle SES English-speaking professional who is not afraid to go after what she wants for her son. She is well mannered and diplomatic, but she is determined to do whatever it takes to get her son into the school of her choice. Mark's mother is virtually swimming in cultural and social capital, and the outcomes for her son clearly demonstrate this.

Marcos, on the other hand, if he is very fortunate, will receive special education through the school because an SLP is willing to give up some of her personal time to advocate for him. But what if the SLP was not willing to do this? Marcos would fall through the cracks, another victim of a system where the rich get richer and the poor get poorer.

In terms of social and cultural capital among African American families, according to a study by Pungello et al. (2009), the African American subjects they studied in a large urban area were more likely to come from single-parent homes headed by mothers than the White subjects, who more often came from married, two-parent households. Hale (2004) states that 85% of African American households that send children to school are headed by females.

When a mother must concern herself with keeping food on the table and a roof over her children's heads, she has a limited amount of time to support her children's academic achievement and negotiate the ins and outs of school. White upper-income parents are a part of the culture that makes school rules, so these parents function with ease. However, regardless of SES, many African American parents don't know the nuances of what Hale calls a "game of hide and seek in elementary and secondary schools" (p. 37). They lack cultural capital.

Hale (2004) writes that many African American parents have very little exposure to the world of highly competitive upper-middle-class schooling because of their own educational backgrounds and the settings in which they raise their children. In addition, White upper-income parents are more likely to have the resources to obtain "test prep" courses for their children and to hire expensive private tutors to help their children meet high academic standards. Hale points out that schools inappropriately place teaching responsibilities on parents, many of whom are not trained to help their children at home.

Hale recommends that instead of excoriating African American parents for their lack of effort and involvement, those who want to support these families need to figure out what the "village" can do to accomplish this. For example, agencies could provide education advocates and provide high-quality, affordable tutoring for low SES African American children, as well as other low SES children from various ethnic backgrounds. Other interventions also may be effective, as illustrated in the following real-life case example.

I will always remember Wilma, the African American mother of Latisha. Latisha was an African American child with learning difficulties that could not be effectively addressed because she often was absent from school. The school team knew that Wilma often kept Latisha home from school. When I called Wilma to chat with her, she confessed that she often kept the child home from school because Latisha cried and begged to stay home. It was very difficult for her to resist Latisha's tears and pleas, she said, so she frequently let her stay home. I gently shared with Wilma that this created a vicious cycle; the more often Latisha was absent, the further she fell behind academically. The further behind she fell, the less she wanted to come to school because she had missed so much information. Wilma confirmed her own role in the problem and agreed that she needed to be "stronger" and send Latisha to school on a regular basis. I also discussed some supportive interventions at school to help Latisha catch up academically. Wilma expressed support and appreciation for these interventions.

Parental involvement in their children's education as a whole has declined in the United States for several reasons: the fast pace of modern society as a whole, more parents in the workforce, and the declining role of the family (Lichter & Wethington, 2010). Nevertheless, professionals know that it is extremely important to involve the families of children from low SES backgrounds in their education as much as possible. This is especially true when the families have some cultural and linguistic differences that make it challenging for them to gain access to schools and services for their children.

LOW SES, CLD FAMILIES: SPECIAL CONSIDERATIONS IN SERVICE DELIVERY

Some General Considerations

The primary focus of this book is on SES and parents' educational level as these variables relate to children's linguistic and academic achievement in school. However, as discussed elsewhere, CLD persons in the United States tend to be more vulnerable to poverty and its effects than mainstream White persons (Battle, 2012; Iglesias & Rojas,

2012). Accordingly, professionals need to be aware of some special considerations in meeting the needs of CLD students and families from low SES backgrounds.

In the 21st century, the face of the United States is changing rapidly. According to the U.S. Bureau of the Census (2010), the number of foreign-born residents is projected to rise from 31 million in the year 2000 to 48 million in 2025. It is projected that in 2030, 43% of U.S. citizens will be from a culturally diverse background. By midcentury, the Hispanic population is expected to triple (Table 9–1).

From the 1997–1998 school year to the 2008–2009 school year, the general population of students in the United States grew by 7.2% to 49.5 million ((Education Week, 2012). During the same time period, the number of English Language Learners (ELLs) enrolled in America's public schools increased from 3.5 million to 5.3 million, or by 51% (National Clearinghouse for English Language Acquisition, 2011). Children from linguistically and culturally diverse backgrounds who are ELLs sometimes perform quite well in school; being a proficient bilingual has many cognitive, linguistic, and social advantages (Grech & McLeod, 2012). Children who become proficient bilingual adults enrich society in a wide variety of ways. They are very attractive as potential employees both in the United States and abroad.

However, some ELLs experience difficulty in school (Hernandez, 2011; Kayser, 2012; Paradis, Genesee, & Crago, 2011; Rosa-Lugo, Mihai, & Nutta, 2012; Roseberry-McKibbin, 2008). Nationwide, only 12% of students with limited English scored "at or above proficient"

Table 9–1. Percentage of U.S. Population by Ethnicity: 1970–2050

Percentage of U.S. Population:	1970	2000	2050
White	83.7	70	50
Black	10.6	12	13
Hispanic	4.5	13	24
Asian	1.0	4	9
Native Americans	.4	.9	1

in mathematics in 4th grade compared with 42% of students not classified as ELLs. The gap was much wider in 8th grade math, where 5% of ELLs were proficient or above proficient in math, compared with 35% of non-ELLs. In 8th grade, on a national reading test, only 3% of ELLs scored at or above proficiency, compared with 34% of non-ELLs (Education Week, 2012). ELLs struggle in mainstream American schools for a number of reasons.

One major reason is that they come to kindergarten speaking little-to-no English; schools do not support or accommodate them successfully. Most classes in American public schools are taught in English only, with few if any supports or provisions for ELLs. There are few bilingual classrooms. In addition, many ELLs come from low SES environmental and cultural backgrounds that do not match that of the typical middle-class, White public school. The lack of familiarity with English coupled with environmental mismatch issues creates a great deal of vulnerability to school failure (Rosa-Lugo et al., 2012).

The standard of living for those in the bottom 10% of the population is lower in the United States than in any other developed nation except the United Kingdom. Statistics show that nationally, 27% of White children, 30% of Asian children, 61% of African American children, and 63% of Hispanic children come from backgrounds of poverty (National Center for Children in Poverty, 2005). Some states are more impacted than others. For example, in 2011, in California, an estimated 2.2 million children lived in poverty. Children of color in California were four times more likely than White children to be born into economically fragile households. Compared with 32% of White children, 69% percent of Hispanic and 71% of African American children in California were classified as "income poor." Eighty two percent of poor children came from homes where at least one parent was working (Posnick-Goodwin, 2011).

In Chapter 6, we cited Terry et al. (2010), who stated that research shows that there is widely varying achievement among children in American schools, with children from some environments experiencing early difficulty. When these children enter kindergarten, achievement gaps are observable even before they start learning to read. According to Terry et al., the most salient child characteristics that predict academic success are race and socioeconomic status. Low SES, non-White children tend to lag behind White, middle SES children. Students who are ELLs, are from low SES backgrounds, or both are environmentally at risk for academic failure.

In the United States, a majority of children from low SES homes (about 65%) are White, because the total number of low SES White families is greater than for any other ethnic group. However, although the total number of African American and Hispanic American children from low SES homes is smaller than the number of White children from low SES homes, the percentages for the first two groups are higher. African Americans are disproportionately affected by poverty due to a combination of factors, which include prejudice, poverty, and residence in urban ghettoes (Goode et al., 2011; Pungello et al., 2009). According to the U.S. Bureau of the Census (2000), 22.1% of all African Americans and 21.2% of Hispanics live below the poverty level, compared with 7.5% of the non-Hispanic White population. The percentage of African Americans in poverty went from 19.3% in 2000 to 24.2% in 2006. In 2006, 24.2% of African Americans were poor in comparison to 8.2% of Whites (Logan & Westrich, 2008).

Residents of American Indian reservations have the highest poverty rate in the United States at 31%. In 2001, the unemployment rate for American Indians was 46% (Murphy, 2001). Native Americans in the U.S. have less education, higher poverty levels, and more psychological and physical health problems than members of the dominant culture (Westby & Inglebret, 2012). Thus, again, it is clear that CLD children in the United States are more vulnerable to poverty than their White counterparts.

In order to put the United States' situation into an international perspective, it is instructive to briefly describe situations in several other countries in terms of findings regarding poverty and ethnic minorities. As one example, a study in England, conducted by Lucinda Platt of Essex University, asked why ethnic minority groups were poorer than members of the White population. Platt found that many ethnic minority groups are younger than the White population, and they have more children. Basically, more children means more poverty. In some communities in England, 43% of Bangladeshi and 33% of Pakistani families have four or more children, compared with 4% of White families (National Literacy Trust, 2005).

Single parenthood, which is closely associated with poverty, is particularly pronounced among some ethnic groups. For example, in England, half of Caribbean-origin mothers are single and have never married. In addition, in England, 54% of all women are economically active; 27% of Bangladeshi and Pakistani women are economically active.

Platt also found that, in Britain, ethnic minority workers are more concentrated in lower pay sectors and in inner cities, where unemployment is greater (National Literacy Trust, 2005).

Unfortunately, it is evident from the foregoing that, in both the United States and other countries, persons from CLD groups appear to be especially vulnerable to the effects of poverty. How can professionals provide support for such persons and their families, especially in terms of helping them facilitate their children's oral and literate language development? How can professionals especially provide support for low SES students and families from immigrant and refugee backgrounds?

Providing Services for Students and Families from Immigrant/Refugee Backgrounds

Many professionals work with students from low SES backgrounds whose families are immigrants or refugees. The number of immigrants and refugees living in the United States has more than tripled in 30 years, from 9.6 million in 1970 to 28.4 million in the year 2000. The United States adds a new immigrant approximately every 31 seconds (U.S. Bureau of the Census, 2000; Weekly Reader, 2006). Current estimates indicate that one of every five children in the United States is the child of immigrants (Lichter & Wethington, 2010). The decade of 2000–2010 may have been the highest for immigration in our nation's history; more than 13 million new legal and illegal immigrants arrived in the United States. It is estimated that at this time, there are 11.5 million undocumented immigrants in the United States In 2008 and 2009 alone, 2.4 million new immigrants settled in the United States. (Camarota, 2011).

According to Lichter and Wethington (2010), poverty rates for these children are nearly twice the national average. Sixty-one percent of children of immigrant parents (8.1 million) live in low SES families, whereas 41% of children of native-born parents live in poverty (Addy & Wight, 2012). New immigrant families, mostly from Asia and Latin America, are poorer and less skilled than they were in the past. They frequently live in highly congested, impoverished urban ethnic enclaves, where they are residentially segregated from native-born non-Hispanic Whites; there, they are cut off from mainstream society and employment opportunities. Immigrant and refugee children are especially likely to experience chaos at home. Refugee children are the most likely to manifest the sequelae of chaos. They often have experienced forced abandonment of their home culture, and have undergone (and continue to undergo) cultural bereavement, social isolation, and economic deprivation (Lustig, 2010). In terms of refugees, a total of 56,384 persons were admitted to the United States in 2011. The leading countries of nationality were Burma, Bhutan, and Iraq (Martin & Yankay, 2012).

Immigrants and refugees to the United States experience a great deal of poverty. For most recent immigrants and refugees, the median income is approximately 58% of the income earned by U.S. natives. The proportion of immigrant and refugee households that receive welfare benefits is 30% to 50% higher than that of native households (Center for Immigration Studies, 2001). One in five young children of immigrant parent families lives below the federal poverty level. This is triple the rate for children whose parents are born in the United States. Even for immigrant children who have two working parents, almost one-fourth of the children of immigrants live in homes in which the overall income is below 200% of the federal poverty level.

As a result of recent rapid immigration, children with immigrant/refugee parents make up an increasingly large share of the nation's population of young children (under age 6). Thirty-four percent of refugees admitted to the United States in 2011 were under 18 years of age; they are, on average, younger than the U.S. native-born population. In 2011, the median age of refugees arriving on our shores was 24 years old; in contrast, the median age of the native-born population in the United States was 34 years of age. In 2011, the leading states of residence for refugees were California (38%), Florida (17%), and New York (15%). Approximately two thirds of persons granted asylum reside in these three states (Martin & Yankay, 2012).

The higher poverty rate of children of immigrants/refugees is associated with a greater likelihood of living in crowded housing, having less food and poorer nutrition, having poorer health, and having lower rates of health insurance coverage. Young children of immigrants and refugees are twice as likely as children of natives to be uninsured. They are much less likely than native-born children to receive housing assistance, cash welfare, and food stamps (Center for Immigration Studies, 2001).

Children of immigrants and refugees exhibit many risk factors associated with low academic achievement (Kayser, 2012). They are much more likely than native-born children to live in low SES families where caregivers have limited English skills. The parents are much less likely than native-born parents to have a high school education; 45% of children of low SES, recent immigrants or refugees live with parents who don't have high school degrees, compared with 18% of children of low SES, native-born parents. Children of low SES, recent immigrants or refugees to the West are especially likely to have parents with low levels of education (Douglas-Hall & Koball, 2004). These children also are read to less regularly by their parents (Roseberry-McKibbin, 2007).

In addition, immigrant and refugee children are less likely than native children to be in center-based child care or preschool programs; they are much more likely than native children to be in parental care. Availability of and access to prekindergarten programs are issues for many immigrant and refugee families. It has been found that when these programs are offered through public schools, Hispanic and Asian children are more likely than those from other ethnic groups to participate (Takanashi, 2006).

As noted previously, high-quality early education programs such as Head Start have many benefits, for both parents and children. These programs can link parents to their communities, increase families' access to health care and other benefits, and provide parents with educational opportunities. High-quality early educational programs for children benefit their socialization and overall development, increase their language skills, ease the transition from home to school, and help them adapt to a new language and culture. Educators and other professionals who work with children need to encourage parents who are immigrants or refugees to enroll their children in high-quality programs before kindergarten.

One issue professionals may encounter is that some immigrant and refugee parents may come from cultures where it is considered unsafe and unloving to separate a young child from his or her caregivers for any length of time. The belief is that young children belong at home with family members, who will give them ideal amounts of love and support. In addition, it is my personal experience that American facilities such as daycare centers and schools encourage parents to "drop off your child on the first day and just leave." Parents are assured that their children will be "just fine." Although this is probably true, many CLD parents from various cultures don't believe that their children will be "just fine" after having been abruptly dropped off in a new place with unfamiliar caregivers.

To increase these caregivers' comfort levels, it can be helpful to allow and even encourage them to volunteer at the child care center that their child is attending. If caregivers are allowed to be on the premises for even a few of the hours that their children are there, they will feel more comfortable in allowing their children to be separated from them. There are several benefits to this situation. First, caregivers will be more willing to allow their children to spend time in child care centers which can provide much-needed cognitive and linguistic stimulation. Second, through volunteering at the centers, caregivers may be exposed to ideal practices such as reading with children and playing learning games with them. Caregivers can implement these practices at home, further facilitating their children's oral and literate language skills.

Language and Literacy Practices in CLD Families: Facilitating an Optimal Language Learning Environment for Children

Because of the documented achievement gap between White, middle SES students and low SES CLD students, it is especially important for professionals to get families involved with implementing optimal language and literacy practices in the home. Research has shown that children in poverty whose parents provide engaging learning environments at home do not start school with the readiness gaps that are so often found among low SES children (Education Week, 2011). In working with children from low SES backgrounds, they and their families must be viewed as part of a larger family system; in working with CLD low SES families, an appreciation of this larger family system is critical to success. Recommendations to families for working in the home to enhance their children's oral and literate language must be sensitive to the language, culture, and language practices of the home.

It is important to keep in mind that caregivers from various CLD backgrounds may interact with their children differently from the way White, mainstream, English-speaking caregivers interact with their children. The ways in which these CLD caregivers interact with their children often are different from what many professionals would consider "mainstream," and professionals from mainstream backgrounds must be careful never to imply to these families that their way of doing things is wrong or inadequate. For example, a common assumption is that parents who do not encourage their children to talk as much as possible are doing things "wrong." van Kleeck (1994) addresses this issue:

> Parent programs focused on parent-child interactions often have as either an explicit or implicit goal that parents should try to encourage the child to communicate as frequently as possible. This aligns well with the mainstream culture generally valuing a relatively high degree of verbosity in children. Indeed, an entire line of social science research views reticence as a social deficiency. . . . For example, as compared to their more talkative peers, reticent children are viewed by their teachers as significantly less likely to do well in all academic areas, and less likely to have positive relationships with other students. . . . Indeed, quietness in the classroom may lead to a speech-language pathology referral. (p. 69)

van Kleeck goes on to point out that in many cultures, people value quietness in children. For example, American Indians value a child's ability to observe and wait silently (Joe & Malach, 2011). Many Asian parents also value quietness in children (Chan & Chen, 2011). In one study, Johnston and Wong (2002) surveyed English-speaking North American and Chinese mothers regarding their discourse practices with their children. These researchers found clear differences between the two groups.

The Chinese mothers in this study were much less likely to report that they often talked with their children about nonshared events of the day, allowed their children to converse with adults who were nonfamily members, and prompted their children for personal narratives. Activities such as these would treat the child as an equal conversational partner, reflecting an expectation that the child would exhibit early verbal competence as well as independence. But these are not the child-raising goals of many Chinese parents, who value social interdependence (as opposed to independence) and hold only modest performance expectations for preschool-aged children (Chan & Chen, 2011; Fung & Roseberry-McKibbin, 1999). Johnston and Wong (2002) also found that only 30% of the Chinese mothers reported that they frequently read books to their young children. Chinese mothers disagreed more strongly than the Western mothers that children learn through play, and agreed more strongly that children learn best with instruction (e.g., use of flashcards to teach children).

Based on the results of their survey, Johnston and Wong (2002) made several recommendations for professionals who work with Chinese families, and these recommendations can be extrapolated to other CLD groups as well. First, when a currently recommended Western practice (e.g., reading with children) is not found in a particular culture, professionals can recommend "functional equivalents." For example, for families who do not have a tradition of reading books to their children when they are young, clinicians may recommend using family photo albums or oral storytelling in place of reading. Second, professionals may recommend that Chinese parents create explicit language lessons for their children, rather than embedding their language teaching in play as Western experts usually recommend.

Research also has addressed the language and literacy practices of Hispanic families (Hammer & Rodriguez, 2012; Iglesias & Rojas, 2012). As previously stated, Hispanics are a rapidly growing group in the United States. Hispanics are the largest minority group in the United States, and the Hispanic population increased 43% between 2000 to 2010 (U.S. Bureau of the Census, 2010). Based on data from the census in the year 2000, 40% of U.S. children in immigrant families are from Mexico (U.S. Bureau of the Census, 2000). Thus, because so many more children in our school system come from Hispanic backgrounds, it is of utmost importance for us to understand and reach this population in ways that are culturally sensitive, appropriate, and facilitative of success, especially in literacy.

It has been found that some Hispanic caregivers do not believe that it is important for their children to know such concepts as letters, numbers, or colors; rather, respect and courtesy are emphasized (Roseberry-McKibbin, 2013). As mentioned earlier in this book, in a longitudinal study of Mexican mothers conducted by Madding (2000), most mothers showed reticence toward reciprocal interactions with their children. When asked who would teach their children such concepts such as colors, shapes, and body parts, the mothers most often responded that teachers would do that. Many mothers in Madding's study believed that it was not appropriate to begin reading with children until they were of kindergarten age (5 years old). Many did not have books in their homes.

A study by Carta and Atwater (2003) examined expressive language development in Hispanic children from low SES homes. These children were part of a longitudinal study that was carried out in an Early Head Start program in the Midwest. The researchers gathered information regarding bilingual language development in 20 children, 12 girls and 8 boys, who were observed and assessed on multiple occasions from the ages of 14 to 36 months, and their families. Measurements were conducted every 4 to 6 months in many language areas such as semantics, social communication, morphosyntactic skills, and others.

The results of the study revealed that Spanish-dominant families spent less time in verbal interactions with their children; this was especially true if the families had five sociodemographic risk factors (e.g., low SES, low educational level of parents). The English-dominant families in this study with three and four sociodemographic risk factors spent more time in verbal interactions with their children. The researchers found that children's language performance on the Preschool Language Scale-3 (Zimmerman, Steiner, & Pond, 1992) was directly related to the amount of language interaction they had with their caregivers. Children with higher language scores were more likely to have caregivers who interacted with them more often.

In this sample, the Spanish-dominant caregivers had lower educational levels and larger families than the English-dominant families. The researchers speculated that perhaps the sociodemographic risks of larger family size and lower educational levels of caregivers, as well as other risk factors, increased the chances that fewer linguistic interactions occurred in these families.

Carta and Atwater (2003) stated that it is positive for children to be raised in a bilingual environment; this is consistent with the findings of many other experts (e.g., Kayser, 2012; Roseberry-McKibbin, 2013). However, although children benefit from being raised in a bilingual environment, they may still be at risk for some delays in language development if their caregivers are of low SES status and have low educational attainment (Hammer & Rodriguez, 2012). The challenges faced by Hispanic families from low SES backgrounds are similar to those that affect low SES families from other cultural and linguistic groups. Professionals must support parents in providing oral and literate language stimulation for their children.

Hernandez (2011) emphasizes that we need to model to parents ideal practices for reading with children. As one example of how this was implemented, one school district in Texas has used some of its grant money to send a bilingual aide to each child's home during the summer to read with children, model good reading strategies for parents, and help parents learn good reading habits with their children. Aides leave books for children and parents to read together (Jachman, 2006).

Kayser (2006) discussed other ways to support Hispanic families in providing enriching literacy experiences for their children in the home. According to Kayser, research shows that if family caregivers are given literature to read that is not interesting or relevant to their lives, they will not want to read with their children. They are more likely to view reading as a chore and as a reminder of their own past failures in school (e.g., "When I was a kid, reading was a punishment"). But when families are given books to read that reflect their values and who they are as people, the caregivers are much more likely to read to their children frequently and with enjoyment. Although these conclusions may seem obvious, it is important especially for White, middle SES professionals to look carefully at the books they provide for families to read. Do these books reflect only White, middle-class values, or are they relevant for low SES, CLD families and their children? Kayser (2006) states:

> Children do not learn to love books and the knowledge they hold if they are asked to bring books home for their parents to read aloud. Parents may need to learn to love books also, and not to think of books as past failures, past punishments, and joyless times in school. . . . How we engage "la familia" will require innovation, creativity, energy, and understanding of parents' experiences with literacy and schools. (p. 23)

Researchers have found that when working with low SES Hispanic families, there are several things professionals can do to increase their effectiveness in interacting with these families. First, it is ideal to provide access to parents who are already receiving services and to paraprofessionals from the Hispanic culture (Blevins, 2012; Kummerer, 2012; Larrotta & Ramirez, 2009). Second, professionals need to do their best to come across as warm, personable, and approachable. Kummerer (2012) states that:

> A central problem in effective service delivery with CLD families is a failure to establish respectful and trusting relationships . . . Relationships are extremely important to Hispanic families, and the SLP's personal qualities such as respectfulness, approachability, and personal interest are often perceived as more valuable than technical qualifications. (p. 86)

Technical qualifications can be important too, however. Many Hispanic families have great respect for not only educational institutions, but for medical institutions as well. One research project capitalized on this, studying the impact of pediatrician-recommended reading programs for Hispanic children (Diener, Hobson-Rohrer, & Byington, 2012).

Diener et al. (2012) sampled 40 low SES Hispanic immigrant mothers and their children. Children's medical records were reviewed to determine the level of exposure they had had to a program called Reach Out and Read (ROR; mentioned in Chapter 5). This program is a pediatric, primary-care intervention designed to promote emergent literacy skills. There are three components: (1) Pediatricians provide advice about shared book reading during preventative care visits, (2) children receive a free book at each well-child check between 6 months and 5 years of age, and (3) volunteers model effective shared book reading techniques. Pediatricians are key in this method because parents typically place a great deal of faith in their children's pediatricians; many also see the pediatricians fairly regularly during their children's preschool years. ROR has been implemented at over 4500 clinics since 1989, reaching almost 4 million American children (Neuman, 2009).

In this study, children had begun the ROR program when they were six months old. The subjects' home literacy environment was assessed through maternal interview. Children's emergent literacy skills were assessed before kindergarten through interviews with the children and through the Dynamic Indicators of Basic Early Literacy Skills (DIBELS); at the end of kindergarten, children's emergent literacy skills were evaluated through teacher questionnaires. These questionnaires provided teachers with opportunities to rate each child in early literacy areas such as producing rhyming words, naming letters, using complex sentence structure, understanding conventions of print, and others.

Diener et al. (2012) completed descriptive analyses, creating composite scores of children's print awareness, teacher-rated literacy skills, and ROR exposure. Partial correlations controlling for childhood age and maternal education were conducted between the composite score of ROR exposure and children's literacy skills. Maternal education and child age were controlled.

Home literacy environments of families were strong as demonstrated by parent-reported adult-child reading and number of books in the home (received from pediatricians using the ROR program).

Evaluation of early literacy skills demonstrated that children had good familiarity with print. Greater ROR exposure was related to significantly greater phonemic and print awareness before kindergarten entry. During the interview in the summer before kindergarten, 76% of the children could identify a favorite book by name.

Prior to kindergarten, DIBELS testing identified 37 to 45% of the children as at risk for reading difficulties. At the end of kindergarten, teachers reported that 60% of the $N = 40$ children studied were at an intermediate or proficient level in reading. Teachers rated the literacy skills of 77% of the children exposed to ROR as average, above average, or far above average when compared to all (including non-Hispanic) students in the same grade (Diener et al., 2012).

Diener et al. (2012) concluded that even though the subjects in their study had some risk factors (poverty, low educational level of mothers, parents who did not speak English), they had good home literacy environments and average or above average literacy skills by the end of kindergarten. Thus, it was seen that a pediatrician-implemented program, Reach out and Read, helped to create positive outcomes for these at-risk children.

Paul and Norbury (2012) and Davis and Banks (2012) give some additional specific suggestions for working with CLD families to encourage them to enhance emergent literacy skills in their young children. Like Johnston and Wong (2002), they point out that many families are more comfortable telling stories orally than reading to their children. In these cases, professionals can encourage parents to tell as many stories as possible and to re-tell them frequently.

If parents are nonliterate in English but are comfortable with books, professionals can encourage them to engage in literacy-related activities such as looking at wordless books with their children and discussing the stories. Gillam (2011) explained how in one study, low SES parents (some Hispanic) were given wordless books to discuss with their children; others were given children's books with print. The results of the study found that in parent-child dyads, wordless books generated richer language than the books with print in them. Parents "reading" wordless books with their children were more animated and discussed the books' contents more creatively than parents who were using books with print when interacting with their children. Gillam suggested that professionals can encourage parents to discuss wordless books with their children, as these discussions can generate verbal exchanges and discourse that support oral language development as a foundation for emerging literacy skills.

Parents also can be encouraged to take their children to the local library to look at and check out books, as well as to look for good-quality, inexpensive books at flea markets and garage sales. In many developing countries, garage sales and flea markets are unknown concepts, and parents may need to be alerted to these sources of literacy materials. Professionals also can invite parents to literacy events at the school such as book fairs. If appropriate, parents can be directed to local English classes.

Allen (2010) describes a highly successful Australian program that reached out to low SES families in remote, isolated locations in the outback of Western Australia. Better Beginnings, a universal literacy program targeting children from 0 to 3 and their families, started as a pilot program in 2004. At the time of the publication of the results (2010), 6 years after Better Beginnings started, over 70,000 families across Western Australia had been served; in 2009/2010, the program reached the families of approximately 96% of the babies born in Western Australia. Bright Beginnings had strong government support and used several successful strategies which are described here.

In the Better Beginnings programs, public libraries were made into community hubs, where families were supported in practical strategies to build the confidence of adults in reading with their children. Libraries provided parenting information, children's books, and other resources to promote family literacy. The libraries ran story time sessions and rhyming sessions that provided parents opportunities to share action songs, rhyming activities, and simple picture books with their babies and children. Parent workshops featured guest speakers such as health nurses and speech pathologists to talk with parents in a comfortable, non-medical, informal setting about various aspects of their children's wellbeing and development.

In addition to featuring varied, relevant, and interesting programs in the libraries, Better Beginnings gave each family a story kit with puppets, books, and other resources for conducting early literacy activities with their children. The story kits helped parents implement, at home, activities that they had learned in sessions in the libraries. Community health nurses were given story kits as well, and they were able to share these with families who came to clinics for health services. A striking feature of Better Beginnings was the strong and ongoing, reciprocal relationship between libraries/educators and health care practitioners.

In terms of results of this program, several were reported in a previous paragraph. In addition to those results, it was found that before receiving the story kits, only 14% of caregivers reported reading with their children at home; 85% of mothers reported that, since receiving the story kits, they read to their children. After being involved in the program, 62% of mothers reported that they had increased confidence in sharing books with their children; 79% reported that Better beginnings had influenced their beliefs about the importance of sharing books with young children. Ninety-six percent of these caregivers believed that sharing books with their children was "very important." Before involvement in Better Beginnings, over half (56%) of mothers indicated that their children were not interested in books; after involvement in the program, 94% of mothers indicated that their children were interested in books. As an unanticipated benefit of the Better Beginnings program, over half the mothers reported reading more to their older children as well as to their infants and toddlers. In 2010, the Australian State Library is working to extend Better Beginning story kits with reading packs for children ages 4 to 5 years old, and literacy backpacks of books, audio CDs, literacy resources, and literacy skill development games for families to borrow.

The success of the West Australian Better Beginnings program can be attributed to several features, First, this program reached out to families in remote areas: families who traditionally would not have access to literacy materials. Literacy programs were tied to local libraries, child-friendly, comfortable places where parents could bring their children. Parents were not just trained in literacy techniques, although that was important; they were given physical literacy resources to take home. Nurses/medical professionals were involved with the program; these nurses helped parents learn to meet their children's health as well as literacy needs. American professionals can partner with local libraries and medical agencies to provide literacy training and materials for low SES, CLD parents.

As a last suggestion for encouraging low SES CLD parents to engage in literacy activities with their children, American professionals can consider the use of technology. Low SES parents may not have access to technological devices; however, many seem to have such devices. For example, professionals anecdotally report that almost all the low SES parents they work with have iPhones. There are many "apps" (applications) for iPads and iPhones which depict children's books. In most of these apps, the book is read aloud to the child as part of the app experience. For instance, I have used the app, "Miss Spider's Tea Party" in both Spanish and English. Children love these apps, and parents do not need to read. For families where English literacy is an issue for parents, books on apps can be an excellent resource to enhance children's literacy experiences without parents needing to read to them directly (although this is ideal).

In many cultures, infants and young children spend more time in the care of older siblings than they do in the company of their parents. Professionals can take advantage of this, training siblings in oral language stimulation strategies and also in use of basic literacy practices with their younger siblings.

Facilitating Overall Involvement of Low SES, CLD Families in Children's Education

Hammer and Rodriguez (2012) discuss considerations in working with Mexican-American families, stating that many of these families believe that the role of the school and the home should not interfere with each other. Many Mexican American families believe that they are being helpful by maintaining a respectful distance from the educational system. Hammer and Rodriguez conclude that Hispanic families in general are very interested in and supportive of their children's education; however, they often believe that they should not interfere with the educational process. In my own clinical experience, families from other CLD backgrounds often believe and behave similarly. For example, in the Philippines, teachers teach; parents train character and good behavior. Parents do not question the teachers, who are viewed as authority figures.

It is ideal to team up with persons from the families' cultures, who can help the families understand that in the United States, school professionals welcome and encourage family involvement. Convincing these families to alter their thinking on this issue may be challenging; in any case, maintaining a balance between respecting families' beliefs and encouraging them to participate in their children's education may be the best approach.

Of relevance, Zuniga (2011) points out that most immigrant and refugee CLD parents come to the United States to provide better lives for their children than they themselves had. In keeping with this goal, American professionals, although they wish to be sensitive, also need to provide these parents with information and suggestions that will help their children succeed in U.S. schools and ultimately in the world of work. A Vietnamese father I worked with did not like my suggestion that he talk more with his son Kevin, who had a language impairment. I told him that I genuinely respected his perspective, especially because I was raised in Southeast Asia myself. But I shared with him that I knew that he and his wife wanted a good life in the United States for Kevin, and that in this country, schools expect children to be verbally participatory. I expressed my empathy with his cultural feelings of discomfort but pointed out that to help Kevin fit in better and succeed in school; he needed more verbal interaction at home.

When professional teams encounter challenges in working with low SES, CLD families, it can be helpful to use the services of a *cultural mediator*. Roles and responsibilities of the cultural mediator include acting as a liaison between parents and professionals as well as being an advocate for the family. Cultural mediators also often serve as interpreters during assessments and meetings with parents, and they may translate written documents for the parents.

It is important for professionals to recognize that the services of cultural mediators can considerably increase the comfort level of low SES, CLD parents. It can be both instructive and humbling for professionals to see the critical role that cultural mediators can play in the work setting. Sometimes I have done my very best to work with a family and had limited success until the cultural mediator showed up. Professionals need to be open to help from these team members; often, not much can be accomplished without them, as seen in the following case example.

I remember meeting with the mother of Louis C., a very bright and active first grader from a Cantonese-speaking home, who was referred for a language screening. Results of the screening revealed that Louis' language learning ability was within normal limits. He definitely did not have a language impairment; however, because of his status as an English language learner, he was somewhat academically behind his classmates.

To address this issue, I met with his mother, Tao, an immigrant from Hong Kong, who cried for the better part of an hour as I handed her tissue after tissue. She said that her husband was not supportive at home and let Louis stay up till all hours watching TV. Her husband gambled away much of her earnings. She had a full-time job outside the home, working at a cookie store. She was a computer programmer in Hong Kong but could not find a commensurate job in the United States.

Tao sobbed as she talked about how patronizing many customers were, and how they treated her as though she were stupid. The loss of vocational status was very hard to endure. She was exhausted when she got home at the end of a long day. Her English, she said, was not good enough to even help Louis with his homework at the first grade level. She said that she felt so much despair that she did not know where to turn. None of my suggestions seemed to make a difference.

Fortunately, at the end of the conference as Tao was leaving, a Chinese interpreter who worked with some of the children at the school happened to be walking by. I introduced Tao to the interpreter, who also was a native Cantonese speaker. Tao immediately grasped the opportunity for real communication and could not stop talking to the interpreter. After an animated conversation, the interpreter ended up inviting Tao to a local Chinese church. The Chinese interpreter did for Tao what I could not: provided her with encouragement from a member of her own culture.

In addition to providing cultural mediators, another way in which professionals can be encouraging, empathetic, and supportive to low SES, CLD families is to emphasize the positive and interact in a personable manner as we said before. Many CLD families expect the professional to be somewhat like a friend (Chan & Chen, 2011; Sharifzadeh, 2011; Zuniga, 2011). The professional can take advantage of this (within appropriate boundaries, of course) and show an interest in the family as a whole, rather than just in the child in question.

In my own clinical practice, for example, I ask parents about the child's siblings and, if time allows, a little bit about how the family came to the United States and how they like it here. Much can be learned by this approach, and the families generally are very appreciative of any interest expressed in them. Although self-disclosure should be limited, many CLD families appreciate knowing a little bit of personal information about the professionals who are serving them (Chan & Chen, 2011; Roseberry-McKibbin, 2013).

Last year, I worked with an Indian family who was experiencing challenges coming to terms with the fact that their kindergarten son needed special education services. I briefly shared that my own son Mark had received occupational and vision therapy, doing my best to keep my sharing time short. It was amazing how the parents visibly became more receptive when they realized that the professional's child had been diagnosed with special needs, and that she was not ashamed to admit that he had received extensive special services. They became far more open to signing paperwork that would permit me and the rest of the special education team to assess their son in depth so that he could receive needed interventions.

In terms of helping low SES CLD families feel comfortable, another consideration is manner of dress. As a point of personal preference, for meetings with these parents, I dress professionally but inexpensively. I often wear a professional-looking white jacket that cost around $30. I wear some costume jewelry. Expensive clothing or jewelry may convey an inaccurate impression or even be intimidating to low SES parents, thereby creating an even greater gulf than the one that already exists between many low SES, CLD caregivers and the White, middle SES professionals who serve their children. Each professional has to decide for himself or herself what works best.

A personal experience supports my recommendation that less is more in this context: At a professional meeting, another SLP administrator was present. She was wearing several large diamond rings, diamond earrings, and a very expensive suit with perfectly matching expensive shoes. I realized that I felt intimidated in her presence. In my $20 dress from a mall sale and my costume jewelry, I felt a gulf between us, even though she was very cordial. If I felt this way, how much more so must low SES families feel when trying to relate to professionals who appear very expensively dressed by comparison.

In attempting to relate well to low SES, CLD families and help them feel comfortable, it often is helpful to praise their child's behavior or nature or character or mention that the child is well-behaved, obedient, and respectful (if this indeed is the case!). Even if a student is having difficulties, or has been diagnosed with a special education need, professionals can still find many good things to say about the children, and families appreciate hearing such validation. I frequently find that when I am sharing the results of diagnostic reports and recommendations for treatment, for example, it is highly effective to begin with a statement like, "I really enjoyed working with Jardin. He was hardworking and respectful and had a great attitude. You must be very proud of him! Let me share with you what I found during my assessment of his language skills."

Another way to help low SES families and students feel more comfortable is by showing interest in their linguistic and cultural backgrounds. I have worked with Russian middle school students who were thrilled when I learned three or four words in Russian. When I volunteered in my son's third grade Sunday school class, there was a new Mexican girl named Lilia Z. who spoke some English; Spanish was her dominant language, and she was the only Hispanic child in the class. Each Sunday when Lilia's father dropped her off, I greeted her and had her teach me a new word en Español. I mentioned to Lilia and her father that I took Spanish in college and really needed a brush-up! I asked Lilia to teach me a new word in Spanish every Sunday. I kept a running written list of new Spanish words that I showed Lilia each week. I thanked her for her help, and she would beam proudly at her contribution to my fledgling Spanish skills. I was very happy that she kept coming to Sunday school and was reminded of how much it can mean to CLD students and families when professionals take just a little bit of time and effort to acknowledge them and make them feel special.

An unfortunate finding in my own clinical practice is the belief of many low SES, CLD parents that school personnel will scold them for speaking a language other than English in the home. (Parents may actually lie to school personnel, maintaining that they speak only English at home.) It is critical for professionals who work with parents of CLD students to emphasize that being bilingual is a great asset in today's society. Professionals need to stress to parents that fluent bilingualism is highly desirable. Parents should speak to their children in the language in which they (the parents) are most fluent. Parents need to provide rich linguistic models for their children. The following case example highlights this special concern.

I will never forget Jesse M., a third grader who was on my speech-language caseload. His parents were from Mexico. His mother's English was quite fluent; his father's was rudimentary and showed many patterns of grammatical transfer from Spanish. Somewhere along the line, he had been told to speak only English to Jesse—which he obediently did. Jesse was confused; as he told me, "My mom speaks English one way, my dad speaks it another way, and my teacher speaks it even a different way" (the classroom teacher was Dutch). Jessie's father was providing him with a nonstandard English model that was doing more harm than good, and also was depriving him of the opportunity to be competently bilingual. I met with Jesse's parents and emphasized that exposing Jesse to his father's fluent Spanish at home was exactly the right thing to do to help Jesse with his language skills.

It is *always* best for children to hear grammatically sound, semantically rich language models, instead of models that have many errors and are quite basic.

It is crucial to encourage families to work with school professionals in a collaborative manner. However, as noted earlier, some low SES, CLD families may not want to do this because they feel that the child's education is the school's responsibility. In many countries, the teacher is the authority figure, and parents respect this boundary. They would consider it rude and out of line to make suggestions or give input into their child's education. Professionals who work with these kinds of families need to sensitively share that in the United States, parents are expected to be part of the team, and their input is welcome. How can professionals help parents to be more involved in their children's education, both regular and special education? Some suggestions follow (Roseberry-McKibbin, 2007, 2013):

- *When meeting with parents at the school site or conducting home visits, bring samples of the student's work to show.*
- *Send home pictures of children doing school activities.* For many low SES, CLD parents who are not able to come to their children's schools, this helps them feel more connected.

▦ *Help parents understand the academic/curricular expectations of United States schools.* Parents who have not been educated in the United States may have very little idea of what actually goes on in their children's classrooms. For example, because I was raised in the Philippines, it's been a steep learning curve for me in terms of finding out what is expected of my son in American schools. I have been very fortunate to volunteer in his classroom on a regular basis. Classroom volunteer experience can be revealing, helpful, and very rewarding in helping parents understand what is expected of their children in American classrooms.

▦ *Help parents understand common American school routines such as waiting in line, volunteering to speak in class, and eating lunch in a cafeteria.* In an example that probably is stretching this point, at Mark's first elementary school, the principal told me to "keep off the grass." Having been raised in a tropical island country (where I rarely wore shoes), I never would have thought of this as a possible school rule.

▦ *Help parents understand their role in helping their children with homework.* As the parent of a kindergartner, I was shocked to discover my son had at least a half-hour to an hour of homework each night, and I was expected to help him with all of it. Not that I minded, but when my family and I lived in the Philippines, my sisters and I did not have homework (at least on the islands my family and I lived on during those years). We worked very hard in school, but our schoolwork was the teacher's responsibility, not the parents'. Parents accustomed to this situation need to become oriented to American schools' expectations of their role in actively helping children with homework.

▦ *Invite parents to observe in the classroom.*

▦ *Ask parents to do activities at home to support the classroom* (e.g., collate and staple papers, cut out projects).

▦ *Invite parents to school functions such as book fairs.*

It is a privilege to work with the families of students from low SES, CLD backgrounds. I have often found that the parents of these students have made great sacrifices to create better lives for their children than they themselves had. As noted earlier, many parents are struggling to provide their children with the basics of life such as food, shelter, and clothing. They often have low-paying jobs and may work two jobs (per parent) to support their families. I have come to have profound respect for these families, the challenges they face, and their desire and drive to help their children succeed in the United States. These families inspire me to be deeply grateful for all my own blessings, and to work even harder to make sure that their children receive the services that they deserve.

POSSIBLE VALUE CONFLICTS BETWEEN LOW SES FAMILIES AND MIDDLE SES PROFESSIONALS

As mentioned, many professionals in U.S. schools today are from middle-class backgrounds and have difficulty understanding the social norms of students and families from low SES backgrounds. Children who come to school from middle SES backgrounds are decreasing in number, and students who come from low SES backgrounds are increasing in number. Middle SES professionals need to remember that schools operate from middle-class norms and follow the hidden rules of the middle class. As emphasized by Adler (1979):

> The American school system . . . is predominantly a middle-class institution. It not only teaches middle-class values and ideas, but it operates in a middle-class fashion and uses middle-class methods in performing its role in American society. This is inevitable since the official ideology of the United States is a middle-class ideology, and the school system is an institutionalized arm of that middle-class society. The educators . . . are themselves largely middle class . . . since they are products of the system, that is to be expected. (p. 142)

Differences may exist between the values of low SES children and families and the middle class professionals who provide services for them; several of these differences are described here. Some of these, discussed in Chapter 1, are revisited in this section.

First, mainstream middle SES professionals tend to be proactive, valuing planning for the future and setting goals. For example, these professionals may recommend early intervention for a young child who is at risk for a language delay. In a low SES family, however, the present may be valued as the most important aspect of living; decisions are made in the moment based on survival today. The future is uncertain and therefore not important. Thus, if the child is surviving as a 3-year-old in the neighborhood, the family may not see the importance of planning for two years from now when the child enters kindergarten.

A second and related area of potential value conflicts between the middle SES professional and the low SES family is in locus of control. Middle SES professionals typically have an internal locus of control and a strong sense of personal efficacy. They believe that they can affect both present and future by good choices that they make today. It is an attitude of "God helps those who help themselves." But many low SES families believe that there is little they can do to work against chance. Their current circumstances are their fate, and little or nothing can be done to change it. Hard work and perseverance are ineffective against problems created by poverty (Sue & Sue, 2013). Thus, these families may not follow through with recommendations for home carryover programs or perhaps even bringing a child to an SLP for much needed speech and language intervention.

Many students and their families from low SES backgrounds have an external locus of control and a limited sense of personal efficacy (Lynch, 2011). Owing in large part to the harshness of their circumstances, and the myriad discouragements that they have endured, many low SES families may seem uninvolved and behave as if they do not care: about school, homework, special education, their children's health, or anything else. To reiterate, it is essential for middle SES professionals to view these families with compassion and provide them the support they need *at the level that is usable for them.*

An SLP and the school intervention team were meeting with a migrant Hispanic family to share suggestions that they could implement with their language-impaired child at home. She and the rest of the team felt very pleased with themselves as they described detailed, specific, successful academic and language strategies with the family. The intervention team provided pages of information and suggestions. The family nodded politely for an hour. At the end of the hour, the father said: "We live in our car. Can you help understand how to implement your suggestions under these conditions?"

This case example illustrates the point that before making recommendations, professionals need to know the circumstances and life situations of the children's caregivers. Recommendations must be tailored to their ability to carry out these recommendations. Professionals must work with children and families where they are, even in less-than-ideal circumstances, as illustrated in yet another case example.

I worked with Faloah S., a 10-year-old child of low SES parents, who was born in American Samoa and came to the United States with her family as a toddler. She had recently transferred from another school district and was being evaluated for special services for a number of problems. Faloah had a history of allergies (for which she was not receiving any known treatment) and probable vision and hearing problems (which also had never been addressed). In her previous school district, the IEP team had made many recommendations for management of these problems, but her family had never followed up on any of these recommendations.

At age 10, Faloah was found to have the language and cognitive skills of a child half her age. A large, friendly girl, Faloah had severe dental/occlusal problems that made it difficult for her to speak intelligibly. I recommended that next time Faloah's mother (no father was in the picture) took her to the dentist, the possibility of orthodontia be discussed. In the mean time, in speech therapy, we decided to try to "work around" Faloah's dental/occlusal problems, doing the best we could under the circumstances to help this child sound as intelligible as possible. The success of this approach would necessarily be very limited.

The evaluation team met with Faloah's mother, repeating the previous school district's recommendations for evaluations of Faloah's hearing, vision, and allergies as well as her dentition. Even if all of these evaluations could be accomplished, this child's school records suggested that she and her mother would soon move again. Nevertheless, we recognized that it was our job to nonjudgmentally work with Faloah while she was at the school site, making

> the most of the time we had with her. (note: Faloah and her family moved again, and are no longer at our school site).

A third area in which middle SES professionals and low SES families may differ is in the area of communication styles. As noted earlier in this book, formal register, used by middle SES professionals, is linear, sequential, and to the point, whereas casual register is characterized by a more oblique style of communication in which it is normal to "beat around the bush." If professionals conduct meetings with parents by getting right to the point, parents from low SES homes may be offended; they may view professionals as noncaring and rude. As recommended before, it often is ideal to engage in a little preliminary "chit-chat" before getting down to business. Many families from backgrounds of generational poverty view institutions and "the establishment" with mistrust (Payne, 2003). Professionals may have to work hard to secure the trust of these families, and engaging in a little social conversation can help them feel more comfortable.

FACILITATING FOUNDATIONAL SUPPORT SERVICES FOR LOW SES FAMILIES: PRACTICAL SUGGESTIONS

Supporting Low SES Families in Meeting Basic Needs

Educators frequently cite lack of parent involvement as a problem in low SES schools (Perlman & Fantuzzo, 2010; Woolfolk, 2008). Many low SES parents are labeled "uninvolved," "uncaring," and worse. Certainly it is frustrating when parents appear uninvolved and do not follow through. Landsman (2006) discussed a California middle school in which teachers were frustrated that parents were not showing up at school for conferences or performances. The school social worker asked how many teachers had cars. All teachers, administrators, and assistants raised their hands. The social worker then told them that 89% of the parents at the school had no car. If parents were to come to conferences, they would need to take time off work (not easy in low-wage jobs) and negotiate bus schedules to get to the school.

As a consequence of this exercise, teachers began to think of new ways to reach parents. They would phone them or hold conferences in locations closer to students' homes. They would visit homeless shelters where families lived. Many teachers began to use staff release days before the beginning of the school year to go into the homeless shelters and neighborhoods where their students lived and talk to the parents about what they wanted for their children. Teachers frequently said that these were the most useful preparation days they spent all year.

Some teachers have found that home visits are effective in helping parents feel more involved in their children's education. These visits are especially effective when teachers report children's positive accomplishments. In one school district, if parents do not feel comfortable having teachers in their homes, teachers meet the parents at a mall or a local restaurant (Haberman, 1999).

As Landsman (2006) points out, realizing the difficult conditions experienced by students and families from low SES backgrounds can help professionals suspend judgment about their behavior. "If we look at a student whose head is on the desk each day or whose clothes are dirty and decide that that student is deficient in character, we will lose that student from the start" (p. 30).

I mentioned previously that one of my former school principals, Mr. Gulden, who had been in the field of education for 18 years, had repeatedly encountered the situation where teachers (usually White, middle-class teachers) would say that a certain student could not progress due to lack of family involvement. He emphasized that, although professionals need to try to involve parents fully in their child's educational experience, obtaining parent involvement was not always possible. Lack of parent involvement cannot be made a scapegoat for all of a child's problems, nor should teachers just "write a child off" because parental involvement is lacking.

An instructive example is my experience working with Jamal, a fourth grade student who was not learning because he literally was unable to pay attention. The school's special education professionals all thought that unless Jamal could receive medication to help him pay better attention in class, he might have to repeat fourth grade because his academic achievement was so very low. It took months to get a signed Request for Assessment form back from his mother, who stated that she took him to a pediatrician who said he was "just fine." Jamal's scores in all language areas tested were steeply below age level. He scored at a kindergarten–first grade level on most language skills assessed. It was pretty evident that not much progress could be expected with Jamal until his medical issues were resolved. Jamal's mother could not or would not address this issue. The situation was very frustrating, and Jamal's mother was a target of that frustration.

A situation in my personal life has helped me to recognize that many factors may underlie lack of parental involvement. To serve as volunteers in our son's classroom at his new school, my husband and I were required to be fingerprinted and tested for tuberculosis (TB), according to the school district's policy. So on my way home from work one day, I got my TB test at the district office approximately 20 miles away. I went back the next day to have the result read (first I had to take my son to his karate lesson, which ended at 4:30 PM). Then I discovered that the district's machine for fingerprinting was broken, so I had to travel to a sheriff's station, even farther away. The hours of the sheriff's station were Monday through Friday, 9 AM to 12 noon and 1 to 4 PM. Thus, the fingerprinting had to be accomplished on a completely separate trip. Then I stood in line for the fingerprints and took them back to the school district office. All of this took 3 to 4 hours of time, juggling tasks, and driving more than 50 miles.

Without the resources I am fortunate enough to have, the requirements for volunteering in my son's classroom probably would make it impossible to get involved as a parent. Many low SES mothers, for example, would not have the transportation to go to the district office and get TB tested. Even if they did have transportation, how would they arrange to go to the sheriff's station to get fingerprinted at the designated hours? Low SES mothers who work outside the home frequently have jobs with little or no flexibility in hours—certainly they do not have jobs that allow them to leave at the hours that the sheriff's station is open.

This situation alone has been a true eye-opener regarding the resources it takes to be an "involved parent." Am I more involved with my son's education because I am morally and intellectually superior to low SES, "uninvolved" mothers? Do I love my child more than they love theirs? Am I diligent in contrast to their laziness and clear lack of motivation to help their children?

Or do they love and want to help their children just as much as I do but lack the resources to do so? As an exercise, I created Table 9–2, which shows the resources that I possess as a middle SES parent that enable full involvement in my child's scholastic life to volunteer in the classroom and to help Mark boost his reading scores as well as provide overall support for homework that is assigned nightly. As I consider this list, I somehow feel much less judgmental of "uninvolved" low SES caregivers. Those of us from middle SES backgrounds take a great deal for granted.

In addition to the ideas described at the beginning of this section, professionals can reach out in still other ways to families of low SES children to support them in meeting their basic needs. One practical thing that professionals can do to support low SES families is to have available comprehensive lists of low-cost or free local health services for families and information about transportation.

Even if health services are available, families may not have transportation to the sites where services are provided. . In addition, professionals must keep in mind that the U.S. health care system is difficult to navigate, especially when parents' English abilities are limited and they cannot communicate their concerns to health providers (Battle, 2012).

This can be a problem in instances in which a child experiences multiple episodes of otitis media or ear infections that affect hearing, language, and other aspects of communication. If that child cannot get to an appropriate service provider, the ear infections may continue unabated, with have negative long-term consequences on language development and other areas. Thus, again, professionals need to be prepared to help low SES families by providing suggestions for transportation to low-cost or free clinics where their health needs can be met. Professionals can also do their best to refer low SES CLD families to clinics where health care personnel speak their language.

Another intervention that professionals can use to support low SES caregivers is to conduct training through use of DVDs, as well as YouTube videos, mentioned previously. Payne (2003) states that in many low SES communities, caregivers cannot come to meetings or inservice training sessions because they don't have transportation. However, despite their poverty, many caregivers do own DVD

Table 9-2. A Middle-SES Parent's Resources for School Involvement

- Can speak fluent English
- Can read and write fluent English
- Owns car to drive to school site and other necessary places
- Car runs well and does not break down
- Able to drive
- Can afford gas, even at current prices
- Lives close enough to school to go there; school is not geographically out of reach
- Not intimidated by classroom teacher—able to communicate with him/her easily
- Can walk across the street; can sit in chair in classroom; no physical handicap that prevents these activities
- Can see well
- Can hear
- Not addicted to a substance, therefore able to show up regularly when needed
- Healthy and well-nourished; therefore energetic enough to volunteer and interact with teacher
- Owns a computer
- Computer-literate enough to e-mail teacher (who prefers e-mail)
- Owns appropriate clothes to wear to school and district office
- Owns washer and dryer
- Can afford laundry detergent to have clean clothes to wear
- Clean enough to go to the school because have money for self-care products (soap, shampoo)
- Able to afford toothpaste and toothbrush, so not self-conscious about having bad breath when talking with teacher or other parents
- Owns shoes that are sturdy enough that pebbles and sticks don't hurt feet on walking to the classroom from car
- Has job; job is flexible enough to permit involvement in son's school
- Has supportive spouse and two incomes, allowing the time to volunteer and be involved, as well as the money to support child's school activities
- Has paper, pencils, crayons, tape, and glue for child's homework assignments
- Has the time and skills/educational background to help child with homework assignments
- House has clean, well-lighted space for child to complete homework assignments
- House is in safe neighborhood where family does not have to fear violence, thus distracting parents and child from schoolwork

players. Many own iPhones. Payne shared the story of a low-income school that served children, 95% of whose parents were on welfare. The school principal and the teachers were successfully able to reach these parents by providing information and instructions on 15-minute videotapes. Professionals who want to train caregivers in language stimulation techniques or other educationally beneficial activities may consider sending home short, simple videos or DVDs that caregivers can watch repeatedly in their own homes

If families have computers and internet access, they can watch instructional videos on YouTube for free. Some experts have begun to broadcast short YouTube video clips depicting strategies for successfully reading with children. The advantages of YouTube clips are that: (1) they are free, (2) they can be watched over and over again, and (3) they are available to families at any time of day or night.

In terms of supporting children and families from low SES backgrounds, professionals also need to consider situations in which children are being raised by their grandparents. A growing number of grandparents are caring for their grandchildren because of parental abandonment and incarceration, mental illness, divorce, and death. Generations United (2012) reported that more than 6.7 million children across our country live in households maintained by grandparents or other relatives. Twenty-two percent of grandparents raising their children have incomes below poverty level, and 63% are still in the workforce. Many are over the age of 60 years.

One study in Virginia found that 98% of grandparents raising their children were worried about financial matters. Housing and food were grandparents' greatest expenses. Almost half (40%) of grandparents indicated that they had a chronic or serious illness. Many grandparents cut back on the amount of food that they themselves ate so that there would be enough for their grandchildren to eat. Almost 48% reported going for a whole day without eating. Henderson (2004) recommended that professionals who work with children living with their grandparents help these caregivers find support for their daily necessities such as food.

Supporting Children from Homes Characterized by Abuse or Neglect

According to Neuman (2009), because of the irreplaceable importance of early relationships in young children's development, we must do everything possible to help parents to establish good relationships with their children from the very beginning of their lives. Unfortunately, these relationships are sometimes characterized by abuse and neglect. Many low SES parents neglect their children because they are literally unable to provide health care, food, clothing, or shelter for them. *Neglect* usually indicates a failure to provide for a child's basic needs, and it may be emotional, educational, physical, or some combination of those. Emotional neglect can involve exposure to domestic violence or inattention to a child's emotional needs. Research has found that children who are severely emotionally neglected may have cognitive problems, including difficulty with problem-solving skills and impulse control (Hildyard & Wolfe, 2002).

Educational neglect can involve the caregivers' failure to attend to a child's general or special education needs. Physical neglect can be characterized by lack of food, shelter, or medical care; it also can involve lack of appropriate supervision (e.g., leaving young children at home alone). Children who have been severely ignored and neglected may be apathetic and lethargic (Hardman et al., 2006). Parents may neglect their children for a variety of reasons; one of the major ones is a lack of financial resources.

In my own clinical experience, a fourth grade girl from a low SES family literally had to be sent home from school several times because her clothing was so soiled from urine that the penetrating odor prevented the classroom teacher and other children from attending to classroom activities. Conducting language intervention with her in a small therapy room with no windows was particularly challenging. In winter, the girl had no sweater, so some of us brought sweaters from home for her to wear. At the same school, a 7-year-old boy from a low SES home had been referred for testing. As I was conducting the assessment, I could hear his stomach growling; he said he had not had breakfast. I obtained a snack for him so that he could focus and perform to the best of his capability during the assessment session.[1]

Low SES parents are often are severely stressed, which can result in abuse of their children. The abuse can be physical, verbal, emotional, or a combination of these. As a chronic stressor, poverty often is associated with acrimonious relationships between parents. This in

---

[1]In general, professionals should be extremely careful about feeding children, and some readers may feel that children should never been given food at all, no matter how hungry they are. An important consideration is that many children have food allergies; school professionals may be unaware of these.

turn can lead to irritability, hostility, and verbal, physical, or emotional abuse between parents. Often, this may be extended to include children. Stressed parents tend to abuse their children more, which leads to higher rates of depression in children. Early experiences of child abuse have a long-term, encompassing impact on children's academic achievement. The parents are more likely to feel like they have less social support, to feel isolated, and to believe that it is appropriate to use aggression as a means of problem solving.

In this country, on the average, child abuse is reported every 10 seconds. Each day in the United States, more than four children die as a result of abuse in the home (Safe Horizon, 2006). In the Preface of this book, I mentioned a little boy from a school where I used to work. He came in one day absolutely distraught. Finally, he told us that his father had made him watch as he beat the family dog to death. I'm sure you hate reading this; I sure hate writing about it. But it reminds us of the traumatic circumstances in which some of our students live.

I'll never forget Christina, a sweet, shy, sixth grade girl with some minor speech difficulties on my caseload in a low SES neighborhood. In January, after Christmas break, Christina would not speak at all. She had been fine in December. We discovered that an uncle had moved into the house and was sexually molesting her. Proper steps were taken to help Christina become safe again. Table 9–3 offers some suggestions for professionals who try to help families increase the effectiveness of child-caregiver interactions in which neglect or abuse exists.

Research shows that low SES caregivers tend to issue commands and orders, and to use more physical punishment with their children (Hart & Risley, 1995). Children of low SES parents are more likely to receive harsh discipline at home (Perlman & Fantuzzo, 2010). As described in Table 9–3, professionals can help caregivers learn how to use positive discipline, including using language instead of corporal punishment, to manage their children's behavior. Families from some countries may believe that corporal punishment is effective and will use it often with their children. Professionals can be instrumental in helping these families (often through the assistance of a cultural mediator) understand that laws in the United States forbid certain types of corporal punishment (Roseberry-McKibbin, 2007, 2013).

Effective ways of accomplishing this are available; parent training often is very helpful (Neuman, 2009; Swick, 2010). Devall (2004)

Table 9–3. Intervention Strategies for Increasing Effectiveness of Caregiver-Child Interaction When the Caregiver Abuses Substances and/ or Mistreats or Neglects the Child

1. Ask caregivers about their own needs, and attempt to meet these needs or guide them to professionals who can help (e.g., adult English classes, parenting classes, food stamp programs).

2. Provide key information about overall child development.

3. Provide respite care so that the caregiver can get a break.

4. Make caregivers feel good about their parenting skills. Point out what they are already doing right (e.g., "I noticed that when Benny obeyed you, you said, 'Good job!'")

5. Provide support groups of other caregivers who are experiencing the same life challenges. Provide on-site child care for the child and siblings.

6. Organize play groups where caregivers' positive behaviors are pointed out as good examples ("Look, when Josefina bumped her knee and started to cry, Mary picked her up and started to comfort her immediately.")

7. Use DVDs of good examples of communication and successful parenting strategies. If possible, contrast the ideal way of communicating with a way that is less than ideal. For example, show a child knocking over a glass of juice. In scenario #1, the mother scolds and berates him, then cleans up the mess herself. In scenario #2, the mother empathizes calmly with the accident and has the child help her clean up the mess.)

8. Model language stimulation strategies (such as using recasts and extensions) that are free, effective, and easily incorporated into the caretaker's daily routine.

9. Encourage reading in the home. Model techniques that are effective with reading to children, and share examples of books that are appropriate for children of various ages.

10. Encourage parents to have their children attend school regularly.

11. For immigrant parents especially, help them recognize what constitutes child abuse in the United States.

Source: Adapted from La Paro et al., 2004; Paul and Norbury, 2012; Payne, 2003; Roseberry-McKibbin, 2007; Safe Horizon, 2012.

reported on a parent training program implemented in New Mexico, a state that has high numbers of low SES, CLD parents. The population of New Mexico is 42% Hispanic and 10% Native American (U.S. Bureau of the Census, 2000). Devall noted that parent training effectiveness research has been conducted primarily with White, middle SES families; she and her colleagues wanted to empirically evaluate the effectiveness of a family-centered parenting program for high-risk families using scientifically based curricula and evaluation tools. The families in this project primarily lived in poverty, lacked social support, and experienced high levels of stress. Many were from CLD groups.

The Nurturing Parent (NP) program (Bavolek & Bavolek, 2002) was used. This program addresses parenting and self-nurturing skills. Classes met once a week and lasted for 2 ½ hours. Interactive teaching strategies were used to present information on life skills, nutrition, and parenting. Parents were given class time to practice new skills, and homework assignments were given to reinforce the new skills. Classes for children were run concurrently with classes for parents. Children participated in drama, music, art, and games designed to teach program concepts at developmentally appropriate levels. During family nurturing time, parents and children came together for activities such as games and songs to promote family bonding.

NP classes were held in community centers, schools, and local agencies. Classes for incarcerated parents were held at state and federal prisons. To help retain families in the program, several strategies were used. Each week, parent educators mailed postcards to parents to thank them for coming to meetings, announce the topic for the upcoming class, and let absent parents know that they were missed.

To encourage attendance, each family also was called before meetings. A graduation ceremony was held for parents who completed at least 75% of class sessions. The number of classes for the NP series ranged from 9 to 24. The average completion rate of the NP classes was 60%.

The results of the NP program showed that parents demonstrated significant improvement in their knowledge of positive discipline techniques and empathy for their children's needs. They reported significant decreases in belief in corporal punishment, inappropriate expectations of children, and restriction of children's independence. Devall (2004) concluded that group parent education is an effective format for high-risk families. Parents experience social support, decreased levels of stress, and decreased likelihood of abusing their children. Other researchers have reported that providing parent training can help parents interact with their children in more positive, constructive ways (Blevins, 2012; Ispa et al., 2006; Neuman, 2009).

Neuman (2009) discusses Early Head Start, a program that began in 1994. It has been established in many high-poverty communities, and focuses on helping pregnant mothers and low SES families and toddlers get the strongest possible support. Early Head Start providers are willing to visit mothers and children in their homes; center-based visits are also possible. These providers are highly qualified professionals who help caregivers in every possible area, including parenting skills training. Results of Early Start interventions have been highly positive; in one area, children from multirisk environments whose families participated in Early Start were scoring equal to or above district and state averages on state tests four or five years later. Among the positive effects documented for Early Head Start programs: higher scores for children on standardized tests; greater parent involvement in language and literacy activities; lower levels of family stress and conflict; milder disciplinary techniques (e.g., time-outs rather than spanking); and, perhaps best of all, greater security and attachment for children. Children feel secure and are better able to experience attachment with caregivers when the home atmosphere is supportive.

Helping Caregivers Provide a Supportive Home Atmosphere

Research has shown that maternal warmth and responsive mother-child interaction patterns are critical factors in children's language outcomes (Aikens & Barbarin, 2008; Hamer, 2012). Because stress and depression are common among low SES mothers especially, professionals can be aware of this and do their best to provide support (Turnbull & Justice, 2012). When parents feel supported and less stressed, they usually will be more receptive to suggestions regarding facilitating optimal language activities and interactions with their children. Increased support for parents helps improve their sense of personal efficacy, which leads to willingness to take action to change and improve circumstances (Lynch, 2011). The improved family dynamics will open the way for better communication in the home. Previous chapters have presented ways in which caregivers can stimulate and facilitate their children's oral and written language development.

Professionals also can teach caregivers how to provide an emotionally supportive home atmosphere for their children.

The importance of helping caregivers who are at risk for neglecting or abusing their children has been emphasized. We also said that is important to help all caregivers by supporting them in general parenting skills (Swick, 2010). In some language and early literacy programs, professionals such as speech-language pathologists and their colleagues are taking child development classes so they can support parents in using positive discipline with their children (Blevins, 2012). Although many professionals might legitimately believe that teaching parenting and positive discipline skills is not "our job," they are finding that it is almost impossible to provide supportive services without giving at least basic support in this area. As one of my former school principals wryly told me, many parents are so young that we have "children raising children."

In terms of successful parenting styles, researchers in Illinois found that among low SES African American parents, those whose children succeeded in school usually were married couples who imposed routines that reinforced the message that school came first: before any other distractions such as video games, TV, or friends. In the homes of students who were low achievers, mothers came home from work and either did not mention homework at all or were quickly distracted from the subject (Hymowitz, 2005).

Research indicates that higher control parenting is associated with better grades for African American and Asian students (Glasgow, Dornbusch, Troyer, Steinberg, & Ritter, 1997). Higher academic achievement for inner-city children has been associated with parenting that is strict and directive, with clear rules and consequences, that is combined with high levels of emotional support and warmth. Such parenting can be achieved even by a caregiver without an advanced education or much money, as seen in the following real-life case example.

> At a school where I work part-time a speech-language evaluation had been scheduled for Rashida, a 4-year-old. She was brought to the evaluation by her older African American foster mother, "Grandma." She had come from a home where she had been abused and neglected. Although a sweet child, Rashida clearly had difficulties with behavior,

attention, and focus, as well as with speech and language, and I was concerned that the assessment process would be very prolonged, unproductive, or even unpleasant. Much to my surprise, the evaluation went very well because Grandma was extremely strict and firm with Rashida and gave more hugs, kisses, and affirmations than I see from most biological parents.

Along with the fact that she was well loved, Rashida knew her boundaries. She was allowed to get away with nothing. If Rashida began to misbehave, consequences were swift, immediate, and very clear. When she obeyed Grandma, Grandma would enfold her in a huge hug, kiss her, and tell her what a good girl she was and how proud she was. Never before or since have I seen such a truly masterful combination of love, limits, and discipline. I wished I had a video camera. I don't think Grandma had an advanced education or much money, but I believe that many educated, middle and upper SES parents could have taken parenting lessons from this gifted older woman. Grandma was my most poignant lesson in my whole career in directive parenting accompanied by love and warmth.

Positive parenting skills combined with supportive language interaction styles provide children with the foundation they need to be successful. As discussed earlier in this book, research has shown that in some low SES homes, caregivers do not interact in ways that support children's optimal language development.

In our university clinic, we serve children and adults with communication disorders and their families. One of my graduate students, Lisa, was serving Mindy, a 10-year-old girl from a low SES home. Mindy had a language impairment, was doing poorly in school, and appeared to have very low self esteem. Mindy had been struggling with weight issues for most of her childhood. Lisa worked hard to help Mindy feel better about herself, because Lisa was so moved by Mindy's depressed demeanor and self-put-downs. One day when Lisa came to pick Mindy up in the clinic waiting room, she overheard Mindy's parents tell her that she was fat and would never "get a husband." Lisa concealed her shock, greeted Mindy's parents, and brought Mindy back to the therapy room. There, Lisa gently told Mindy that she had overheard what was said, and asked Mindy if her parents commonly told her those things. "All the time," Mindy replied. "I'm fat, and no man will ever want to marry me." Lisa eventually talked diplomatically with Mindy's parents, suggesting that her self-image was suffering due to hearing how she was fat and would never marry because no man would ever want her. Mindy's parents were genuinely shocked. They had no idea, they told Lisa, that it was negative for Mindy to hear those words. They thanked Lisa for her insight, and said they would try to change their behavior.

In terms of caregivers' interactions with children, Hart and Risley (1995) observed that in the families where the affect was positive during interactions, the children were more motivated to explore new topics, to listen and practice, and to notice facts and relationships.

Hart and Risley (1995) found that by the age of 4, the average child in a welfare family might had had 144,000 fewer encouragements and 84,000 more discouragements of behavior than the average child from a working class family. Hart and Risley (1995) extrapolated that to keep the confidence-building experiences of welfare children equal to those of working class children, the welfare children would need to be given 1,100 more instances of affirmative feedback per week. In all, 40 hours a week of substituted experience would be needed to keep the welfare children's ratio of lifetime experience with encouragement (relative to discouragement) equal to that of children from working-class homes. This type of program would need to start at birth and run continuously all year long.

Hart and Risley (1995) stated that what children hear affects their self-image, which influences expectations for success and motivation to try. Although later experience can provide pockets of success in which children can feel good and confident about themselves, it is unlikely that these pockets of success will replace cumulative feelings of incompetence or inferiority that have been contributed to by such statements as, "Bad boy!" or "I hate you" or "You're so stupid." It is my clinical experience that any parents, regardless of SES, can say negative things to their children. However, my clinical experience echoes the data-based findings of Hart and Risley. In my career, I have tended to hear more negative statements from low SES caregivers (mothers, fathers, grandparents) than from middle-and upper SES caregivers.

It is easy for professionals who work with low SES students to focus on training mothers to interact with their children more effectively. Little research focuses directly on low SES fathers. However, one study examined the interactions of low SES dads and their children, evaluating the impact of fathers' parenting involvement.

Using data from a study of 261 children in three cities, analyses assessed whether fathers' parenting practices during early childhood showed long-term links with their children's cognitive skills through middle childhood. Results of the study found that fathers' caring and warm parenting predicted enhanced math and reading skills for their children in middle childhood; fathers' restrictive discipline predicted lower math and reading skills. Interestingly, these links were independent of mothers' parenting and emerged even when the researchers controlled for a range of child and family characteristics. Associations between children's cognitive skills and fathers' parenting were similar across both nonresident and resident fathers and across Hispanic and African American families (Coley, Lewin-Bizan, & Carrano, 2011). The results of this study can encourage professionals to, when possible, emphasize inclusion of fathers in education and training.

Professionals can provide education and training for caregivers in the areas of parenting skills and ways to provide a supportive home atmosphere. If caregivers can be provided with the support and training they need, children's lives will be greatly enhanced. Lugo-Gil and Tamis-LeMonda (2008) investigated reciprocal associations among measures of parenting quality, family resources, and child cognitive performance in a low-income, ethnically diverse sample of 2,089 children and families. Parenting quality and family resources uniquely contributed to children's cognitive performance at 14, 24, and 36 months of age; parenting quality mediated the effects of family resources on children's performance at all ages. Parenting quality continued to be related to children's cognitive performance at 24 and 36 months of age after controlling for earlier measures of family resources, parenting quality, and child performance. In sum, Lugo-Gil and Tamis-LeMonda showed that parenting quality was a key variable in the cognitive development of low SES young children.

Some years ago I worked with Jeffrey G., a kindergarten boy from a low SES family. With his white-blond hair and blue eyes, he looked like an angel. One day during therapy, I asked him to do something a little more difficult than usual. He responded: "Forget it, b-tch." After I had recovered from my shock, I firmly told Jeffrey that this language was inappropriate in school, and that if he said that again, he would need to go to the principal's office. He was stunned. He told me he was sorry, adding: "My dad always calls my mom that. I didn't know it was a bad thing to say."

CONCLUSIONS

Low SES families in the United States today have many challenges to overcome as they try to raise their children to be successful adults. Professionals also can support families in meeting their fundamental needs and give them training that will encourage positive parenting practices, as well as helping them provide emotionally supportive home environments for their children. To reiterate the chapter opening quote from Cesar Chavez, once social change begins, it cannot be reversed. You cannot un-educate the person who has learned to read. You cannot humiliate the person who feels pride. You cannot oppress the people who are not afraid any more. All school professionals who work with children and families from low SES backgrounds have a mandate to be part of this social change.

CHAPTER HIGHLIGHTS

■ Low SES families often lack the social and cultural capital of middle SES families. This lack of capital prevents families from making the connections that can help their children access ideal services and opportunities in school and in society in general.

- Low SES, culturally and linguistically diverse (CLD) families may experience challenges due to their CLD status. For example, if CLD students come to school not speaking any English, and schools do not support them, these students are at risk for educational and eventual vocational failure.

- CLD students and their families are statistically documented to experience poverty at a much higher rate than White students and families, with poverty's resulting impacts in every area of life. Internationally, CLD persons also may experience disadvantages compared to the country's mainstream majority.

- Children of immigrants and refugees in the U.S. are highly likely to experience poverty. In addition, these children are less likely than native-born children to receive high quality, center-based, early child care with its advantages. Professionals can support caregivers in becoming more comfortable placing their children in these centers through allowing them to volunteer, thus being close to their children.

- Language and literacy practices of various cultures may differ from those espoused by mainstream American professionals. Professionals can recommend functional equivalents, or practices from parents' cultures that promote language and literacy skills while simultaneously being culturally appropriate.

- Many CLD parents relate better to professionals who come across as warm, caring, and interested in them as people. It can be helpful if professionals discretely and very briefly share a little personal information; families tend to feel more connected to these professionals, and thus more open to implementing recommendations which will benefit their children.

- Studies show that in order to help parents engage in literacy activities with their children, professionals can team up with libraries and medical facilities to provide children's books and instruction in best reading practices.

- To facilitate low SES CLD parents' involvement in their children's education, it is ideal to use cultural mediators. These mediators are people from the parents' own culture who can serve as liaisons between families, professionals, and agencies that provide services for children.

- Professionals and low SES parents in general may experience clashes in values. For example, professionals may want to be proactive in terms of implementing early intervention for young, at-risk children; parents may not see the value in this. Professionals must patiently and sensitively emphasize small, do-able steps that take parents' comfort level into consideration.

- It is ideal if professionals have lists and contacts available that inform low SES families of agencies and persons who can provide practical support (e.g., health and transportation services). It is important to consider the increasingly common situation of children living with their grandparents.

- Low SES caregivers may experience such stress that they neglect and even abuse their children. Parent training in best discipline practices and support for stressed parents can go a long way in helping parents to interact more positively and constructively with their children.

10

Some Words of Encouragement

Let no one be deluded that a knowledge
of the path can substitute for putting
one foot in front of the other.

Mary Caroline Richards, poet

Even professionals who have armed themselves with all known useful strategies and interventions for helping students from low SES backgrounds sometimes find themselves with more questions than answers. As you come to the conclusion of this book, you may feel—as I often did during the writing of this book—overwhelmed as you truly realize the magnitude of the challenges faced by these children and their families. Most of us in the helping professions, teachers, SLPs, and others are middle SES professionals and we are aware of the steep uphill climb faced by many of the families and children we serve. As identified in relevant research, the vast array of problems encountered in this climb may make it very daunting: this book may have helped you realize that the hill is even steeper than you thought.

A major reason many of us experience burnout as we attempt to support children from low SES families is that we work from a level 3 perspective. We feel very alone as individuals, doing all we can to help, often spending money out of our own pockets and a great deal of time from our personal lives. We feel as though we have a teaspoon to deal with an ocean of need. Can we really make a difference?

It is this question that led me to write this book. I've made every effort in this book to provide encouragement, support, and some research-based practical strategies to use with the low SES students we work so hard to help. When I feel discouraged, I think of stories like the one told to me by David, an SLP from Nebraska several years ago when I was there to present a workshop. A young American Indian boy was placed onto David's caseload for intervention for a speech-language disorder. The boy's family lived on a reservation where there was a great deal of poverty, hopelessness, and despair. The boy reflected these feelings, believing that he had no future, but David relentlessly encouraged him year after year. He told the young man that he could be somebody; that he had someone who cared for him; that he knew the young man could be successful. Today, that young man is an engineering student at University of Nebraska, Lincoln. It really is true that even if we cannot change the world, we can make a difference to those in our immediate path. Who knows whose lives we could impact?

Consideration of the problems addressed in this book also can provide an opportunity for self-examination of feelings and attitudes about poverty. How do most middle-class people manage to live with the knowledge of the vast social inequities that exist in our country? How can we comfortably drop $50 for a Halloween costume for our child or spend money on a trip to Hawaii when so many American children are barely subsisting? Perhaps at some level, conscious or unconscious, we blame the poor for "doing this to themselves." If they just had better characters, if they would just work harder, if they had more get-up-and-go, they could lift themselves out of their present circumstances and lead more successful lives. After all, that's the American dream, right? Any boy or girl can become president. This is the land of opportunity, where we all can lift ourselves up by our bootstraps. All it takes is determination and perseverance. This is the country in which anybody, whatever his or her racial, ethnic, or socioeconomic origins, can become "somebody"—somebody with at least a comfortable, middle class life, if not outright wealth.

Most people of middle SES backgrounds do not want to admit that our nation has moved far, far away from those ideals of our forefathers. For increasing numbers of America's children, the American dream has become the American nightmare in which they are trapped in a vicious downward spiral that they cannot escape from by themselves. What will we do to change the lives of these children? Will we continue to blame the poor for their predicament and turn our backs on their plight? Or will we rise up, take action, and refuse to tolerate the perpetration of rank injustice in our society?

In describing citizens in the United States today, one author refers to an "empathy deficit." We would not tolerate schools that don't teach, schools that are understaffed and underfunded, he points out, if we thought that the children in these schools were like our children. None of us as middle SES professionals would want our children in these schools.

It's essential to keep in mind that each of us must continually work to address the needs of children of low SES families at all three levels described in Chapter 1: (1) the macroeconomic state and federal policy level, (2) the school district and site level, and (3) the individual level. Many of us, no doubt, operate predominantly at level 3, with an occasional foray into level 2. But for real change to occur in the lives of the children we serve, each of us must do even more-contribute to the foundational, critical levels 1 and 2. At first, it might be hard to imagine what each of us can do on an individual basis to improve state and federal policies. Our lives are crowded enough-who among us busy professionals has the time or energy to run for office or otherwise get heavily involved in politics?

For one thing, we can vote in favor of policies that increase resources to low SES families in the areas of tax breaks, health care, affordable housing, and employment. We can support policies that help defray the costs of basic life necessities so that these families can have more disposable income. Such policies include housing vouchers, food stamps, and extension of Medicaid coverage to all children from low SES homes and their caregivers. Statistics show that women earn less than men for comparable work; moreover, many of these children come from single, female-headed households. Accordingly, we can support policies that improve women's relative earnings; these policies include affirmative action and equal opportunity.

Sheer politics aside, each of us should think honestly about our choices in state and federal elections. Do we vote down universal preschool because we are afraid our comfortable, middle SES lifestyles will change for the worse with increased taxes? Do we vote for lawmakers and politicians who routinely oppress the poor and give tax advantages to the rich? Or do we lend our voices and ardent support to lawmakers and politicians who have the best interests of our children at heart?

If we ignore our own potential small contribution to level 1, then we are not doing all we can to benefit children from low SES families and help them to become productive members of society who can further support that society as tax-paying citizens. We can make all the personal sacrifices of time and money that we want to, but without change at level 1, we truly will be trying to use teaspoons to spoon out an ocean of need.

What schools cannot do is to offset the inequities in society that disproportionately place some children at much greater risk for negative outcomes. Resilience is not a cure for inequitable risk conditions. These conditions can be changed only through shifts in level 1. School reform alone is bound to be frustrating and ultimately unsuccessful. In order to succeed, school improvement must be combined with level 1 policies that narrow economic and social differences between children. As Neuman (2009) points out, we need to implement successful programs that: (1) begin early on in children's lives, (2) are comprehensive in nature, providing a multitude of services and networks, (3) employ highly trained professionals, and (4) are intensive enough to make a genuine difference.

At the school site–based level, level 2, we also need to examine our own deep-seated attitudes. When the principal wants to institute a new program to help disadvantaged children, do we shrink away because we will have to make the time and effort to learn something new? If the district wants our school sites to cut programs that benefit children from low SES families, do we stand up and fight? Or do we sit in passive resignation, figuring that you can't fight City Hall? It is very important to be involved in strengthening services at level 2.

If we are supporting low SES children through participation in levels 1 and 2, then we can know that at level 3, we have already contributed at levels 1 and 2. When we go to the teacher supply store to purchase small Christmas gifts and toys for our students from low SES homes, for example, we can comfort ourselves with the thought that although this is "just a level 3" contribution, we have made a contribution to the foundation of addressing the problem of poverty in our nation.

It's been suggested that contributions we make at level 3 constitute a "Band-Aid" approach (e.g., DiFazio, 2006). It's true that many of our interventions at this level benefit only the child who receives that intervention. But when I give a third grader a health food bar, for example, because she is hungry, I don't view my health bar as a Band-Aid. I view it as carrying away a very small stone that shows *this* child that someone at the school cares and wants her to succeed. Awareness that the child knows this simple fact can give us the strength to continue to work to level the playing field for all of America's children.

It is up to educators and other professionals to show caring and to teach the skills that allow students and families from low SES backgrounds to make choices about their lives.

> It is time for us to shift our thinking from resigned helplessness to activism, pressing for what our students need in classrooms and schools . . . we can keep our hearts and minds open to the potential of our students. We can expand our concern beyond our own life situation to the broader concerns of equity in employment, education, and material resources in our communities. The heart of being a teacher who makes a difference to students in poverty is compassion. . . . We must believe that all students can learn challenging material and gain complex skills. . . . If we start from there and persist in thinking in this way, we cannot help but become bearers of hope for all students. (Landsman, 2006, pp. 31–32)

It is my prayer that all of us who work with children will be bearers of hope for all students. Thank you for being on this journey with me.

References

Abudarham, S. (1980). The role of the speech therapist in the assessment of language-learning potential and proficiency of children with dual language systems or backgrounds. *Journal of Multilingual and Multicultural Development, 1,* 187–205.

Accelerated Reader Enterprises. (2006). *Accelerated Reader.* Retrieved November 11, 2006, from http://www.renlearn.com/ar/

Ackerman, B. P., & Brown, E. D. (2010). Physical and psychosocial turmoil in the home and cognitive development. In G.W. Evans & T. D. Wachs (Eds.), *Chaos and its influence on children's development: An ecological perspective* (pp. 35–48). Washington, DC: American Psychological Association.

Adams, J. L., & Ramey, C. T. (1980). Structural aspects of maternal speech to infants reared in poverty. *Child Development, 51,* 1280–1284.

Adams, M. J. (1990). *Beginning to read: Thinking and learning about print.* Cambridge, MA: MIT Press.

Addy, S., & Wight, V. R. (2012, May 20). *Basic facts about low-income children, 2010 (children under age 18).* Retrieved from http://www.nccp.org/publications/pub_1049.html

Adler, S. (1979). *Poverty children and their language: Implications for teaching and treating.* New York, NY: Grune & Stratton.

Adler, S., & Birdsong, S. (1983). Reliability and validity of standardized testing tools used with poor children. *Topics in Language Disorders, 3,* 76–87.

Aikens, N. L., & Barbarin, O. (2008). Socioeconomic differences in reading trajectories: The contribution of family, neighborhood, and school contexts. *Journal of Educational Psychology, 100,* 235–251.

Allen, N. (2010). Making a difference: The Western Australia Better Beginnings family literacy program. *Aplis, 23,* 33–37.

Alliance for Excellent Education. (2011). *The high cost of high school dropouts: What the nation pays for inadequate high schools.* Retrieved from http://www.all4ed.org/files/GraduationRates_FactSheet.pdf

American Community Survey. (2006). *A survey of American communities.* Retrieved from http://www.census.gov/acs/www

American Institute for Research. (2005). *Similar students, different results: Why do some schools do better? A large-scale survey of California elementary schools serving low-income students.* Mountain View, CA: EdSource.

American Psychological Association. (2012). *Facing the school dropout dilemma.* Retrieved from http://www.apa.org/pi/fammilies/resources/ school-dropout-prevention.aspx

American Speech-Language-Hearing Association. (2005). *Introduction to evidence-based practice: What it is (and what it isn't).* Retrieved from http:// www.asha.org/members/ebp/default

Anastasiow, N. J., & Hanes, M. L. (1976). *Language patterns of poverty children.* Springfield, IL: Charles C Thomas.

Anastasiow, N. J., Hanes, M. L., & Hanes, M. (1982). *Language and reading strategies for poverty children.* Baltimore, MD: University Park Press.

Anderson-Yockel, J., & Haynes, W. O. (1994). Joint book-reading strategies in working class African American and White mother-toddler dyads. *Journal of Speech and Hearing Research, 37,* 583–593.

Antoniadis, A., Gilbert, S. G., & Wagner, M. G. (2006). Neurotoxicants: Environmental contributors to disability in children. *ASHA Leader, 11*(13), 6–39.

Archer, A. L., Gleason, M. M., Vachon, V., & Isaacson, S. (2007). *Rewards reading program.* Retrieved from http://www.rewardsreading.com

Armstrong, J. (2011, August). Serving children with emotional-behavioral and language disorders: A collaborative approach. *ASHA Leader,* pp. 1–7.

Armstrong, T. (2011). *Multiple intelligences.* Retrieved from http://www. thomasarmstrong.com/multiple_intelligences.php

Aud, S., Hussar, W., Johnson, F., Kena, G., Roth, E., Manning, E., Wang, X., & Zhang, J. (2012). *The Condition of Education 2012* (NCES 2012-045). U.S. Department of Education, National Center for Education Statistics. Washington, DC. Retrieved from http://nces.ed.gov/pubsearch

Auman, M. (2003). *Step up to writing* (2nd ed.). Self-published book. To order: 800-547-6747.

Baggerly, J., & Jenkins, W. W. (2009). The effectiveness of child-centered play therapy on developmental and diagnostic factors in children who are homeless. *International Journal of Play Therapy, 18,* 45–55.

Baggerly, J., & Zalaquett, B. (2006). A descriptive study of single adults in homeless shelters: Increasing counselors' knowledge and social action. *Journal of Multicultural Counseling and Human Development, 34,* 155–167.

Bailey, D., & Harbin, G. (1980). Nondiscriminatory evaluation. *Exceptional Children, 46,* 590–595.

Baker, L., Mackler, K., Sonnenschein, S., & Serpell, R. (2001). Parents' interactions with their first-grade children during storybook reading and relations with subsequent home reading activity and reading achievement. *Journal of School Psychology, 39,* 415–438.

Bardige, B.S. (2009). *Talk to me, baby! How you can support young children's language development*. Baltimore, MD: Paul H. Brookes.

Barone, D. M. (2006). *Narrowing the literacy gap: What works in high-poverty schools*. New York, NY: Guilford Press.

Barrett, A. E., & Turner, R. J. (2005). Family structure and mental health: The mediating effects of socioeconomic status, family process, and social stress. *Journal of Health and Social Behavior, 46,* 159–169.

Barton, P. E. (2004). Why does the achievement gap persist? *Educational Leadership, 62,* 8–13.

Basham, L.B. (1994). *Active learning and the at-risk student: Cultivating positive attitudes toward science and learning*. (ERIC Document Reproduction Service No. ED 374 088).

Battle, D. E. (2012). Communication disorders in a multicultural and global society. In D. E. Battle (Ed.), *Communication disorders in multicultural and international populations* (4th ed., pp. 2–19). St. Louis, MO: Mosby.

Battle, D. E., & Anderson, N. (1998). Culturally diverse families and the development of language. In D. E. Battle (Ed.), *Communication disorders in multi- cultural populations* (2nd ed., pp. 213–246). Newton, MA: Butterworth-Heinemann.

Bavolek, S. J., & Bavolek, J. D. (2002). *Nurturing Parent program: Parents and their infants, toddlers, and preschoolers (birth to 5 years)*. Retrieved from http://www.nurturingparenting.com

Bayley, N. (1993). *Bayley Scales of Infant Development*. New York, NY: Psychological Corporation.

Beals, D. E. (1997). Sources of support for learning words in conversations: Evidence from mealtimes. *Journal of Child Language, 24,* 673–694.

Beck, I., McKeown, M., & Kucan, L. (2002). *Bringing words to life*. New York, NY: Guilford Press.

Beitchman, J., & Brownlie, E. (2011). Language development and its impact on children's psychosocial and emotional development. *Encyclopedia of Literacy Development*. Retrieved from http://literacyencyclopedia.ca/index.php?fa=items.show&topicId=3

Bureau of Labor Statistics. (2012). *Household data*. Retrieved from http://www.bls.gov/news.release/pdf/empsit.pdf

Bell, N. (1991). *Visualizing and verbalizing for language comprehension and thinking*. Paso Robles, CA: Academy of Reading Publications.

Bender, W. N. (2004). *Learning disabilities: Characteristics, identification, and teaching strategies*. Boston, MA: Allyn & Bacon.

Benner, A. D., & Graham, S. (2009). The transition to high school as a developmental process among multiethnic urban youth. *Child Development, 80,* 356–376.

Bennett, C. I. (1995). *Comprehensive multicultural education: Theory and practice* (3rd ed.). Boston, MA: Allyn & Bacon.

Bernstein, B. (1964). Elaborated and restricted codes: Their social origins and some consequences. *American Anthropologist, 66,* 55–69.

Biemiller, A. (1999). *Language and reading success.* Cambridge, MA: Brookline.

Biemiller, A. (2003). Vocabulary: Need if more children are to read well. *Reading Psychology, 34,* 323–335.

Blachman, B. A. (1991). Early intervention for children's reading problems: Clinical applications of the research in phonological awareness. *Topics in Language Disorders, 12,* 51–65.

Blachman, B. A. (2000). Phonological awareness. In M. L. Kamil, P. B. Mosenthal, P. D. Pearson, & R. Barr (Eds.), *Handbook of reading research* (Vol. 3). Mahwah, NJ: Lawrence Erlbaum Associates.

Blackwell, L. S., Trzesniewski, K. H., & Dweck, C. (2007). Implicit theories of intelligence predict achievement across an adolescent transition: A longitudinal study and intervention. *Child Development, 78,* 246–263.

Blair, C., Granger, D. A., Willoughby, M., Mills-Koonce, R., Cox, M., Greenberg, M. T., Kivilgan, K. T., & Fortunato, C. K. (2011). Salivary cortisol mediates effects of poverty and parenting on executive functions in early childhood. *Child Development, 82,* 1970–1984.

Blevins, D. (2012, March). *Enhancing preschool speech-language services: Implementing RtI using SLP-SLPA teams.* Paper presented at the annual convention of the California Speech and Hearing Association, San Jose, CA.

Bloom, L., & Lahey, M. (1978). *Language development and disorders.* New York, NY: Macmillan.

Bohannon, J. N., & Bonvillian, J. D. (2009). Theoretical approaches to language acquisition. In J. B. Gleason & N. J. Ratner (Eds.), *The development of language* (7th ed., pp. 227–284). Boston, MA: Pearson Education.

Borrell, L. N., Beck, J. D., & Heiss, G. (2006). Socioeconomic disadvantage and periodontal disease: The dental atherosclerosis risk in communities study. *American Journal of Public Health, 96*(2), 332–339.

Bradley, R. H. (2010). From home to day care: Chaos in the family/child-care mesosystem. In G. W. Evans & T. D. Wachs (Eds.), *Chaos and its influence on children's development: An ecological perspective* (pp. 135–153). Washington, DC: American Psychological Association.

Bradley, R. H., Corwyn, R. F., Pipes-McAdoo, H., & Garcia-Coll, C. (2001). The home environments of children in the United States Part I: Variations by age, ethnicity, and poverty status. *Child Development, 72,* 1844–1867.

Breaden, N.C. (2008) *Teacher-quality gap examined world wide.* Retrieved from http://www.edweek.org

Brice, A. E. (2002). *The Hispanic child: Speech, language, culture, and education.* Boston, MA: Allyn & Bacon.

Brinton, B., & Fujiki, M. (2011). *Facilitating social communication in children with autism spectrum disorders and language impairment: Interventions to enhance social and emotional competence.* Workshop presented at the University of the Pacific, Stockton, CA.

Britto, P. R., Brooks-Gunn, J., & Griffin, T. M. (2006). Maternal reading and teaching patterns: Associations with school readiness in low-income African American families. *Reading Research Quarterly, 41,* 68–89.

Bronfenbrenner, U., McClelland, P., Wethington, E., Moen, P., & Ceci, S. (1996). *The state of Americans: This generation and the next.* New York, NY: Free Press.

Bronson, P., & Merryman, A. (2009). *NurtureShock: New thinking about children.* New York, NY: Hachette Book Group.

Brooks, J. E. (2006). Strengthening resilience in children and youths: Maximizing opportunities through the schools. *Children and Schools, 28*(2), 69–76.

Brooks-Gunn, J., Johnson, A. D., & Leventhal, T. (2010). Disorder, turbulence, and resources in children's homes and neighborhoods. In G. W. Evans & T. D. Wachs (Eds.), *Chaos and its influence on children's development: An ecological perspective* (pp. 155–170). Washington, DC: American Psychological Association.

Brown, J. L., & Pollitt, E. (1996). Malnutrition, poverty, and intellectual development. *Scientific American, 2*(96), 38–44.

Buckner, C. J. (2008). Understanding the impact of homelessness on children: Challenges and future research directions. *American Behavioral Scientist, 51,* 721–736.

Burke, L. M. (2012). *Freedom to succeed: How using school choice can help narrow the achievement gap.* Retrieved from http://www.spotlightonpoverty.org/ExculsiveCommentary.aspx

Bureau of U.S. Labor Statistics. (2012). *Household data.* Retrieved from http://www.bls.gov/news.release/pdf/empsit.pdf

Cabell, S. Q., Justice, L. M., Plasta, S. B., Curenton, S. M., Wiggins, A., Turnbull, K. P., & Petscher, Y. (2011). The impact of teacher responsitivity education on preschoolers' language and literacy skills. *American Journal of Speech-Language Pathology, 20,* 315–330.

Cain, J. (2004). Effective hours after school. *New Horizons for Learning.* Retrieved August from http://www.newhorizons.org

Camarota, S. A. (2011). *Immigrant gains and native losses in the U.S. job market, 2000 to 2010.* Center for Immigration Studies. Retrieved from http://cis.org/print/2649

Campbell, L. R. (1993). Maintaining the integrity of home linguistic varieties: Black English vernacular. *American Journal of Speech-Language Pathology, 2,* 85–86.

Campbell, T., Dollaghan, C., Needleman, H., & Janosky, J. (1997). Reducing bias in language assessment: Processing-dependent measures. *Journal of Speech, Language, and Hearing Research, 40,* 519–525.

Carlson, K. T. (2006). Poverty and youth violence exposure: Experiences in rural communities. *Children and Schools, 29*(2), 87–96.

The Carolina Abecedarian Project. (2006). *Home executive summary.* Retrieved from http://www.fpg.unc.edu/~abc/

Carta, J. J., & Atwater, J. B. (2003, September). *The impact of an early intervention program on parent-child interactions and children's developmental trajectories.* In J. Carta (Chair), Panel on parent-child interactions. Panel presented at the meeting of the International Society of Early Intervention, Rome, Italy.

Castellani, J., & Jeffs, T. (2001). Emerging reading and writing strategies using technology. *Teaching Exceptional Children, 33,* 60–67.

Castillo, R. (2012). *Migrant education Region IV.* Retrieved from http://migrant.fcoe.org/

Center for Immigration Studies. (2001). *Immigration trends.* Retrieved from http://www.cis.org/articles/2001/back101.html

Centre for Social Justice. (2011, February). *Mental health: Poverty, ethnicity, and family breakdown.* Interim Policy Briefing. Artillery Row, London, UK: The Centre for Social Justice.

Chall, J. S., & Jacobs, V. A. (2003). Research round-up: Poor children's fourth grade slump. *American Educator,* Spring 2003. Retrieved from http://www.aft.org/pubs-reports/american_educator/spring2003/chall.html

Chall, J. S., Jacobs, V. A., & Baldwin, L. E. (1990). *The reading crisis: Why poor children fall behind.* Cambridge, MA: Harvard University Press.

Chan, S., & Chen, D. (2011). Families with Asian roots. In E. W. Lynch & M. J. Hanson (Eds.), *Developing cross-cultural competence: A guide for working with young children and their families* (4th ed., pp. 234–318). Baltimore, MD: Paul H. Brookes.

Chen, E., Martin, A. D., & Matthews, K. A. (2006). Understanding health disparities: The role of race and socioeconomic status in children's health. *American Journal of Public Health, 96*(4), 702–708.

Child Trends DataBank. (2003). *School communication in parents' native language.* Retrieved from http://www.childtrendsdata bank.org

Chiu, M. M., & Khoo, L. (2005). Effects of resources, inequality, and privilege bias on achievement: Country, school, and student level analyses. *American Educational Research Journal, 42*(4), 575–603.

Christakis, D. A., Gilkerson, J., Richards, J. A., Zimmerman, F. J., Garrison, M. M., Xu, D., . . . Yapanel, U. (2009). Audible television and decreased adult words, infant vocalizations, and conversational turns: A population-based study. *Archives of Pediatrics and Adolescent Medicine, 163,* 554–558.

Christakis, D. A., Zimmerman, F. J., DiGuiseppe, D. L., & McCarty, C. A. (2004). Early television exposure and subsequent attentional problems in children. *Pediatrics, 113,* 708–713.

Clark, P. (2012). *Recent research on all-day kindergarten.* Retrieved from http://www.education.com/reference/article/Ref_Recent_Research_All/

Cognitive Concepts. (1997–2003). *Earobics: Sound foundations for reading and spelling.* Evanston, IL: Cognitive Concepts.

Coleman, L. J., & Southern, W. T. (2006). Bringing the potential of under-served children to the threshold of talent development. *Gifted Child Today, 29,* 35–39.

Coley, R. L., Lewin-Bizan, S., & Carrano, J. (2011). Does early paternal parenting promote low income children's long-term cognitive skills? *Journal of Family Issues, 32,* 1522–1542.

Commission on Excellence in Special Education. (2001). *Revitalizing special education for children and their families.* Retrieved from http://www.ed.gov/inits/commissionsboards/whspecialeducation

Conger, R. D., Conger, K. J., & Elder, G. (1997). Family economic hardship and adolescent academic performance: Mediating and moderating processes. In G. Duncan & J. Brooks-Gunn (Eds.), *Consequences of growing up poor* (pp. 288–310). New York, NY: Russell Sage Foundation.

Corcoran, M. (2001). Mobility, persistence, and the consequences of poverty for children: Child and adult outcomes. In S. H. Danziger & R. H. Haveman (Eds.), *Understanding poverty* (pp. 127–161). New York, NY: Russell Sage Foundation.

Coulton, C. J., Crampton, D. S., Irwin, M., Spilsbury, J. C., & Korbin, J. E. (2007). How neighborhoods influence child maltreatment: A review of the literature and alternative pathways. *Child Abuse and Neglect, 31,* 1117–1142.

Covington, M. V., & Teel, K. M. (1996). *Overcoming student failure: Changing motives and incentives for learning.* Washington, DC: American Psychological Association.

Craig, H. K., & Washington, J. A. (2002). Oral language expectations for African American preschoolers and kindergartners. *American Journal of Speech-Language Pathology, 11,* 59–70.

Craig, H. K., & Washington, J. A. (2004a). Language variation and literacy learning. In C. A. Stone, E. R. Silliman, B. J. Ehren, & K. Apel (Eds.), *Handbook of language and literacy: Development and disorders* (pp. 228–247). New York, NY: Guilford Press.

Craig, H. K., & Washington, J. A. (2004b). Grade-related changes in the production of African American English. *Journal of Speech, Language, and Hearing Research, 47,* 450–463.

Crowley, C. J. (2004). The ethics of assessment with culturally and linguistically diverse populations. *ASHA Leader, 9,* 6–7.

Cruzado-Guerrero, J. R., & Carta, J. J. (2006). Assessing vocabulary and the bilingual environment in young Latino children. *Perspectives on Communication Disorders and Sciences in Culturally and Linguistically Diverse Populations, 13,* 8–13.

Curenton, S. M., & Justice, L. M. (2004). African American and Caucasian preschoolers' use of decontextualized language: Literate language features in oral narratives. *Language, Speech, and Hearing Services in Schools, 35,* 240–253.

Cutuli, J. J., Wiik, K. L., Herbers, J. E., Gunnar, M. R., & Masten, A. S. (2010). Cortisol function among early school-aged homeless children. *Psychoendocrinology*, *35*, 833–845.

Davis, P. N., & Banks, T. (2012). Intervention for multicultural and international clients with communication disorders. In D. E. Battle (Ed.), *Communication disorders in multicultural and international populations* (4th ed., pp. 279–295). St. Louis, MO: Mosby.

Darling-Hammond, L., & Ifill-Lynch, O. (2006). If they'd only do their work! *Educational Leadership*, *63*, 8–13.

Dennison, P. E., & Dennison, G. E. (1986). *Brain gym*. Ventura, CA: Edu-Kinesthetics.

Devall, E. L. (2004). Positive parenting for high-risk families. *Journal of Family and Consumer Sciences*, *96*, 22–28.

Diener, M. L., Hobson-Rohrer, W., & Byington, C. L. (2012). Kindergarten readiness and performance of Latino children participating in Reach out and Read. *Journal of Community Medicine and Health Education*, *2*, 1–7.

DiFazio, W. (2006). *Ordinary poverty: A little food and cold storage*. Philadelphia, PA: Temple University Press.

DiLorenzo, K. E., Rody, C. A., Bucholz, J. L., & Brady, M. P. (2011). Teaching letter-sound connections with picture mnemonics: Itchy's Alphabet and early decoding. *Preventing School Failure*, *55*, 28–34.

DiRivera, C., Girolametto, L., Greenberg, J., & Weitzman, E. (2005). Children's responses to educators' questions in day care play groups. *American Journal of Speech-Language Pathology*, *14*, 14–26.

Dilworth-Bart, J. E., & Moore, C. F. (2006). Mercy mercy me: Social injustice and the prevention of environmental pollutant exposures among ethnic minority and poor children. *Child Development*, *77*(2), 247–265.

Dodd, B., & Carr, A. (2003). Young children's letter-sound knowledge. *Language, Speech, and Hearing Services in Schools*, *34*, 128–137.

Dodge, E., Rice, C., & Grimm, D. (2010). *The Kimochi's feel guide: Teacher's edition*. San Rafael, CA: Plushy Feely Corp.

Dollaghan, C. A., & Campbell, T. F. (1998). Nonword repetition and child language impairment. *Journal of Speech, Language, and Hearing Research*, *41*, 1136–1146.

Dolloghan, C. A., Campbell, T. F., Paradise, J. L., Feldman, H. M., Janosky, J. E., Pitcairn, D. N., & Kurs-Lasky, M. (1999). Maternal education and measures of early speech and language. *Journal of Speech, Language, and Hearing Research*, *42*, 1432–1443.

Douglas-Hall, A., & Koball, H. (2004). *Children of low-income, recent immigrants: Fact sheet* (based on the U.S. Current Population Survey [CPS], 2004 Annual Social and Economic Supplement). National Center for Children in Poverty, Columbia University Mailman School of Public Health. Retrieved from http://www.nccp.org/pub_cli04.html

Duncan, G., & Brooks-Gunn, J. (Eds.) (1997). *Consequences of growing up poor.* New York, NY: Russell Sage Foundation.

Duncan, L., & Seymour, P. (2000). Socio-economic differences in foundation-level literacy. *British Journal of Psychology, 91,* 145–166.

Dunn, J. R., Schaefer-McDaniel, N. J., & Ramsay, J. T. (2010). Neighborhood chaos and children's development: Questions and contradictions. In G. W. Evans & T. D. Wachs (Eds.), *Chaos and its influence on children's development: An ecological perspective* (pp. 173–189). Washington, DC: American Psychological Association.

Dweck, C. (2007). The perils and promise of praise. *Educational Leadership, 65,* 34–39.

Eberle, L. (2003). *"Executive functioning"—new research about familiar behavior.* Retrieved from http://www.strugglingteens.com/news/executive functionimg.html

Education Week. (2012). *Achievement gap.* Retrieved from http://www.ed week.org/ew/issues/achievement-gap/

Edwards, P. A. (1989). Supporting lower SES mothers' attempts to provide scaffolding for book reading. In J. Allen & J. Mason (Eds.), *Risk makers, risk takers, risk breakers: Reducing the risks for young literacy learners* (pp. 222–250). Portsmouth, NH: Heinemann.

Ehren, B. J., Lenz, B. K., & Deshler, D. D. (2004). In C. A. Stone, E. R. Silliman, B. J. Ehren, & K. Apel (Eds.), *Handbook of language and literacy: Development and disorders* (pp. 681–670). New York, NY: Guilford Press.

Ehrenreich, B. (2006). Raising wages for low-wage workers will help America's poor. In G. Griffin (Ed.), *How can the poor be helped?* (pp. 39–48). Farmington Hills, MI: Greenhaven Press.

Engel, P., Santos, F. H., & Gathercole, S. E. (2008). Are working memory measures free of socioeconomic influence? *Journal of Speech, Language, and Hearing Research, 51,* 1580–1587.

Engle, J., & Theokas, C. (2010). *Top gap closers: Some public four-year collects and universities have made good progress in closing graduation-rate gaps.* The Education Trust. Retrieved from http://www.csupomona .edu/~research/rsp/documents/top_gap_closers_000.pdf

Enos, L., Kline, L., Guillen-Green, S., Weger, L., Roseberry-McKibbin, C., & O'Hanlon, L. (2005, April). *The influence of poverty and maternal education on children's language.* Paper presented at the annual meeting of the California Speech-Language-Hearing Association, Santa Clara, CA.

ERIC Clearinghouse on Urban Education. (2006). *Facilitating transition to the mainstream: Sheltered English vocabulary development.* Retrieved from http://www.ncela.gwu.edu

Evans, G. W., Eckenrode, J., & Marcynyszyn, L. A. (2010). Chaos and the macrosetting: The role of povety and socioeconomic status. In G. W. Evans & T. D. Wachs (Eds.), *Chaos and its influence on children's development:*

An ecological perspective (pp. 225–238). Washington, DC: American Psychological Association.

Evans, G. W., & Hygge, S. (2007). Noise and performance in children and adults. In L. Luxon & D. Prasher (Eds.), *Noise and its effects* (pp. 549–566). London, UK: Wiley.

Evans, G. W., & Schamber, M. A. (2009). *Childhood poverty, chronic stress, and adult working memory.* Proceedings of the National Academy of Sciences. Retrieved from http://www.pnas.org/contnet/106/16/6545.long

Evans, G. W., & Wachs, T. (2010). *Chaos and its influence on children's development: An ecological perspective.* Washington, DC: American Psychological Association.

Evard, B., & Sabers, D. (1979). Speech and language testing with distinct ethnic-racial groups: A survey of procedures for improving validity. *Journal of Speech and Hearing Disorders, 44,* 271–281.

Fagundes, D. D., Haynes, W. O., Haak, N. J., & Moran, M. J. (1998). Task variability effects on the language test performance of southern lower socioeconomic class African American and Caucasian five-year-olds. *Language, Speech, and Hearing Services in Schools, 29,* 148–157.

Farah, M. J., Noble, K. G., & Hurt, H. (2005). *Poverty, privilege, and brain development: Empirical findings and ethical implications.* Retrieved from http://www.psych.upenn.edu/~mfarah

Fazio, B. B., Naremore, R. C., & Connell, P. (1996). Tracking children from poverty at risk for specific language impairment: A 3-year longitudinal study. *Journal of Speech and Hearing Research, 39,* 611–624.

Federal Interagency Forum on Child and Family Statistics. (2003). *America's children: Key national indicators of well-being.* 2003 (Federal Interagency Forum on Child and Family Statistics). Washington, DC: U.S. Government Printing Office.

Fey, M. E., Long, S. H., & Finestack, L. H. (2003). Ten principles of grammar facilitation for children with specific language impairment. *American Journal of Speech-Language Pathology, 12,* 3–5.

Fey, M. E., Windsor, J., & Warren, S. F. (1995). *Language intervention: Preschool through elementary years* (Communication and Language Intervention Series, Vol. 5). Baltimore, MD: Paul H. Brookes.

Fiese, B. H., & Winter, M. A. (2010). The dynamics of family chaos and its relation to children's socioemotional well-being. In G. W. Evans & T. D. Wachs (Eds.), *Chaos and its influence on children's development: An ecological perspective* (pp. 49–66). Washington, DC: American Psychological Association.

Fish, M., & Pinkerman, B. (2003). Language skills in low-SES rural Appalachian children: Normative development and individual differences, infancy to preschool. *Journal of Applied Developmental Psychology, 23,* 539–585.

Fisher, D., Frey, N., & Williams, D. (2002). Seven literacy strategies that work. *Educational Leadership, 60,* 70–73.

Fiske, A. P. (2002). Using individualism and collectivism to compare cultures —A critique of the validity and measurements of the constructs: Comment on Oyserman et al. (2002). *Psychological Bulletin, 128,* 78–88.

Flores, R. L. (2007). Effect of poverty on urban preschool children's understanding of conventional time concepts. *Early Child Development and Care, 177,* 121–132.

Fogle, P. T. (2013). *Essentials of communication sciences and disorders.* Clifton Park, NY: Cengage/Delmar.

Forum on Child and Family Statistics. (2011). *America's children: Key national indicators of well-being, 2011.* Retrieved from htto://www.child stats.gov/americaschildren/famsoc3.asp

Foster, E. M. (2002). How economists think about family resources and child development. *Child Development, 73,* 1904–1914.

Fowler, W. (1995). *Talking from infancy: How to nurture and cultivate early language development.* Cambridge, MA: Center for Early Learning and Child Care.

Fowler, W., Ogston, K., Roberts-Fiati, G., & Swenson, A. (1995). Patterns of giftedness and high competence in high school students educationally enriched during infancy: Variation across educational and racial/ethnic backgrounds. *Gifted and Talented International, 10,* 31–36.

Francis, D. J., Fletcher, J. M., Shaywitz, B. A., Shaywitz, S. E., & Rourke, B. P. (1996). Defining learning and language and disabilities: Conceptual and psychometric issues with the use of the IQ test. *Language, Speech, and Hearing Services in Schools, 27,* 132–143.

Fraser, J. (1997). *Children, youth, and family background: When children grow up poor.* University of Pittsburgh Office of Child Development, Fall 1997 issue, Report #1.

Friedlander, D., & Martinson, K. (1996). Effects of mandatory basic education for adult AFDC recipients. *Educational Evaluation and Policy Analysis, 18,* 327–337.

Friere, P. (1970). *The pedagogy of the oppressed.* Harmondsworth, UK: Penguin.

Friere, P. (1995). *Pedagogy of hope: Reliving pedagogy of the oppressed.* New York, NY: Continuum.

Fry, E.B. (2004). *The vocabulary teacher's book of lists.* San Francisco, CA: Jossey-Bass.

Fung, F., & Roseberry-McKibbin, C. (1999). Service delivery considerations in working with clients from Cantonese-speaking backgrounds. *American Journal of Speech-Language Pathology, 8,* 309–318.

Furey, J. (2010). Production and maternal report of 16- and 18-month-olds' vocabulary in low-and middle-income families. *American Journal of Speech-Language Pathology, 20,* 38–46.

G.A.T.E. Resources. (2012). *Ways to support gifted minority students.* Retrieved from http://gateresources.blogspot.com

Gandara, P. (2004). Building bridges to college. *Educational Leadership, 62,* 56–60.

Gardner, H. (1993). *Multiple intelligences: The theory and practice.* New York, NY: Harper & Row.

Geiss, S. A. (2011). *Language and literacy issues in children who are homeless or living in poverty.* Paper presented at the annual convention of the California Speech and Hearing Association, Los Angeles, CA.

Generations United. (2002). *Fact Sheet—Grandparents and other relatives raising children: Challenges of caring for the second family.* Washington, DC: Author.

Generations United. (2012). *Grandfamilies statistics.* Retrieved from http://www2.gu.org/OURWORK/Grandfamilies/GrandfamiliesStatistics.aspx

Genesee, F., Paradis, J., & Crago, M. B. (2004). *Dual language development and disorders: A handbook on bilingualism and second language learners.* Baltimore, MD: Paul H. Brookes.

Genesee, F., & Riches, C. (2006). Literacy development: Instructional issues. In F. Genesee, K. Lindholm-Leary, W. Saunders, & D. Christian (Eds.), *Educating English language learners: A synthesis of research evidence.* Washington, DC: Center for Applied Linguistics.

Geoffroy, M., Cote, S. M., Borge, A. I. H., Larouche, F., Seguin, J. R., & Rutter, M. (2007). Association between nonmaternal care in the first year of life and children's receptive language skills prior to school entry: The moderating role of socioeconomic status. *Journal of Child Psychology and Psychiatry, 48,* 490–497.

German, D. J., Schwanke, J. H., & Ravid, R. (2012). Word finding difficulties: Differentiated vocabulary instruction in the speech and language room. *Communication Disorders Quarterly, 33,* 146–156.

Gerwitz, A., Hart-Shegos, E., & Medganie, A. (2008). Psychosocial status of homeless children and youth in family supportive housing. *American Behavioral Scientist, 51,* 810–823.

Gibbons, P. (2002). *Scaffolding language, scaffolding learning: Teaching second language learners in the mainstream classroom.* Portsmouth, NH: Heinemann.

Gillam, R. (2011, March). *Putting the practice into evidence-based practice.* Paper presented at the annual convention of the California Speech and Hearing Association, Los Angeles, CA.

Gillam, R. B., & van Kleeck, A. (1996). Phonological awareness training and short-term working memory: Clinical implications. *Topics in Language Disorders, 17,* 72–81.

Gillon, G. T. (2004). *Phonological awareness: From research to practice.* New York, NY: Guilford.

Gimpel, G. A., & Holland, M. L. (2003). *Emotional and behavioral problems of young children.* New York, NY: Guilford Press.

Ginsberg, M. B. (2004). *Motivation matters: A workbook for school change.* San Francisco, CA: Jossey-Bass.

Girolametto, L., Weitzman, E., & Greenberg, J. (2004). The effects of verbal support strategies on small-group peer interactions. *Language, Speech, and Hearing Services in Schools, 35,* 254–268.

Girolametto, L., Weitzman, E., & Greenberg, J. (2012). Facilitating emergent literacy: Efficacy of a model that partners speech-language pathologists and educators. *American Journal of Speech-Language Pathology, 21,* 47–63.

Glasgow, K. L., Dornbusch, S. M., Troyer, L., Steinberg, L., & Ritter, P. I. (1997). Parenting styles, adolescents' attributions, and educational outcomes in nine heterogeneous high schools. *Child Development, 68,* 507–523.

Goldstein, B. A. (2000). *Cultural and linguistic diversity resource guide for speech-language pathologists.* San Diego, CA: Singular/Thomson Learning.

Goldsworthy, C. L. (2003). *Developmental reading disabilities: A language based treatment approach* (2nd ed.). Clifton Park, NY: Thomson-Delmar Learning.

Goldsworthy, C. L., & Pieretti, R.A. (2012). *Sourcebook of phonological awareness activities, Volume 3: Children's core literature grades 3 through 5* (2nd ed.). Clifton Park, NY: Delmar.

Goode, T. D., Jones, W., & Jackson, V. (2011). Families with African American roots. In E. W. Lynch & M. J. Hanson (Eds.), *Developing cross-cultural competence: A guide for working with children and their families* (4th ed., pp. 140–184). Baltimore, MD: Paul H. Brookes.

Gopaul-McNichol, S., & Armour-Thomas, E. (2002). *Assessment and culture: Psychological tests with minority populations.* San Diego, CA: Academic Press.

Gravel, J. S., & Wallace, I. F. (2000). Effects of otitis media with effusion on hearing in the first 3 years of life. *Journal of Speech, Language, and Hearing Research, 42,* 631–644.

Graves, M. F. (2006). *The vocabulary book: Learning and instruction.* New York, NY: Teacher's College Press; Newark, DE: International Reading Association; and Urbana, IL: National Council of Teachers of English.

Grech, H., & McLeod, S. (2012). Multilingual speech and language development and disorders. In D. E. Battle (Ed.), *Communication disorders in multicultural and international populations* (4th ed., pp. 120–147). St. Louis, MO: Elsevier/Mosby.

Greenwood, C. R., Theiman-Bourque, K., Walker, D., Buzhardt, J., & Gilkerson, J. (2011). Assessing children's home language environments using automatic speech technology. *Communication Disorders Quarterly, 32,* 83–92.

Grzywacz, J. G., Almeida, D. M., Neupert, S. D., & Ettner, S. L. (2004). Socioeconomic status and health: A micro-level analysis of exposure and vulnerability to daily stressors. *Journal of Health and Social Behavior, 45,* 1–16.

Guiterrez-Clellen, V. F. (1999). Language choices in intervention with bilingual children. *American Journal of Speech-Language Pathology, 8*, 291–302.

Guiterrez-Clellen, V. F., & Pena, E. (2001). Dynamic assessment of diverse children: A tutorial. *Language, Speech, and Hearing Services in Schools, 32*, 212–224.

Gustafson, J. P. (2002). Missing the mark for low-SES students. *Kappa Delta Pi Record, 38*, 60–63.

Haberman, M. (1999). *Star principals serving children in poverty.* Indianapolis, IN: Kappa Delta Pi, International Honor Society in Education.

Haberman, M. (2005). *Star teachers: The ideology and best practice of effective teachers of diverse children and youth in poverty.* Houston, TX: The Haberman Educational Foundation.

Hadley, P. A., Simmerman, A., Long, M., & Luna, M. (2000). Facilitating language development for inner city children: Experimental evaluation of a collaborative, classroom-based intervention. *Language, Speech, and Hearing Services in Schools, 31*, 280–295.

Hale, J. E.(2004). How schools shortchange African American children. *Educational Leadership, 62*, 34–38.

Hallahan, D. P., Lloyd, J. W., Kauffman, J. M., Weiss, M. P., & Martinez, E. A. (2005). *Learning disabilities: Foundations, characteristics, and effective teaching* (3rd ed.). Boston, MA: Allyn & Bacon.

Hamer, C. (2012, March). NCT research overview: Parent-child communication is important from birth. *Perspective—NCT's Journal on Preparing Parents for Birth and Early Childhood*, pp. 15–20.

Hamilton, B. E., Martin, J. A., & Ventura, S. J. (2007). *Births: Preliminary data for 2006.* Retrieved from http://www.cdc.gov/nichs/data/nvsr/nvsr56/nvsr56_07.pdf

Hammer, C. S. (2012). From the editor: More than just talk. *American Journal of Speech-Language Pathology, 21*, 1–2.

Hammer, C. S., Farkas, G., & Maczuga, S. (2010). The language and literacy development of Head Start children: A study using the family and child experiences database. *Language, Speech, and Hearing Services in Schools, 41*, 70–83.

Hammer, C. S., & Rodriguez, B. (2012). Bilingual language acquisition and the child socialization process. In B. A. Goldstein (Ed.), *Bilingual language development and disorders in Spanish-English speakers* (2nd ed., pp. 31–46). Baltimore, MD: Paul H. Brookes.

Hammer, C. S., & Weiss, A. (1999). Guiding language development: How African American mothers and their infants structure play interactions. *Journal of Speech, Language, and Hearing Research, 42*, 1219–1233.

Hammer, C. S., & Weiss, A. (2000). African American mothers' views of their infants; language development and language-learning environment. *American Journal of Speech-Language Pathology, 9*, 126–140.

Hardman, M. L., Drew, C. J., & Egan, M. W. (2011). *Human exceptionality: School, community, and family* (10th ed.). Belmont, CA: Wadsworth.

Hart, B., & Risley, T. R. (1995). *Meaningful differences in the everyday experience of young American children.* Baltimore, MD: Paul H. Brookes.

Hart, B., & Risley, T. R. (2003). The early catastrophe: The 30 million word gap. *American Educator, 27,* 4–9.

Hartman, C. (2006). Students on the move. *Educational Leadership, 63,* 20–25.

Haycock, K. (2001). Closing the achievement gap. *Educational Leadership, 58,* 6–11.

Haynes, W. O., & Pindzola, R. H. (2012). *Diagnosis and evaluation in speech pathology* (8th ed.). Boston, MA: Allyn & Bacon.

Hearne, J. D. (2000). *Teaching second language learners with learning disabilities: Strategies for effective practice.* Oceanside, CA: Academic Communication Associates.

Heath, S. B. (1983). *Ways with words.* Cambridge, UK: Cambridge University Press.

Heath, S. B. (1986). What no bedtime story means: Narrative skills at home and at school. In B. B. Schieffelin & E. Ochs (Eds.), *Language socialization across cultures* (pp. 97–124). New York, NY: Cambridge University Press.

Hecht, S., Burgess, S., Torgeson, J., Wagner, R., & Rashotte, C. (2000). Explaining social class differences in growth of reading skills from beginning kindergarten through fourth-grade: The role of phonological awareness, rate of access, and print knowledge. *Reading and Writing: An Interdisciplinary Journal, 12,* 99–127.

Heckelman, R. G. (1978). *Using the neurological impress reading technique: Solutions to reading problems.* Novato, CA: Academic Therapy.

Hegde, M. N., & Maul, C. A. (2006). *Language disorders in children: An evidence-based approach to assessment and treatment.* Boston, MA: Allyn & Bacon.

Henderson, T. L. (2004). Grandparents rearing grandchildren on TANF: A study in Virginia. *Journal of Family and Consumer Sciences, 96,* 10–12.

Hepp, N. (2011). Protecting children from toxicants. *ASHA Leader,* Nov. 22, 2011.

Herman, D. B., Susser, E. S., Struening, E. L., & Link, B. L. (1997). Adverse childhood experiences: Are they risk factors for adult homelessness? *American Journal of Public Health, 87,* 249–255.

Hernandez, D. J. (2011). *How third-grade reading skills and poverty influence high school graduation.* Retrieved from http://fcd-us.org/resources/double-jeopardy-how-third-grade-reading-skills-and-poverty-influence-high-school-graduatio

Hernandez, R. (2011). Literacy starts in the family. *California Educator, 15,* 10.

Hildyard, K. L., & Wolfe, D. A. (2002). Child neglect: Developmental issues and concerns. *Child Abuse and Neglect, 26,* 679–695.

Hirsch, E. D. (2003). Reading comprehension requires knowledge of words and the world. *American Educator, 27,* 1328–1348.

Hoff, E. (2003). The specificity of environmental influence: Socioeconomic status affects early vocabulary development via maternal speech. *Child Development, 74,* 1368–1378.

Holcomb-McCoy, C. (2011, April). A smoother transition for Black teens. *Educational Leadership,* pp. 59–63.

Holloway, J. H. (2003). Addressing the needs of homeless students. *Educational Leadership, 60,* 89–90.

Holt, J. K., & Smith, M. C. (2005). Literacy practices among different ethnic groups: The role of socioeconomic and cultural factors. *Reading Research and Instruction, 44,* 1–21.

Homes for the Homeless: The Institute for Children and Poverty. (2005). *Jump-start child development centers and early childhood development programs.* Retrieved from http://www.homesforthe homeless.com

Hoover, J. R., & Storkel, H. L. (2005). Understanding word learning by preschool children: Insights from multiple tasks, stimulus characteristics, and error analysis. *Perspectives on Language Learning and Education, 12,* 8–12.

Horton-Ikard, R., & Weismer, S. E. (2007). A preliminary examination of vocabulary and word learning in African American toddlers from middle and low socioeconomic status homes. *American Journal of Speech-Language Pathology, 16,* 381–392.

Hosp, J. L., & Reschly, D. J. (2004). Disproportionate representation of minority students in special education: Academic, demographic, and economic predictors. *Exceptional Children, 70,* 185–199.

Howard-Hobson, J. (2002, June). Living on the edge: Why too many Sacramento children live in poverty and the toll it takes on them. *Parents Monthly,* pp. 14–17.

Hubner, J. (2006, Spring). Discarded lives: Children sentenced to life without parole. *Amnesty International Magazine.* Retrieved from http://www.amnestyusa.org

Huntington, N., Buckner, J. C., & Bassuk, E. L. (2008). Adaptation in homeless children: An empirical examination using cluster analysis. *American Behavioral Scientist, 51,* 737–755.

Hwa-Froelich, D., & Matsuo, H. (2005). Vietnamese children and language-based processing tasks. *Language, Speech, and Hearing Services in Schools, 36,* 230–243.

Hymowitz, K. S. (2005). What's holding black kids back? *City Spring Journal.* Retrieved from http://www.city-journal.org/html

Hyun, J. K., & Fowler, S. A. (1995). Respect, cultural sensitivity, and communication: Promoting participation by Asian families in the individualized family service plan. *Teaching Exceptional Children, 28*, 25–28.

Iglesias, A., & Rojas, R. (2012). Bilingual language development of English Language Learners: Modeling the growth of two languages. In B. A. Goldstein (Ed.), *Bilingual language development and disorders in Spanish-English speakers* (2nd ed., pp. 3–30). Baltimore, MD: Paul H. Brookes.

Individuals with Disabilities Education Improvement Act of 2004 (IDEA). (2004). Public Law 108-446, 108th Congress. Retrieved from http://www.copyright.gov/legislation/al108-446.html

Infoture, Inc. (2008). *Patterns of talk in the language environment of American children, 2–26 months.* Paper presented at the Child Language Development Symposium, Department of Language and Hearing Sciences, University of Colorado, Boulder.

Ingram, D., & Seashore, K. (2003). *Arts for academic achievement: Summative evaluation report.* Unpublished report. Center for Applied Research and Education Improvement, College of Education and Human Development, University of Minnesota.

Invernizzi, M., & Robey, R. R. (2001). *Phonological Awareness Literacy Screening: Technical manual and report.* Charlottesville, VA: University of Virginia.

Ispa, J. M., Thornburg, K. R., & Fine, M. A. (2006). *Keepin' on: The everyday struggles of young families in poverty.* Baltimore, MD: Paul H. Brookes.

Jachman, A. (2006). Reading and the migrant student. *SEDL Letter Volume XIV, Number 3: Putting Reading First.* Retrieved from http://www.sedl.org

Jacobs, E. L., & Coufal, K. L. (2001). A computerized screening instrument of language learnability. *Communication Disorders Quarterly, 22*, 67–75.

Jensen, E. (2009). *Teaching with poverty in mind: What being poor does to kids' brains and what schools can do about it.* Alexandria, VA: ACSD.

Jeynes, W. H. (2003). A meta-analysis: The effects of parental involvement on minority children's academic achievement. *Education and Urban Society, 35*, 202–218.

Joe, J. R., & Malach, R. S. (2011). Families with American Indian roots. In E. W. Lynch & M. J. Hanson (Eds.), *Developing cross-cultural competence: A guide for working with young children and their families* (4th ed., pp. 110–139). Baltimore, MD: Paul H. Brookes.

Johnson, A. D., Martin, A., Brooks-Gunn, J., & Petrill, S.A. (2008). Order in the house! Associations among household chaos, the home literacy environment, maternal reading ability, and children's early reading. *Merrill-Palmer Quarterly, 54*, 445–472.

Johnson, D. D., & Johnson, B. (2002). *High stakes: Children, testing, and failure in American schools.* Oxford, UK: Rowman & Littlefield.

Johnston, J., & Wong, M. Y. (2002). Cultural differences in beliefs and practices concerning talk to children. *Journal of Speech, Language, and Hearing Research, 45*, 916–926.

Jones, C. B. (2002). *The source for brain-based learning.* East Moline, IL: LinguiSystems.

Jozefowicz-Simbeni, D. M. H., & Israel, N. (2006). Services to homeless students and families: The McKinney-Vento Act and its implications for school social work practice. *Children and Schools, 28*(1), 35–44.

Justice, L. M., Chow, S. M., Capellini, C., Flanigan, K., & Colton, S. (2003). Emergent literacy intervention for vulnerable preschoolers: Relative effects of two approaches. *American Journal of Speech-Language Pathology, 12*, 320–332.

Justice, L. M., & Ezell, H. K. (2000). Enhancing children's print and word awareness through home-based parent intervention. *American Journal of Speech-Language Pathology, 9*, 257–269.

Justice, L. M., & Ezell, H. K. (2001). Written language awareness in preschool children from low-income households: A descriptive analysis. *Communication Disorders Quarterly, 22*, 123–134.

Justice, L. M., & Ezell, H. K. (2002). Use of storybook reading to increase print awareness in at-risk children. *American Journal of Speech-Language Pathology, 11*, 17–29.

Justice, L. M., & Ezell, H. K. (2004). Print referencing: An emergent literacy enhancement strategy and its clinical applications. *Language, Speech, and Hearing Services in Schools, 35*, 185–193.

Justice, L. M., Invernizzi, M. A., & Meier, J. D. (2002). Designing and implementing an early literacy screening protocol: Suggestions for the speech-language pathologist. *Language, Speech, and Hearing Services in Schools, 33*, 84–101.

Justice, L. M., Kaderavek, J. N., Fan, X., Sofka, A., & Hunt, A. (2009). Accelerating preschoolers' early literacy development through classroom-based teacher-child storybook reading and explicit print referencing. *Language, Speech, and Hearing Services in Schools, 40*, 67–85.

Justice, L. M., McGinty, A. S., Cabell, S. Q., Kilday, C. R., Knighton, K., & Huffman, G. (2010). Language and literacy curriculum supplement for preschoolers who are academically at risk: A feasibility study. *Language, Speech, and Hearing Services in Schools, 41*, 161–178.

Justice, L. M., McGinty, A. S., Piasta, S. B., Kaderavek, J. N., & Fan, X. (2010. Print-focused read-alouds in preschool classrooms: Intervention effectiveness and moderators of child outcomes. *Language, Speech, and Hearing Services in Schools, 41*, 504–520.

Justice, L. M., Meier, J., & Walpole, S. (2005). Learning new words from storybooks: An efficacy study with at-risk kindergartners. *Language, Speech, and Hearing Services in Schools, 36*, 17–32.

Justice, L. M., Pullen, P., & Pence, K. (2008). Influence of verbal and nonverbal references to print on preschoolers' visual attention to print during storybook reading. *Developmental Psychology, 44,* 855–866.

Justice, L. M., Skibbe, L., & Ezell, H. (2006). Using print referencing to promote written language awareness. In T. A. Ukrainetz (Ed.), *Contextualizing language intervention: Scaffolding PreK–12 literacy achievement* (pp. 389–428). Eau Claire, WI: Thinking Publications.

Kaderavek, J. N. (2011). *Language disorders in children: Fundamental concepts of assessment and intervention.* Upper Saddle River, NJ: Pearson Education.

Kaderavek, J. N., & Boucher, D. N. (2006). Temperament profiles in children: Implications for academic performance and literacy learning. *HEARSAY Journal of the Ohio Speech-Language-Hearing Association, 18,* 14–20.

Kaderavek, J. N., & Justice, L. M. (2002). Shared storybook reading as an intervention context: Practices and potential pitfalls. *American Journal of Speech-Language Pathology, 11,* 395–406.

Kahlenberg, R. D. (2006). The new integration. *Educational Leadership, 63,* 22–27.

Kaiser, A. P., Qi, X., Hancock, T. B., & Foster, E. M. (2002). Teacher-reported behavioral problems and language delays in boys and girls enrolled in Head Start. *Behavioral Disorders, 28,* 23–39.

Kamil, M. L., & Walberg, H. J. (2005). *Kamil Op-Ed: The scientific teaching of reading.* Stanford University School of Education News Bureau. Retrieved from http://ed.stanford.edu/suse/news-bureau

Kaufman, C. (2010). *Executive functions in the classroom: Practical strategies for improving performance and enhancing skills for all students.* Baltimore, MD: Brookes.

Kayser, H. (2006, August 15). Parent programs in literacy: Differences for Latinos. *ASHA Leader,* pp. 8–23.

Kayser, H. (2012). Hispanic and Latino cultures in the United States and Latin America. In D. E. Battle (Ed.), *Communication disorders in multicultural and international populations* (4th ed., pp. 102–118). St. Louis, MO: Mosby.

Kitano, M. K. (2003). Gifted potential and poverty: A call for extraordinary action. *Journal for the Education of the Gifted, 26,* 292–303.

Klotz, M. B., & Nealis, L. (2005). *The new IDEA: A summary of significant reforms. National Association of School Psychologists.* Retrieved from http://nasponline.org

Kohn, M. L. (1969). *Class and conformity: A study in values.* Homewood, IL: Dorsey Press.

Kohnert, K., & Windsor, J. (2004). The search for common ground: Part II. Nonlinguistic performance by linguistically diverse learners. *Journal of Speech, Language, and Hearing Research, 47,* 891–903.

Kornman, S. (2004). *Reading mentors help kids break cycle of poverty.* Retrieved from http://www.experiencecorps.org

Koutsoftas, A. D., Harmon, M. T., & Gray, S. (2009). The effect of Tier 2 intervention for phonemic awareness in a response-to-intervention model in low-income preschool classrooms. *Language, Speech, and Hearing Services in Schools, 40*, 116–130.

Kozol, J. (1995). *Amazing grace: The lives of children and the conscience of a nation.* New York, NY: Crown.

Kozol, J. (2005). *The shame of the nation: The restoration of apartheid schooling in America.* New York, NY: Three Rivers Press.

Kratcoski, A. (1998). Guidelines for using portfolios in assessment and evaluation. *Language, Speech, and Hearing Services in Schools, 29*, 3–10.

Kummerer, S. E. (2012). Promising strategies for collaborating with Hispanic parents during family-centered speech-language intervention. *Communication Disorders Quarterly February, 33*, 84–95.

La Cerva, V. (1996). *Pathways to peace: Forty steps to a less violent America.* Memphis, TN: Heal Foundation Press.

Laing, S. P., & Kamhi, A. (2003). Alternative assessment of language and literacy in culturally and linguistically diverse populations. *Language, Speech, and Hearing Services in Schools, 34*, 44–55.

Landsman, J. (2006). Bearers of hope. *Educational Leadership, 63*, 26–33.

Laosa, L. M. (1982). School, occupation, culture, and family: The impact of parental schooling on the parent-child relationship. *Journal of Educational Psychology, 74*, 791–827.

La Paro, K. M., Justice, L., Skibbe, L. E., & Pianta, R. C. (2004). Relations among maternal, child, and demographic factors and the persistence of preschool language impairment. *American Journal of Speech-Language Pathology, 13*, 291–303.

Larrotta, C., & Ramirez, Y. (2009). Literacy benefits for Latina/o parents engaged in a Spanish literacy project. *Journal of Adolescent and Adult Literacy, 52*, 621–630.

Lareau, A. (2002). Invisible equality: Social class and childrearing in black families and white families. *American Sociological Review, 67*, 747–776.

Lee, J. S., & Bowen, N. K. (2006). Parent involvement, cultural capital, and the achievement gap among elementary school children. *American Educational Research Journal, 43*(2), 193–218.

Lichter, D.T., Qian, Z., & Mellott, L. (2006). Marriage or dissolution? Union transitions among poor cohabiting women. *Demography, 43*, 223–240.

Lichter, D. T., & Wethington, E. (2010). Chaos and the diverging fortunes of American children: A historical perspective. In G. W. Evans & T. D. Wachs (Eds.), *Chaos and its influence on children's development: An ecological perspective* (pp. 15–34). Washington, DC: American Psychological Association.

Link, J., & Bohannon, J. (2003). *Negative evidence in Spanish.* Paper presented at the biennial meeting of Society for Research in Child Development, Tampa, FL.

Loban, W. (1976). *Language development: Kindergarten through grade twelve.* Urbana, IL: National Council of Teachers of English.

Lochman, J. E., & Szczepanski, R. (1999). Externalizing conditions. In V. L. Schwean & D. Saklofske (Eds.), *Psychosocial correlates of exceptionality* (pp. 110–136). New York, NY: Plenum.

Locke, A., Ginsborg, J., & Peers, I. (2002). Development and disadvantage: Implications for the early years and beyond. *International Journal of Language and Communication Disorders, 37,* 3–15.

Loeb, S., Fuller, B., Kagan, S. L., & Chang, Y. W. (2004). Child care in poor communities: Early learning effects of type, quality, and stability. *Journal of Child Development, 25,* 47–65.

Logan, A., & Westrich, T. (2008). *The state of minorities: How are minorities faring in the economy?* Center for American Progress. Retrieved from http://www.americanprogress.org/issues/2008/04/minorities_economy.html

Lohr, S. (2010, March 16). Online hate sites grow with social networks. *New York Times.* Retrieved from http://bits.blogs.mytimes.com

Long, E. (2012, April 3). Integrating dynamic assessment and response-to-intervention in reading instruction. *ASHA Leader.* Retrieved from http://www.asha./org/Publications/leader/2012/120403/Integrating-Dynamic-Assessment-and . . .

Long, S. H. (2005). Language and linguistically-culturally diverse children. In V. A. Reed, *An introduction to children with language disorders* (3rd ed., pp. 301–334). Boston, MA: Allyn & Bacon.

Lopez, L. M. (2005). A look into the homes of Spanish-speaking preschool children. In J. Cohen, K. McAlister, K. Rolstad, & J. McSwan (Eds.), *ISB4: Proceedings of the 4th International Symposium on Bilingualism* (pp. 1378–1383). Somerville, MA: Cascadilla Press.

Lopez, L. M. (2012). Language and the educational setting. In B. A. Goldstein (Ed.), *Bilingual language development and disorders in Spanish-English speakers* (2nd ed., pp. 267–284). Baltimore, MD: Paul H. Brookes.

Lovelace, S., & Stewart, S. (2009). Effects of robust vocabulary instruction and multicultural text on the development of word knowledge among African American children. *Language, Speech, and Hearing Services in Schools, 18,* 168–179.

Lubliner, S. (2005). *Getting into words: Vocabulary instruction that strengthens comprehension.* Baltimore, MD: Paul H. Brookes.

Lubliner, S., & Smetana, L. (2005). The effects of comprehensive vocabulary instruction on Title I students' metacognitive word-learning skills and reading comprehension. *Journal of Literacy Research, 37,* 163–200.

Lugo-Gil, J., & Tamis-LeMonda, C. S. (2008). Family resources and parenting quality: Links to children's cognitive development across the first three years. *Child Development, 79,* 1065–1085.

Lund, N. J., & Duchan, J. F. (1993). *Assessing children's language in naturalistic contexts* (3rd ed.). Englewood Cliffs, NJ: Prentice-Hall.

Luster, T., Bates, L., Vandenbelt, M., & Peck Key, J. (2000). Factors related to successful outcomes among preschool children born to low-income adolescent mothers. *Journal of Marriage and the Family, 62,* 133–146.

Lustig, S. L. (2010). An ecological framework for the refugee experience: What is the impact on child development? In G. W. Evans & T. D. Wachs (Eds.), *Chaos and its influence on children's development: An ecological perspective* (pp. 239–251). Washington DC: American Psychological Association.

Lynch, E. W. (2011). Conceptual framework: From culture shock to cultural learning. In E. W. Lynch & M. J. Hanson (Eds.), *Developing cross-cultural competence: A guide for working with children and their families* (4th ed., pp. 20–41). Baltimore, MD: Paul H. Brookes.

Lynch, E. W., & Hanson, M. J. (Eds.) (2011). *Developing cross-cultural competence: A guide for working with children and their families* (4th ed.). Baltimore, MD: Paul H. Brookes.

Lyon, C. R. (2006). Demonstrating poverty in a multicultural education course: Buying school supplies with limited funds. *Multicultural Education, 13,* 46–48.

Madding, C. C. (2000). Maintaining focus on cultural competence in early intervention services to linguistically and culturally diverse families. *Infant-Toddler Intervention: The Transdisciplinary Journal, 10,* 9–18.

Manson, T. J. (Ed.). (2005). *How to teach children at risk of educational failure: Coping with poverty, bullying, disease, crime, and ethnicity.* Lewiston, NY: Edwin Mellen Press.

Martin, D. C., & Yankay, J. E. (2012). Refugees and asylees: 2011. *Annual Flow Report.* Office of Immigration Statistics, Homeland Security, May 2012. Retrieved from http://www.dhs.gov/immigrationstatistics

Marvin, C. A., & Mirenda, P. (1993). Home literacy experiences of preschoolers enrolled in Head Start and special education programs. *Journal of Early Intervention, 17,* 351–367.

Matsumoto, M., & Brown-Welty, S. (2009). Ase study of leadership practices and school-community interrelationships in high-performing, high-poverty, rural California high schools. *Journal of Research in Rural Education, 24,* 1–18.

Maxwell, L. A. (2012). Study: Pediatric early literacy effort a boon to English learners. *Education Week.* Retrieved from http://blogsedweek.org/edweek/learning-the-language/2012/04/study_pediatric_early_liter . . .

Maxwell, L. E. (2010). Chaos outside the home: The school environment. In G. W. Evans & T. D. Wachs (Eds.), *Chaos and its influence on children's development: An ecological perspective* (pp. 83–95). Washington, DC: American Psychological Association.

McCormack, J., Harrison, L. J., McLeod, S., & McAllister, L. (2011). A nationally representative study of the association between communication impairment at 4–5 years and children's life activities at 7–9 years. *Journal of Speech, Language, and Hearing Research, 54,* 1328–1348.

McDowell, K. D., Lonigan, C. J., & Goldstein, H. (2007). Relations among socioeconomic status, age, and predictors of phonological awareness. *Journal of Speech, Language, and Hearing Research, 50,* 1079–1092.

McGregor, K. K. (2004). Developmental dependencies between lexical semantics and reading. In C. A. Stone, E. R. Silliman, B. J. Ehren, & K. Apel (Eds.), *Handbook of language and literacy: Development and disorders* (pp. 302–317). New York, NY: Guilford Press.

McLaughlin, S. (2006). *Introduction to language development* (2nd ed.). Clifton Park, NY: Thomson-Delmar Learning.

McLoyd, V. C. (1998). Economic disadvantage and child development. *American Psychologist, 53,* 185–204.

McNeilly, L. G., & Coleman, T. J. (2000). Early intervention: Working with children within the context of their families and communities. In T. J. Coleman (Ed.), *Clinical management of communication disorders in culturally diverse children* (pp. 77–100). Boston, MA: Allyn & Bacon.

Miles, S. B., & Stipek, D. (2006). Contemporaneous and longitudinal associations between social behavior and literacy achievement in a sample of low-income elementary school children. *Child Development, 77*(1), 103–117.

Miller, M. (2006). Where they are: Working with marginalized students. *Educational Leadership, 63,* 50–51.

Montgomery, J. K. (2007). *The bridge of vocabulary.* Minneapolis, MN: NCS Pearson.

Moore, J. (2007). *A look at child welfare from a homeless education perspective.* Greensboro, NC: National Center for Homeless Education at SERVE. Retrieved from http://www.serve.org/nche

Moore-Brown, B., & Montgomery, J. K. (2006). *Response to intervention: An alternative to special education* [Audio CD and manual]. Rockville Pike, MD: American Speech-Language-Hearing Association.

Moran, M. (2010, March). *The early literacy crisis.* Retrieved from http://www.parenting.org

Morris, K. (2011, February). *Practical strategies for therapists working with sensory disorders in children and adolescents.* Workshop presented in Sacramento, CA.

Morrison, G. S. (2003). *Teaching in America* (3rd ed.). Boston, MA: Allyn & Bacon.

Murphy, J. (2011). Homeless children and youth at risk: The educational impact of displacement. *Journal of Education for Students Placed at Risk, 16*, 38–55.

Nathan, L., Stackhouse, J., Goulandris, N., & Snowling, M. J. (2004). The development of early literacy skills among children with speech difficulties: A test of the "Critical Age Hypothesis." *Journal of Speech, Language, and Hearing Research, 47*, 377–391.

National Alliance to End Homelessness. (2012). *An emerging framework for ending unaccompanied youth homelessness.* Retrieved from http://www.endhomelessness.org/content/article/detail/4486

National Association for the Education of Homeless Children and Youth. (2011). *Facts about homeless education.* Retrieved from http://www.naehcy.org/facts.html

National Center for Children in Poverty. (2005). *Basic facts about low-income children: Birth to age 18.* Retrieved from http://nccp.org. pub_lic06.html

National Center for Children in Poverty. (2012, May 20). *National Center for Children in Poverty statistics.* Retrieved from http://www.naccchildlaw.org/news/84535/news-National-Center-for-Children-in-Poverty

National Center for Education Statistics. (2005). Rates of computer and Internet use by children in nursery school and students in kindergarten through twelfth grade: 2003. *U.S. Department of Education Institute of Education Sciences, NCES 2005-111, Issue Brief, 1–3.*

National Center for Education Statistics. (2011). *Condition of education, 2011.* Retrieved from http://www.ecs.org

National Center for Homeless Education. (2006). *Housing agency and school district collaborations to serve homeless and highly mobile students. Best Practices in Homeless Education.* Greensboro, NC: National Center for Homeless Education at SERVE. Retrieved from http://www.serve.org/nche

National Center for Policy Analysis. (2009). *Poverty—2009/2010 topic.* Retrieved from http://www.debate-central.org

National Center on Family Homelessness. (2008). *The characteristics and needs of families experiencing homelessness.* Retrieved from http://community.familyhomelessness.org/sites/default/files/NCFH

National Center on Family Homelessness. (2009). *America's youngest outcasts: State report card on child homelessness.* Newton, MA: Author. Retrieved from http://community/familyhomelesschildrenamerica.porg/pdf/rc_full_report.pdf

National Center on Response to Intervention. (2012). *RtI: Considerations for English Language Learners (ELLs).* Retrieved from http://www.rti4success.org

National Clearinghouse for English Language Acquisition. "*The Growing Numbers of English Language Learner Students,*" 1998/99–2008/09. February, 2011.

National Coalition for the Homeless. (2006). *Who is homeless?* Retrieved from http://www.nationalhomeless.org

National Center for Policy Analysis. (2009, June). Poverty—2009/2010 topic. Retrieved from http://www.debate-central.org

National Dissemination Center for Children with Disabilities. (2004). *Visual impairments: Fact Sheet 13.* Retrieved from http://www. cichcy.org

National Institute for Early Education Research. (2005). *New study shows high quality state pre-K programs improve language and math abilities of children from all backgrounds.* Retrieved from http://nieer.org/media center/index.php

National Institute of Child Health and Human Development. (2006). *Child health indicators.* Retrieved from http://www.nichd.gov/publications

National Literacy Trust. (2005). *Ethnic minority issues and poverty.* Retrieved from http://www.literacytrust.org.uk

National Women's Law Center. (2011). *Closing the wage gap is especially important for women of color.* Retrieved from http://www.nwlc.org/ resource/closing-wage-gap-especially-important

Nelson, N. W. (2010). *Language and literacy disorders: Infancy through adolescence.* Boston, MA: Pearson.

Nelson, P., Kohnert, K., Sabur, S., & Shaw, D. (2005). Classroom noise and children learning through a second language: Double jeopardy? *Language, Speech, and Hearing Services in Schools, 36,* 219–229.

Neuman, S. B. (2001). The role of knowledge in early literacy. *Reading Research Quarterly, 36,* 468–475.

Neuman, S.B. (2009). *Changing the odds for children at risk: Seven essential principles of educational programs that break the cycle of poverty.* Westport, CT: Praeger.

Neuman, S. B., & Celano, D. (2001). Access to print in middle- and low-income communities: An ecological study of four neighborhoods. *Reading Research Quarterly, 36,* 8–26.

Neuman, S. B., & Celano, D. (2006). The knowledge gap: Implications of leveling the playing field for low-income and middle-income children. *Reading Research Quarterly, 41,* 176–201.

Nippold, M. A., Duthie, J. K., & Larson, J. (2005). Literacy as leisure activity: Free-time preferences of older children and adolescents. *Language, Speech, and Hearing Services in Schools, 36,* 93–102.

Nittrouer, S. (1996). The relation between speech perception and phonemic awareness: Evidence from low-SES children and children with chronic OM. *Journal of Speech-Language-Hearing Research, 39,* 1059–1070.

Norris, J. (2011). *Using phonic faces in a RtI service delivery model.* Paper presented at the annual meeting of the SPALS conference, Baton Rouge, LA.

Nungesser, N. R., & Watkins, R. V. (2005). Preschool teachers' perceptions and reactions to challenging classroom behavior: Implications for speech-language pathologists. *Language, Speech, and Hearing Services in Schools, 36,* 139–151.

Obama, B. (2006). *The audacity of hope: Thoughts on reclaiming the American dream.* New York, NY: Crown.

Ogbu, J. U. (1995). Literacy and Black Americans: Comparative perspectives. In V. L. Gadsden & D. A. Wagner (Eds.), *Literacy among African-American youth: Issues in learning, teaching, and schooling* (pp. 83–100). Cresskill, NJ: Hampton Press.

Ogbu, J. U. (1997). Understanding the school performance of urban blacks: Some essential background knowledge. In H. Walberg, O. Reyes, & R. P. Weissberg (Eds.), *Children and youth: Interdisciplinary perspectives* (pp. 190–240). Norwood, NJ: Abex.

Olsen, J. Z. (2003). *Handwriting without tears.* Cabin John, MD: Handwriting Without Tears, Inc.

Olszewski-Kublius, P., Lee, S. Y., Ngoi, M., & Ngoi, D. (2004). Addressing the achievement gap between minority and nonminority children by increasing access to gifted programs. *Journal for the Education of the Gifted, 28,* 127–158.

O'Neill-Pirozzi, T. M. (2003). Language functioning of residents of family homeless shelters. *American Journal of Speech-Language Pathology, 12,* 229–242.

O'Neil-Pirozzi, T. M. (2006). Comparison of context-based interaction patterns of mothers who are homeless with their preschool children. *American Journal of Speech-Language Pathology, 15,* 278–288.

O'Neil-Pirozzi, T. M. (2009). Feasibility and benefit of parent participation in a program emphasizing preschool child language development while homeless. *American Journal of Speech-Language Pathology, 18,* 252–263.

Owens, R. E. (2004). *Language disorders: A functional approach to assessment and intervention* (4th ed.). Boston, MA: Allyn & Bacon.

Owens, R. E. (2012). *Language development: An introduction* (8th ed.). Boston, MA: Pearson.

Owens, R. E., Metz, D. E., & Farinella, K. A. (2011). *Introduction to communication disorders: A lifespan evidence-based perspective* (4th ed.). Boston, MA: Pearson.

Packer, L. E. (2004). *What are executive functions?* Retrieved from http://www.schoolbehavior.com/conditions_edfoverview.htm

Palacio, M. (2001). Language wellness for inner-city preschoolers. *ADVANCE for Speech-Language Pathologists, 11,* 5–9.

Pan, B. A., Rowe, M. L., Spier, E., & Tamis-Lemonda, C. (2004). Measuring productive vocabulary of toddlers in low-income families: Concurrent and predictive validity of three sources of data. *Journal of Child Language, 31*, 587–608.

Paradis, J., Genesee, F., & Crago, M. (2011). *Dual language development and disorders: A handbook on bilingualism and second language learning* (2nd ed.). Baltimore, MD: Paul H. Brookes.

Paris, S. G. (1991). Assessment and remediation of metacognitive aspects of children's reading comprehension. *Topics in Language Disorders, 12*, 32–50.

Paterson, P. O., & Elliott, L. N. (2006). Struggling reader too struggling reader: High school students' responses to a cross-age tutoring program. *Journal of Adolescent and Adult Literacy, 49*, 378–389.

Paul, R., & Norbury, C.F. (2012). *Language disorders from infancy through adolescence: Listening, speaking, reading, writing, and communicating* (4th ed.) St. Louis, MO: Mosby/Elsevier.

Payne, A. C., Whitehurst, G. J., & Angell, A. L. (1994). The role of home literacy environment in the development of language ability in preschool children from low-income families. *Early Childhood Research Quarterly, 9*, 427–440.

Payne, R. K. (2003). *A framework for understanding poverty* (4th ed.). High lands, TX: Aha! Process, Inc.

Payne-Johnson, J. (1992). A case for understanding African Americans who are elderly. *Asha Magazine, 34*, 41–44.

Pena, E. D., Iglesias, A., & Lidz, C. S. (2001). Reducing test bias through dynamic assessment of children's word learning ability. *American Journal of Speech-Language Pathology, 10*, 138–154.

Perkins-Gough, D. (2004). A two-tiered education system. *Educational Leadership, 62*, 87–90.

Perlman, S., & Fantuzzo, J. (2010). Timing and influence of early experiences of child maltreatment and homelessness on children's educational well-being. *Children and Youth Services Review, 32*, 874–883.

Peterson, C., Jesso, B., & McCabe, A. (1999). Encouraging narratives in preschoolers: An intervention study. *Journal of Child Language, 26*, 49–67.

Picucci, A. C., Brownson, A., Kahlert, R., & Sobel, A. (2004). Middle school concept helps high-poverty schools become high-performing schools. *Middle School Journal, 36*, 4–11.

Podhajski, B., & Nathan, J. (2005). Promoting early literacy through professional development for childcare providers. *Early Education and Development, 16*, 23–42.

Posnick-Goodwin, S. (2001). Once looked upon as child's play, preschool education is now serious business. *California Educator, 5*, 6–8.

Posnick-Goodwin, S. (2006). NCLB gets an F. *California Educator, 11*, 6–9.

Posnick-Goodwin, S. (2011, November). Living and learning in poverty. *California Educator, 16*, 10–21.

Proctor, B., & Dalaker, J. (2002). *Poverty in the United States: 2001, Current population reports*, P60–219. Washington, DC: U.S. Government Printing Office.

Pruitt, S. L., Oetting, J. B., & Hegarty, M. (2011). Past participle marking by African American English-speaking children reared in poverty. *Journal of Speech, Language, and Hearing Research, 54*, 598–607.

Pungello, E. P., Iruka, I. U., Dotterer, A. M., Mills-Koonce, R., & Reznick, J. S. (2009). The effects of socioeconomic status, race, and parenting on language development in early childhood. *Developmental Psychology, 45*, 544–557.

Qi, C. H. (2006). Beyond assessment: Issues of assessing language and behavior of African American children from low-income backgrounds. *Special Interest Division 14 Newsletter, American Speech-Language-Hearing Association, 13*, 14–18.

Qi, C. H., & Kaiser, A.P. (2004). Problem behaviors of low-income children with language delays: An observation study. *Journal of Speech, Language, and Hearing Research, 47*, 595–609.

Rabkin, N., & Redmond, R. (2006). The arts make a difference. *Educational Leadership, 63*, 60–65.

Rafferty, Y. (1995). The legal rights and educational problems of homeless children and youth. *Educational Evaluation and Policy Analysis, 17*, 39–61.

Raikes, H., Pan, B. A., Luze, G., Tamis-LeMonda, C. S., Brooks-Gunn, J., Constantine, J., . . . Rodriguez, E. T. (2006). Mother-child bookreading in low-income families: Correlates and outcomes during the first three years of life. *Child Development, 77*, 924–953.

Rashid, F. L., Morris, R. D., & Sevcik, R. A. (2005). Relationship between home literacy environment and reading achievement in children with reading disabilities. *Journal of Learning Disabilities, 38*(1), 2–10.

Reardon, S. F. (2011). *The widening achievement gap between the rich and the poor: New evidence and possible explanations.* New York, NY: Russell Sage Foundations Press.

Reach Out and Read. (2012). *At-risk Latino children in Reach Out and Read have strong kindergarten literacy skills.* Retrieved from http://www.reachoutandread.org/newsroom/press_article.aspx?id=373

Redmond, S. M. (2011). Peer victimization among students with specific language impairment, attention-deficit/hyperactivity disorder, and typical development. *Language, Speech, and Hearing Services in Schools, 42*, 520–535.

Reed, V. A. (2005). *An introduction to children with language disorders* (3rd ed.). Boston, MA: Pearson Education.

Reinstein, D. (1998). Crossing the economic divide. *Educational Leadership*, *55*, 28–29.

Reuters (2011). *Poor schools don't get "fair share": Education Department*. Retrieved from http://www.reuters.com/article/2011/11/30/us-usa-states-education

Reynolds, M. E., & Fish, M. (2010). Language skills in low-SES rural Appalachian children: Kindergarten to middle childhood. *Journal of Applied Developmental Psychology*, *31*, 238–248.

Riley, K.G., & McGregor, K.K. (2012). Noise hampers children's expressive word learning. *Language, Speech, and Hearing Services in Schools*, *43*, 325–337.

Roberts, J., Jurgens, J., & Burchinal, M. (2005). The role of home literacy practices in preschool children's language and emergent literacy skills. *Journal of Speech, Language, and Hearing Research*, *48*, 345–359.

Roberts, M. Y., & Kaiser, A. P. (2011). The effectiveness of parent-implemented language interventions: A meta-analysis. *American Journal of Speech-Language Pathology*. Retrieved from http://www.asha.org

Robila, M., & Krishnakumar, A. (2005). Effects of economic pressure on marital conflict in Romania. *Journal of Family Psychology*, *19*, 246–251.

Robinson, J. L., & Acevedo, M. C. (2001). Infant reactivity and reliance on mother during emotional challenges: Prediction of cognition and language skills in a low-income sample. *Child Development*, *72*, 402–415.

Robinson, N. B., & Robb, M. P. (2002). Early communication assessment and intervention. In D. K. Bernstein & E. Tiegerman-Farber, *Language and communication disorders in children* (5th ed., pp. 126–180). Boston, MA: Allyn & Bacon.

Rodriguez, E. T., Tamis-LeMonda, C., Spellman, M. E., Pan, B. A., Raikes, H., Lugo-Gil, J., & Luze, G. (2009). The formative role of home literacy experiences across the first three years of life in children from low-income families. *Journal of Applied Developmental Psychology*, *30*, 677–694.

Rosa-Lugo, L.I., Mihai, F.M., & Nutta, J.W. (2012). *Language and literacy development: An interdisciplinary focus on English Learners with communication disorders*. San Diego, CA: Plural.

Roseberry-McKibbin, C. (2000). Multicultural matters. *Communication Disorders Quarterly*, *21*, 242–245.

Roseberry-McKibbin, C. (2001). Serving children from the culture of poverty: Practical strategies for speech-language pathologists. *ASHA Leader*, *6*, 4–16.

Roseberry-McKibbin, C. (2003). *Assessment of bilingual learners: Language difference or disorder?* [Video]. Rockville, MD: American Speech-Language-Hearing Association.

Roseberry-McKibbin, C. (2007). *Language disorders in children: A multicultural and case approach*. Boston, MA: Allyn & Bacon.

Roseberry-McKibbin, C. (2008). *Multicultural students with special language needs: Practical strategies for assessment and intervention* (3rd ed.). Oceanside, CA: Academic Communication Associates.

Roseberry-McKibbin, C. (2013).Playing the classroom game: Supporting students who are environmentally at risk. In T. A. Ukrainetz (Ed.), *Schoolage language intervention: Principles and procedures for oral and written language.* Austin, TX: Pro-Ed.

Roseberry-McKibbin, C., Brice, A., & O'Hanlon, L. (2005). Serving English language learners in public school settings: A national survey. *Language, Speech, and Hearing Services in Schools, 36,* 48–61.

Roseberry-McKibbin, C., & Hegde, M. N. (2011). *Advanced review of speech-language pathology: Preparation for PRAXIS and comprehensive examination* (3rd ed.). Austin, TX: Pro-Ed.

Roseberry-McKibbin, C., Pena, A., Hall, M., & Stubblefield-Smith, S. (1996, November). *Health care considerations in serving children from migrant Hispanic families.* Paper presented at the annual convention of the American Speech-Language-Hearing Association, Seattle, WA.

Rossetti, L. M. (2001). *Communication intervention: Birth to three* (2nd ed.). Albany, NY: Delmar.

Rothstein, R. (2004). The achievement gap: A broader picture. *Educational Leadership, 62,* 40–43.

Rothstein, R. (2006). The social and economic realities that challenge all schools. *Independent School, 65,* 18–26.

Rudebusch, J., & Wiechmann,, J. (2011). How to fit Response to Intervention into a heavy workload. *ASHA Leader.* Retrieved from http://www.asha .org/Publications/leader/2011

Ruiz, N. T., Rueda, R., Figueroa, R. R., & Boothroyd, M. (1995). Bilingual special education teacher's shifting paradigms: Complex responses to educational reform. *Journal of Learning Disabilities, 28,* 622–635.

Rumberger, R. W., & Palardy, G. J. (2005). Does segregation still matter? The impact of student composition on academic achievement in high school. *Teacher's College Record, 107,* 1999–2045.

Ruston, H. P., & Schwanenflugel, P. J. (2010). Effects of a conversation intervention on the expressive vocabulary development of prekindergarten children. *Language, Speech, and Hearing Services in Schools, 41,* 303–313.

Rvachew, S., Ohberg, A., Grawburg, M., & Heyding, J. (2003). Phonological awareness and phonemic perception in 4-year-old children with delayed expressive phonology skills. *American Journal of Speech-Language Pathology, 12,* 463–471.

Safe Horizon. (2006). *Ten ways to stop child abuse.* Retrieved from http:// www.safehorizon.org

Safe Horizon. (2012) *Child and Family Traumatic Stress Intervention Forum 2012.* Retrieved from http://www.safehorizon.org

Saint-Laurent, L., & Giasson, J. (2001). Effects of a multicomponent literacy program and of supplemental phonological sessions on at-risk kindergartners. *Educational Research and Evaluation, 7,* 1–33.

Sanger, D., Moore-Brown, B., Montgomery, J., & Hellerich, S. (2004). Speech-language pathologists' opinions on communication disorders and violence. *Language, Speech, and Hearing Services in Schools, 35,* 16–29.

Sapp, J. (2006). *Rigor + Support = Success.* Retrieved August 15, 2006, from http://www.tolerance.org/teach

Saxton, M. (2000). Negative evidence and negative feedback: Immediate effects on the grammaticality of child speech. *First Language, 20,* 221–252.

Saxton, M., Gallaway, C., & Backley, P. (1999). *Negative evidence and negative feedback: Long-term effects on the grammaticality of child speech.* Paper presented at the VIIIth International Congress for the Study of Child Language, San Sebastian, Spain.

Saxton, M., Kulcsar, B., Marshall, G., & Rupra, M. (1998). Longer-term effects of corrective input: An experimental approach. *Journal of Child Language, 25,* 701–721.

Schwartz, S., & Miller, J. E. H. (1988). *The language of toys: Teaching communication skills to special-needs children: A guide for parents and teachers.* Bethesda, MD: Woodbine House.

Sharif, I., Reiber, S., & Ozuah, P. (2002). Exposure to Reach Out and Read and vocabulary outcomes in inner city preschoolers. *Journal of the National Medical Association, 94,* 171–177.

Sharifzadeh, V.-S. (2011). Families with Middle Eastern roots. In E. W. Lynch & M. J. Hanson (Eds.), *Developing cross-cultural competence: A guide for working with young children and their families* (4th ed., pp. 392–436). Baltimore, MD: Paul H. Brookes.

Sherman, A. (1994). *Wasting America's future: The Children's Defense Fund report on the costs of child poverty.* Boston, MA: Beacon Press.

Shipley, K. G., & Roseberry-McKibbin, C. (2006). *Interviewing and counseling in communicative disorders: Principles and procedures.* Austin, TX: Pro-Ed.

Shinn, M., Schteingart, J.S., Williams, N.C., Carlin-Mathis, J., Bialo-Karagis, N., Becker-Klein, R., & Weitzman, B.C. (2008). Long-term associations of homelessness with children's well-being. *American Behavioral Scientist, 51,* 789–809.

Sibka, R. J., Poloni-Staudinger, L., Simmons, A. B., Feggins-Azziz, R., & Chung, C. G. (2005). Unproven links: Can poverty explain ethnic disproportionality in special education? *Journal of Special Education, 39*(3), 130–144.

Silliman, E. R., Wilkinson, L. C., & Brea-Spahn, M. R, (2004). Policy and practice imperatives for language and literacy learning: Who will be left behind? In C. A. Stone, E. R. Silliman, B. J. Ehren, & K. Apel (Eds.), *Handbook of language and literacy: Development and disorders* (pp. 97–129). New York, NY: Guilford Press.

Singer, B. D., & Bashir, A. S. (1999). What are executive functions and self-regulation and what do they have to do with language-learning disorders? *Language, Speech, and Hearing Services in Schools, 30,* 265–273.

Smith, K. E., Landry, S. H., & Swank, P. R. (2000). Does the content of mothers' verbal stimulation explain differences in children's development of verbal and nonverbal cognitive skills? *Journal of School Psychology, 38,* 27–49.

Snow, C. (2005, July/August). From literacy to learning. *Harvard Education Letter.* Retrieved from http://www.edletter.org/past/issues/2005-ja/snow.shtml

Snow, C. E. & Juel, C. (2005). Teaching children to read: What do we know about how to do it? In M. J. Snowling & C. Hulme (Eds.), *The science of reading: A handbook* (pp. 501–520). London, UK: Blackwell.

Solley, B. A. (2005). *When poverty's children write: Celebrating strengths, transforming lives.* Portsmouth, NH: Heinemann.

Southern Poverty Law Center. (2012). *Active U.S. hate groups.* Retrieved from http://www.splcenter.org/get-informed/hate-map

Sparks, S. (1993). *Children of prenatal substance abuse.* San Diego, CA: Singular.

Sparks, S. D. (2011). *Study finds gaps remain large for Hispanic students.* Retrieved from http://www.edweek.org/ew/issues/achievement-gap/

Stipek, D. (2006). No Child Left Behind comes to preschool. *Elementary School Journal, 105,* 455–466.

Storch, S. A., & Whitehurst, G. J. (2002). Oral language and code-related precursors to reading: Evidence from a longitudinal model. *Developmental Psychology, 38,* 934–947.

Sue, D. W., & Sue, D. (2003). *Counseling the culturally diverse: Theory and practice* (4th ed.). New York, NY: John Wiley & Sons.

Sunburst Technology Corporation. (2002). *Type to learn.* Pleasantville, NY.

Swanson, J. D. (2006). Breaking through assumptions about low-income, minority gifted students. *Gifted Child Quarterly, 50,* 11–25.

Swanson, T. J., Hodson, B. W., & Schommer-Aikins, M. (2005). An examination of phonological awareness treatment outcomes for seventh-grade poor readers from a bilingual community. *Language, Speech, and Hearing Services in Schools, 36,* 336–345.

Swick, K. J. (2010). Responding to the voices of homeless preschool children and their families. *Early Childhood Education Journal, 38,* 299–304.

Tabors, P. O. (2008). *One child, two languages: A guide for preschool educators of children learning English as a second language.* (2nd ed.) Baltimore, MD: Paul H. Brookes.

Takanishi, R. (2006). Leveling the playing field: Supporting immigrant children from birth to eight. *Future of Children, 14,* 61–79.

Talbert-Johnson, C. (2004). Structural inequities and the achievement gap in urban schools. *Education and Urban Society, 37,* 22–36.

Tamis-LeMonda, C. S., Bornstein, M. H., & Baumwell, L. (2001). Maternal responsiveness and children's achievement of language milestones. *Child Development, 72,* 748–767.

Tamis-LeMonda, C. S., Shannon, J. D., Cabrera, N. J., & Lamb, M. E. (2004). Fathers and mothers at play with their 2- and 3-year-olds: Contributions to language and cognitive development. *Child Development, 75,* 1806–1820.

Tavernise, S. (2012). *Education gap grows between rich and poor, study says.* Retrieved from http://www.nytimes.com/2012/01/10/education/education -gap-grows-between-rich-and-poor

Terrell, S. L., & Jackson, R. S. (2002). African Americans in the Americas. In D. E. Battle (Ed.), *Communication disorders in multicultural populations* (3rd ed., pp. 113–134). Boston, MA: Butterworth-Heinemann.

Terry, N. P., Connor, C. M., Thomas-Tate, S., & Love, M. (2010). Examining relationships among dialect variation, literacy skills, and school context in first grade. *Journal of Speech, Language, and Hearing Research, 53,* 126–145.

Thomas-Tate, S., Washington, J., & Edwards, J. (2004). Standardized assessment of phonological awareness skills in low-income African American first graders. *American Journal of Speech-Language Pathology, 13,* 182–190.

Thordardottir, E., Kehayia, E., Mazer, B., Lessard, N., Majnemer, A., Sutton, A., . . . Chillingaryan, G. (2011). Sensitivity and specificity of French language and processing measures for the identification of primary language impairment at age 5. *Journal of Speech, Language, and Hearing Research, 54,* 580–597.

Trelease, J. (2006). *Chapter 1: Why read aloud?* Excerpted from J. Trelease, *The Read-Aloud Handbook.* Retrieved from http:// www.trelease-on-read ing.com

Turnbull, K. L. P., & Justice, L. M. (2012). *Language development: From theory to practice* (2nd ed.). Boston, MA: Pearson.

Ukrainetz, T. A. (Ed.). (2013). *Schoolage language intervention: Principles and procedures for oral and written language.* Austin, TX: Pro-Ed.

Ukrainetz, T., Harpell, S., Walsh, C., & Coyle, C. (2000). A preliminary investigation of dynamic assessment with Native American kindergartners. *Language, Speech, and Hearing Services in Schools, 31,* 142–154.

Ukrainetz, T. A., Ross, C. L., & Harm, H. M. (2009). An investigation of treatment scheduling for phonemic awareness with kindergarteners who are at risk for reading difficulties. *Language, Speech, and Hearing Services in Schools, 40,* 86–100.

University of Michigan Health System. (2012). *Your child: Television and children.* Retrieved 6/18/12 from http://www.med.umich.edu/yourchild/ topics/tv.htm

The Urban Institute. (2005). *Young children of immigrants in two-parent families have triple the poverty rate of children with U.S.-born parents.* Retrieved from http://www.urban.org/publications/900779.html

U.S. Bureau of the Census. (2000). *Statistical abstract of the United States, 2000* (120th ed.). Washington, DC: U.S. Department of Commerce.

U.S. Bureau of the Census. (2005). *Statistical abstract of the United States 2005* (125th ed.). Washington, DC: U.S. Department of Commerce.

U.S. Bureau of the Census. (2010). *Statistical abstract of the United States 2010* (130th ed.). Washington, DC: U.S. Department of Commerce.

U.S. Census Bureau Newsroom. (2009, July 15). *Facts for features.* Retrieved from http://www.census.gov/Press-release/www/releases/archives/facts_for_features

U.S. Department of Agriculture. (2012). *Rural labor and education: Farm labor.* Retrieved from http://www.ers.usda.gov/Briefing/LaborAndEducation/FarmLabor.htm

U.S. Department of Education. (2001). *23rd annual report to Congress on the implementation of IDEA.* Washington, DC: Author.

U.S. Department of Education. (2002). *The No Child Left Behind Act Title I: Improving the academic achievement of the disadvantaged—Summary of final regulations.* Retrieved from http://www.ed.gov/nclb

van Broekhuizen, D. (2006). *Sheltered English: Techniques for ensuring comprehension.* Retrieved from http://prel.org/products/paced/oct04/re_sheltered.htm

Van Hook, J., Brown, S. L., & Kwenda, M. N. (2003, May). *One step forward, two steps back: The increase in immigrant child poverty from 1970 to 2000.* Paper presented at the annual meeting of the Population Association of America, Minneapolis, MN. Retrieved from http://paa2003.princeton.edu/abstractViewer.asp

van Keulen, J. E., Weddington, G. T., & DeBose, C. E. (1998). *Speech, language, and learning and the African American child.* Boston, MA: Allyn & Bacon.

van Kleeck, A. (1994). Potential cultural bias in training parents as conversational partners with their children who have delays in language development. *American Journal of Speech-Language Pathology, 3,* 67–78.

van Kleeck, A., Gillam, R. B., Hamilton, L., & McGrath, C. (1997). The relationship between middle-class parents' book-sharing discussion and their preschoolers' abstract language development. *Journal of Speech, Language, and Hearing Research, 40,* 1261–1271.

van Kleeck, A., Lange, A., & Schwarz, A. L. (2011). The effects of race and maternal education level on children's retells of the Renfrew Bus Story—North American edition. *Journal of Speech, Language, and Hearing Research, 54,* 1546–1561.

van Kleeck, A., Vander Woude, J., & Hammett, L. (2006). Fostering literal and inferential language skills in Head Start preschoolers with language impairment using scripted book-sharing discussions. *American Journal of Speech-Language Pathology, 15,* 85–95.

Venkatagiri, H. S. (2002). Speech recognition technology applications in communication disorders. *American Journal of Speech-Language Pathology*, *11*, 323–332.

Vernon-Feagans, L., Garrett-Peters, P., Willoughby, M., & Mills-Koonce, R. (2011). Chaos, poverty and parenting: Predictors of early language development. *Early Childhood Research Quarterly*, *27*(3), 339–351.

Vernon-Feagens, L., Pancsofar, N., Willoughby, M., Odom, E., Quade, A., & Cox, M. (2008). Predictors of maternal language to infants during a picture book task in the home: Family SES, child characteristics and the parenting environment. *Journal of Applied Developmental Psychology*, *29*, 213–226.

Wachs, T. D., & Evans, G. W. (2010). Chaos in context. In G. W. Evans & T. D. Wachs (Eds.), *Chaos and its influence on children's development: An ecological perspective* (pp. 3–13). Washington, DC: American Psychological Association.

Walker, D., Greenwood, C., Hart, B., & Carta, J. (1994). Prediction of school outcomes on early language production and socioeconomic factors. *Child Development*, *65*, 606–621.

Wallace, I. F., Roberts, J. E., & Lodder, D. E. (1998). Interactions of African American infants and their mothers: Relations with development at 1 year of age. *Journal of Speech, Language, and Hearing Research*, *41*, 900–912.

Wang, S. (2001, April). *Do child-rearing values in the US and Taiwan echo their cultural values of individualism and collectivism?* Paper presented to the Society for Research in Child Development, Minneapolis, MN.

Washington, J. A. (2001). Early literacy skills in African-American children: Research considerations. *Learning Disabilities Research and Practice*, *16*(4), 213. Retrieved from http://www.blackwell-synergy.com

Wasik, B. A, Bond, M. A., & Hindman, A. (2006). The effects of a language and literacy intervention on Head Start children and teachers. *Journal of Educational Psychology*, *98*, 63–74.

Watson, C., & Weitzman, E. (2000). *It takes two to talk: The Hanen Program for Parents*. Ontario, Canada: The Hanen Centre.

Week of the Young Child. (2003). *Guide to WOYC celebrations: Key facts and resources*. Retrieved from http://www.naeyc.org/woyc.guide/woyc_facts .asp

Weekly Reader. (2006). 300 million and counting. *WR News*, *3*(76), 2–3.

Weiner, C. (2001). *Preparing for success: Meeting the language and learning needs of young children from poverty homes*. Youngtown, AZ: ECL Publications.

Weisner, T. S. (2010). Well-being, chaos, and culture: Sustaining a meaningful daily routine. In G. W. Evans & T. D. Wachs (Eds.), *Chaos and its influence on children's development: An ecological perspective* (pp. 211–224). Washington, DC: American Psychological Association.

Weiss, A. (2002). Planning language intervention for young children. In D. K. Bernstein & E. Tiegerman-Farber (Eds.), *Language and communication disorders in children* (5th ed., pp. 256–314). Boston, MA: Allyn & Bacon.

Weissman, D. (2004). You can't get much better than that. In N. Rabkin & R. Redmond (Eds.), *Putting the arts in the picture: Reframing education in the 21st century* (pp. 17–48). Chicago, IL: Columbia College.

Weitzner-Lin, B. (2004). *Communication assessment and intervention with infants and toddlers.* St. Louis, MO: Butterworth-Heinemann.

Wells, G. (1986). *The meaning makers: Children learning language and using language to learn.* Portsmouth, NH: Heinemann.

Westby, C. (1997). There's more to passing than knowing the answers. *Language, Speech, and Hearing Services in Schools, 28*(3), 274–287.

Westby, C. (2006). There's more to passing than knowing the answers: Learning to do school. In T. A. Ukrainetz (Ed.), *Contextualized language intervention: Scaffolding PreK–12 literacy achievement* (pp. 319–388). Eau Claire, WI: Thinking Publications.

Westby, C. E. (2011, March). *Language and literacy learning for the 21st century: Culture, multiliteracies, and differentiated instruction.* Paper presented at the annual convention of the California Speech and Hearing Association, Los Angeles, CA.

Westby, C. E., & Inglebret, E. (2012). Native American and worldwide indigenous cultures. In D. E. Battle (Ed.), *Communication disorders in multicultural and international populations* (4th ed., pp. 76–101). St. Louis, MO: Mosby.

White, T. G., Graves, M. F., & Slater, W. H. (1990). Growth of reading vocabulary in diverse elementary schools: Decoding and word meaning. *Journal of Educational Psychology, 82,* 281–290.

Whitehurst, G. J., Arnold, D. S., Epstein, J. N., Angell, A. L., Smith, M., & Fischel, J. E. (1994). A picture book reading intervention in day care and home for children from low-income families. *Developmental Psychology, 30,* 679–689.

Whitehurst, G. J., & Lonigan, C. J. (2001). Emergent literacy: Development from prereaders to readers. In S. B. Neuman & D. K. Dickinson (Eds.), *Handbook of early literacy research* (pp. 11–29). New York, NY: Guilford Press.

Wilcox, K. (1982). Differential socialization in the classroom: Implications for equal opportunity. In G. Spindler (Ed.), *Doing the ethnography of schooling* (pp. 454–488). New York, NY: Holt, Rinehart, & Winston.

Williams, J. P. (2002). Using the Theme Scheme to improve story comprehension. In C. C. Block & M. Pressley (Eds.), *Comprehension instruction: Research-based best practices* (pp. 126–139). New York, NY: Guilford Press.

Williams, K. T. (2001). *Expressive Vocabulary Test*. Circle Pines, MN: American Guidance Service.

Williams, K.T. (2007). *Expressive Vocabulary Test* (2nd ed.). San Antonio, TX: Pearson.

Willis, W. O. (2004). Families with African American roots. In E. W. Lynch & M. J. Hanson (Eds.), *Developing cross-cultural competence: A guide for working with young children and their families* (pp. 1–2). Baltimore, MD: Paul H. Brookes.

Wilson, F. W., Wilson, J. R., & Coleman, T. J. (2000). *Culturally appropriate assessment: Issues and strategies*. Boston, MA: Allyn & Bacon.

Wilson, W. J. (2006). Social theory and the concept "underclass." In D. B. Gresky & P. England (Eds.), *Poverty and inequality* (pp. 103–116). Stanford, CA: Stanford University Press.

Windsor, J., & Kohnert, K. (2004). The search for common ground: Part I. Lexical performance by linguistically diverse learners. *Journal of Speech, Language, and Hearing Research, 47*, 877–890.

Wolfe, P. (2001). *Brain matters: Translating research into classroom practice*. Alexandria, VA: Association for Supervision and Curriculum Development.

Wolfram, W. (1983). Test interpretation and sociolinguistic differences. *Topics in Language Disorders, 3*(3), pp. 21–34.

Woolfolk, A. (2008). *Educational psychology* (11th ed.). Boston, MA: Allyn & Bacon.

Woolfolk Hoy, A., Demerath, P., & Pape, S. (2002). Teaching adolescents: Engaging developing selves. In T. Urdan & F. Pajares (Eds.), *Adolescence and education* (Vol. I, pp. 119–169). Greenwich, CT: Information Age.

Wright, V.R., Chau, M., & Aratani, Y. (2010). *Who are America's poor children? The official story*. New York, NY: National Center for Children in Poverty, Manhattan School of Public Health, Columbia University.

Wulbert, M., Inglis, S., Kriegsman, E., & Mills, B. (1978). Language delay and associated mother-child interaction. In *Readings in childhood language disorders* (pp. 148–159). Hoboken, NJ: John Wiley & Sons.

Wyatt, T. (2002). Assessing the communicative abilities of clients from diverse cultural and language backgrounds. In D. E. Battle (Ed.), *Communication disorders in multicultural populations* (3rd ed., pp. 415–460). Woburn, MA: Butterworth-Heinemann.

Wyatt, T. (2012). Assessment of multicultural and international clients with communication disorders. In D.E. Battle (Ed.), *Communication disorders in multicultural and international populations* (4th ed., pp. 243–278). St. Louis, MO: Mosby.

Xu, D., Yapanel, U., Gray, S., & Baer, C. T. (2009). *Reliability of the LENA Language Environment Analysis System in young children's natural home environment*. Boulder, CO: LENA Foundation. Retrieved from http://www.lenafoundation.org/Research/TechnicalReports.aspx

Yan, W., & Lin, Q. (2005). Parent involvement and mathematics achievement: Contrast across racial and ethnic groups. *Journal of Educational Research, 99*, 116–127.

Young, P. (1987). *Drugs and pregnancy*. New York, NY: Chelsea House.

Yu, M., North, C. S., LaVesser, P. D., Osborne, V. A., & Sptiznagel, E. L. (2008). A comparison study of psychiatric and behavior disorders and cognitive ability among homeless and housed children. *Community Mental Health Journal, 44*, 1–10.

Zimmerman, I. L., Steiner, V. G., & Pond, R. E. (1992). *PLS-3: Preschool Language Scale-3*. San Antonio, TX: Psychological Corporation.

Zimmerman, I. L., Steiner, V. G., & Pond, R. E. (1993). *Preschool Language Scale-3*. San Antonio, TX: Psychological Corporation.

Ziolkowski, R. A., & Goldstein, H. (2011). Kevin: A school-age child with behavioral disorders and language-learning disabilities: Applying contextualized written language and behavioral supports. In S. S. Chabon & E. R. Cohn, *The communication disorders casebook: Learning by example* (pp. 291–302). Upper Saddle River, NJ: Pearson Education.

Zuniga, M. E. (2011). Families with Latino roots. In E. W. Lynch & M. J. Hanson (Eds.), *Developing cross-cultural competence: A guide for working with young children and their families* (4th ed., pp. 190–233). Baltimore, MD: Paul H. Brookes.

Index

B

Behavior characteristics of children
from low-SES homes
first three grades, 70
Head Start attendance, 69
maternal influence, 70–72
overview, 72–74

C

Chaos, 24–28
and American children, 298–299
characteristics
and impact of disorder,
294–296
and impact of turbulence,
296–298
and high mobility in schools/
classroom, 300–301. *See also*
Homeless student service
main heading; Migrant
student service *main
heading*
classroom routines/scripts
learning, 327
executive functioning, 319–336
self-reflection/planning: taking
responsibility for choices
and consequences, 327–336
structure/routine/time concept
sense development, 322–327

Characteristics of children and
families from mainstream
and culturally diverse
backgrounds, 67
Contextualizing language
contextual cue emphasis, 256–264
contextual cues increased to
enhance learning, 256–264
increasing student language as
possible, 255–256
and relevance of classroom
activities, 256
standardized testing out-of-sync
with language of low-SES
students' lives, 254
Wolfe levels of learning, 253
Culture of resistance
culture defined, 265
groups at risk for membership in
culture, 265–267
Project EXCITE, 271–272
role model need, 267–273

D

Daily Goal Sheet, 329
Dynamic assessment
obtaining optimal results,
99–100
overview, 97–99
test-teach-test format basis,
99–100

E

Environment optimization, 244
clutter/distraction elimination,
244
signal-to-noise ratio, 244
specifics for K–12, 246–247

F

Families, low-SES
CLD (culturally, linguistically
diverse)
service delivery considerations,
347–370
conflicts with middle-SES
professionals, 370–373
cultural/social capital, 339–347
helping caregivers provide
a supportive home
atmosphere, 383–388
supporting children in homes
characterized by abuse or
neglect, 378–383
supporting children in meeting
basic needs, 373–378
Fetal alcohol syndrome, 15–17
FLP (Family Life Progress), 27
Forms
Daily Goal Sheet, 329
Tracking Consequences of
Choices: My Choice Chart,
330
Work Plan Contract, 333

H

Handwriting Without Tears, 195
Hart and Risley research, 49–55,
108–109, 256
Homeless student service
characteristics/needs of students
and families, 309–313

demographics, 306–309
McKinney-Vento Act, 310
supporting students and family,
313–319

I

IDEA 2004 (Individuals with
Disabilities Education
Improvement Act of 2004),
78
nonstandardized informal
assessment measures, 86,
98–99
Independence/self-direction
building
basic principles, 279–281
effort over ability emphasis,
282–285
multiple intelligences use,
285–288
Individuals with Disabilities
Education Improvement Act
of 2004
CLD (culturally and linguistically
diverse) students over-
represented in special
education, 78
K–3, 78
Integrating schools by student
socioeconomic status,
216–220
iPads, 133–134, 179

L

Language assessment for low-SES
students
assessment for special education
preliminary components
case history gathering, 82
screening, 79–80
language sampling, 94

informal evaluation of
language use, 95–97
overview, 76–77
programs affecting assessment of
low-SES family children for
special education, 78
Individuals with Disabilities
Education Improvement Act
of 2004. *See also* IDEA 2004
(Individuals with Disabilities
Education Improvement Act
2004) *main heading*
No Child Left Behind (NCLB)
Act, 78–79
RTI (response to intervention),
79–80
standardized assessment
alternatives
dynamic assessment, 97–100
IDEA 2004, 97–99. *See also*
IDEA 2004 (Individuals
with Disabilities Education
Improvement Act of 2004)
main heading
information processing skills
assessment, 101–103
legal considerations, 97–99
portfolio assessment, 100
standardized tests
bias sources with CLD
students, 91–92
considerations for students
from low-SES backgrounds,
86–88
modifying tests, 92–94
Language skills of children
factors affecting/characteristics
of literacy skills of low-SES
children
books in homes, 61–62
family reading, 63–65
letter knowledge on entering
school, 65

letter sound development, 65
phonological/print awareness
skills, 65–68
print access in home, 65–66
reading to children in home,
66
factors affecting/characteristics
of oral language skills of
children
children allowed unreasonable
voices and choices, 52–53
children strictly told what
to do, with no verbal
alternatives permitted, 53
cortical development stages, 55
ethnic background/language
skill, 47, 49
Greenwood and colleagues
Hart and Risley follow-up,
56–57
Hart and Risley research, 49–55
higher-SES parent/child
talking, 50
language use differences that
reflect parental cultural
priorities, 53–54
Loban oral language
production studies, 46–47
low-SES/language skill, 47–48
middle-SES child benefiting
from verbal elaboration, 48
middle-SES child language
skills, 48–49
and mothers, 47–48
oral language stimulation
parental attitudes, 60–61
overview, 45–46
and parental education, 47–48
and parental job, 57–59
parental reprimands/
encouragment, 51
SES categories (Hart and Risley
research), 50

Language skills of children;
factors affecting/characteristics
of oral language skills of
children *(continued)*
    SES/language skill, 47–48
    skills differences among
      children on entering school,
      55
    social opportunities of upper-
      SES families *versus* welfare
      families, 54
    young children/number of
      parent-child utterances in
      given time, 50–51
    young children/number of
      words heard by children,
      51–52
  first three years as crucial in
    language/reading, 55
  overview, 44–45, 72–74
Literacy skill enhancement
    strategies for low-SES
    background students
  early preliteracy/literacy skills
    phonological awareness skills,
      165–167
    principles, 164–165
    print awareness, 167–175
    reading comprehension,
      175–179
  elementary years +
    increasing vocabulary skills for
      reading success, 185–190
    NIM (Neurological Impress
      Method), 190–191
    NIM (Neurological Impress
      Method) for visual tracking,
      190–191
    overview, 179–183
    REWARDS (reading excellence:
      word attack and rate
      development strategies,
      183–184

    writing skills, 192, 194–195
  overview, 156–158
  young childhood book reading
    optimization
    increasing daily book-reading
      routines, 159–161
    measures of home literacy
      programs, 161–162
    overview, 158–159
    potential YouTube video
      promoting shared reading,
      162–163
    Reach Out and Read (ROR),
      163

M

McKinney-Vento Act, 310
Migrant student service
  families, 303–304
  and limited English skills, 303
  model of school services,
    304–305
  overview, 301
  service follow-through, 302

N

No Child Left Behind (NCLB) Act,
  78, 205–206

O

Oral language skills enhancement
    for children from low-SES
    families
  grammatical language skills in
    formal register, 138–142
  infant language development
    stimulation
    book use with babies, 114–116
    general principles, 109–114
    overview, 108–109

pragmatic language skills in
formal register, 142–149
toddler/preschooler language
development stimulation
early child care provider
appropriate training
importance, 122–126
high-quality preschool
importance, 116–122
toddler/preschooler language
skill promotion in natural
settings
formal language register,
135–137
milieu teaching techniques,
129–131
overview, 126–127
principles of successful
stimulation, 127–129
specific incidental learning,
129–131
vocabulary skill enhancement,
131–134

P

Poverty overview, 33
childhood poverty, U.S., 4–6
brain development, overall
effects of, 18–19
children of color, 6–8
and dropping out of high
school, 10
environmental issue effects on,
23–25
and family structure, 8–9
fetal alcohol syndrome, 15–17
health care access effects on,
21–23
hearing/vision deficits of,
29–31
home atmosphere emotionality
effect of, 31–33

hunger/malnutrition effects of,
17–18
instability/chaos effects on,
25–28. *See also* Chaos *main
heading*
and juvenile justice system, 10
male unemployment, 10
and middle ear infections, 31
neurotoxicants' exposure
effects on, 23–25
physical/psychological effects,
12–33
prenatal/birth issues, 12–17
at risk status, 10
safety issues as effects of,
19–21
single-parent families, 9–10
and teen births, 10
and TV viewing, 19–21, 27–28
educational professionals' roles in
attacking poverty, 39–41
employment future, 4
family educational levels, 5–7
generational *versus* situational
poverty, 33, 35–39
Great Recession (2007)
aftermath, 4
middle-SES values/practices
contrasts with same for low-
SES, 34–35
single-parent families, 9–10
and intergenerational support,
10
support levels for low-SES
(socioeconomic status)
children/families, 11–12
PPVT-R (Peabody Picture
Vocabulary Test-Revised),
137

R

Reach Out and Read (ROR), 163

S

School enhancement: supportive
    programs/relationships
    arts implementation, 222–223
    gifted students from low-SES
        backgrounds, 232
        AAMSUS (Accelerating
            Achievement in Math and
            Science in Urban Schools),
            235–236
        GATE (gifted and talented
            education), 234–235
        general, 232–234
    kindergarten, all-day, 221–222
    parallel education systems,
        220–221
    schools partnering with
        community resources,
        228–232
    supplemental program provision,
        224–228
School environment optimization
    for optimal student
    environment
    conditions in low-SES schools,
        currently, 207–211
    helping create change climate,
        207–208
    No Child Left Behind (NCLB) Act,
        205, 206
    overview, 203–204
    school factors associated with
        student achievement, 215
    school reform efforts currently,
        205
    teacher preparation/
        professionalism, 211–215
    Title 1 of the Elementary and
        Secondary Education Act,
        207
School factors associated with
    student achievement

school environment optimization
    for optimal student
    environment, 215
Self-esteem and motivation
    incentives
    dealing with shabby clothing/
        grooming, 277–279
    overview, 273–274
    positive reinforcement behavior
        management, 276–277
    positive self-talk, 275
Service delivery considerations
    involving in children's education,
        363–370
    optimal language learning
        environment fostering,
        354–363
    overview, 347–351
    services for immigrant/refugee
        backgrounds, 351–354
Standardized tests
    bias sources with CLD students,
        91–92
    considerations for students from
        low-SES backgrounds, 86
    biases, 87–88
    IQ tests, 87
    need for MAE (Mainstream
        American English) fluency, 88
    test selection, 86–87
    modifying tests, 92–94
Standardized tests alternatives
    dynamic assessment, 97–100
    overview, 97–99
    test-teach-test format basis,
        99–100
    IDEA 2004, 97, 98–99. *See also*
        IDEA 2004 (Individuals
        with Disabilities Education
        Improvement Act of 2004)
        main heading
    information processing skills
        assessment, 101–103

legal considerations, 97–99
portfolio assessment, 100

T

Tracking Consequences of Choices:
My Choice Chart, 330

W

Whole-brain-learning enhancement
memory skills, 249–252

ACE (association, color,
exaggeration), 250
reducing stress, 247–249
Work Plan Contract, 333
Writing skills
enhancement, 192, 194
handwriting, 194
Handwriting Without Tears, 195